THE KASSEL MANUSCRIPT
OF BEDE'S
'HISTORIA ECCLESIASTICA
GENTIS ANGLORUM'
AND
ITS OLD ENGLISH MATERIAL

THE KASSEL MANUSCRIPT
OF BEDE'S
'HISTORIA ECCLESIASTICA
GENTIS ANGLORUM'
AND
ITS OLD ENGLISH MATERIAL

by

T.J.M. VAN ELS

ASSEN, 1972

VAN GORCUM & COMP. N.V. - DR. H. J. PRAKKE & H. M. G. PRAKKE

The publication of this book was made possible through a grant from the Netherlands Organization for the Advancement of Pure Research (Z.W.O.)

ISBN   90 232 0962 1

Printed in the Netherlands by Royal VanGorcum Ltd.

PREFACE

The significance of *Kassel MS. Theol. Qu. 2* as one of the very early copies of Bede's *Historia Ecclesiastica Gentis Anglorum* was first registered by W. M. Lindsay when he consulted it for *Notae Latinae* (Cambridge 1915). Owing to the availability of other early copies of the *Historia Ecclesiastica*, editors of the text had little use for the Kassel MS, because it lacked the first three Books of the text. The first to use part of the Old English material of this ancient and very accurate copy was G. Storms in an article in *English Studies* (1956). Colgrave and Mynors (1969) used it for their edition of the text.

The present study edits and discusses the Old English material, almost exclusively onomastic, of the Kassel MS. Since linguistic material is not abundantly available for the early period of Old English, it is desirable that even such material should be made available in critical editions. Although the name-material of Bede's *Historia Ecclesiastica* has been edited and discussed before, a separate edition of the material of the Kassel MS appears to be justified, because the Kassel MS is the most accurate early copy of one of the two recensions of the *Historia Ecclesiastica* and consequently must be regarded as one of the main sources for a definite settlement of the appearance of the name-material of the History, at any rate of the final two Books.

In order to facilitate a close comparison of the name-material of the Kassel MS with that of the four main eighth-century MSS, the names from all five MSS are presented in parallel columns. With a view to an exact definition of the material, the Kassel MS is dated and placed as closely as possible, and its position in the tradition of the text is established. Etymological notes provide the necessary background to the phonological discussion.

I wish to express my thanks to the authorities of the *Murhardsche Bibliothek der Stadt Kassel und Landesbibliothek* for permission to reproduce a number of folios of the MS, and to the staff of the Library for assistance of various kinds. Thanks are also due to the authorities of the British Museum and Cambridge University Library for permission to use the manuscripts in their possession, and to the staff of Nijmegen University Library for their unfailing helpfulness.

The subject of the present study was suggested to me by Professor Dr. G. Storms of the University of Nijmegen, who supervised the preparation of the study as a doctoral dissertation. I want to thank Professor Storms for his invaluable assistance and for his stimulating criticism. I am also under obligation to Professor T. A. Birrell, M. A., and Dr. A. Gruijs, also of Nijmegen University, for reading the work in manuscript and for various suggestions concerning its improvement.

The Netherlands Organization for the Advancement of Pure Research (Z.W.O.) has enabled me to do part of my research in the libraries in London, Cambridge, and Kassel.

To my wife and children

To my mother

To the memory of my father

CONTENTS

ABBREVIATIONS

Abbreviated literature is arranged alphabetically under BIBLIOGRAPHY, pp. 245 ff.

B	MS. London British Museum, Cotton Tiberius A. XIV
C	MS. London British Museum, Cotton Tiberius C. II
el.	element
els.	elements
EPNS	English Place-Name Society
HE	*Historia Ecclesiastica Gentis Anglorum*
K	MS. Kassel Theol. Qu. 2
L	MS. Leningrad Public Library Lat. Q.v. I. 18
M	MS. Cambridge University Library Kk.5.16
ME	Middle English
MHG	Middle High German
MS	manuscript
MSS	manuscripts
N	MS. Namur Public Library, Fonds de la Ville 11
OE	Old English
OHG	Old High German
O.S.	Original Series

INTRODUCTION

The life of the Venerable Bede, as it comes to us from the small number of biographical data furnished by Bede himself at the end of the *Historia Ecclesiastica Gentis Anglorum,* strikes the reader as a fairly uneventful one. The main facts may be briefly summarised as follows[1]. When in 731 Bede completed his *Historia* with this short sketch of his life, he was probably 59 years old; the year of his birth may thus be 672 or 673. He was born in the territory of the monastery of St. Peter at Wearmouth. At the age of seven he was put by his kinsmen into the charge of Benedict Biscop, who had founded the monastery in 673 or 674. When Benedict Biscop founded the twin monastery of Jarrow in the vicinity of Wearmouth in 681 or 682, Bede moved to the new foundation together with Ceolfrid, its new Abbot. At the age of 19 he was ordained a deacon and, when 30, he was ordained a priest. His education consisted mainly of a constant study of the Scriptures. He observed the Rule and performed the daily offices, and besides, in his own words, his great delight was "to learn or to teach or to write". From the time of his ordination as a priest one of his occupations was "to make brief extracts from the works of the venerable fathers or the holy scriptures, or to add notes of my own to clarify their sense and interpretation"[2]. It is not known whether he

---

[1] For more detailed accounts of Bede's life and times the reader may be referred to PLUMMER I, "Introduction"; S. J. Crawford, *Anglo-Saxon Influence on Western Christendom 600-800,* Oxford 1933 (repr. Cambridge 1966); A. Hamilton Thompson (ed.), *Bede. His Life, Times and Writings,* Oxford 1935 (repr. 1969); R. W. Chambers, "'Bede', Annual Lecture on a Master Mind", *Proceedings of the British Academy* XXII (1936), 129-156; E. S. Duckett, *Anglo-Saxon Saints and Scholars,* New York 1947; M. L. W. Laistner, *Thought and Letters in Western Europe, A.D. 500-900* (rev. ed.), London 1957 (first publ. 1931); W. F. Bolton, *A History of Anglo-Latin Literature 597-1066, vol. I: 597-740,* Princeton, N.J., 1967; CO & MY, "Historical Introduction"; and P. Hunter Blair, *The World of Bede,* London 1970. For bibliographical information the reader is advised to consult especially W. F. Bolton, "A Bede Bibliography: 1935-1960", *Traditio* XVIII (1962), 436-445, and P. Hunter Blair, *op. cit.*

[2] Cf. HE V, 24; Latin text and translation in CO & MY 567.

ever left his monastery for any length of time. Although we may assume that Bede took a lively interest in what went on at home and abroad in those troubled times, he, the monastic scholar, did so as an observer from outside. On 25 May 735 he died. A later Abbot of Wearmouth and Jarrow, Cuthbert, has left us an eye-witness account of Bede's last days in the well-known letter to his friend Cuthwini[3].

From the picture drawn by Cuthbert, Bede emerges as "the very model of the saintly scholar priest"[4]. It may seem somewhat strange, then, that the epithet to his name has always remained 'venerabilis', i.e. 'reverend', the more so because we know of a cult of Bede at a fairly early date. The reason for this may be that Bede has always been looked upon first and foremost as the scholar – the author of many biblical commentaries, of scientific works, and of the *Historia Ecclesiastica*, a course of things which would most certainly have been to Bede's own liking and is, for example, wholly in keeping with the fact that he appended to his short biography in HE an extensive list of all his works[5].

The greater part of Bede's writings, about 45 of them, consist of Old and New Testament commentaries, which were studied all over Western Europe and which have come down to us in over 950 MSS. In addition to these there are his scientific works, such as one on Orthography and two on Chronology. The latter subject was suggested to Bede by the controversy between the Roman and the Celtic Churches over the Paschal question, which was settled for England at the Synod of Whitby in 664; most of HE V,21 is also taken up by a discussion of this matter. Finally, he composed a number of historical works, among them the *Lives of the Abbots of Wearmouth and Jarrow* and also the work with which Bede's name is primarily associated, the *Historia Ecclesiastica Gentis Anglorum*.

HE was completed at the end of a life-time devoted to studies in many fields. The work may have undergone a revision from the hand of the author himself. Such a revision is reflected in the two versions distinguished by Plummer and more about it will be said below in PART I, Chapter 2. The popularity HE enjoyed both in

[3] Cf. PLUMMER I, lxxii-lxxviii and PLUMMER I, clx-clxiv for translation and original Latin text respectively of this letter.
[4] Cf. *op. cit.*, lxxviii f.
[5] Cf. also Paul Lehmann, "Mittelalterliche Beinamen und Ehrentitel", *Historisches Jahrbuch* 49 (1929), 215-239 (repr. in: Paul Lehmann, *Erforschung des Mittelalters I*, Leipzig 1959; 129-154. Cf. especially 137 ff.)

England and on the Continent must have been very great even from a very early date. Of it over 160 MSS have been preserved, and a great many other unidentified MSS are mentioned in medieval library catalogues[6]. At least six of the MSS preserved to this day can be dated to the eighth century. One of these, *MS. Theol. Qu. 2* of the Landesbibliothek of Kassel, Germany, is the subject of the present study.

A. The Aim of the Present Edition

Bede's HE has been published in print from the second half of the 15th century, at first a number of times on the Continent and then in 1643 for the first time in England by Abraham Whelock, who gave the Latin text and the OE version in parallel columns[7]. The first really critical edition, based mainly on the Moore MS (see below), was published by George Smith in 1722, who completed the work of his father John Smith (1659-1715). Most 19th-century editions were based mainly on Smith's work, until Charles Plummer brought out his *Venerabilis Baedae Opera Historica* in 2 volumes (Oxford 1896). Plummer consulted a great number of MSS, and accompanies his text, largely based on the Moore MS, with a critical apparatus of variant readings from other MSS, with a full commentary and an extensive introduction[8]. The latest edition is that of Bertram Colgrave and

---

[6] More detailed information on how Bede composed HE is provided in the relevant passages of the works mentioned above, note 1, particularly by Wilhelm Levison, "Bede as Historian", Chapter V of A. Hamilton Thompson (ed.), *op. cit.* Besides, reference can be made to Charles W. Jones, "Bede as Early Medieval Historian", *Medievalia et Humanistica* 4 (1946), 26-36; Margaret W. Pepperdene, "Bede's Historia Ecclesiastica: A New Perspective", *Celtica IV* (1958), 253-262; P. Hunter Blair, *Bede's "Ecclesiastical History of the English Nation" and its importance today* (Jarrow Lecture), Jarrow: The Rectory 1959; Hugh Farmer, "The Studies of Anglo-Saxon Monks (A.D. 600-800)", in: *Los Monjes Y Los Estudios, IV Semana de Estudios Monásticos (Poblet 1961)*, Abadía de Poblet 1963, 87-103; and D. P. Kirby, "Bede's Native Sources for the *Historia Ecclesiastica*", *Bulletin of the John Rylands Library* 48 (1965/1966), 341-371. An elaborate discussion of the history of the tradition of the text is to be found in CO & MY xxxix ff.

[7] For a survey of the history of the publication of HE see PLUMMER I, cxxix ff. and CO & MY lxx ff.

[8] R. W. Chambers, *op. cit.*, p. 155, says of Plummer: "Charles Plummer seemed the reincarnation of Bede, if ever one man seemed the reincarnation of another, in his vast learning, his humility, his piety, his care for the young."

R. A. B. Mynors, *Bede's Ecclesiastical History of the English People* (Oxford 1969). Colgrave and Mynors set out to offer an accurate text on the basis of the best MSS including the Leningrad MS (see below) and the Kassel MS, which had not been used by Plummer, and an adequate translation from the Latin on facing pages[9].

In the present study the material of the Kassel MS is presented, not with a view to a further settlement of the Latin text of HE, to which very little could be added after the editions of Plummer and Colgrave and Mynors, but in order to discuss the OE name-material contained in it. When a linguist finds himself confronted with a historical period of a language for which only very little language-material is in evidence, he will have to avail himself of whatever evidence he can find for an assessment of the phonological features of that language or of dialects of that language, including such problematic material as names. What the eventual value of name-material may be, will be gone into in greater detail later in this INTRODUCTION. For the moment we would like to point out that as regards OE and its dialects of the eighth century we are concerned with one of these historical periods deficient in linguistic material. As R. I. Page has rightly said: "There is room for a lot of detailed study of some of the early OE texts, work of the nature, scope and quality of Anderson's study of the Leningrad Bede. The other early *Historia Ecclesiastica* texts and the *Liber Vitae* of Durham are obvious subjects for such study"[10]. Moreover, it is of prime importance for the study of place-names that the oldest occurrences of names are established as accurately as possible. In this connection the great place-name scholar Ekwall has stressed the importance of HE as a source of historical forms of English place-names[11].

The interest taken by the linguist in name-material goes beyond the purely text-oriented interest of the editors of the Latin text of Bede's HE. For the latter the exact appearance of the names in HE has always been only of minor interest, whereas the linguist will want to know how the names appear in each of the MSS. The editors of HE have not hitherto paid any linguistically relevant attention to the spelling of the names, with the exception of Plummer, who,

[9] According to CO & MY xli, n. 1, "A text with a critical apparatus is planned for the series *Corpus Christianorum*".
[10] Cf. R. I. Page, "Language and Dating in OE Inscriptions", *Anglia* 77 (1959), p. 405.
[11] EKWALL VC 7.

however, as indicated above, has not used the Kassel MS. An edition of the name-material of the Kassel MS is for that reason fully justified.

In a broader context, too, a specific edition of the name-material of the Kassel MS would seem to be justified. As will be seen below in PART I, Chapter 2, the Kassel MS contains a text of the so-called C-type, which is different from the Moore MS and the Leningrad MS, which show the M-type version. The existence of two versions of the text poses the problem of the priority, and also of the appearance of the original text. A comparison of the two versions often yields an answer to the latter question. In those cases where items of one version correspond with items in the other version, or with items in one of the MSS of the other version, we may generally assume that we are dealing with original material (with regard to this see also PART I, Chapter 2, § 1). This means that, if in the case of the name-material of HE such correspondence exists between MSS of the two different versions, we may look upon such material as stemming from Bede himself, i.e. as material that was written down by him – which does not necessarily imply that such material represents Bede's own Northumbrian dialect. For it is a well-known fact that Bede sometimes quotes literally from his sources, many of which were from other dialect-areas than his own (for more information about this see PART V, D). With a view to assessing the appearance of the OE name-material in Bede's original, an edition of the Kassel MS is required because so far the C-type version has only been represented by one eighth-century MS, viz. *British Museum MS. Cotton Tiberius C II* (see below). The availability of a second independent MS of the C-version makes it possible to assess which of the deviating spellings of the Cotton MS may truly be considered as typical of the C-type version and which not. Moreover, as will appear from the discussion of PART I, Chapter 2, the Kassel MS is a much more accurate MS than the Cotton MS. Its accuracy is such that where certain corresponding spellings are assessed as typical of the C-type version, as a whole such spellings gain more weight than when they were based on the Cotton MS only. For in the latter case they could still be discarded as the indiosyncracies of a relatively inaccurate copy.

We have decided to supplement the edition of the name-material of the Kassel MS with an edition of the corresponding name-material from four other eighth-century MSS of HE. These four other MSS are the Moore MS, the Leningrad MS, the Cotton MS, and *British Museum MS. Cotton Tiberius A XIV*. The name-material of the

Kassel MS is subjected to a direct confrontation with the name-material from these MSS, both with a view to an assessment of the difference between M-type and C-type texts and with a view to the localisation of the phonological features of the name-material. Two other MSS of HE which because of their early date might also have laid claim to inclusion, have not been utilized. They are the eighth-century *Wolfenbüttel, Herzog-August Bibliothek Weissenburg 34*[12] and the ninth-century *Namur, Public Library, Fonds de la ville 11*. Both these MSS contain an M-type text (which by some of the scribes of the Namur MS is treated very unskilfully[13]), and both MSS were copied in Continental scriptoria. Insertion of the name-material from these MSS would at best have been an unnecessary enlargement of the number of M-type texts already available, while at the same time the name-material of these MSS would no doubt show Continental features and thus be of little value within the framework of the present study[14].

For reasons of direct availability it has seemed necessary to embody the name-material of the MSS with which that of the Kassel MS has been constantly compared in this edition. It should be added that the material of the other MSS, if edited or otherwise available at all, will not normally be found arranged alphabetically as is the material of this edition. Furthermore, the embodiment of the material from the other MSS serves another purpose. It has been found that

---

[12] This MS is described by CLA IX, no. 1385 and CO & MY xcix f.

[13] A description of the Namur MS is provided by Charles Plummer, "Mémoire sur un manuscrit de l'Histoire Ecclésiastique du Peuple Anglais de Bède, dit le Vénérable. Appartenant à la Ville de Namur", *Annales de la Société Archéologique de Namur* 19 (1891), 393-400, and by PLUMMER I, lxxxvi ff. Plummer stresses the worthlessness of the text of this MS, "with an asperity which is most unlike him and is not warranted" according to CO & MY xiv. But by CO & MY too the weaknesses of the MS are granted and the value of the MS for a settlement of the text is thought to be negligible, as so many other good very early MSS are available. Cf. also DAHL 4 and STRÖM xxvi.

[14] At one stage we have considered inserting the name-material of the Wolfenbüttel MS in order to find out in how far OE name-material of a Latin MS is actually affected when it is transmitted by non-natives, assuming of course that the Wolfenbüttel MS, which is written in an early Caroline minuscule, was not actually copied on the Continent by scribes of Anglo-Saxon origin. For example, the name-material of this MS shows an almost universal use of svarabhakti vowels in such name-themes as **berct/berht/berict**, which may be an indication of its Continental origin. Such an undertaking would have led too far and could not possibly be incorporated in the present study. The question itself is interesting enough to warrant separate treatment.

the editions of the variant readings of the Moore MS and especially of the two Cotton MSS, as provided by Plummer's work and by Henry Sweet's *The Oldest English Texts*, are not reliable enough for our purpose, as will appear from the critical apparatus of PART II. In the present edition the name-material of the Moore MS and of the Cotton MSS is derived from a collation of the MSS themselves[15]. For the Moore MS P. Hunter Blair's facsimile edition was also used, as was O. Arngart's facsimile edition of the Leningrad MS and the edition of the OE material of this MS by the same scholar under the name of Anderson (see note 15). The accuracy of Anderson's edition of the OE material is remarkable; only in one instance has an incorrect reading been found, viz. *sexuulfum* instead of *sᴇxuulfum* on p. 43[16].

B. The OE Material and its Interpretation

Unlike the Moore MS and the Leningrad MS the Kassel MS has no OE version of the Hymn composed by Caedmon[17]. The only OE

[15] In the past most scholars using HE name-material have relied for their data on Sweet's and Plummer's editions. Of those who specifically study this name-material KÖHLER 1 states that he has used Plummer's edition; STRÖM names both editions as his sources, and so does ANDERSON LB. Anderson remarks (p. 10) that he has noticed differences between the two editions, but that "... a projected collation of the earliest MSS. in order to establish a complete critical edition of the Old English Material in Bede's History had to be abandoned owing to difficulties caused by the war". DAHL xi had noticed the deficiencies of the two editions before that, and for his study undertook a collation of the two Cottonian MSS. His work, however, is arranged in such a way that, what with the absence of an Index, the name-material is not very easy to retrace. Of those who have gone to HE for early forms of English place-names, most have quite understandably relied on PLUMMER and OET. So much is clear from the lists of sources used in the works of Ekwall, von Feilitzen, Tengvik, Tengstrand and Sandred (see elsewhere for further bibliographical details). A complete new collation of all the earliest MSS, i.e. of all the five Books of HE, such as intended by Anderson, is still a desirability, but would be outside the frame-work of the present study.

[16] The MS places are: Leningrad MS 91v,b and Kassel MS 10r, 12.

[17] Cf. HE IV, 24 and CO & MY 416 f. In the Latin text Bede presents only the general sense of the Hymn: "Hic est sensus, non autem ordo ipse verborum, quae dormiens ille canebat;...". There are seventeen MSS in which Caedmon's Hymn is contained, either in Northumbrian or in West Saxon dialect. Cf. E. van K. Dobbie, *The Manuscripts of Caedmon's Hymn and Bede's Death Song* (Columbia University Studies in English and Comparative Literature 128),

word in the Kassel MS that does not form part of a name is *gae* 'yes', which occurs on 26 v, 1. An account of the policy pursued in the present study with regard to the question which names to include and which to exclude is presented in the Editorial Note to PART II.

The application of name-material in historical-phonological research has always been considered a hazardous enterprise. The orthography of place-names and personal names is as a rule fairly stable and thus quickly tends to be archaic[18]. If the name-material is incorporated in a Latin text, heed should be given to the influence of the Latin orthography[19]. There are more factors that confuse the issue. For example, name-material may find its way into a text through written or oral tradition, and accordingly be represented differently. Moreover, do the author and those who copy his work have a different attitude towards names known to them from names unknown to them? It may be surmised that unknown names, if transmitted from written sources, will be recorded in the form they had in the original source. On the other hand, familiar names, especially if taken down from oral tradition, will probably appear in the language or dialect of the writer of the text. Indeed, even in this case it should be taken into account that, if a name is also common in the language or dialect of the writer, the writer may decide to give the name the form it takes in the dialect of the bearer, especially if the latter is widely known. Moreover, in cases where MSS are written by copyists, the way in which familiar names are transmitted will in general depend to a great extent on the strictness with which scriptorium discipline was exacted and to some extent on the personal attitude of the copyist.

New York 1937, pp. 10 ff. Cf. also A. H. Smith, *Three Northumbrian Poems. Caedmon's Hymn, Bede's Death Song and the Leiden Riddle*, London 1933; John C. Pope (ed.), *Seven Old English Poems*, Indianapolis 1966; and dr. Elisabeth Okasha, "The Leningrad Bede", *Scriptorium* 22 (1968), 35-37.

[18] Cf. Robert P. Stockwell and C. Westbrook Barritt, *Some Old English Graphemic-Phonemic Correspondences... ae, ea, and a* (Studies in Linguistics; Occasional Papers 4), Washington, D.C., 1951, p. 31.

[19] Cf. James W. Marchand, "Names of Germanic Origin in Latin and Romance Sources in the Study of Germanic Phonology", *Names* (Journal of the American Name Society) VII (1959), 167-181. Marchand shows himself very reserved as to the usefulness of this kind of material in linguistic studies: "At best, using names to determine the pronunciation (phonetics) of a language is a hazardous business; at worst, as in the case of most of the name-material dealt with in this paper, it is hopeless". It should be borne in mind, however, that Marchand is concerned with Latin texts composed by Romans, which constitutes an essential difference with the origin of our material.

At any rate, what should under all circumstances be taken into account is the linguistic background of the copyist(s)[20]. All this forms a complex of factors to be reckoned with in a discussion of name-material for historical-phonological purposes, but is not so insuperable as Sprockel's statement in its generality suggests: "Place-names and names of rivers and persons can seldom be used as reliable evidence"[21]. In any case such a verdict seems to be less valid for material from an eighth-century MS, such as ours, than for the name-material of *Domesday Book*, which, judging from Sprockel's reference to von Feilitzen's study[22], was the occasion for his statement.

The above summary enumeration of problems of name-material research may suffice to account for the way in which PART I of the present study has been worked out. In this PART an attempt is made to define as closely as possible time and place of the MS from a palaeo-graphical and codicological point of view. At the same time an attempt is made to place the Kassel MS in the tradition of the text, assuming that name-material of a near-original text will display linguistic characteristics of a near-original, i.e. near-Bedan, nature. Also the possibility of different scribes is investigated, and the overall relia-bility of the copy, and thus of the name-material, is established. Furthermore, a number of features of the orthography of the Latin is examined in order to isolate their effect on the appearance of the names[23]. In so far as these influences have been at work, they are discussed again in the phonological discussion of PART IV. In this PART, attention will also be given to a possible influence of Bede's sources on the way in which the names appear. In PART III the

[20] The statement of ANDERSON LB 2: "The question of the different hands having no bearing on the Old English material, except in so far as the change of hand may affect the orthography..." is as it stands a bit puzzling, to say the least, unless Anderson means to say that the different hands noticed by him in the Leningrad MS do not exhibit any deviation in spelling beyond a greater or less variety in the use of *ae* and *ę*.

[21] Cf. C. Sprockel, *The Language of the Parker Chronicle*, vol. I, *Phonology and Accidence* (Dissertation Amsterdam), The Hague 1965, p. 4.

[22] Cf. FEILITZEN DB 38. It is hard to see, however, how Sprockel's generalizing statement can be based on von Feilitzen's treatment of this matter.

[23] It has, for example, long been realised that the absence in the Latin alphabet of symbols to represent some of the palatal consonants has constituted a problem for the OE scribes. Cf. Yakov Malkiel, "Initial Points Versus Initial Segments of Linguistic Trajectories", in: Horace G. Lunt (ed.), *Proceedings of the Ninth International Congress of Linguists* (Cambridge, Mass., August 27-31, 1962), The Hague 1964; 402-406.

etymological derivations of names and name-elements are discussed. The etymological discussion is not an end in itself, but serves its purpose in the framework of the phonological description. It is exhaustive in that all the name-material of the edition is accounted for etymologically and that as a rule a complete picture is presented of scholarly opinion on these matters (see also the Introductory Note to PART III).

Once the name-material has been defined as precisely as possible as linguistically relevant OE material, i.e. when things such as "all kinds of palaeographical, psychological, mechanical, or associational factors"[24] have been isolated, the question arises to what use it can be put in a phonological description. What do the spellings found represent? Are we dealing with a phonemic spelling, or are we dealing with a spelling that is phonetic in character so that the pronunciation of the language or dialect involved can be narrowly reconstructed from it? McLaughlin[25], following in the main McIntosh[26], distinguishes two views with respect to writing. In the one a direct correspondence between spelling system and phonological system is assumed, and in the other it is held that "writing, like speech, is an independent manifestation of language"[27]. He who analyses a living language will first analyse and describe the spoken system and the written system of the language separately, and will then try to establish the relationship between the two[28]. It will appear that not all features of the writing system that reveal something significant of the language involved are also significant on the level of the spoken system; the capital letter *A* of *Archer*, for instance, marks the word as a family-name against the common noun *archer* with a small letter, whereas the two words are indistinguishable when spoken[29]. In historical studies, where we do not have direct access to the spoken system, the analysis of a language is much more complicated. Mc-

---

[24] Cf. C. L. Wrenn, "The Value of Spelling as Evidence", *Transactions of the Philological Society 1943*, London 1944, p. 30.
[25] Cf. John McLaughlin, *A Graphemic-Phonemic Study of A Middle English Manuscript*, The Hague 1963.
[26] Cf. Angus McIntosh, "The Analysis of Written Middle English", *Transactions of the Philological Society 1956*, Oxford 1956, 26-55.
[27] Cf. John McLaughlin, *op. cit.*, p. 23. C. E. Bazell, "The Grapheme", *Litera* 3(1956), 43-46, warns against overemphasizing the independent status of the written system, and against drawing too close a parallel between phonemics and graphemics.
[28] Cf. John McLaughlin, *op. cit.*, pp. 27 f.
[29] *op. cit.*, p. 26.

Laughlin finds it impossible to indicate how the phonological structure should be discovered in historical studies of language, but stresses that the written system can only be a starting-point for such an analysis and should never be "assumed to represent the structure of the spoken language"[30]. The analysis of the written system in itself may provide valuable information and may thus lead to valid conclusions about dialect divisions, as McIntosh has stressed for ME texts, but features of the written system do not of necessity have correspondences on the phonological level.

Nevertheless, the material we are dealing with in the present study appears in an alphabetical writing system, and especially for the earlier phases of such a system the assumption is justified that its users would attempt to achieve the closest possible correlation between spelling and pronunciation. The MSS with which McIntosh and Mc-Laughlin are concerned were composed 700 to 800 years after the period of our MS, by which time the number of non-correlating features of the writing-system had, no doubt, increased greatly. Although one does wisely to deal with a writing system as a system of graphs in the first place and to look for what is systematic in it on the graphic level without too readily drawing conclusions as to the phonological structure of the language or dialect involved, we may assume for MSS of our period that the writing-system fairly closely represented the spoken system. Thus we may expect that a change of spelling is generally an indication of a change on the phonological level.

The exact interpretation of such changes on the phonological level is a moot point among historical linguists. There are those, like Hockett[31] and Penzl[32], who believe that spellings and hence spelling changes can only be phonemic. Others, like Daunt[33] and

[30] op. cit., p. 36.
[31] Cf. Charles F. Hockett, "The Stressed Syllabics of Old English", *Language* 35 (1959), p. 579.
[32] Cf. Herbert Penzl, "A Phonemic Change in Early Old English", *Language* 20 (1944), p. 87; *idem*, "Orthographic Evidence for Types of Phonemic Change", *Proceedings of the Eighth International Congress of Linguists*, Oslo 1958, p. 147. Penzl is a bit less outspoken about this in "The Phonemic Split of Germanic *k* in Old English", *Language* 23 (1947), p. 34: "... orthographic evidence and occasional naive spellings lend themselves primarily to phonemic, hardly ever to a purely phonetic interpretation".
[33] Cf. Marjorie Daunt, "Old English Sound-Changes Reconsidered in Relation to Scribal Tradition and Practice", *Transactions of the Philological Society 1939*, London 1939, 108-137.

Stockwell and Barritt[34], apparently assume that orthographical features may be employed both for phonemic and allophonic distinctions. For without this neither Daunt nor Stockwell and Barritt could have proposed their re-interpretations of the OE 'short diphthongs' (see below). Hockett, to prove his point that a difference in spelling cannot "correlate with a merely *allophonic* difference in pronunciation", refers to the random application of the symbols þ and *đ* for both the voiced and the voiceless allophone of the spirant /þ/, whereas an allophonic writing-system would have applied each of the two available symbols to one of the two allophones. However, Hockett's example is not a very apt one, even apart from the fact that one negative proof cannot suffice to base a general rule on. The difference between the voiced and voiceless variants of the spirant /þ/ was as a rule "evident from the position in the word"[35]; the need to distinguish between them by orthographical means cannot have been felt very strongly, even if for historical reasons the writing-system happened to possess two different symbols for the spirant. What Hockett calls a "fairly regularly maintained distinction of spelling"[36] should, therefore, not be interpreted *a priori* as an indication in this case of a phonemic difference in the spoken system.

The interpretation of the graphs of historical texts presents considerable difficulties and the two views just described lead to divergent treatments. In the last few decades, for instance, scholars have given much attention to the so-called OE 'short diphthongs', which usually appear in OE MSS as *io*, *eo* and *ea*. In the traditional view, represented also in the main grammars of OE, these short diphthongs have always been looked upon as the phonemes /io/, /eo/, and /æa/, distinguished from the corresponding long diphthongs /īo/, /ēo/, and /ǣa/ mainly by length. Contrary to this it has been suggested that the symbols *o* and *a* of the three digraphs should be seen in relation to the following consonants only, in that *o* and *a* indicate the particular dark quality of allophonic variants of these consonants[37].

---

[34] Cf. Robert P. Stockwell and C. Westbrook Barritt, *op. cit.*; *idem*, "The Old English Short Digraphs: Some Considerations", *Language* 31 (1955), 372-389; *idem*, "Scribal Practice: Some Assumptions", *Language* 37 (1961), 75-82.
[35] Cf. CAMPBELL 20.
[36] Cf. *loc. cit.*
[37] Cf. Marjorie Daunt, *op. cit.*; Fernand Mossé, *Manuel de l'Anglais du Moyen Age, I. Vieil-Anglais* (Bibliothèque de Philologie Germanique VIII), Paris 1945 (repr. 1950), p. 41; and Marjorie Daunt, "Some Notes on Old English Phonology. A reply to Mr. M. Samuels' paper", *Transactions of the Philological Society 1952*, Oxford 1953, 48-54.

The Anglo-Saxon monks would, in this view, have taken over this way of symbolizing consonant quality by pre-consonantal vowel-symbols from their masters, the Irish. Quite rightly it has been objected to this that, if the Irish taught the Anglo-Saxons how to spell Latin, it does not follow that they also taught them how to spell their own native language; that, moreover, these digraphs do not appear in the oldest OE MSS, i.e. the MSS that would be most under Irish influence, and, finally, that precisely the most common of these Irish diacritics, viz. the symbol *i*, has left no trace in OE MSS. Stockwell and Barritt[38] acknowledge the conditioning influence of the consonants, and look upon *io* and *eo* (at any rate for the earlier period) and *ea* as allophones of the sort vowels /i/, /e/, and /æ/, allowing for considerable differences on the phonetic level, even to the point of diphthongal pronunciation of the allophones. Independently from them Reszkiewicz[39] arrives at a similar conclusion, differing only in that according to him the 'short diphthongs' were always monophthongal variants of the short vowels. Hockett[40] interprets *io*, *eo*, and *ea* as short vowels, phonemically distinct from /i/, /e/, and /æ/. In this controversy the traditional view has been upheld by Kuhn and Quirk, and many others[41].

The conclusion from this short survey may be that, however much scholars differ in their interpretations of the digraphs *io*, *eo* and *ea*, they all start from the assumption that the introduction of different

[38] See Note 34. Cf. also A. J. Van Essen, "Some Remarks on Old English Phonology", *Linguistics* 32 (1967), 83-86.
[39] Cf. A. Reszkiewicz, "The Phonetic Interpretation of Old English Digraphs", *Biuletyn Polskiego Towarzystwa Językoznawczego* 12 (1953), 179-187.
[40] Cf. *op. cit.*
[41] Cf. Sherman M. Kuhn and Randolph Quirk, "Some recent interpretations of Old English digraph spellings", *Language* 29 (1953), 143-156; and *idem*, "The Old English Digraphs: a Reply", *Language* 31 (1955), 390-401. (Both these articles have been reprinted in: Randolph Quirk, *Essays on the English Language, Medieval and Modern*, London 1968, 38-54 and 55-69 respectively). Cf. also M. L. Samuels, "The Study of Old English Phonology", *Transactions of the Philological Society 1952*, Oxford 1953, 15-47; C. E. Bazell, (review of Stockwell & Barritt (1951)), *Litera* 1 (1954), 75-77; Gerd Bauer, "The Problem of Short Diphthongs in Old English", *Anglia* 74 (1956), 427-437; C. E. Bazell, "The Phonemic Interpretation of the Old English Diphthongs", *Litera* 3 (1956), 114-120; Y. Krupatkin, "Old English Breaking. A Step to a Phonemic Approach", *Philologica Pragensia* VII (1964), 62-64; C. Sprockel, *op. cit.*, p. 133; James W. Ney, "Old English Vowel Digraph Spellings", *Linguistics* 45(1968), 36-49; and PILCH 64 ff.

spellings for /i/, /e/, and /æ/ points to changes on the phonological level. In historical-linguistic studies, therefore, an inventory of the graphs of the writing-system and of "the conditions under which certain graphs are used"[42] is a first requirement. Brunner stresses that as long as a clear picture with regard to the phonemic and/or phonetic significance cannot be attained for the relevant "fairly regularly maintained distinctions of spelling" there is little harm in preserving such terms as 'Breaking', 'Front Mutation', and 'Back Mutation' in OE studies. The view that the historical linguist should start from a systematic inventory of the orthography is also shared by Stockwell and Barritt[43]. The next step in the study, according to them, should be a search for phonemic contrasts, and then an attempt to derive from these the underlying phonemic structure with the help of external information, such as etymological data[44], and finally a phonetic interpretation may be attempted. It should be kept in mind, however, that the absence of minimal contrastive pairs may sometimes be due to the deficiencies of the written material, and cannot in itself always be taken to imply absence in the spoken system of a particular phonemic contrast[45].

The aim of the present historical-linguistic study is a restricted one. In the first place, as has been said before, it is an edition of the OE name-material in the Kassel MS; in addition the value of the material is defined in a discussion of a number of factors that may have influenced the appearance of the names; and finally a phonological description is provided on the basis of the etymological

[42] Cf. Karl Brunner, "The Old English Vowel Phonemes", *English Studies* 34 (1953), p. 247.
[43] Cf. Robert P. Stockwell and C. Westbrook Barritt, "The Old English Short Digraphs: Some Considerations", *Language* 31 (1955), p. 384.
[44] For phonemic interpretations of the OE vowel-system cf. Robert P. Stockwell, "The Phonology of Old English: A Structural Sketch", *Studies in Linguistics* 13 (1958), 13-24; Charles F. Hockett, *op. cit.*, p. 576; and Sherman M. Kuhn, "On the Syllabic Phonemes of Old English", *Language* 37 (1961), 522-538. Cf. also Herbert Pilch, "Altenglische historische Lautlehre als phonologisches Problem", *Word* 24 (1968; *Linguistic Studies Presented to André Martinet*, Part Two: *Indo-European Linguistics*), 350-370. For a phonemic interpretation of the OE consonant-system cf. Sherman M. Kuhn, "On the Consonantal Phonemes of Old English", in: James L. Rosier (ed.), *Philological Essays. Studies in Old and Middle English Language and Literature in Honour of Herbert Dean Meritt*, The Hague 1970, 16-49.
[45] Cf. Sherman M. Kuhn and Randolph Quirk, "Some recent interpretations of Old English digraph spellings", *Language* 29 (1953), p. 153.

information available. The phonological description departs from the West-Germanic and Primitive OE vowel and consonant phonemes. From an inventory of their representations in the Kassel MS a further definition of the material as to date and dialect will be attempted, on the basis of what is known about the OE dialects and their developments. Conclusions will have validity primarily on the level of the graphic representation. When called for, questions of phonemic and also phonetic interpretation of the material will be gone into indirectly. The aim of this study, restricted as it is by the limitations of the name-material, cannot be an altogether fresh review of OE phonology as a whole. The addition to the store of OE material of another portion of early OE material that is precisely defined is a sufficient aim in itself.

C. The Manuscripts

1. *The Kassel MS*. Because of a number of reasons which we have already gone into in the previous section, a thorough and extensive description of the Kassel MS from a palaeographical, codicological and textual point of view is required. For this the reader is referred to PART I. From now on the Kassel MS will be K for short.

2. *The Moore MS*. The Moore MS, *Cambridge University Library Kk. 5.16*, which will be referred to as M, is named after Bishop John Moore of Ely, who owned it before his library was given to the University of Cambridge by King George I in 1715. From the chronological entries at the end of the work the date of composition of the MS has been set at 737. Despite the fact that as early as the ninth century it was in France, it is usually assumed that it was copied in a Northumbrian monastery. The occasional uncial script of the MS, which is reminiscent of Wearmouth-Jarrow but is very irregular in appearance, leads Wright[46] to assume that M was copied from a

---

[46] Cf. David H. Wright (review of P. Hunter Blair, *The Moore Bede, etc.* ....), *Anglia* 82 (1964), 110-117. Some of the other more or less extensive descriptions of M are given by PLUMMER I, lxxxix ff.; E. van K. Dobbie, *op. cit.*, pp. 11 ff.; CLA II, no. 139; DAHL 2 ff.; STRÖM XXVII; M. L. W. Laistner and H. H. King, *A Hand-list of Bede Manuscripts*, Ithaca New York 1943, p. 95; P. Hunter Blair, *The Moore Bede, Cambridge University Library, MS. Kk.5.16* (Early English Manuscripts in Facsimile, Ninth Volume), Copenhagen 1959, pp. 11 ff.; and CO & MY xliii ff.

Wearmouth-Jarrow MS at another northern Northumbrian monastery. The whole of M was copied in Anglo-Saxon minuscule by one scribe, who produced a good copy which, however, is marked by a fairly great number of minor mistakes of spelling (see also PART I, Chapter 2).

3. *The Leningrad MS.* The Leningrad MS, *Leningrad Public Library Lat. Q. v.I.18*, from now on referred to as L, was taken to Russia from France, where its last-known home was the Benedictine Abbey of Saint Germain des Prés, some time during the French revolution. It may have been in France from the 12th century onwards. L, not used by PLUMMER, has been the subject of a great number of studies since the publications of Anderson/Arngart[47]. The marginal chronological entries, a feature that L shares with M, point to A.D. 746 as its date of composition, which recently has come to be looked upon as the date *non post quem*, as some scholars reckon with the possibility that L was copied during Bede's own life-time. Its importance is enhanced by the fact that from a palaeographical point of view there can be little doubt that it was copied at Wearmouth or Jarrow. Therefore, it must have been very close to Bede both in time and place, although Lowe's interesting suggestion that in the phrase

[47] Cf. ANDERSON LB, and O. Arngart, *The Leningrad Bede, an Eighth Century Manuscript of the Venerable Bede's Historia Ecclesiastica Gentis Anglorum In the Public Library, Leningrad* (Early English Manuscripts in Facsimile, Second Volume), Copenhagen 1952. Before this L had been used by LINDSAY 487, and it had been described by E. Heinrich Zimmermann, *Vorkarolingische Miniaturen*, Berlin 1916, pp. 145 and 169; by O. Dobiache-Rojdestvensky, "Un manuscrit de Bède à Leningrad", *Speculum* 3(1928), 314-321; E. van K. Dobbie, *op. cit.*, pp. 16 f.; and STRÖM XXXI f. The other main recent contributions to the study of this MS are: E. A. Lowe, "A Key to Bede's Scriptorium. Some Observations on the Leningrad Manuscript of the 'Historia Ecclesiastica Gentis Anglorum'", *Scriptorium* 12 (1958), 182-190; *idem*, "An Autograph of the Venerable Bede?", *Revue Bénédictine* 68 (1958), 200-202; M. Schapiro, "The Decoration of the Leningrad Manuscript of Bede", *Scriptorium* 12 (1958), 191-207; D. Misonne, "'Famulus Christi'. A Propos d'un Autographe de Bède le Vénérable", *Revue Bénédictine* 69(1959), 97-99; David H. Wright, "The Date of the Leningrad Bede", *Revue Bénédictine* 71(1961), 265-273; P. Meyvaert, "The Bede 'Signature' in the Leningrad Colophon", *loc. cit.*, 274-286; M. Bévenot S.J., "Towards Dating the Leningrad Bede", *Scriptorium* 16 (1962), 365-369; David H. Wright, (review of P. Hunter Blair, *The Moore Bede, etc....*), *Anglia* 82 (1964), p. 115; P. Meyvaert, *Bede and Gregory the Great* (Jarrow Lecture), Jarrow: The Rectory 1964, pp. 3 f.; and CLA XI, no. 1621. Cf. also CO & MY xliv.

Beda famulus Christi indignus at the end of the work on 161r we may have Bede's own signature has been refuted on palaeographical grounds by Bévenot, who thinks it is a late eighth-century forgery. L is written in Anglo-Saxon pointed minuscule and is fairly elaborately ornamented[48]. Four scribes have been at work on this copy of HE; the last executed the bulk of the MS, viz. 68v to 161r (the end of the MS), which also covers the complete text of Books IV and V, the Books that mainly interest us. Lowe[49] suggests that Hand IV is distinguishable from the preceding three Hands in that it betrays features of someone who was trained outside Wearmouth and Jarrow and in an older epoch than the other three. All four scribes produced a very exact copy.

4. *London British Museum, Cotton Tiberius C. II*. This MS, to be referred to as C, has for a long time been one of the important MSS on which editors based their texts of HE. To Plummer it was the oldest representative of one of the two versions of the text, which version he therefore called the C-type version. K, as we shall see in PART I, is another old MS of this version. The date of C has never caused much difference of opinion; it is generally assigned to the second half or the end of the eighth century. Scholars have, however, differed in opinion on its origin. Plummer[50], on textual evidence, would assign it to Durham. According to recent opinion, following Zimmermann[51], the South of England provides a likelier origin, although Kuhn[52] has tried to prove that the group of MSS to which C clearly belongs and which Zimmermann had named the 'Canterbury School' all stem from Mercia. C is a well-written copy in Anglo-Saxon minuscule, probably all by one hand, with more minor textual deviations than the other MSS we have discussed so far (see below, PART I, Chapter 2).

---

[48] E. Heinrich Zimmermann, *op. cit.*, p. 145, because of its ornamentation assigns L to southern England.
[49] Cf. E. A. Lowe, "A Key to Bede's Scriptorium. Some Observations on the Leningrad Manuscript of the 'Historia Ecclesiastica Gentis Anglorum'", *Scriptorium* 12 (1958), p. 188.
[50] Cf. PLUMMER I, xciii f.
[51] Cf. E. Heinrich Zimmermann, *op. cit.*, p. 135 and p. 294. Cf. also CLA II, no. 191; STRÖM XXVIII f.; David H. Wright, *op. cit.*, p. 116; CO & MY xlii.
[52] Cf. Sherman M. Kuhn, "From Canterbury to Lichfield", *Speculum* 23 (1948), 591-629.

5. *London British Museum, Cotton Tiberius A. XIV*. This MS was badly damaged in the Cottonian fire of 1731 and was for that reason designated B (= burnt) by Plummer, in which we will follow him. Because of the severe damage, B was neglected by scholars until Plummer discovered its great merits. It has been dated early ninth century[53], but Plummer[54] dates it eighth century. Wright[55] thinks that it cannot have been copied long after 746, because the dates of the marginal entries to the chronological summary at the end of HE for the greater part yield 746, as in L. The Anglo-Saxon minuscule script and the ornament are of high quality. As far as can be made out, only one hand has been at work at it. B was probably copied in the same scriptorium as L.

6. The relations between K and the other MSS discussed above will be gone into in PART I, Chapter 2.

In the case of C any direct parentage between it and any of the three M-type MSS, i.e. M, L, and B, is out of the question.

With regard to the relation between M and B, PLUMMER I, xci concludes that "B is a sister MS to M", which means that despite their closeness neither of them can be said to be derived from the other. M and B go back to a common original. The same conclusion ANDERSON LB 10 draws for M and L. As to the relationship between L and B, Anderson defines it as "fairly close", a closeness that had also been noticed by Zimmermann[56]. Further scrutiny of the two MSS has revealed that they are so close to each other that the conclusion seems inescapable that B is a direct copy of L. Definite proof, however, is hard to find[57].

---

[53] Cf. *Catalogue of Ancient Manuscripts in the British Museum*, Part II, Latin, London 1884, p. 79. B was omitted altogether from CLA II, a mistake acknowledged by E. A. Lowe in "The Script of the Farewell and Date Formulae in Early Papal Documents, as reflected in the oldest manuscripts of Bede's Historia Ecclesiastica", *Revue Bénédictine* 69 (1959), p. 22 note. It will now be incorporated in CLA, *Supplement*, as no. 1703. DAHL 11 and ANDERSON LB 6, 141 f. also date it early ninth century and Arngart, *op. cit.*, p. 35, dates B considerably later than L, although the close relationship is recognized.
[54] Cf. PLUMMER I, xci ff.; cf. also STRÖM XXX f.
[55] Cf. David H. Wright, *op. cit.*, pp. 115 ff. A similar view is expressed by CO & MY xlvi.
[56] Cf. E. Heinrich Zimmermann, *op. cit.*, p. 145.
[57] Cf. CO & MY xlvi f., and cf. also David H. Wright, *loc. cit.*

D. The Plan of the Study

The arrangement of the separate PARTS of the present study follows logically from what we have set out to do. PART I gives a more or less complete description of both the MS itself and of its text. PART II contains the name-material of K, arranged alphabetically for ease of reference in connection with the subsequent phonological discussion and accompanied by the name-material from M, L, C, and B in parallel columns. The critical apparatus of this PART provides detailed information on palaeographical points concerning the name-material on the one hand, and on the way in which the material has been treated in the previous editions in OET and PLUMMER on the other. The discussion of the name-material opens with PART III which contains etymological notes on names and name-elements, also in alphabetical order. The phonological discussion proper is given in PART IV in which the West-Germanic or Primitive OE vowel and consonant phonemes and their corresponding representations in K are dealt with systematically. Then PART V follows with Sections on the possible influences of the different Hands, of the orthography of the Latin of the text, of the position of K among the MSS; of the local origin of the name-material; and finally with Sections on the dialectal features and the date of the name-material. The BIBLIOGRAPHY has been arranged alphabetically. All the names of the edition also appear in the INDEX.

PART I
KASSEL MS. THEOL. QU. 2

Chapter 1

THE MANUSCRIPT

§ 1. General

MS. Theol. Qu. 2 of the Kassel Landesbibliothek[1] contains Books IV and V of Bede's *Historia Ecclesiastica Gentis Anglorum*, beginning with the capitulum of Chapter 1 of Book IV, which runs "Ut defuncto deusdedit uigheard ad suscipiendum episcopatum romam sit missus", and ending with the final line of Bede's request for his readers' prayers, viz. "Apud omnes fructum pię intercessionis inueniam ,,, ,,,". On the front-cover of the pigskin envelope a fifteenth-century hand has written *xxxiiii or.* ∧ (see below, § 6) and a ninth-century minuscule hand *historia angloru̅ ƀ.* The inside of the front-cover carries some heterogeneous material. In handwriting of modern times it has *Continet folia L* and by a different hand, in four successive lines, *Deficit in hoc codice | Bedæ de Historia | Anglorum Liber I.II. | et III.* Of a somewhat earlier date are the drawings of two faces, very poorly

---

[1] The MS is no. 1140 of CLA VIII. Gustav Struck gives a fairly full description of it in "Handschriftenschätze der Landesbibliothek Kassel", in: Dr. Wilhelm Hopf (ed.), *Die Landesbibliothek Kassel 1580-1930*, Part II, Marburg 1930, pp. 25 f. Less detailed references are given by Karl Christ, *Die Bibliothek des Klosters Fulda im 16. Jahrhundert. Die Handschriftenverzeichnisse* (Zentralblatt für Bibliothekswesen, Beiheft 64), Leipzig 1933, p. 184; G. Storms, "The Weakening of O.E. Unstressed *i* to *e* and the Date of Cynewulf", *English Studies* 37 (1956), p. 108; Dorothy Whitelock, *After Bede* (Jarrow Lecture), Jarrow: The Rectory 1960, p. 10; and David H. Wright, (review of P. Hunter Blair, *The Moore Bede, etc....*), *Anglia* 82 (1964), p. 116. Short references to the MS by Georg Baesecke, *Der Vocabularius Sti. Galli in der Angelsächsischen Mission*, Halle 1933, p. 99, n. 13; by Karl Christ, "Karolingische Bibliothekseinbände", in: *Festschrift Georg Leyh*, Leipzig 1937, p. 85 and p. 104; by C. W. M. Grein, *Das Hildebrandslied... nebst Bemerkungen über die ehemaligen Fulder Codices der Kasseler Bibliothek*, 2nd ed., Kassel 1880, p. 13; by F. G. C. Gross, "Über den Hildebrandslied-Codex der Kasseler Landesbibliothek, nebst Angaben und Vermuthungen über die Schicksale der alten Fuldaer Handschriften-Bibliothek überhaupt", *Zeitschrift des Vereins für hessische Geschichte u. Landeskunde*, N.F. 8 (1880), p. 165; by Montague R. James, "The Manuscripts of Bede", in: A. Hamilton Thompson (ed.), *Bede. His Life, Times, and Writings*, Oxford 1935 (repr. 1969), p. 236, n. 1; by M. L. W. Laistner and H. H. King,

done, at the bottom of the page[2]. Of equally obscure origin and meaning are the numbers *i.ii.iii.iiii.*, which are written three times, one above the other, in the middle of the inside of the front-cover. There too a modern hand has written in pencil, again in successive lines, *4º MS. theol. | 2 | Beda | Schaup I,10.* And finally, also in pencil, the inside of the front-cover has *Blatt 1-50.* The hand by which this was written is probably also the source of the other matter in pencil of the MS: 1. the numbering of the folios; 2. the numbering of the Chapters; 3. *Caput 14 deficit* in the margin of 11r; 4. the rectangular bracket in line 35 of the same folio preceding "Interea"; 5. the two cross-strokes of 50r,27, which separate Bede's request for his readers' prayers from the preceding text; 6. *Finis* at the end of Book V, on 48r[3]. Neither 50v – the text ends on 50r – nor the inside and outside of the back-cover show much of interest. 50v shows some pen-trials, viz. a ninth-century (?) minuscule *a* almost right in the middle, below it two figures resembling the figure *8* lying horizontally, and to the right of these near the inner edge, on one line, the letters *a b c d e f g h i k* in pre-caroline minuscule of somewhat later date it seems than those of the front-cover, which line of letters is written a second time below it[4].

A Hand-list of Bede Manuscripts, Ithaca New York 1943, p. 94 and p. 97; by Paul Lehmann, *Johannes Sichardus und die von ihm benutzten Bibliotheken und Handschriften* (Quellen und Untersuchungen zur lateinischen Philologie des Mittelalters 4), München 1911, p. 114; by Emile Lesne, *Les Livres, "Scriptoria", et Bibliothèques du commencement du VIIIe à la fin du XIe siècle (Histoire de la Propriété ecclésiastique en France,* vol. 4), Lille 1938, p. 63; by W. M. Lindsay, *Palaeographia Latina,* Part II (St. Andrews University Publications XVI), Oxford 1923, p. 34; by R. A. B. Mynors, "The Early Circulation of the Text", in: P. Hunter Blair, *The Moore Bede, Cambridge University Library,* MS. *Kk. 5.16* (Early English Manuscripts in Facsimile, Ninth Volume), Copenhagen 1959, p. 33; by G. H. Pertz, "Handschriften der Churfürstlichen Bibliothek zu Kassel", *Archiv der Gesellschaft für ältere deutsche Geschichtskunde* 6 (1838), p. 203; by August Potthast, *Wegweiser durch die Geschichtswerke des europäischen Mittelalters bis 1500* (Bibliotheca Historica Medii Aevi I), 2nd ed., Berlin 1896, p. 138; by Friedrich Prinz, *Frühes Mönchtum im Frankenreich,* Kultur und Gesellschaft in Gallien, den Rheinlanden und Bayern am Beispiel der monastischen Entwicklung. 4. bis 8. Jahrhundert, München-Wien 1965, p. 517; and by Dorothy Whitelock, *English Historical Documents I, c. 500-1042,* London 1955, p. 587.
[2] See Gustav Struck, *op. cit.,* p. 25.
[3] Points 2, 3, 4, and 5 will be discussed in further detail below, Chapter 2, § 1.
[4] Also referred to by Karl Christ, "Karolingische Bibliothekseinbände", in: *Festschrift Georg Leyh,* Leipzig 1937, p. 85.

4

The offset of these is to be seen on the inside of the back-cover, which was evidently inadvertently laid against 50v, before the ink of the pen-trials had dried up, for the ink of the second line of these letters has run out both on 50v and the inside of the back-cover. In the middle of the top half of the latter there are, moreover, to be found some rather indistinct characters of modern date to all appearances representing *stpite*. There is nothing of interest on the outside of the back-cover.

The text itself of Book IV and Book V and of the *recapitulatio chronica totius operis* of the *Historia Ecclesiastica* covers 99 folios. There are six gatherings of eight leaves each, and a separate sheet constituting two leaves for 49 and 50. Book IV covers the first three gatherings, Book V the whole of the next three gatherings, 48v excepted, and the *recapitulatio* covers 48v, 49r, 49v and 50r. If the arrangement of Books IV and V into separate sets of gatherings was not deliberate, it probably was made use of when the MS was taken from the shelves for such purposes as copying. Particular gatherings or sets of gatherings could be taken from the body of the Codex. The first two or three folios of Book IV show severe fading of script, and so to a lesser degree do 24v, which is the last folio of Book IV, and 25r, which is the first folio of Book V. It is quite possible that the explanation of the loss of the first three Books lies in such a taking apart of gatherings. When the MS still held five Books, it probably consisted of 110 to 115 leaves according to David H. Wright[5]. When one takes into account the amount of material lost with the first three Books and when one assumes regular gatherings of eight for these as well, a total number of eight gatherings for the first three Books can be calculated, which would amount to 114 leaves for the complete MS.

Both Book IV and Book V open with a full list of their capitula, or chapter-headings, on 1r-1v and 25r-25v respectively. There is a difference in the way the capitula of the two Books have been arranged on the folio. Those of Book V are marked off from one another by the fact that each capitulum starts on a new line with a capital letter for its first letter. Capital letters are also used for the first letters of the capitula of Book IV, but some of these have been given a distinctive feature that one does not come across elsewhere in the MS, viz. a comma inside the main body of the capital letter, used when the

[5] *op. cit.*, p. 116.

capitulum simply follows its predecessor in the middle of a line and does not start on a fresh line.

Capitula are not numbered, nor originally were chapters. In this respect K differs from M, L, C, and B, as it also does in that all *explicits* and *incipits* are wanting. There are no colophons nor any glosses. Indeed, K is a very sober copy of the *Historia Ecclesiastica*, a "utilitarian book" as Wright quite rightly calls it[6]. Where chapter-division is concerned, the normal practice is for chapters to be concluded by a set or several sets of three consecutive commas to fill out the final line in so far as that was necessary, after which one full line is left open and the new chapter starts on a new line with an initial capital letter – the only attempt in the MS at some kind of ornament. The third comma of the set is usually much larger than the other two. Exceptional treatment has been noted in a number of cases. There is only one comma at the end of Chapters 7 (7v) and 12 (10v) of Book IV, and of Chapter 5 (28r) of Book V[7]. Chapter 1 (26r) of Book V is concluded by only two commas. No commas are used at the ends of Chapters 15 (11v), and 18 (13r) of Book IV, and of Chapters 6 (29r) and 11 (32v) of Book V. In all these cases there was not enough space to insert the normal set(s) of three commas. Following Chapters 10 (9r), 22 (16r), 24 (19r), and 25 (20r) of Book IV, and Chapters 14 (36r), 15 (36v), and 18 (38r) of Book V no extra line has been left open, apparently because more than half of the concluding line of the Chapter was blank.

The available writing-space is used economically. The folios measure 27,5 cm × 18,0 cm and the area reserved for writing purposes measures 22,0 cm × 13,5 cm. As a rule the top margin takes up 2,2 cm, the bottom margin 1,25 cm and the outer margin 3,25 cm. The writing is done in single columns of long lines, normally 42 lines to a folio. Folios 9r to 16v, the complete second gathering, and 23r and 23v have 41 lines; 24r and 48r (the end of Book V) have 40 lines; and on 24v (the end of Book IV) and on 50r (the end of the MS) what space remains is left blank, 17 lines and 6 lines respectively. As a rule lines are filled out completely. The text shows no paragraph-division. Neither are quotations or extracts from other sources given special prominence as a rule. Special prominence is only given to three of the poems quoted in the text, viz. to the Epitaph for Caedualla in

[6] *loc. cit.*
[7] We follow the chapter-numbering as found in CO & MY. For further comment on the question of chapter-numbering see below, Chapter 2, § 1, note 5.

Book V, Chapter 7, on 29r-29v; to the Epitaph for Theodore, Archbishop of Canterbury, in Book V, Chapter 8, on 29v-30r; and to the Epitaph for Uilfrid 1 (*s.v.*) in Book V, Chapter 19, on 41r. Each of the lines of these poems starts on a new line. The only[8] other poem of the text, Bede's Hymn in Honour of Aedilthryd (*s.v.*), which Bede quotes in Book IV, Chapter 18, on 14v-15r, is not treated in that way.

Three times run-overs, set off by rectangular brackets, occur in K, viz. on 14v, 29v and 43v. Nothing of the margins has been cut away by binders. In the margins there are sixteen instances of corrections of words, syllables, and single letters, executed by a contemporary hand, to all appearances the scribe himself[9]. There are also thirty instances in which either single lines or two intersecting lines of various shapes occur in the margins. Their ink is usually that of the text and only in some cases looks slightly faded. They are probably pen-trials. For the greater part these marginal signs, i.e. 27 out of 30, occur in Book IV. The last three instances are found on 29v, 32r and 34r.

§ 2. *Physical Appearance*

The writing-material used is "vellum of the Insular type, but treated only in part with the pumice-stone"[10]. The feel of the conjugate leaves 3 and 6, and 49 and 50, and of the folios 9r and 16v, 10r and 15v, 11r and 14v, and 28r and 29v, all of them corresponding sides of conjugate leaves, is softer than that of the other folios, and they are less glossy in appearance. The front-cover and back-cover and the leaves 3, 14, 26, 28, 32, 38, 39, 45, and 46 show holes which had fallen into the vellum before it was written on, since no part of the text has been lost owing to them. The pigskin envelope is badly damaged at its sides. Wormbores pierce front-cover and back-cover and penetrate a number of leaves.

As has been said, there are six gatherings of eight leaves each,

---

[8] The Latin text of Caedmon's Hymn in Book IV, Chapter 12, on 18r, is not looked upon as a poem by Bede. See above, INTRODUCTION, note 17.

[9] The total number of marginal corrections is rather small, compared with the number of corrections made in the text itself. Of the latter there are about one hundred and fifty. It is noteworthy that the majority of the marginal corrections occur on folios copied by what will appear to be Hand I (see below), viz. on 6v, 11v, 15r, 15v, 33r, 35r, 41r, 41v, 42r (twice), 42v, 43v, 44v, 45v, 46v, and 48v. This may be an indication that corrections were executed by the scribes themselves.

[10] Cf. CLA VIII, no. 1140.

and a separate sheet was added for leaves 49 and 50. Following Kirchner[11], we could sum up the arrangement of the gatherings in the
formula 6 IV (48) + I (50). Of the six quaternions gathering one
contains leaves 1-8, gathering two leaves 9-16, gathering three leaves
17-24, gathering four leaves 25-32, gathering five leaves 33-40, and
gathering six leaves 41-48, and finally the loose sheet contains leaves
49 and 50. All the gatherings are regular in their make-up, except
for the third gathering, in which leaves 17 and 23, 18 and 22, and
19 and 21 are conjugate leaves and leaves 20 and 24 have been sewn
in as separate leaves (see Figure One). The gatherings are unsigned.

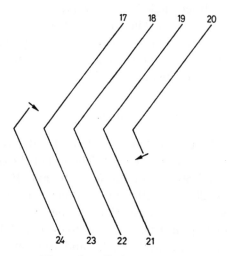

Figure One. Gathering three.

It is not always possible to distinguish between flesh-side and hair-side,
but as far as we can see the normal practice of putting flesh-side to
flesh-side and hair-side to hair-side, with flesh-side opening the
gathering, has been observed in gatherings one, four and five. The
sixth gathering deviates from the normal practice in that it opens
with a hair-side. Gatherings two and three are quite irregular for
obvious reasons: gathering three is altogether irregular in its make-up
as we have just seen, and of gathering two at least three leaves have
been treated with the pumice-stone. MSS of insular vellum thus

[11] Cf. Joachim Kirchner, *Germanistische Handschriftenpraxis*. Ein Lehrbuch
für die Studierenden der deutschen Philologie (2nd ed.), München 1967, p. 15.

8

treated were not arranged strictly according to the rules formulated above[12].

The six gatherings and the separate sheet for leaves 49 and 50 are held in a pigskin envelope (see below, §§ 5 and 6). In the centre of each gathering there are six holes through which uncoloured string is threaded in order to hold the leaves of the gatherings together. These are the holes marked × and o in Figure Two. With the help of the string that goes through the top and bottom holes, marked o, adjacent gatherings are linked together in pairs. The complete set of six gatherings is bound in with the pigskin envelope with the help of the string that goes through the four central holes, marked ×. This is to be seen on the back of the Codex, where there are four bands of uncoloured string (whose positions correspond with those of the four central holes of the six gatherings) interlaced with blue string, the ends of which appear in the centre of the sheet constituting leaves 49 and 50 where they are knotted. Beside the six holes through which string is threaded each gathering also shows in its centre four holes, marked ⟨, which are not put to any purpose, but which may have been used with a previous binding. For these holes there are no corresponding ones on the back of the cover, which is an indication that there must have been an earlier cover. See also below, § 5[13].

Prickings occur in both margins. Most of the gatherings were pricked after folding, one gathering at a time. This can be deduced from the fact that the slant of the lines on all folios of a gathering is the same, and the lines actually cover each other when the gathering is folded up. There is nothing in any of the folios of gatherings one, two, four, five, and six which would make pricking in one operation seem unlikely. On the contrary, there are points which seem to corroborate it. The irregularity found in gathering two is shared by all the folios of that gathering; they show 42 prickings in the outer margins (which is the rule for the whole of the MS), but only 41 in the inner margin. The folios of gathering four all show an irregular extra pricking in the inner margin near the first line. Only of gathering three, whose basic irregularity has already been pointed out above, can it be proved that the folios were not pricked in a single operation. Leaf

---

[12] See Bernhard Bischoff, "Paläographie, Mit Berücksichtigung des deutschen Kulturgebietes", in: Wolfgang Stammler (ed.), *Deutsche Philologie im Aufriss*, 3 vols. (2nd ed.), Berlin-Bielefeld-München 1962, column 385.
[13] Much of the description of the binding I owe to Dr. Maria Möller of the *Murhardsche Bibliothek der Stadt Kassel und Landesbibliothek*, Kassel.

Figure Two.
Outline of
Binding.

17 has an irregularity not found elsewhere in the gathering. The same is true of leaves 21 and 22. Leaf 23 has double rows of prickings in inner and outer margins, of which those in the outer margin are only 41 in number. And leaf 24 has 41 prickings in the inner margin. Gathering three, therefore, is a very irregular quaternion from a point of view of prickings and was apparently made up of sheets which had already been pricked before being put together. Throughout the MS the distance between the prickings is almost uniformly 0,5 cm. The punctures are round and small.

Ruling was done after folding and, according to Lowe[14], "probably a quire at a time, and re-ruled when necessary". A dry-point was used for the purpose. The one instance in the MS where the ruling had to be corrected, on leaf 25, would seem to make it very unlikely that, in general, a whole quire was ruled at a time, for the impression of the wrong ruling of leaf 25 on leaf 26, although present, is very slight indeed and is totally absent on 27. The horizontal ruling does not go to the edge anywhere and leaves margins. There are single bounding lines. On leaf 23 vertical ruling has been laid on very heavily, even so as to cut through part of the leaf. All leaves have 42 ruled lines, except 9 to 16 of gathering two, and leaves 23 and 24 of gathering three, which all have 41 ruled lines.

The ink used is brown, black or brown to black. This is true of the main body of the text and also of corrections, of *signes de renvoi* and other correction-signs. In no part of the MS do striking contrasts in the shades of ink occur.

§ 3. Script

The script is a small and rapid Anglo-Saxon minuscule, skilfully execut-ed. According to CLA "by more than one hand", while Struck[15] does not commit himself any further than to speak in general terms of "einheitliche Schreiberhand". The script is clearly of the same general type all through the MS, and if more scribes have contributed to the completion of the MS, the similarity between the scripts produced by these skilled scribes is so great that it is difficult to distinguish

[14] Cf. CLA VIII, no. 1140. Plates of 5v, 15r, 21r, 24r, and 31r are given on pp. 267 ff., which the reader is invited to consult for the relevant passages of the following discussion.
[15] Gustav Struck, *op. cit.*, p. 25.

between them and the danger of discerning more hands than actually took part in the copying is a very real one[16]. A close scrutiny of the handwriting seems to bring to light that certain peculiarities of script are shared by some folios against others. On palaeographical grounds which will be gone into presently three types of script have been distinguished. Further distinctions in these types may have to be made, but of these only that in the third type will be taken into account in the further discussions, because in this case other evidence than that of a palaeographical kind seems to corroborate our first impression[17]. We therefore reckon with the possibility of four hands, the third and fourth of which exhibit the same type of script. Hand I covers 1r to 13v; 14v; 15v; 21r, 6-30; and 34r,8-42, to 50r. Hand II covers 14r; 15r; and 16r to 21r,1-4. Hand III covers 21r,31-42, to 24v. And Hand IV covers 25r to 34r,1-8. If a general characterisation of the types of script is asked for, it may be said that the first type, i.e. Hand I, is very regular and invariably shows a slight forward slant; that the second type, i.e. Hand II, is more compressed and shows shorter descenders; and that type three, i.e. Hands III and IV, is characterised by a certain "looseness" in the formation of the characters, showing a slight forward slant on one folio and standing upright on another. The characteristic features which contribute to the creation of these general impressions will emerge in the following detailed discussion. A general reference may be made to the Plates reproduced at the end of this work.

The letter *a* is closed at the top. Of open *a* there are only two (corrected) instances, viz. in the word *farne* of 26r,7 and the word *emendaret* of 34v,33. In both cases the correction is the scribe's.

The ascenders of *b*, *h*, *k*, and *l* are of normal length in all three types of script. The tops are usually clubbed, i.e. thickened into triangles, whenever these letters occur, although this phenomenon occurs more often and in a more outspoken way in type three than in the other two. The thickened top has not always been filled out completely so that the parchment sometimes shows through. *l* has a rounded

---

[16] In a personal communication (1965) Dom Pius Engelbert O.S.B. of the Benedictine Abbey of Gerleve, Germany, informs me that after studying the MS he is not able to express a definite opinion on this matter, but that he is inclined to disagree with Lowe's view that more hands have been at work on it.

[17] See below, § 4. Evidence of another than a palaeographical kind for the settlement of the differences between the Hands is also adduced above, § 1, note 9, and below, Chapter 2, §§ 2 and 3.

foot. The bow of *b* and *d* is closed as a rule. The stem of the latter is turned back. Upright *d* occurs only twice, viz. in the word *dignus* of 15v,30 and *de* of 25v,7. Normally *c* is not raised above the line; at times it is hard to distinguish this letter from the letter *o*, namely when the two ends almost touch. About half of the times that the letter *e* occurs its top is raised above the line: in many cases the top is separated from the main body. The general character of Hand II is to some extent determined by the fact that the smaller type of this letter outnumbers the elongated type. The descenders of *f*, *p*, *q*, *r*, *y*, and especially of *s* are usually long. In the script of Hand II they are perceptibly shorter than elsewhere in the MS. Particularly that of the letter *r* is at times almost non-existent so that the letter becomes indistinguishable from the letter *n*. The *p* is open, its bow usually ending in a thickening. Of the letter *q* there are two types, the normal minuscule type and a *q* the bow of which resembles a "prancing". This characterisation is taken from Lowe[18], who refers the reader for instances of it to the Plate reproducing part of 29v. Lowe's statement that this type is used at the beginning of sentences is not entirely accurate. It is true, it is used exclusively at the beginning of words like *qui, quo, quamuis* etc., which for the greater part open sentences or sub-clauses, but it would be wrong to conclude that this type of *q* was looked upon by the scribes as a capital letter only. For the scribes apply this letter with the peculiar bow in two ways. There is the type which rises high above the line and is used as a capital letter throughout the MS, and there is the type of which the main body does not rise above the line and which to all appearances is just another form of the letter available for use at the beginning of words. The smaller type occurs on those folios where the other type is also much in evidence. There are many instances of the *q* whose bow resembles a "prancing" on 26r to 30v, and on 32r and 32v. The smaller type occurs on the folios just mentioned as well as on 22v, 23r, 33v, 34v, 36r, 36v, 38r and 39r. Quite a number of the folios of Hand I and Hand II do not have any instances of this type of letter. It is noteworthy that the only three occurrences of superscript *u* in the whole of the MS are with this type of letter *q*, viz. *q^{u}o* on 26v,18, *q^{u}em* on 28r,30 and *q^{u}od* on 29r,2. As has already been remarked above, the length of the descender of *r* varies considerably and has some bearing on the difference in hands. The side-arm of this minuscule

---

[18] Cf. CLA VIII, no. 1140.

letter also varies considerably in the way it is formed, but there is no one variation which can be said to be typical of any one Hand in particular; at all times it ends in an upward stroke of the pen. The small variety of uncial *r* is used five times instead of minuscule *r*, viz. on 2v,23, 9r,23, 19r,36, 19v,14 and 39r,35. Also with regard to long *s* there is some variation in the length of the descender, and in the height of the side-arm, which always ends in a downstroke. Uncial *s* in the middle of a word is evidenced once, viz. in the word *esse* on 32v,9, where it was possibly placed because of a misreading of the exemplar by the scribe[19]. The letter *g* invariably has a curved top. It is in the formation of the bow that differences are noticeable. There is one line to connect the top of this letter with the bow and to form the bow itself, but this line now descends in a graceful curve, then again turns right at a sharp angle at the point where it passes into the bow. The two types are generally met with indiscriminately on all folios of the MS, except on 25r to 33v where an almost exclusive predilection is shown for the latter type. In either type the bow is closed as a rule. Initial *i-longa* is frequently used by all Hands. It is hardly ever a straight downstroke and nearly always has a break at the foot[20]. Subscript *i* occurs only ten times, viz. on 20v,19, 27r,15, 29v,3,39, and 40, 30r,30 and 33, 35r,9, 45v,27 and 49v,37. The letters it occurs with are *h* and *c* once, *m* twice and *n* six times. The letters *m* and *n* are of the regular minuscule type. Half-uncial *N* is only used once, viz. in the word *adamnanum* on 36v,8. The letter *o* is always fairly small and roundish, with thickening of both top and bottom. Both the bottom half and the top half have been executed from left to right. The cross-stroke of *t* is straight. When *t* occurs in final position, the cross-stroke is frequently long and in a great many cases the point of the curve ends in a dot. The letter has a different shape when it is in ligature with *e*. Letter *u* has the regular minuscule form. Only when it is the Roman numeral for five does one fairly regularly come across a *v*-shaped one, instances of which are to be found on a number of folios written by Hand I and 20v of Hand II. The latter and 47v, 48v and 49r each have three instances of it; 49v even has four. Usually the upper right limb and lower left limb of *x* do not constitute one stroke. The lower left limb, if it does not stop at the line, frequently

[19] See below, p. 18.
[20] W. M. Lindsay, *Palaeographia Latina*, Part II (St. Andrews University Publications XVI), Oxford 1923, p. 34, states that of *i-longa* K has "none (unless *i-longior* in *in, iuxta*)".

13

turns in. The descender of *y* varies in length; both left and right side-arms end in a down-stroke. Anglo-Saxon þ (= thorn) for *th* and ᚹ (= wynn) for *uu* are not in evidence.

Ligatures are found of the letters *e* and *u* in combination with following *i* and certain consonant-symbols, and of the letter *i* in combination with preceding consonant-symbols. Ligatures in which the centre bar of the *e* serves as a bond are very common, especially in the combinations *ei*, *er*, *es*, *et*, and *ex*, but also in the combinations *ef*, *eg*, *em*, and *en*. The combinations of *h*, *m*, or *n* and subscript *i* have already been mentioned. The letter *i* commonly enters into ligature with a preceding *t*, and occasionally with preceding *l* or *r*. In the ligature of *u* with following *r* or *s* the second downstroke of *u* is covered by the descender of *r* or *s*. This ligature is applied by the scribes when they are pressed for space in the last word of a line that ends in *-ur* or *-us*. It occurs on the following folios: 2r, 2v, 3v (twice), 4r, 4v, 9r, 12r, 17v (twice), 21r, 21v (three times), 22v (twice), 27v (twice), 36v, 37r, 40r, 40v, 41r, 41v (twice), 42r (twice), 44r, 47r, 47v and 48v (twice). The only time that it occurs in the middle of a line is in the word *usq·* on 34v,11. And the last ligature of which instances occur in the MS, and that very rarely, is the *æ*-ligature. Twice its occurrence concerns Anglo-Saxon names, viz. *ærconuald* on 1r,14 and *æadberctum* on 47v,5; twice it is incorrectly used instead of *e*, viz. in the word *speciæ* on 31r,28 and the word *decennouæn-nalib·* on 45r,12-13; and finally it is found in *sæcula* on 29r,26 and in *ecclesiæ* on 47r,20.

Decoration and illumination are lacking in the MS. The only relief in its sober lettering is offered by the initial capitals at chapter openings, to which a little more space and attention is devoted than to the other letters. Beginnings of other sentences are marked out as a rule by the use of slightly enlarged minuscule letters. The initials of the MS are of the Insular type[21], having what Lowe calls "the inevitable wedge-shaped shafts of tall letters"[22]. That this thickening of shafts was executed with two downward strokes and one transverse stroke of the pen is clear from those initials whose upper parts show blank holes in the middle. This trait can be said to be mainly a characteristic of Hand I, in which 1v, 5r, 7r and 12v have it in the capital letter *I*, 10v and 11v in the upper part of the stem of capital *P*

[21] Cf. CLA VIII, no. 1140.
[22] Cf. CLA II, Introduction, p. XI.

and 46v in the top of the left ascender of N. The parchment is also partly visible through the upper parts of the stems of the capitals H and P of 26r and 31v respectively, but the impression is that in these cases it is accidental. On the other hand it is an intrinsic part of the capital in the letter U of 31r, in which also the top of the left ascender exhibits it. Another remarkable feature of capital letters in the MS has also been pointed out by Lowe[23], viz. the crescent finial as seen in the capital letter A of 29v (see his Plate); this feature is also found in L and Lowe says that it is "presumably a product of Jarrow". The crescent finial forms part of nearly all capital letters A of the MS. It is tacked on to the top end as well as the bottom end of the gracefully curving right ascender of capital A on 13r, 29r, 34v and 47v. On 15r one encounters a differently shaped variety of capital A whose top end forks out into two thinly drawn-out lines which end in and are linked up by a crescent finial. Moreover crescent finials conclude the long drawn-out descenders of two capital letters Q of the enlarged minuscule type on 25r and the bottom end of the left hand stem of capital letter N on 28r. And the most elaborate capital letter of the MS, the capital letter Q of 36r, has one crescent finial at the end of the thinly drawn-out left part of the stem and a string of three crescent finials to conclude the "prancing" top.

Having dealt with two features which some capitals have in common we shall now review in alphabetical order all the capital letters at chapter openings. Capital letter A, which is clearly based on the uncial prototype and whose more or less exact counterparts – but without crescent finials – one comes across regularly in the volumes of CLA, opens chapters on 5v, 13r, 15r, 16r, 20r, 27r, 27v, 29r, 29v, 34v, 37v, 38r, 41r and 47v. It can be said to be common to all three types of script. The employment, however, of this initial (either with or without crescent finial) in *inside-text* position is mainly restricted to the folios of type three, for on 23v to 33v extensive use is made of it whereas the other folios on which it occurs, viz. 14v, 21r, 39r, 40v, 42r and 42v, use it only once each. To a great extent, therefore, its use runs parallel to that of the second type of the q with the bow that resembles a "prancing". The only occurrence of capital letter C is on 8r. On 22v and 37r enlarged minuscule letters d open new chapters. Of initial capital E there are seven instances. The minuscule elongated type, enlarged to various degrees of bigness, is used on 3r, 7v, 9r, 21v, 23v, and 30r, being linked to a following r on 7v and

[23] Cf. CLA VIII, no. 1140.

23v and to a following *x* on 21v. Noteworthy is the closed capital *E* of 41v. Initial *H*, which is of the uncial type, opens chapters on 12r, 19r, 26r and 32v. We have already noted above that the wedge-shaped tops of the initial capitals *I* on 1v, 5r, 7r, and 12v have inkless openings in the middle. The tops of the other samples of this capital on 15r, 18r and 21r have been filled out completely. All seven instances are of the *i-longa* type covering three to four lines. An enlarged min-uscule *m* serves as the initial capital letter of a chapter on 2v. There are six chapters in the MS that open with a capital letter *N*, on 7r, 24r, 26v, 28r, 35v and 46v. They are all of the same general type. The two uprights have wedge-shaped tops; the left stem descends below the line and gradually fades away; and the linking bar is almost horizontal and on a level with the bottom line, and descends in a gentle curve from left to right. Now the letters of 7r, 35v and 46v clearly belong to the same hand differing from those of 26v and 28r in that the latter have straight uprights, the left one of which only makes a gentle curve to the left when below the line. The letter of 24r re-sembles those of 7r, 35v and 46v. The opening in the thickened top of the letter of 46v and the crescent finial of that of 28r have been mentioned above. The three initial capital letters *P* that open chapters and occur on 10v, 11v, and 31v are all three of the same enlarged minuscule type with a gently curving long drawn-out shaft and a bow that is not quite closed. The openings in the thick parts of the top of the shafts have already been commented upon above. Initial capital *Q* occurs twice in the MS at the beginning of chapters. On 9v a regular heavy capital is used; on instances of similar letters we have already remarked above. In that context the other capital letter *Q*, that of 36r, was also mentioned[24]. Initial capital letter *S* opens three chapters, on 8v, 25v, and 36v; those of 25v and 36v are of the uncial type, that of 8v is an enlarged minuscule long *s*. Six times initial capitals of the letter *U* stand at the beginning of chapters, on 1r, 14v, 23r, 25r, 31r and 48v. They are all of the same general type, but those of 1r and 14v look heavier. The initial of 31r has already been mentioned in another context above. The capital letters *U* used in the MS in other positions are all of this type, but as a rule a little smaller.

[24] A great number of instances of this letter *q*, whether used as a capital or as a small letter, can be gleaned from the Plates of MSS reproduced in the volumes of CLA. It may be noted that this type only seems to be known to scribes who write Insular or Continental Anglo-Saxon minuscule.

16

Something has already been said on punctuation in connnection with chapter-division, and on the use of commas inside some of the capital letters at the beginning of the capitula of Book IV in § 1. Dots are used to set off the second component in *homel·ea·* on 12r,10, the personal name *·ini·* on 11v,2 and 29v,15, and the OE word *·gae·* on 26v,1. The most common punctuation mark employed in the MS is the comma, used either singly, in twos or in threes. More often than not no punctuation marks are employed at all, and main pauses are indicated by leaving space between two consecutive words and by magnifying to a greater or lesser degree the opening letter of the new sentence. Spacing also serves to keep words apart and although, indeed, crowding of words does sometimes occur, it is hardly ever difficult to discriminate words in the process of reading. Ligaturing of the last and first letters of adjacent words, as found in *de terrenis* of 3v,18, is extremely rare. When commas are used, their position is medial. Clusters of two or three consecutive commas are only evidenced, apart from when they conclude chapters, in the text of the Hymn in Honour of Aedilthryd (*s.v.*), on 14v and 15r, and after some of the capitula of Book IV on 1r and 1v. Occasionally numerals are marked out as such by commas that immediately precede and follow them.

Corrections may be of several types. We have already dealt with marginal corrections[25]. Misspellings are simply overdrawn whenever it could be done without any serious objection. Otherwise the scribe either put a *punctum delens* underneath the wrong letter and wrote the correct letter above it, or he erased the wrong letter and then inserted the correct one. Rubs, however, are not very common, whereas the *punctum delens* occurs frequently throughout the MS. Letters that had been left out by mistake were often inserted above the word. The combined number of instances of all these types of corrections does not exceed 150 in the whole of the MS. The question whether corrections were made by the scribes themselves or a contemporary corrector cannot be answered definitely. We have seen above in § 1, note 9, that the distribution of marginal corrections in the MS points to a connection between the use of these and Hand I. Definite proof of correction by a later hand can be said to be very scanty; on 1v a later hand has supplied the missing word *episcopus* in between lines 15 and 16 in the form of *ēpīs*. The hand in question is probably

---

[25] See above, § 1.

the same hand that has also overdrawn some of the letters of 1r and 1v which had become too indistinct owing to fading.

Omission and insertion are marked with *signes de renvoi*. They take the shape of short and thin slanting lines which occur singly, or in groups of two or three drawn parallel to each other, or singly in combination with a dot. There are 28 instances of them in the MS, 10 of which indicate where marginal corrections should be inserted in the text and 18 of which put right the word-order of the text where it deviates from the reading of the other MSS. Usually the strokes are laid on very thinly, which may be the reason that their ink often looks more faded than that of the rest of the text. There is nothing to prove, however, that they were not the work of the scribes themselves or of a contemporary corrector.

From certain mistakes in the MS conclusions can be drawn regarding the handwriting of the exemplar from which the MS was copied. K has incorrect *a* for *u* about ten times and also, in an even smaller number of cases, incorrect *u* for *a*. Its explanation may be sought in the use of open *a* in the exemplar which made it impossible at times to distinguish between *a* and *u*. Mention has already been made above of the occurrence of uncial *s* in the word *esse* on 32v,9. In the text *esse* is completely out of place, for it should be *ergo*. Mistaking *ergo* for *esse* when *ergo* is written in full does not seem to be very likely. Possibly, therefore, the copyist of K was misled by the use in the exemplar of an abbreviated form for *ergo*. The only abbreviation for *ergo* known to Anglo-Saxon scribes, but not used freely by them, is *eḡ* [26]. There is a possibility that the scribe misinterpreted this as an unusual abbreviation *es̄* for *esse*, but only if the exemplar had *eḡ* written with uncial *g*, for uncial *g* resembles uncial *s*. The use of uncial *s* by the scribe in K seems to point to this. There is another indication in K that the exemplar used uncial *g*. In the word *augeretur* of 6v,19 the letter *g* clearly is the corrected form of another letter, to all appearances a long *s* [27]. In this case too the explanation may be sought in the use of uncial *g* in the exemplar. There are instances of two other mistakes of this type in K. Twice the scribe has had to change an *n* he had written into a long *r* by adding a descender, viz. in the word *rumor* on 17r,18 and the word *incorruptae* on 40r,42. The letters

---

[26] Cf. LINDSAY 66; and W. M. Lindsay, "The Abbreviation-symbols of *ergo*, *igitur*", *Zentralblatt für Bibliothekswesen* 29 (1912), p. 59.

[27] In the margin there is minuscule *g* in a contemporary (the scribe's) hand.

r which the exemplar had in these words were probably hardly distinguishable from minuscule *n* owing to the shortness of their descenders. In K itself, as we have seen above, subscript *i* is not very common. Whether it was used extensively in its exemplar we do not know, but certain mistakes in K seem to point to a regular use of it. On the one hand K has a number of words in which *i* was first forgotten and then inserted, and on the other hand it has a number of words in which double *i* is used instead of single *i*. To the first group belong *d^iem* of 4v,9; *u^iolenter* of 6v,1; *clar^iorib·* of 8r,31; *histor^iis* of 18v,19; *d^ieb·* of 18v,29; *p^iissimo* of 29v,13; *conperi^it* of 31v,36; *uestig^iis* of 37r,38; and *diei* of 42v,12, the missing *i* of which has been squeezed in and not inserted above the word. Of the second group there are three words, *coniugii* on 6v,25, *litteriis* on 22r,21 and *peregrinarii* on 29v,19. With the first group subscript *i* of the exemplar was overlooked, with the second *i-longa* was interpreted as *i* plus subscript *i*[28].

A final conclusion drawn from the preceding is that the scribes copied from an exemplar and were not dictated to, since many of the mistakes mentioned above were clearly the result of visual misinterpretation.

§ 4. Abbreviations

In K abbreviations of the suspension-type and of the contraction-type are used. Here follows a full list of them. *ĥ* for "autem"[29]; *-b·* for "-bus"; *x̄p̄s*(-), *x̄p̄o*, *x̄p̄m*, and *x̄p̄e* for "Christus", "Christo", etc.; *ɔ* for "con-", on 44r,17; *d̄s̄, d̄ī, d̄ō,* and *d̄m̄* for "Deus", "Dei", etc.; *d̄ī* for "dicit"; *d̄x̄* and *d̄x̄t̄* for "dixit"; *d̄x̄r̄t̄* for "dixerunt"; *d̄r̄* for "dicitur"; *d̄n̄s̄, d̄n̄ī*(-), *d̄n̄ō* and *d̄n̄m̄* for "Dominus", "Domini", etc.[30]; *#* for "enim"; *episc̄* for "episcopus", "episcopi", "episcopo" and

---

[28] We have also inserted those cases in which the error may have resulted from what is considered to be a normal feature of Latin orthography of this time, viz. the confusion between *i* and *ii*. To which of these two causes the actual confusion is to be attributed, we do not know. The confusion may have been due to a combination of the two.

[29] In the MS itself, as in all MSS of Insular script, the tail of the shorthand sign that is represented by *ĥ* in the present study, is appended directly to the shoulder of *h*. Cf. LINDSAY 13.

[30] For "dominis" K has *domnis* on 12r,22. The form *domno* for "domino" is found twice, on 29v,13 and 14; at this place this form is shared by all other MSS, with the exception of C once, and is also used by PLUMMER I, 294.

"episcopum"; *episcī* for "episcopi"; (-)*episō* for "(-)episcopo"[31]; *eē, eēm, eēt,* and *eēnt* for "esse", "essem", etc.; ÷ for "est"; *frār* for "frater", on 46r,15; *ff* for "fratres"; *ihs/ihūs, ihm/ihum,* and *ihu* for "Iesus", "Iesum", etc.; *kl* for "kalendas", and *kl, klrum* and *kldarūm* for "kalendarum"; *n* for "non"; *nr, nrā, nrae, nrī, nrīs,* and *nrm* for "noster", "nostri", etc.; *nī* on 25v,38 for "nostri", and *nm* on 43r,15 for "nostrum"; *ꝑ* for "per"; *ꝑ*(-) for "prae(-)"[32]; *ꝑ* on 3r,34 for "pro"; *ppꝑ* on 1r,30, *pꝑr* and *ppter* for "propter"; *q;* for "quae"; *-q̥* for "-que"; *qm* for "quem"; *ꝗ* and *qd* for "quod"; *qm* on 3r,16, *qm* on 47r,1, *qn* on 20v,9, *quo* on 45v,16, and *qnm* for "quoniam"; *qq* for "quoque"; *-x* for "-rum"; *-rt* for "-runt"; *sclā* on 14v,21 for "saecula" and *sclī* on 13v,8 for "saeculi"; *scs, scā, scāe, scām, scarūm, scās, scī*(-), *scīs, scm, sco, scorūm, scos,* and *scu-* for "sanctus", "sancti", etc.; *sps, spm,* and *spu* for "spiritus", "spiritum", etc.; *st* for "sunt"; and *ꝧ* for "uel". There are some instances of rather arbitrary suspensions, most of them of words used in connection with dating, viz. *id* for "iduum" on 47v,28, *incarnat* for "incarnatione" on 48v,11, and "incarnationis" on 48v,8, *indict* for "indictione" on 6r,12, *mai* for "maiarum" on 47v,28, *mens* for "menses" on 2v,13 and 47v,37, and *sept* for "septembrium" on 49r,39. Besides, *an* for "anno" (twice), *aug* for "augusto" and *cons* for "consulatus" occur on 29v,13 and 14, where they form part of the text of Caedualla's epitaph which is quoted literally[33]. Finally there are *-ā, -ē,* and *-ū* for "-am", "-em", and "-um". The superscript-stroke for final *-m* is as a rule applied when the word in question stands at the end of a line, and occasionally when in the middle of a line the scribe is pressed for space because of a hole or a rub. The only exception to this is the word *agnoscere* on 34r,21.

Looking at the MS as a whole one must say that abbreviated forms are not overfrequently used considering that the MS is written in Insular minuscule. The scriptorium at which K was copied had clearly made a considered selection from the abbreviations available. Thus,

---

[31] *epis* for "episcopus" occurs in a later hand on 1v (see above, § 3).

[32] The letter-combinations "per" and "prae" may be abbreviated under all circumstances, independent of whether they have the function of prepositions or not. Thus the word "presbyter" and its case-forms, when abbreviated, appear as *ꝑ + sbyter*, etc.

[33] Cf. PLUMMER I, 294. L, M, B, and C have the same abbreviated forms in this place. We may conclude, therefore, that this version of the epitaph goes back to Bede's original and may be identical with the actual words on the tomb.

on the one hand, one encounters no unabbreviated forms in K of the *Nomina Sacra* "Christus", "Deus", and "Iesus", nor any unabbreviated forms of "Spiritus" and only one of "Dominus" when the latter two words are used in their theological sense[34]; and one of "sanctus", viz. *sancte* on 46r,15. Very seldom does one come across unabbreviated forms of "autem", "est", "prae(-)", "propter", "quoniam", "uel" and the syllables "-bus" and "-que". The word "kalendas, -is, etc." is always abbreviated, and "esse, etc.", "non", "per", "quod", "quoque" and "sunt" are frequently abbreviated[35]. On the other hand, words for which abbreviated forms are very common in Insular script, such as "eius", "haec", "hoc", "quam" and "quia", are never abbreviated, and ꝛ for "con-" and ꝑ for "pro" occur only once each. The endings "-ter" and "-tur" are not shortened. Other words such as "apostolus", "ecclesia", "episcopus", "etiam", "iuxta", "nunc", "post", "qua", "quando", "quasi", "qui", "quo", "saeculum", "tamen", "tantum", "tunc" and "uidelicet" seldom or never appear in abbreviated form. On the whole, therefore, one can say that the scribes of K use a system of abbreviation that is well-reasoned and consistent throughout.

This does not mean, however, that the proportion of abbreviated forms and un-abbreviated forms of words is the same all over the MS. Reading through the MS one becomes aware of certain fluctuations which seem to have a consistency of their own. Even a rough count of abbreviated forms against unabbreviated ones indicates that fluctuations may have to be related to the occurrence in the MS of different hands. In order to arrive at as significant results as possible we have selected for a more exact count a number of words of high frequency for which both abbreviated and unabbreviated forms are used, viz. "enim", "esse etc.", "non", "noster etc.", "per",

---

[34] On 46v,3 K reads *dominus dominorum* for "Dominus dominorum", in which by the way it agrees with C against L, M, and B. Cf. CO & MY 550. For the rest a sharp distinction is drawn between the use of "dominus" and "spiritus" in their theological sense and in their non-theological sense, in that these words are invariably abbreviated in the former sense and never in the latter sense. Adjectival "dominicus, -a, -um etc." are usually abbreviated to *dnīcus, -a, -um* etc. "Spiritalis" and related forms are not abbreviated.

[35] In contrast to what one would expect from what LINDSAY 176 ff. says on this matter, K abbreviates "prae" more frequently than "per". Not only does the absolute number of ꝑ̄ for "prae" exceed that of ꝑ for "per", but also the proportion of abbreviated occurrences against unabbreviated occurrences of "prae" is higher than that of "per".

"quae", "quod", "quoque" and "sunt". From this count it appears that of these words notably[36] more unabbreviated forms than abbreviated ones are evidenced on 21v, 22v, 26r, 28r, 28v, 29r, 29v, 30v, 31r, 31v, 32r, 32v, 33r, 33v and 35r, and that of all other folios from 21r to 34r it is only on 23r and 24v that abbreviated forms exceed unabbreviated ones, by one and two respectively. On most of the other folios abbreviated forms outnumber unabbreviated forms, on twenty-one of them by nine or more. The word "enim" is not symbolised on any of the folios between 18v and 34v. Thirteen of the twenty folios that do not abbreviate "esse etc." belong to 21v to 34r. Twelve of them have no abbreviated forms of "non", whereas the other folios of this group use unabbreviated and abbreviated forms side by side, 27v being the only one that, with nineteen others outside the group, uses the abbreviated form exclusively, viz. twice. "Noster etc." occurs on twenty-five folios of the MS, either abbreviated or unabbreviated; of the folios between 21v and 34r only 25v has one instance of abbreviated "noster etc.". On these same folios only six instances occur of the frequent abbreviation p for "per". Another fairly frequent abbreviation, q, for "quae", is equally rare on them: only 21v and 22v have one instance each. To a smaller extent the same picture is offered by the abbreviations of "quod", "quoque" and "sunt". It is clear, therefore, that the scribes whom we have identified as Hands III and IV very much restrict themselves in the use of the abbreviations available to them. With regard to Hand I and Hand II the count has shown that there is not much difference as regards the use of abbreviations, except that on all the folios of Hand II abbreviated forms exceed unabbreviated forms by at least three and that "quod", "quoque" and "sunt" only occur in abbreviated form, as $q\bar{d}$, $q\bar{q}$, and $s\bar{t}$.

In this connection there is one thing that may have some bearing on the exemplar from which K was copied. A close scrutiny of the abbreviation-system of the script of type three leads to the conclusion that, although 21r to 34r as a group are clearly distinguished from all the other folios by their sparing use of abbreviations, a further subdivision of this group into two may have to be made, viz. 21r,31-42, to 24v and 25r to 34r,1-8. For one thing, in all the folios of the latter group unabbreviated forms exceed abbreviated forms by at least

---

[36] The words selected for the count occur on an average between fifteen and thirty times per folio, abbreviated and unabbreviated forms taken together. On the folios mentioned here unabbreviated forms outnumber abbreviated ones by at least nine.

four, with the exception of 25r in which the words selected for the count happen to occur only three times - all three of them unabbreviated. Moreover, $\bar{n}$ for "non" only occurs three times, viz. on 27v and 28r, against eight times on 22r, 23r, and 24r; $\not{p}$ for "per" occurs once, on 30r, against five times on 22r, 24r, and 24v; q', for "quae" does not occur at all against twice on 21v and 22r; for "quod" one finds only q twice, on 28v and 30r, against $q\bar{d}$ fourteen times on 21v, 22r, 22v, 23r, 23v, and 24r; and for "quoque" one finds $q\bar{q}$ four times, on 22r, 22v (twice) and 23r. This seems to corroborate what has been said above[37] about the possibility of there being two hands in this script. It seems noteworthy, however, that a similar tendency to make less use of abbreviations in the first part of Book V, i.e. from 25r onwards, may be seen in at least one of the other eighth-century MSS of HE, viz. B. In this MS the phenomenon may be observed with the words "autem", "esse etc.", "non", "post", "prae", "pro", "quae", "quod", "quoque", and "sunt" and the ending "-ter"[38]. It may be a mere coincidence, but on the other hand it may well be that both the scribe of this part of K, Hand IV, and the scribe of B were influenced by the appearance of their respective exemplars, which in their turn closely reflected the usage of an earlier version of the text.

In the tradition of the text incorrect interpretation of abbreviations in the exemplars at times gives rise to incorrect variant readings. In this respect K is almost free from obvious examples. On 29r,3 there is an instance of an incorrect reading which to all appearances finds its origin in a misinterpretation by one of our scribes (or for that matter by a scribe of the exemplar of K) of $\bar{p}$ as "per", for K reads *per maiore senectute* instead of *prae maiore senectute*[39].

§ 5. Date

"The dating of Insular manuscripts presents problems as difficult as they are delicate. It is best to be candid and to admit that we know very little about the earliest manuscripts". This was said in

---

[37] See § 3, note 17.

[38] The evidence from L, which may point to the same conclusion, is not very reliable, since there are so few instances of these abbreviations in the MS as a whole.

[39] Some of the differences between M-type and C-type texts may be related to misinterpretation of abbreviations. Instances of these will be dealt with in Chapter 2, § 2 note 35, because they do not directly concern the relation of K to its exemplar.

1935 by E. A. Lowe[40], the great expert on Insular palaeography. Words of similar purport come from another great expert in this field, Paul Lehmann, in connection with the dating and placing of Anglo-Saxon MSS found at Fulda at an early date[41]. That K belongs to the category of early Fulda MSS will be seen in the next section. Nevertheless, as regards the date of K there has never been much difference of opinion among those who have been concerned with the MS. Lowe dates it "s.viii²", which is adopted by David H. Wright[42]. Less specifically it is dated "eighth century" by Lindsay, Struck, Christ, Lesne, Laistner and King, and Whitelock[43]. The date *non ante quem* is furnished by the author himself. The chronological summary at the end of Book V, 49r and 49v, is concluded with the annals for the years 733 and 734, so that A.D. 734 would be the earliest possible date for the composition of this MS[44]. At the other end of the scale the date *non post quem* is provided by the pigskin envelope referred to above, §§ 1 and 2, in which the MS has been bound. The front-cover has *historia anglorū ƀ* in minuscule writing which is dated ninth century by CLA. Lehmann states of the bindings of this type, which as we shall see in § 6 are typical of Fulda, that they were made in the middle, and partly even in the first half, of the ninth

---

[40] Cf. CLA II, Introduction, p. XIII.

[41] Lehmann states in *Fuldaer Studien* (Sitzungsberichte der Bayerischen Akademie der Wissenschaften, Philosophisch-philologische und historische Klasse, Jahrgang 1925, 3. Abhandlung), München 1925, p. 22: "So ist es sehr schwer, ja oft unmöglich, allein auf Grund von palaeografischen Beobachtungen zu sagen: das ist ein aus England nach Fulda importiertes angelsächsisches Manuskript, jenes ein im deutschen Kloster selbst mit insularen Schriftzügen geschriebener Codex, diese Hs. stammt aus der zweiten Hälfte des 8., jene aus den ersten Jahrzehnten des 9. Jahrh..."

[42] Cf. CLA VIII, no. 1140, and David H. Wright, (review of *P. Hunter Blair, The Moore Bede etc.,...*), *Anglia* 82 (1964), p. 116.

[43] Cf. LINDSAY 452; Gustav Struck, *op. cit.*, p. 25; Karl Christ, "Handschriftenschätze in der Landesbibliothek Kassel", in: Dr. Wilhelm Hopf (ed.), *Die Landesbibliothek Kassel 1580-1930*, Part II, Marburg 1930, p. 184; Emile Lesne, *op. cit.*, p. 63; M. L. W. Laistner and H. H. King, *op. cit.*, p. 97; and Dorothy Whitelock, *English Historical Documents I, c. 500-1042*, London 1955, p. 585.

[44] As Bede himself states at the end of Chapter 23 of Book V, HE was finished by him in A.D. 731. This is, in one type of recension, also the last year for which in the chronological summary at the end of the last Chapter (i.e. Chapter 24) of this Book an item is given in the body of the text. In the type of recension to which K belongs, the annals for the years 733 and 734 are also incorporated in the text at the end of this final Chapter.

century[45]. Furthermore, there is no reason to assume that the pigskin envelope of K was not specifically made for it after the first three Books had been lost, for it fits the remaining 50 folios tightly. That the MS and its cover belonged together at a very early date is clear from the offset on the inside of the back-cover of the letters of the alphabet written on 50v in pre-caroline minuscule[46]. Within these two limits the general appearance of the Anglo-Saxon minuscule used by the four Hands points to a date in the eighth century rather than the ninth century. This is, moreover, borne out by the abbreviations of the MS. The best criterion Lindsay [47] knew for distinguishing eighth-century MSS from ninth-century ones was the use of $n\overline{i}$, etc. instead of $n\overline{ri}$, etc. for "nostri etc.". Both types occur side by side in eighth-century MSS, but of the former no occurrences are to be found anywhere after A.D. 815. We have seen above, § 4, that K has one instance of $n\overline{i}$ and one of $n\overline{m}$. Of course, isolated occurrences of forms like these should not be relied upon too much, for they may well find their origin simply in very faithful copying of the exemplar by a scribe. Attention has already been drawn to this by D. Bains[48]. But when they occur in the company of other early abbreviations, they certainly constitute a clue for dating. In this connection the first thing to note is that K does not use any abbreviations that are incompatible with an eighth-century date. Moreover, K has two fairly frequent forms which would hardly be used extensively, and exclusively, in ninth-century MSS, viz. $h\hat{}$ for "autem" and $q\colon$ for "quae". Ninth-century scribes avoided the $h\hat{}$-symbol for "autem" and preferred $a\overline{t}$ instead, for fear of confusion resulting from the likeness between

---

[45] Paul Lehmann, *op. cit.*, p. 13: "Was mir daran interessant vorkommt, ist die Tatsache, dass gerade die rohen Einbände Fuldas gewöhnlich in der Mitte, z.T. sogar der 1. Hälfte des 9. Jahrh. angefertigt worden sind. Das erkenne ich an den Federproben und sonstigen Einträgen in angelsächsischer oder kontinentaler Minuskel, die mir aussen und innen auf den Umschlagseiten aufgefallen sind."

[46] See above, § 1. That the two Books which constitute K were for some time without any cover at all, seems to be the explanation for the more serious fading of the letters on the first folios of Book IV than on the first folios of Book V. The four holes in the centre of the six gatherings (referred to above, § 2) which do not play a part in the present binding and for which there are no counterparts in the back of the cover, should probably be associated with an older binding.

[47] Cf. LINDSAY 152.

[48] Cf. Doris Bains, *A Supplement to Notae Latinae, Abbreviations in Latin MSS. of 850 to 1050 A.D.*, Cambridge 1936, p. 26.

$\hat{h}$ for "autem" and h, or h' for "hoc"[49]; and although q', had not disappeared completely by A.D. 850, it was more and more replaced by the ancient Nota $\bar{q}$ owing to confusion with $-q$' or $-q$', or $-q$', for "-que"[50].

In the absence of any other definite clues it does not seem very likely that a more accurate dating than the one arrived at by Lowe will ever be possible. It is only the expert palaeographer who might possibly, from his many dealings with MSS of our period, tentatively come to a more accurate dating. It may be significant, therefore, that Lowe dates K "VIII²" and not "VIIIex.", thus leaving the possibility of a date between A.D. 750 and A.D. 780.

§ 6. Place

There is nothing in K that would justify an unconditional allocation of its origin to one particular place. Various elements, however, in its physical make-up and its script enable us to ascribe it with a high degree of probability to Northumbria, possibly to one of the twin monasteries of Wearmouth-Jarrow[51]. This view is held by Lowe, in which he is followed by Wright and Dorothy Whitelock[52]. In earlier days people generally ascribed it to Fulda, following Pertz, who had stated in 1838: "wohl aus Hersfeld oder Fulda stammend"[53], a view still held by Laistner and King, notwithstanding the non-committal words of Struck on the subject[54]. The evidence for defining the origin of the MS may be summarized as follows.

[49] Cf. LINDSAY 98.

[50] Cf. LINDSAY 208.

[51] In the case of the Leningrad Bede Lowe gives the preference to Jarrow, because Bede himself lived and wrote his works there. Cf. E. A. Lowe, "A Key to Bede's Scriptorium. Some Observations on the Leningrad Manuscript of the 'Historia Ecclesiastica Gentis Anglorum'", *Scriptorium* 12 (1958), p. 186.

[52] Cf. CLA VIII, no. 1140, and Introduction, p. VI; David H. Wright, *op. cit.*, p. 116; and Dorothy Whitelock, *After Bede* (Jarrow Lecture), Jarrow: The Rectory 1960, p. 10.

[53] Cf. G. H. Pertz, *op. cit.*, p. 203; C. W. M. Grein, *op. cit.*, p. 13; F. G. C. Gross, *op. cit.*, p. 165; and Emile Lesne, *op. cit.*, p. 63. We assume that when these scholars speak of "stammend aus" or "provenant de" they refer to origin and not to provenance, the latter being the first known place where a MS was preserved and the former being the place where it was written. For this distinction see CLA VI, Introduction, p. X.

[54] Cf. M. L. W. Laistner and H. H. King, *op. cit.*, p. 97; and Gustav Struck, *op. cit.*, p. 26.

That K is Insular rather than Continental may be seen from its vellum, script and initials. In keeping with an Insular origin are the pricking of both inner and outer margins, and ruling of a quire at a time, which although not exclusive features of Insular script, may certainly be said to be characteristic of it[55]. The application of *signes de renvoi* is not uncommon in Insular MSS (which nevertheless also use other omission and insertion marks[56]), and although the ink of K is not always black and very fresh, which is typical of many Insular MSS, it is not always brown-hued either as in Continental MSS[57]. The abbreviations *ĥ* for "autem", *-//-* for "enim", *-÷-* for "est", *q̓,* for "quae" and *sł* for "sunt" are peculiar to, if not restricted to, Insular script[58]. It is also particularly on the basis of the abbreviations used that we can clearly attribute K to the Anglo-Saxon rather than the Irish type of Insular minuscule. The abbreviations *ꝑ* for "per", *qm̄* for "quem", *qđ* for "quod", *qn̄/qn̄m̄/quō* for "quoniam" and *sclī*, etc. for "saeculi, etc." are typical of Anglo-Saxon minuscule as opposed to Irish minuscule[59]; abbreviation of other words, such as "etiam", "haec", "hoc", and especially "omnes", which as appears from Lindsay's statistics is mainly typical of Irish script, is altogether absent from K[60]. We may also refer to the neatness and the orderliness of the script, distinctive characteristics of Anglo-Saxon script as opposed to Irish script which is "less bound to rules and regulations than the English type modelled upon it"[61]. Moreover, the *q* with the bow which resembles a "prancing" (see above, § 3), whether of the small type or the capital type, only occurs in specimens of Anglo-

---

[55] Cf. Leslie W. Jones, "Prickings as Clues to Date and Origin: the Eighth Century", *Medievalia et Humanistica* 14 (1962), p. 15; and CLA II, Introduction, p. VI.

[56] See E. A. Lowe, "The Oldest Omission Signs in Latin Manuscripts: Their Origin and Significance", in: *Miscellanea Giovanni Mercati*, Vol. VI (Studi e Testi 126), Vatican City 1946, p. 78.

[57] Cf. CLA II, Introduction, p. VIII; and Bernhard Bischoff, *op. cit.*, column 384.

[58] Cf. LINDSAY 23, 63, 69, 207, and 293.

[59] Cf. LINDSAY 181f., 233f., 255, 263, and 275.

[60] Cf. LINDSAY 77, 98, and 173. Of course, we should keep in mind Lindsay's warning (p. 4) that: "The argument "ex silentio" is not always safe in the case of abbreviation-symbols", but this argument may gather weight when other evidence can be adduced in support.

[61] Cf. CLA II, Introduction, p. XII.

Saxon script in the volumes of CLA[62]. More specifically the type of script used in K may be classified as Northumbrian, "to judge from certain palaeographical features" as Lowe says[63]. Among these features may certainly be reckoned the "crescent finial in A(...), also found in the Leningrad Bede, presumably a product of Jarrow"[64], the letter *x* "with the lower left limb turning in or stopping at the line" and the fact that the Roman numeral for five is regularly *v*-shaped. The script of K shares the latter two features with the first three Hands of the Leningrad Bede and with the Codex Amiatinus, two MSS which Lowe has proved to have been composed at Wearmouth-Jarrow[65]. The conclusion, therefore, would be that K was written in the Northumbrian area and that of the monasteries of that area Wearmouth-Jarrow is its most likely home. But this does not seem to be in keeping with what we know of the provenance of the MS.

MS. Theol. Qu.2 is one of a group of MSS that were acquired by the Kassel Landesbibliothek some time in the seventeenth century. That it must have belonged to the library of the old monastery of Fulda from an early date we know with certainty because of the pigskin envelope by which it is covered; this type of binding has been proved to be typical of the Fulda library in the first half of the ninth century[66]. But long before this a Fulda provenance for K and other

---

[62] It occurs in MSS of Anglo-Saxon script of both English and Continental origin. The specimens we have noted occur in: II, no. 220; IV, nos. 517, 519 and 606; VI, nos. 714 and 750; VII, nos. 844 and 983; VIII, no. 1055; IX, nos. 1405, 1436 and 1439; X, no. 1451; and XI, nos. 1600, 1621 (= L), and 1662.

[63] Cf. CLA VIII, no. 1140.

[64] *loc. cit.*, and see also above, § 3.

[65] Cf. E. A. Lowe, "A Key to Bede's Scriptorium. Some Observations on the Leningrad Manuscript of the 'Historia Ecclesiastica Gentis Anglorum'", *Scriptorium* 12 (1958), p. 188, and *idem, English Uncial*, Oxford 1960, pp. 6ff. The identification of the script of the first three Hands of L with that of the Wearmouth-Jarrow scriptorium brings Lowe in conflict with the views generally held with regard to Anglo-Saxon minuscule, since this script of L, because of its pointed and compressed character, would generally be looked upon as Mercian and not as Northumbrian as Lowe does. The first to put forward the arguments for distinguishing between the two scripts was W. Keller, *Angelsächsische Paläographie* (Palaestra XLIII), Berlin 1906, and they are also discussed by N. Denholm-Young, *Handwriting in England and Wales*, Cardiff 1954, p. 20, note. Lowe suggests in his article (p. 187) that the only way out of this dilemma is to assume that "the type was probably in use in Northumbria as well as in Mercia".

[66] Cf. Paul Lehmann, *op. cit.*, p. 13; Karl Christ, "Karolingische Bibliothekseinbände", in: *Festschrift Georg Leyh*, Leipzig 1937, p. 84; and Berthe van Regemorter, "La Reliure Souple des Manuscrits Carolingiens de Fulda", *Scriptorium* 11 (1957), 249-257.

Kassel MSS had been assumed, because it was thought that a direct link could be established between the mysteriously sudden and almost complete disappearance of the rich MS collection of the Fulda monastery in the seventeenth century and Wilhelm V, *Landgraf* of Hessen (1627-1637), who had his residence in Kassel. For in February 1632 Gustav Adolf of Sweden granted the Fulda monastery and the Convents of Corvey and Paderborn to the *Landgraf* for services rendered in the King's campaign in the Thirty Years' War. The removal to Kassel of the Fulda MSS was looked upon as a direct result of this. After some time, however, the question arose why in that case the *Landgraf* contented himself with only a selection of about twenty-five MSS and why with this particular selection. As long ago as 1892 C. Scherer had noted that many of the old printed books of the Kassel library bear the pressmark of the library of the Jesuits College at Fulda. This point was gone into in some detail by Hopf in 1930 and his conclusion was that the Jesuits, who had founded their Convent in Fulda in 1573 and who had often played the part of users of the library or of mediators between the library and other users, had a number of MSS from the old library of the Fulda monastery in their Convent. Owing to the war they had to leave Fulda during the years 1632/'33 and a great part of their own library, including the old MSS, was taken to Kassel. Part of it was first kept in the Kassel Castle itself and was not placed with the other books in the Prince's library until 1661[67]. Thus K came to be one of the few MSS of the old Fulda library that have been preserved[68].

More conclusive evidence as to provenance and history of the MS

[67] Cf. C. Scherer, "Die Kasseler Bibliothek im ersten Jahrhundert ihres Bestehens (16. und 17. Jahrhundert)", *Zeitschrift des Vereins für hessische Geschichte und Landeskunde* 27, N.F. 17 (1892), 224-259; Paul Lehmann, *Johannes Sichardus und die von ihm benutzten Bibliotheken und Handschriften* (Quellen und Untersuchungen zur lateinischen Philologie des Mittelalters 4), München 1911, p. 108; Dr. Wilhelm Hopf, "Die Landesbibliothek Kassel in ihrer geschichtlichen Entwicklung", in: Dr. Wilhelm Hopf (ed.), *Die Landesbibliothek Kassel 1580-1930*, Part I, Marburg 1930, p. 14. Cf. also C. W. M. Grein, *op. cit.*, p. 12; F. G. C. Gross, *op. cit.*, p. 157; Gustav Struck, *op. cit.*, p. IV; and Friedrich Israel, "Die Landesbibliothek in Kassel", *Hessenland, Zeitschrift für die Kulturpflege des Bezirksverbandes Hessen* 53 (1942), p. 2.
[68] So far only about 70 MSS and MS fragments of the old Fulda library have been traced in various European libraries. See Paul Lehmann, *op. cit.*, pp. 131 ff. Little wonder, therefore, that scholars interested in the library speak of its mysterious disappearance, since catalogues show that the library held over 900 MSS as late as the second half of the sixteenth century.

may be provided by the old catalogues and catalogue-fragments of the Fulda library[69]. Catalogue-fragments of early date have come down to us in a number of MSS, viz. *Basle MS. F. III. 15a*, 17v and 18r (eighth century)[70]; *Basle MS. F. III. 15b*, the inside of the front-cover (end of ninth century); *Vatican Library MS. Cod. Pal. lat. 1877*, 36r to 43v (A.D. 840-850); and *Fulda MS. B. 1*, 31v (end of ninth century). As they are only fragments, they do not afford a clear indication as to the number of volumes and the kind of works in the possession of the library at the time of their composition. A clearer picture is presented by three other catalogues that date from the

---

[69] For almost a century and a half catalogues of the old Fulda library have had the attention of scholars. Here follows a list of publications in which Fulda-catalogues are dealt with: Anonymous (= N(ikolaus) K(indlinger)), *Katalog und Nachrichten von der ehemaligen aus lauter Handschriften bestandenen Bibliothek in Fulda*, Leipzig und Frankfurt a.M. 1812; F. G. C. Gross, *op. cit.*; C. W. M. Grein, *op. cit.*; G. Becker, *Catalogi bibliothecarum antiqui*, Bonn 1885; Theodor Gottlieb, *Ueber mittelalterliche Bibliotheken*, Graz 1890; Paul von Winterfeld, "De Germanici Codicibus", in: *Festschrift Johannes Vahlen zum siebzigsten Geburtstag gewidmet von seinen Schülern*, Berlin 1900, 391-407; C. Scherer, "Der Fuldaer Handschriftenkatalog aus dem 16. Jahrhundert", Beilage zu Franz Falk, *Beiträge zur Rekonstruktion der alten Bibliotheca fuldensis und bibliotheca laureshamensis* (Zentralblatt für Bibliothekswesen, Beiheft 26), Leipzig 1902; Paul Lehmann, *Franciscus Modius als Handschriftenforscher* (Quellen und Untersuchungen zur lateinischen Philologie des Mittelalters III,1), München 1908; *idem, Johannes Sichardus und die von ihm benutzten Bibliotheken und Handschriften* (Quellen und Untersuchungen zur lateinischen Philologie des Mittelalters 4), München 1911; *idem*, "Quot et quorum libri fuerint in libraria Fuldensi", in: *Bok- och Bibliotheks-Historiska Studier tillägnade Isak Collijn*, Uppsala 1925, 47-57; *idem, Fuldaer Studien* (Sitzungsberichte der Bayerischen Akademie der Wissenschaften, Philosophisch-philologische und historische Klasse, Jahrgang 1925, 3.Abhandlung), München 1925; Karl Christ, "Die Handschriftenverzeichnisse der Fuldaer Klosterbibliothek aus dem 16. Jahrhundert", in: Dr. Joseph Theele (ed.), *Aus Fuldas Geistesleben*, Fulda 1928, 24-39; *idem, Die Bibliothek des Klosters Fulda im 16. Jahrhundert. Die Handschriften-Verzeichnisse* (Zentralblatt für Bibliothekswesen, Beiheft 64), Leipzig 1933; and Gustav Binz, "Ein bisher unbekannter Katalog der Bibliothek des Klosters Fulda", in: *Mélanges offerts à M. Marcel Godet*, Neuchâtel 1937, 97-108.

[70] First discovered and discussed by Paul Lehmann, *Fuldaer Studien* (Sitzungsberichte der Bayerischen Akademie der Wissenschaften, Philosophisch-philologische und historische Klasse, Jahrgang 1925, 3.Abhandlung), München 1925, pp. 4 ff., 48 ff. and photocopy.

sixteenth century[71]. The first of these is to be found in *Vatican Library MS. Cod. Pal. lat. 1928,* which offers a selective catalogue that was compiled about A.D. 1550 and numbers 585 items. The second catalogue, composed about a decade later and to all appearances aiming at a full enumeration of the MSS in the possession of the Fulda library, has come down to us in three copies, viz. *Marburg, Staatsarchiv R 38; Fulda, Landesbibliothek MS. B 18.4⁰,* and *Hannover, Vormals Königliche und Provinzialbibliothek, MS. 1837.* This second catalogue lists 791 items, whereas the third, i.e. *Paris, Bibliothèque National MS. Lat. nouv. acq. 643,* a copy of a seventeenth-century selective catalogue, lists 348 items. The number of separate MSS listed by these three catalogues amounts to 929 items, but it is very doubtful whether even this presents an exhaustive picture of the possessions of the library in the sixteenth century, for even catalogue number two, which purports to be an Inventory, can be added to from the other catalogues. Moreover, Karl Christ's attempts to identify the extant Fulda MSS with items of the three catalogues have been successful in only two thirds of the cases[72].

As regards the older catalogue-fragments, in none of them is mention made of MSS of HE. In the sixteenth-century catalogues the work is mentioned four times, once in both the Vatican and the Paris catalogue and twice in the second catalogue, i.e. the one aiming at a more or less exhaustive listing. Identity of K with any or all of these

---

[71] We will leave out of consideration the early sixteenth-century catalogue to which Gustav Binz, *op. cit.,* was the first to draw attention, because it has not been made available so far and because it appears from Binz's description that this catalogue does not supply any information of interest to us that has not already been gathered from the other catalogues by Karl Christ.

[72] Cf. Karl Christ, *Die Bibliothek des Klosters Fulda im 16. Jahrhundert. Die Handschriften-Verzeichnisse* (Zentralblatt für Bibliothekswesen, Beiheft 64), Leipzig 1933, p. 63. When Christ (p. 65) counts the Fulda MSS preserved to this day, he takes into consideration only those MSS which at least with a great degree of probability can be ascribed to the Fulda monastery in the sixteenth century. He thus bases his count on 49 MSS and of these he has been able to identify no more than 34 with catalogue items. Assuming a similar proportion of MSS not mentioned in the sixteenth-century catalogues when the library was still intact, we may infer from the outcome of Christ's count that the library must have held over a thousand MSS at the end of the sixteenth century. Furthermore, from the fact that the greater part of the MSS that have been preserved to this day date back to before A.D. 1000, we may assume that this held good for most of the MSS of the library. This means that the monastery library had its hey-day in that period, being a very rich library indeed.

items cannot be established, although it can be made to seem likely with one of them. We have seen above, § 1, that on the front-cover of K the title of the work is given in ninth-century minuscule as *historia angloꝛ ƀ*. This may point to identity with the second mention of HE in the second catalogue, which in the Fulda copy (under X 2,8) records HE with the identical title *Historia Anglorum*, whereas the first mention of HE (under IV 3,10) appears as *Beda in historiam Anglorum*, which is the same as that of no. 172 of the Vatican catalogue and no. 217 of the Paris catalogue. Besides, from the information given by the Vatican catalogue about the contents of MS. no. 172 it transpires that this was a complete copy of HE. The Fulda library to all appearances possessed two copies of HE and in that case the absence of a defective copy like K from selective catalogues such as the Vatican and the Paris ones does not seem extraordinary. There is another thing in these catalogues that enhances the credibility of the attribution of K to the Fulda library. Catalogue two is an Inventory of the library. It lists the MSS in the order in which they happened to be found on the shelves, and re-numbers them accordingly; this accounts for the haphazard arrangement of MSS in this catalogue. But this catalogue also bears traces of the original arrangement of the library, for a great number of items are not only preceded by shelf-numbers but are also followed by such numbers. Where these latter shelf-numbers occur, they correspond to the numbers still found on the existing Fulda MSS and apparently reflect the old ordering. The old shelf-number has not been given either with item X 2,8 or with item IV 3,10, but it is clear from a comparison with similar inscriptions on the other Fulda MSS that have come down to us that *xxxiiii or.* ⋀ found on the front-cover of K is the shelf-number which the MS had at the time of the old arrangement, when the library was divided into forty-eight *ordines*. The script of the inscription is fifteenth century, which is also borne out by the symbol ⋀ which stood for the number 7 in the twelfth to fifteenth century[73]. K, therefore, was no. 7 of *ordo* 34. This fits in with the conclusion arrived at above that K cannot be identified with no. 172 of the Vatican catalogue, for in that catalogue, in which the old division of the

---

[73] Cf. A. Cappelli, *Dizionario di Abbreviature Latine ed Italiane* (sixth ed.), Milan 1961, p. 426. For a long time scholars have followed both Gross's misinterpretation of this symbol as *4* and his identification of K with IV 3,10. Gustav Struck, *op. cit.*, p. 26 even states that IV 3,10 is to be found on the front-cover of K.

library into forty-eight *ordines* is still reflected, no 172 forms part of *ordo* 14. The arrangement of the library into forty-eight *ordines* in all probability goes back to the Benedictine monk Johannes Knöttel – who died in 1505 – of whom a sixteenth-century chronicler states that he put the library in order[74]. The shelf-number, therefore, definitely proves that K belonged to the Fulda library around A.D. 1500.

MS. Theol. Qu. 2 may have formed a part of the Fulda library from a very early date and probably remained in that library throughout the centuries until the library was dispersed in the seventeenth century. The early connections with Fulda raise the question whether the MS may not actually have been written in the scriptorium of the Fulda monastery itself. The fact that in 1925 Lehmann admitted that very often it is simply impossible with MSS of this type to tell an Insular origin from a continental origin[75], explains why K has been attributed to Fulda by scholars. There are clear indications, however, that make a Fulda origin of the MS very unlikely. The three great centres of learning Fulda, Mainz and Würzburg have long been recognized as basically forming part of one writing province in this early period, showing strong Anglo-Saxon influence in their script[76]. Of late this Anglo-Saxon element has been associated more specifically with the South of England where both Boniface and his successor Lullus came from[77]. The irrefutable Northumbrian features we have spoken of above would hardly seem to be reconcilable with a Fulda origin, unless one would assume the presence in the monastery of a number of Northumbrian monks. But one would imagine that the presence of some four scribes of Northumbrian extraction[78] would certainly have left its mark on the scriptorium. Moreover, when one compares the script of K with what Lowe calls the type of Anglo-Saxon script in vogue at Fulda, as shown by the whole series of Fulda MSS now at Basle[79], it transpires that K is not of that type. It seems to be fair

[74] Cf. Paul Lehmann, *op. cit.*, p. 10.

[75] See above, § 5, note 41.

[76] Cf. Paul Lehmann, "Lateinische Paläographie. Bis zum Siege der karolingischen Minuskel", in: Alfred Gercke and E. Norden (eds.), *Einleitung in die Altertumswissenschaft*, 3 vols. (3rd ed.), Leipzig u. Berlin 1927, I, 10; pp. 55 f.

[77] Cf. Bernhard Bischoff, *op. cit.*, column 405; and Herbert Hunger, "Antikes und mittelalterliches Buch- und Schriftwesen", in: Dr. M. Meier and others (eds.), *Geschichte der Textüberlieferung der antiken und mittelalterlichen Literatur*, vol. I, Zürich 1961, p. 120.

[78] At least as many scribes as one distinguishes Hands in K.

[79] Cf. CLA XI, Introduction, p. X. Beside Kassel, Basle is the only other library which houses a considerable number of Fulda MSS.

then to conclude that the MS had come to Fulda from another place at a very early date. As no direct connections with continental centres under Northumbrian influence, such as Echternach, can be established, importation from the North of England seems to be the way K reached Germany. Importation is a very common procedure, for we know that the Anglo-Saxon missionaries were in the habit of taking books with them when they went abroad and we know that in answer to requests from missionaries a great many books were sent from England to the Continent. For instance, in letters of the years 746/747 Saint Boniface asks Archbishop Ecgberct of York, who was a pupil of Bede, and Abbot Hwaetberct of Wearmouth-Jarrow for works of Bede. Boniface's pupil and countryman Lullus, Bishop of Mainz, who died in 786, asks for works of Bede in a letter to Cuthbert, Abbot of Wearmouth-Jarrow, who was also a former pupil of Bede, and he does the same in a letter to Coena (alias Aedilberct), who succeeded Ecgberct as Archbishop of York[80]. Now, as Dorothy Whitelock has pointed out[81], it may be significant that Saint Boniface asks for works by Bede in general terms, whereas Lullus in both letters "describes the works he requires in precisely the words used by Bede in the list of his writings which he gives at the end of his Ecclesiastical History". From this it may be concluded that Lullus by the time he asked for Bede's works, must have had a copy of HE at hand. Could this copy of Bede's HE possibly have been K? The way Bede's works are entitled in the Vienna MS of Lullus's correspondence (for which MS the drafts and originals in the Mainz archives may have been used[82]) is not different from their wording in K which, it is true, can also be said of the other older MSS, M excluded. The argument for such an identification is, therefore, very slender, although on the other hand this identification should not be ruled out solely because a close personal relationship between Lullus and the Fulda monastery

[80] Cf. Michael Tangl, *Bonifatii et Lulli Epistolae* (Monumenta Germaniae Historica, Epistolae Selectae, I), Berlin 1916, nos. 76, 91, 125, and 126; and E. Emerton, *The Letters of Saint Boniface*, New York 1950.

[81] Cf. Dorothy Whitelock, *After Bede* (Jarrow Lecture), Jarrow: The Rectory 1960, p. 7. Before her Wilhelm Levison, *England and the Continent in the Eighth Century*, Oxford 1946, p. 140, had come to the same conclusion. Appendix VII of Levison's work is devoted wholly to the correspondence of Boniface and Lullus.

[82] Cf. Dorothy Whitelock, *English Historical Documents I, c. 500-1042*, London 1955, p. 573.

did not exist[83]. For we know that most of the time there was a very lively exchange of MSS between writing-centres in the area of which Fulda, Mainz and Würzburg were the most important centres, and there is the possibility that K was at one of these other centres for some time before finding its permanent home at Fulda. In this connection it may be interesting to draw attention to the oldest catalogue of the Chapter Library of the Würzburg bishopric, which has come down to us on 260r of *Bodleian MS. Laud. Misc. 126*. This catalogue bears witness to the lively exchange of books between Würzburg and Fulda in that it specifically notes of four of its items that they were lent out to Fulda[84]. But, what is more, it records as no. 5 of the catalogue a MS of HE with a similarly phrased title as that found on the front-cover of K, viz. *historia anglor̄*[85]. The catalogue is written in Anglo-Saxon script of around A.D. 800. Identity of K with the *historia anglor̄* of the catalogue, therefore, is not improbable, although there is no definite proof.

[83] Karl Christ, "Bibliotheksgeschichte des Mittelalters. Zur Methode und zur neuesten Literatur", *Zentralblatt für Bibliothekswesen* 61 (1947), 38-56, 149-166, and 233-252, states on p. 243 that Lullus may not be numbered among the supporters of Fulda and that he preferred Hersfeld.

[84] The presence of the words *ad fultu* at first led scholars to believe that the catalogue itself must be attributed to Fulda, a view which seemed to be corroborated by the presence in the same Codex, on 1r, of a copy of Charlemagne's famous letter *De Litteris Colendis* addressed to Abbot Baugulf of Fulda in A.D. 787. See for instance Paul Lehmann, *Franciscus Modius als Handschriftenforscher* (Quellen und Untersuchungen zur lateinischen Philologie des Mittelalters III,1), München 1908, p. 65. Lowe was the first to interpret the words *ad fultu* at the head of the four works as standing for "lent out to Fulda", cf. E. A. Lowe, "An eighth-century list of books in a Bodleian MS. from Würzburg and its probable relation to the Laudian *Acts*", *Speculum* 3 (1928), pp. 10 f., and also Paul Lehmann, *Fuldaer Studien*, Neue Folge (Sitzungsberichte der Bayerischen Akademie der Wissenschaften, Philosophisch-philologische und historische Klasse, Jahrgang 1927, 2. Abhandlung), München 1927, pp. 6 f., who reconsiders the views expressed by him in the earlier work after reading the draft of Lowe's article. The latter's views are also accepted by Bernhard Bischoff and Joseph Hofmann, *Libri Sancti Kyliani. Die Würzburger Schreibschule und die Dombibliothek im VIII. und IX. Jahrhundert*, Würzburg 1952, pp. 13, 97 and 142.

[85] The similarity of the two titles also seems to have struck Georg Baesecke, because when discussing the catalogue in *Der Vocabularius Sti. Galli in der Angelsächsischen Mission*, Halle 1933, p. 99, he refers in note 13 "5. (Bedas) *Historia Anglorum*" to "Fulda Kassel Th. q. 2" and to "Christ S. 184". The reference "Christ S. 184" is to Karl Christ, *Die Bibliothek des Klosters Fulda*

Until definite proof is found of any such links, there will always be many possible routes along which K reached Fulda. For Fulda had contacts with monasteries in many parts of the western world from an early date. We know of special relations with the territory West of the Rhine under Abbot Baugulf (779-802), attested by Charlemagne's letter *De Litteris Colendis* and the fact that many young Fulda monks were sent to Alcuin for further education[86]. Fulda also had its connections in southern direction with monasteries like St. Gallen and Reichenau. There is evidence of frequent exchange of books between Fulda and Reichenau particularly when Hrabanus Maurus (780-856) was Abbot of Fulda, i.e. from A.D. 842 to 856, and when Walahfrid Strabo (808/9-849), his pupil, had returned to Reichenau. Reichenau is mentioned not because a borrowing of K by Fulda from Reichenau is more likely than any of the other possibilities suggested so far[87], but because Reichenau may be the monastery to which the missing first three Books of K were lent and where they subsequently were somehow lost. For in an old catalogue of the Reichenau library composed in A.D. 821-822 there appears under the general heading of *De libris Bedae presbyteri* the item *de historia ecclesiastica gentis Anglorum libri III in codice I*[88]. We have

im 16. Jahrhundert. Die Handschriften-Verzeichnisse (Zentralblatt für Bibliothekswesen, Beiheft 64), Leipzig 1933, p. 184, where Christ on the strength of identity in title, i.e. *historia anglorum*, identifies K with item X 2,8 of the Fulda copy of the second catalogue and not with the other MS of HE, i.e. item IV 3,10, whose title *Beda in historiam Anglorum* also occurs elsewhere. See also above.

[86] Cf. Paul Lehmann, *op. cit.*, pp. 4 and 12.

[87] One encounters Anglo-Saxon MSS in the possession of the Reichenau library less frequently than MSS from other areas. Paul Lehmann, "Die mittelalterliche Bibliothek der Reichenau", in: *Erforschung des Mittelalters*, vol. IV, Stuttgart, 1961, 26-39 (reprinted from Konrad Beyerle (ed.), *Kultur der Abtei Reichenau*, vol. 2, München 1925, 645-656), says on p. 28: "Vor allem ist es in frühkarolingischer Zeit ausser den Klöstern und Kirchen der Schweiz und der benachbarten deutschen Gebiete wohl Frankreich gewesen, aus dessen reichen Bibliotheken man emsig für die Reichenau geschöpft hat".

[88] This catalogue was reproduced from a rotulus, now lost, by T. Neugart, *Episcopatus Constantiensis Alemannicus*, Partis I Tom. I, St. Blasien, 1803, 536-544. It was then published by G. Becker, *Catalogi bibliothecarum antiqui*, Bonn 1885, no. 6; Alfred Holder, *Die Reichenauer Handschriften*, 3. Band, Leipzig-Berlin 1918, 70-81; and Paul Lehmann, *Mittelalterliche Bibliothekskataloge Deutschlands und der Schweiz*, 1. Band, Die Bistümer Konstanz und Chur, München 1918, no. 49, 240-252. Except for an anonymous *Gesta anglorum*, *volumen I* – probably Bede's HE – in another ninth-century catalogue (see

cited above, § 1, Wright's view that the MS may well have been taken apart for copying purposes per Book since the two remaining Books are bound in separate sets of gatherings. It is possible, therefore, that at one time K and the three Books mentioned in the Reichenau catalogue formed one whole. It is impossible to say how and when the MS was taken apart in that case. We have no concrete evidence of the exchange of MSS between Fulda and Reichenau at such an early date. All we know is that a "Saxon" named Edefridus became a brother at Reichenau under Abbot Johannes (759-782) or Abbot Petrus (782-786) bringing with him "Saxon" MSS. Whether we have to interpret "Saxon" as North German or as Anglo-Saxon we do not know[89].

We may, therefore, conclude that K came to Fulda from North England, possibly via Würzburg and/or other intermediary stages in the same area, and possibly at a time long enough before A.D. 821-822 for the first three Books to be lent to Reichenau and for them to be incorporated in a catalogue of that monastery as if forming an integral part of the library in that year, and possibly before the time of the Würzburg catalogue. Identification of it with the copy of HE of the latter catalogue would push the date *non post quem* further back to about A.D. 800. That it reached the Fulda area as early as Saint Boniface's days is an inviting conclusion for which there is no definite proof.

§ 7. Summary

Kassel MS. Theol. Qu. 2 contains Books IV and V of Bede's *Historia Ecclesiastica Gentis Anglorum*. Nothing of the text of these two Books has been lost nor on the other hand has any extraneous matter been incorporated. Book IV covers three gatherings of eight leaves each, and Book V and the additional *recapitulatio chronica totius operis* cover three gatherings of eight and an extra sheet of two leaves. This arrangement of the MS in which the Books cover separate sets of gatherings must have facilitated the lending to other scriptoria of separate Books for copying purposes, and may indirectly have caused the loss of Books I, II, and III. No trace of the lost part has been found except a possible link with Reichenau, a catalogue of which monastery, composed A.D. 821-822, bears the intriguing

op. cit., no. 54, 262-266) no further references to Bede's work occur in medieval catalogues of Reichenau.
[89] Cf. Paul Lehmann, *op. cit.*, p. 223.

item *de historia ecclesiastica gentis Anglorum libri III in codice I* under the general catalogue heading *De libris Bedae presbyteri*.

K presents a neat and sober copy. Chapter-numbering, *incipits* and *explicits* are wanting. It is written in single columns and the writing-space is used economically. Illumination and decoration are lacking, and Chapters are opened with simple uncoloured initials. The script is a skilful and rapid Anglo-Saxon minuscule, whose general appearance is one of great uniformity. Nevertheless, we think that four Hands can be distinguished, viz. Hand I covering 1r-13v, 14v, 15v, 21r,6-30, and 34r,8-42, to 50r; Hand II covering 14r, 15r and 16r to 21r,1-4; Hand III covering 21r,31-42, to 24v; and Hand IV covering 25r to 34r,1-8. The distinction between Hands III and IV is partly based on differences in the use of abbreviations on their respective folios. Those of Hand IV make an even more sparing use of them than of Hand III. The system of abbreviation as applied in the whole of the MS may be said to be one that is completely in keeping with the Anglo-Saxon character of the script and with its neatness in that the scribes only avail themselves of a limited number of the abundance of abbreviations at their disposal. What evidence as to origin of the MS can be derived from such things as vellum, initials, and pricking and ruling, points to (or at any rate does not preclude) an Anglo-Saxon background of the MS. The use with certain letters of the "crescent finial" may even indicate an association with the scriptorium of Wearmouth-Jarrow.

The problems of dating and placing are not simple. The MS is generally dated eighth century by those who have dealt with it. The date *non ante quem* is provided by the text of the MS, viz. A.D. 734. The date *non post quem* is established by the pigskin envelope in which the MS is held and which is typical of the Fulda scriptorium of the middle of the ninth century. Script and abbreviations point to a Northumbrian origin, notwithstanding the early connections of the MS with Fulda, which is known to have been very much under the influence of Anglo-Saxon minuscule script and theoretically may be taken to have been capable of producing such a MS as K. From a purely palaeographical point of view a more exact dating than "eighth century", and in view of the date *non ante quem*, "second half of the eighth century", is not possible. The actual date of composition of the MS may be any date between A.D. 750 and A.D. 800. Identification of the three lost Books of the MS with those mentioned in the Reichenau catalogue of A.D. 821-822 and identification of the MS itself with

38

the *historia anglō* of the Würzburg catalogue of about A.D. 800 in *Bodleian MS. Laud. Misc. 126* is quite possible, although it cannot be proved. We do not know how early in the eighth century K reached the Continent. A direct connection with the requests to England for Bede's works from Saint Boniface and his successor Lullus cannot be proved, though it should not be excluded.

Chapter 2

THE TEXT

§ 1. Major Textual Differences

Charles Plummer, whose admirable edition of Bede's *Historia Ecclesiastica* has served generations of scholars, based his text on a collation of four of the oldest MSS of HE known to him, viz. M, B, C and *Namur, Public Library, Fonds de la ville 11* (see INTRODUCTION, A.). These were not the only MSS he examined of the great number that were at his disposal[1]. He singled out more MSS for examination than had ever before been selected for a critical edition of the text. His selection of MSS, however, was one-sided, because he mainly restricted himself to copies in the possession of British libraries, which is the reason why in his otherwise excellent work two of the earliest and, as we shall see, most reliable MSS, viz. L and K, have not been taken into consideration. Where such a great number of MSS was studied, it is natural that some attention should also be given to the relations between them, and although this part of the investigation was not pursued in any great detail, it nevertheless enabled Plummer to see that the texts as found in M and C were representatives of two distinct versions of HE to which all other MSS studied by him could somehow be related. For obvious reasons these versions were called by Plummer the M-type and C-type respectively. The M-type text is more common on the Continent, whereas the C-type text "has a monopoly of the

---

[1] The number of MSS and MS fragments of this text enumerated by M.L.W Laistner and H. H. King, *A Hand-list of Bede Manuscripts*, Ithaca New York 1943, pp. 94-102, is 159. Of the MSS mentioned by other writers they think that two are doubtful, and three they have not been able to trace. They also mention over a hundred MSS in which extracts from HE appear. To their list of 159 items another two MSS should be added, to which attention was drawn by N. R. Ker in a review of *A Hand-list...* in *Medium Aevum* XIII (1944), p. 40.

circulation in England"[2]. The greater number of MSS, however, show a conflate text which is basically a C-type text with corrections and insertions taken from the M-type text. Plummer has found that there are five passages in which MSS of the C-type text have a reading in common that differs from that shared by MSS of the M-type text[3]. When the text of K is examined on these five points, it appears that without any doubt it is a MS of the C-type, for in all five points it exhibits a C-type text reading.

1. The clause in which Bede asks for the prayers of his readers, viz. "Praeterea omnes... inueniam", is placed at the end of the work on 50r,27-36[4].

2. The Chapter that is numbered [XIV] in Book IV of Plummer's edition, viz. "In quo tunc monasterio.... missarum celebratione uenerari", is omitted in K. There is no division on 11r,35 between the Chapters XIII and [XV] [5].

3. On 12v,27 "cuius supra meminimus" is not added to the sen-

---

[2] Cf. R. A. B. Mynors, "The Early Circulation of the Text", in: P. Hunter Blair, *The Moore Bede, Cambridge University Library, MS. Kk.5.16* (Early English Manuscripts in Facsimile, Ninth Volume), Copenhagen 1959, p. 33. A much more elaborate treatment of the history of the text, especially of the later MSS, than Plummer's is provided by Mynors in CO & MY xxxix ff. Because K is one of the oldest MSS and because it turns out to have a pure and not a conflate text, the present discussion can in the main be based on Plummer's basic findings only.

[3] Cf. PLUMMER I, xciv f.

[4] Since only the last two Books of HE have been preserved in K, we cannot be absolutely certain that this passage did not also occur where M-type texts have it, viz. at the end of the Preface. A number of conflate MSS of later date have this passage in both places.

[5] Cf. PLUMMER I, 232 ff. and CO & MY 376 ff. This additional piece of text in the MSS of the M-type has led to some diversity in both the numbering and the division of this and the following Chapters in those MSS. From Chapter 13 onwards Plummer uses double numberings, of which the first corresponds to the chapter-division and chapter-numbering found in M and also in C, the additional piece of text being the central part of Chapter 13. The second numbering, in square brackets, is that found in N. This MS numbers the missing part of the C-type texts separately as Chapter 14 and the concluding part of Chapter 13 of M and C as Chapter 15, so that when N comes to what is Chapter 14 in M and C it labels it Chapter 16. CO & MY numbers as N does and adds in brackets the chapter-numbers as found in M. L groups Chapters 14, 15 and 16 of N together as Chapter 14, and B calls Chapters 14 and 15 of N Chapter 14 and then continues with Chapter 15 where M and C have Chapter 14. The chapter-numbers inserted in pencil in K go back to such a usage as that of N,

41

tence ending with "... abbate Biscopo cognomine Benedicto"[6].

4. On 49r,38-39 the second part of the annal for the year 731 is restricted to "Anno eodem tatuini consecratus archiepiscopus" and the annals for the years 733 and 734 are inserted immediately after it[7].

5. Of the list of Bede's works the excerpts from Jerome on the Prophets, which in the M-type text read: "In Isaiam, Danihelem, XII prophetas et partem Hieremiae, distinctiones capitulorum ex tractatu beati Hieronimi excerptas", are missing on 49v,29[8]. The C-type character of the text of K is even more firmly established by a number of other such points in which the reading of K agrees with that of C itself, the main representative of the C-type text.

1. Where K, 1r,26-31, and C have: "Ut uilfrid episcopus prouinciam australium saxonum ad Christum conuerterit, *quae tamen illo abeunte propter aceruam hostium obpressionem proprium episcopum habere nequiuerit*", the complete italicised relative clause is missing in the M-type texts[9].

2. In K, 1v,12-14, and in C the order of the capitula of Chapters 29 and 30 of Book IV is not that of the Chapters themselves, whereas it is in the M-type texts[10]. As a result of this reversal the wording of the capitula is also different. K and C have: "Ut ad reliquias eius quidam nuper fuerit ab oculi languore

---

which may clearly be seen from the fact that "Caput 14 deficit" was added in the margin of 11r against the line in which "Interea superueniens...", the opening of Chapter 15 in N, occurs (see above, Chapter 1, § 1). It is not likely that the MS from which the chapter-numberings in pencil were derived was N itself. For in Book V the numbering of chapters in K deviates a second time from the normal practice, and this time also from that of N. The last paragraph of Chapter 8, on 30r, – following the second stanza quoted from Theodore's epitaph, viz. "Successit autem Theodoro..." to "... lingua atque eruditione multipliciter instructum" (cf. CO & MY 474) – is numbered *C9*, so that from that Chapter onwards the chapter-numberings in pencil are one ahead of those found in the editions. In an Additional Critical Note PLUMMER I, 432 notes that this same deviation is to be found in O7, i.e. *MS. Bodley, e Musaeo 115*. The latter is a conflate text of the twelfth or thirteenth century, according to PLUMMER I, cxxvii.

[6] Cf. CO & MY 388. All our MSS read "cognomine" and not "cognomento", which is the reading of CO & MY.
[7] Cf. CO & MY 566 and 572.
[8] Cf. CO & MY 568.
[9] Cf. CO & MY 324.
[10] Cf. CO & MY 326.

curatus. Ut alter ad tumbam eius sit a paralysi curatus". M, L, and B have: "Ut quidam ad tumbam eius sit a paralysi sanatus. Ut alter ad reliquias eius nuper fuerit ab oculi languore curatus".

3. The sentence "Peruenit autem Theodorus ad ecclesiam suam secundo postquam consecratus est anno sub die VI. kalendarum Iuniarum, dominica, et fecit in ea annos XX et unum menses tres dies XXVI"[11] ends Chapter 1 of Book IV in K, 2v,11-14, and in C, but serves as the opening-sentence of Chapter 2 in M, L, and B.

4. K, 24r,18-22, agrees with C in reading the following sentence, which is given here as it occurs in M, L, and B, without the words *ad pedes usque*: "... sentit, ..., quasi magnam latamque manum caput sibi in parte qua dolebat tetigisse, eodemque tactu totam illam, quae languore pressa fuerat, corporis sui partem, paulatim fugiente dolore ac sanitate subsequente, *ad pedes usque* pertransisse"[12].

5. K, 25r,19, and C have: "multos ad dominum conuerterit", where M, L, and B have "multos ad Christum conuerterit"[13].

6. In K, 25r,21-22, and in C the capitulum for Chapter 11 of Book V reads: "Ut uir uenerabilis Suidberct in Brittaniis, Uilbrod Romae sint in Fresiam ordinati episcopi". M, L, and B have: "Ut uiri uenerabiles Suidberct in Brittaniis, Uilbrord Romae sint Fresiam ordinati episcopi"[14].

7. Whereas the capitulum for Chapter 12, Book V, opens with "Ut quidam..." in both versions[15], there is diversity in the opening of the capitulum of the following Chapter, which in K, 25r,25, and C reads: "Ut econtra alius..." and in M, L, and B: "Ut econtra alter...".

8. K, 25v,26, and C have: "et tanta ingruit tamque fera tempestas hiemis, ut neque...", whereas M, L, and B have: "et tanta ingruit tamque fera tempestatis hiems, ut neque..."[16].

9. A complete sentence, and more, of the M-type texts does not occur in K, 33r,21, nor in C. We give the text as it occurs in M,

---

[11] Cf. CO & MY 332.
[12] Cf. CO & MY 446.
[13] Cf. CO & MY 450.
[14] Cf. CO & MY 450. The *uilbrod*-spelling, which is also a C-type characteristic, will be discussed in PART IV.
[15] Cf. CO & MY 450.
[16] Cf. CO & MY 454.

L, and B and italicise the words missing in K and C: "... nunc ad sublimiora proicerentur, nunc retractis ignium uaporibus relaberentur *in profunda. Sed et fetor incomparabilis cum eisdem uaporibus ebulliens omnia illa tenebrarum loca replebat.* Et cum diutius..."[17].

10. In Abbot Ceolfrid's lengthy letter on the observance of the Easter-date and the right tonsure, which takes up by far the greater part of Chapter 21 of Book V, K, 46r,18-19, and C (in contrast to M, L, and B) drop the italicised words of the following sentence of which they form an indispensable part: "Et si beati Petri consortium quaeris, *cur eius quem ille anathematizauit,* tonsurae imaginem imitaris,...?"[18].

11. Between the annals "Anno DCXC Theodorus archiepiscopus obiit" and "Anno DCCIIII Aedilred, postquam XXX annos Merciorum genti praefuit, monachus factus Coenredo regnum dedit", which occur in K on 49r,26-29, M and B have two annals which are lacking in K and C, viz. "Anno DCXCVII Osthryd regina a suis, id est Merciorum, primatibus interemta" and "Anno DCXCVIII Berctred dux regius Nordanhymbrorum a Pictis interfectus"[19]. Added to Plummer's five criteria for distinguishing M-type texts from C-type texts these eleven points clearly help to establish the very close connection between K and C. The MSS are not, however, closely related in the sense that the one was copied from the other. From certain minor points it appears that such a close relationship is out of the question[20]. Both K and C are independent C-type texts, and the question is: which is nearer the original C-text and, consequently, nearer the original as written by Bede[21]. There is a way of finding out. When in important matters K and C differ from one another and one of the two MSS agrees in its reading with the M-type text, we may infer that this MS renders an earlier recension – possibly

[17] Cf. CO & MY 490.
[18] Cf. CO & MY 550.
[19] Cf. CO & MY 562 ff. In the annal for 704 M and B have "XXXI annos". The passage as a whole is missing in L, a complete folio of which has been lost at this place.
[20] See below, § 2.
[21] It is evident that a text which is nearer to the original from a textual point of view is not necessarily, for that reason, to be looked upon as an older text in the chronological sense. Nor is such a text necessarily the better text in all respects, as later alterations may well be improvements on a former provisional draft.

Bede's original version – from which both M-type text and C-type text stem[22]. This can be demonstrated with the help of the stemmata of Figures Three, Four, and Five. Two assumptions have been the starting-points for these stemmata, viz. that there exist two well-defined recensions of HE, i.e. the M- and the C-version, and that none of the eighth-century MSS have been copied from each other directly, except perhaps B from L. Dependent on whether C- or M-version is considered the earlier, the resulting stemma is that of Figure Three or of Figure Four, unless Plummer's suggestion of a still earlier recension from which both C- and M-version were derived is true, in which case the stemma would be that of Figure Five[23]. C' and M' stand for the common originals of the C-type version and the M-type version respectively.

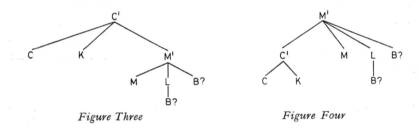

Figure Three   *Figure Four*

It is clear that, barring chance similarity, in cases where K and the MSS of the M-type version share a particular reading against C, the latter MS may be taken to have deviated from the original version. Only when one assumes a derivation of M' from C' through K, does a reading of K that is shared by the MSS of the M-type version against C not necessarily reflect the original (see the stemma of Figure Six).

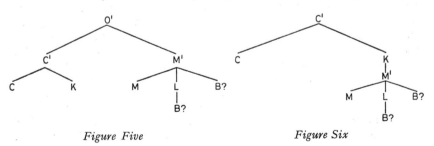

Figure Five   *Figure Six*

[22] Similarly PLUMMER I, xcii stresses the importance of adducing the external testimony of such an independent witness as C, when attempts are made to assess the relative reliability of the texts of M and B on points on which these MSS disagree.
[23] Cf. PLUMMER I, xcvii.

For in that case the M-recension was only made after the text had already been corrupted by the scribes of K. Although there is no conclusive proof against this view of the matter, the available indications all point to the former representation, for a close comparison of K with the MSS of the M-type text has yielded nothing that would fit such a close relation between them as is supposed in this view. It may also be noted that in at least two of the six passages shared by K with the MSS of the M-type against C, viz. no. 4 and no. 5, the reading of C has definitely the air of being an elaboration of the other reading of the other MSS, i.e. of being a later version.

Returning now to the differences between K and C, it is understood, of course, that when we speak of "an important matter" the point of difference should be the result of a conscious attempt at revision of the text or at least be an acceptable alternative reading, and not simply an obvious error that could easily have been corrected by the copyist of a MS later in the line of text-tradition[24]. The following variant readings in the texts of K and C fall into this category and will be compared with the texts of M, L, and B.

---

[24] An example of the kind of variant reading which has clearly been caused by a simple misreading of the exemplar by the scribe is found on 7r,10-14 of K. In this passage the copyist has made the mistake of skipping a number of lines of his exemplar first, and these lines are then without any further comment added at the end of the following sentence. In the other MSS the text runs: "et in loco eius ordinauit episcopum Sexuulfum, qui erat constructor et abbas monasterii quod dicitur Medeshamstedi in regione Gyruiorum. Depositus uero Uynfrid rediit ad monasterium suum, quod dicitur Adbaruae, ibique in optima uitam conuersatione finiuit"; cf. CO & MY 354. K has: "et in loco eius ordinauit episcopum. Depositus uero uynfrit rediit ad monasterium suum quod dicitur adbaruae Ibique in optima uitam conuersatione finiuit saexuulfum qui erat constructor et abbas monasterii quod dicitur medeshamstede in regione gyruio- rum". Probably the scribe was confused by the two occurrences of "quod dicitur" in his exemplar; "episcopum" of the first sentence stands at the end of line 10. From the fact that the mistake is not corrected at all, we may conclude that it was not noticed by the scribe of the MS. This may mean that this scribal blunder was not perpetrated by the scribe of our MS himself, but that the scribe had faithfully copied his exemplar. In this connection an interesting fact for students of the relations between the later MSS of HE may be that PLUMMER I,430 notes exactly the same mistake for *Winchester Cathedral MS. 3*, which is late tenth or early eleventh century. Descriptions of this MS are found in PLUMMER I,cix ff., in E. van K. Dobbie, *The Manuscripts of Caedmon's Hymn and Bede's Death Song* (Columbia University Studies in English and Comparative Literature 128), New York 1937, p. 35, and in CO & MY, Intro- duction, 1 f.

1. K, 9v,1-3, has: "Unde accito ad se praefatae urbis *lundoniae, in qua ipse tunc manebat*, episcopo rogauit, ne...", whereas in C all the italicised words are missing. The reading of K is that of M, L, and B, with this difference that in the latter MSS *praefato* is used instead of *praefatae*[25].

2. On 16r,19 the opening of Chapter 21 of Book IV of K runs as follows: "Anno post hunc sequente, hoc est anno dominicae incarnationis DCLXXX,...". The same opening one finds in M, L, and B[26]. In contrast with this C simply has: "Anno dominicae incarnationis dclxxx".

3. The word "uomeres" in the following passage: "surgentesque duo nequissimi spiritus, habentes in manibus *uomeres*, percusserunt me, unus in capite et alius in pede"[27], appears in the M-type texts either as a marginal note or as an inside-text addition, which it seems is owing to a confusion going back to the MS from which all M-texts have been derived. In K, 35r,27-28, the word is missing altogether, whereas C has a different reading, viz. "surgentesque duo nequissimi spiritus, habentes *cultra* in manibus, percusserunt me, unus in capite et alius in pede".

4. The annal for A.D. 655 in K, 49r,6, agrees with the form it takes in M and B: "Anno DCLV Penda periit, et Mercii sunt facti Christiani"[28]. C has: "Anno dclv Penda rex merciorum occisus est et mercii sunt facti Christiani".

5. The annal for A.D. 705 in K, 49r,29-30, and in M and B reads as follows: "Anno DCCV Aldfrid rex Nordanhymbrorum defunctus est"[29]. This annal reads in C, where it has been added to: "Anno

---

[25] Cf. CO & MY 366. The variation between *praefato* and *praefatae* seems to go back to the distinction between M-type and C-type text. Both London and the Bishop in question are mentioned in the same passage, just a few lines ahead of the one quoted, where Bede relates that King Sebbi of the East Saxons (*s.v.*) went to Ualdheri of London (*s.v.*) when seriously ill at the end of his life: "... uenit ad antistitem Lundoniae ciuitatis, uocabulo Ualdheri, qui Erconualdo successerat,...". In this context it seems more likely that Bede was referring to the Bishop, of whom we hear only at this place in HE, rather than to London. Thus *praefato* is probably a corrected form from *praefatae*, and in the (?earlier) C-version C for some reason or other dropped *lundoniae, in qua ipse tunc manebat.*

[26] Cf. PLUMMER I,252 and CO & MY 404.

[27] Cf. CO & MY 500.

[28] Cf. PLUMMER I, 354 and CO & MY 564. This part of the text is missing in L.

[29] Cf. PLUMMER I, 356 and CO & MY 566. Not in L either.

dccv aldfrid rex nordanhymbrorum defunctus est, et osred regnum su̅s̅ (cepit) et Þilfrid in suam rece̅p̅(tus est) se̅d̅(em)".

6. The following annal, on 49r,30-31, which runs: "Anno DCCVIII Coenred rex Merciorum, postquam quinque annos regnauit, Romam pergit"[30], also occurs in M and – as far as the word *annos* which concludes the MS at this point – in B, but is absent in C.

In five of the six cases the reading of K is the same as that of the representatives of the M-type text, and in one, i.e. no. 3, it is reminiscent of their reading, whereas it differs from the reading of C in all six cases. Moreover, there are no instances of major textual differences between K and C in which the latter agrees in its rendering of the text with M, L, and B against K. This is a strong argument for granting K the possession of a more orthodox text, i.e. one nearer to the original, than C has.

It is very hard to assess how near to the original K may be. K being basically a C-text, this depends to a large extent on how near the C-type text as such is to Bede himself. Opinions differ as to which version is the earlier. PLUMMER I,xcvi f. is inclined to consider the M-version the earlier, whereas according to CO & MY xli[31] it is the later form. It is difficult to find criteria that are generally applicable in this matter. For example, Plummer assumes that "it seems more natural for an author to add to his work in later editions than to make excisions", but then himself has to base the conclusion that the M-version is the earlier mainly on two test-passages, viz. nos. 3 and 4 of the first group of this section, in which the C-version exhibits a less extensive reading. The argument of CO & MY for taking the C-version to be the earlier is that Chapter 14 of Book IV is "clearly authentic, and would never have been removed by a reviser". In connection with Plummer's assumption it may further be noted that a more elaborate text is shown more often by the M-type version than the C-type version. Reference may be made to test-passages nos. 2, 3, 4, and 5 of the first group mentioned above, and of the additional major textual differences to passages nos. 4, 9, 10, and 11. The only occurrence of a more elaborate text in the C-type version is no. 1 of the additional major textual differences. The crux is that one can hardly ever be absolutely certain that what one considers an addition

[30] See note 29.
[31] Cf. also R. A. B. Mynors, *op. cit.*, p. 33.

48

of one version should not as a matter of fact be interpreted as an omission of the other. And although the argument of CO & MY in favour of the C-version is certainly important, the question cannot be taken to be settled definitely one way or the other[32].

For our purpose the question of the priority of the two versions is of less weight than the question at what date the C-type version, of which to all appearances K forms a very authentic copy, came into existence. Should the C-version be the earlier of the two, then the date of its composition may be pushed back to the year in which HE was completed, i.e. A.D. 731, unless there was a still earlier recension, in which case it must have been composed before A.D. 737, the year that the first MS of the M-type version, M, was written. In the other case there is nothing in the C-type version that would be incompatible with a very early date for its composition. Plummer[33] thinks that there is some internal evidence to prove that the C-type recension originated in A.D. 734. However that may be, there is every reason to assume that the text-tradition in which K was written arose, if not during Bede's own life-time and under his supervision, then certainly not long after Bede's death, and therefore bears in it every possibility of a close likeness of its details, such as the spelling of the name-material, with what Bede himself wrote.

[32] Such arguments are very often not as decisive as they may seem to be at first sight. Thus Plummer's view that the absence of "cuius supra meminimus" in K and C, which does not answer to a former reference to Benedict Biscop in HE, should be interpreted as a conscious omission in the revised version may seem convincing. The argument is that in the first version Bede without any further checking inserted "cuius supra meminimus" in the conviction that he had already mentioned Benedict Biscop in HE. This mistake would be conceivable, since Bede had indeed written extensively about Benedict Biscop before, though not in HE but in the *History of Abbots*. However, it is not impossible – though possibly a little less likely – that when an overall revision of HE was undertaken the reviser, whether he was Bede himself or someone else, was in the same way led to believe that Benedict Biscop had already been mentioned and therefore added "cuius supra meminimus". Similarly, the position of the annals for A.D. 733 and A.D. 734 at the end of the *recapitulatio chronica totius operis* in the C-type texts and not, as in the M-type texts, at the end of the completed work, at first sight makes it seem very likely that the M-type version is the earlier. But here too it could be argued that the annals were originally given the positions they have in the C-type version and were afterwards put by a reviser where they are now in the M-type version, because their forming an integral part of the *recapitulatio chronica totius operis* was not in agreement with the date of completion of HE as given by Bede himself at the end of Chapter 23 of Book V (cf. CO & MY 560): in the M-version they are clearly singled out as additional matter.

[33] Cf. PLUMMER I, xcviii

The conclusion of the preceding paragraph that, from a purely textual point of view, K is nearer to the original than C is not invalidated by the presence in K of a number of instances in which a reading is found different from that shown by both C and the M-type texts. They are all differences of a minor order, the main categories of which are the omission and addition of single words, variation as to word-endings, and change of word-order. As a rule these differences result from inattention on the part of the scribe and not from any conscious attempt at altering the appearance of the text. They are very often obvious errors, whose transmission from one MS to another is not as automatic as is sometimes thought. The freedom of the scribes "seems to have included the freedom to correct obvious errors"[34]. The last MS in a line of text-tradition need not necessarily, on top of its own mistakes, incorporate in its text all those mistakes that were ever perpetrated by its ancestors. Nevertheless, the likelihood of a badly contaminated text being later in the line of text-tradition – again not necessarily later in the chronological sense – than a less contaminated one is fairly great, especially since a sharp borderline between a minor error and a conscious change or adaptation must at times have been difficult to draw for a copyist. A number of such changes will, therefore, be transmitted and become distinctive features of a particular side-branch in the tradition of the text. That this is so may be seen from the fact that, when we closely compare our MSS on this point, in over 120 cases K shares such changes with C against the MSS of the M-type version[35]. Seen in this light the number of times that a reading of K differs from the one shared by both C and the MSS of the M-type version, i.e. 42 times, as compared to the number of times that a reading of C differs from the one shared by both K and the MSS of the M-type version, i.e. 105 times, may be said to corroborate the conclusion arrived at in the preceding paragraph. And this can be said in particular of one of the categories of

[34] Cf. E. C. Colwell and E. W. Tune, "Variant Readings: Classification and Use", *Journal of Biblical Literature* 83 (1964), p. 258; and Maurice Bévenot S.J., *The Tradition of Manuscripts. A Study in the transmission of St.Cyprian's treatises*, Oxford 1961, pp. 5 ff.

[35] Some of the differences between M-type texts and C-type texts can be accounted for from the use of abbreviations in the original MS from which both C-type version and M-type version derive or, for that matter, in the original

minor differences mentioned above, viz. change of word-order. Change of word-order is a common feature in K, and also in M and C. What is meant by it is exemplified in "et lindisfarorum episcopatus "p̄ eet "officio" of 5r,36-37, instead of "et lindisfarorum episcopatus officio praeesset" of the other MSS[36]. Change of word-order occurs forty times in K and thirty-four times in C[37]. In K *signes de renvoi*[38] are used (as in the example given) in eighteen out of forty cases. The cases in which they are not used are those in which K agrees with C in having a different word-order from that found in MSS of the M-type version, i.e. the cases in which K renders the C-type version. In sixteen of the cases in which *signes de renvoi* occur they serve to make the reading of K agree with that of both C and the MSS of the M-type version. The remaining two had better be given in full:

1. 7v,28:   puer 'circiter "trium non
   C: puer circiter trium non
   M-texts: puer trium circiter non
2. 45v,30-31: quoque "quam ipse "coronę
   C: quoque ipse quam coronae
   M-texts: quoque coronae quam ipse

Whenever *signes de renvoi* are applied in K, the first element indicates the place where the word, or occasionally the words, preceded by the second element should be inserted. In the foregoing two cases, therefore, the *signes de renvoi* serve to restore the text as found in the M-type version. Change of word-order, especially because it is in many cases an adaptation on stylistic grounds which usually does not entail a change of meaning, would not be easily detected and, consequently, the insertion of *signes de renvoi* would not be called

C-type MS or in the original M-type MS. Such differences as those between *per* and *pro*, and *prae* and *pro*, belong to this category. One of the most striking instances is that in which K, 35v,33, and C have *Audientes h^* (= *autem*) and all the MSS of the M-type text have *Audientes haec*, where the confusion was probably due to the use of the abbreviation *h^* for *autem* or *h̄* for *haec* in the exemplar, the latter of which is fairly frequent in M and is actually used by it in this instance. Cf. CO & MY 504. The forms *h^* and *h̄* were easily confused.
[36] Cf. CO & MY 346.
[37] L has no instances of this phenomenon, whereas B has only 6. M has 48. It is tempting to look for an explanation of this in the way the various MSS came to be copied and to suggest that the scribes of the MSS that show change of word-order were dictated to. On other grounds, however, oral dictation has already been shown to be unlikely. See above, Chapter 1, § 3. Mental dictation would seem to be quite possible.
[38] See Chapter 1, §§ 2 en 3.

for, unless, after completion, the new MS had been closely compared against another MS, e.g. its exemplar. Where the *signes de renvoi* of K are concerned, the text against which K was compared cannot have been an M-type text, although in all eighteen cases this is what the text of K is corrected to, for in that case it would seem unlikely that the twenty-two cases in which K agrees with C against the M-type version would have been left unchanged. On the other hand it cannot have been C or one of its descendants, for under those circumstances there would have been no *signes de renvoi* in the first of the two cases mentioned above, since the uncorrected MS rendered the word-order found in C, and the second element of the *signes de renvoi* of the second case would have preceded *ipse* and not *coronę*. Moreover, twelve times C has a word-order that differs from that shared by K and the MSS of the M-type version without indicating this in any way; it is unlikely that no trace of them should be found in K, if K were a direct descendant of C. The conclusion must be that, whereas the corrections with *signes de renvoi* were no doubt based on a MS of the C-type version, this MS must have been earlier in the text-tradition than C. That the MS against which the text of K was compared was the exemplar of K, we do not know for sure; there are no indications of the opposite[39]. It is clear from what has been said so far about the relation between K and C, in particular from the variations in word-order, that K cannot possibly be directly or indirectly a descendant of C. If further proof for this is looked for, one could point to the many cases in which single words are left out by C against both K and the MSS of the M-type version. One can imagine a scribe occasionally supplying the correct word in an obvious void of the exemplar, but not in forty-five instances, i.e. the number of times that K agrees with the MSS of the M-type text against C. Conversely, the nine instances of loss of essential words in K against both C and the M-type text corroborate the impression already derived from other evidence that C is neither a direct nor an indirect descendant of K.

Keeping in mind what has been stated above about the danger of relying solely on such minor textual differences for the settlement of the relations between the MSS, we may say that they have been

---

[39] Above, Chapter 1, § 3, we have indicated that we believe *signes de renvoi* to be the work of the scribe(s) or of a contemporary corrector. C uses no *signes de renvoi* in contrast to M which corrects 43 of its 48 instances of change of word-order in that way.

of value even in that respect. Their value is much greater, however, when it comes to assessing the relative reliability of the texts and their scribes. And with a view to the discussion in Part IV of the OE material of K, it certainly is of some importance to assess the reliability of the text of K as such, compared with that found in the other MSS. Whether a variant reading of a particular MS is of its own making, or simply derives from its exemplar, is of minor importance in this connection, for in either case the actual appearance of the text is affected, which may provide the right perspective for looking at particular variant readings in the OE material. Two categories of minor textual differences may be distinguished here, viz. one which comprises the cases in which whole words have been left out, added or replaced, and one which concerns the significant changes of single letters[40]. A count of instances of the former category yields the following results: as we have seen above, K and C agree with each other against the other MSS in 120 cases; K differs from all other MSS in 42 cases, C in 105 cases, M in 109 cases, L + B in 17 cases, L in 4 cases, and B in 48 cases. Similarly in the latter category K and C agree with each other in 42 cases; K differs from all other MSS in 43 cases, C in 103 cases, M in 74 cases, L + B in 7 cases, L in 7 cases, and B in 15 cases. If the five texts are to be judged from this as to their reliability, it appears that L is the most reliable MS, rather closely followed by K and B, and then by C and M. When in the category of omission, addition or replacement of single words one considers more closely the instances in which single words have been left out, the picture one gets is, it would seem, even more indicative of relative reliability. For leaving out single words is the result of hasty and inaccurate copying. When the new copy was compared against the exemplar after completion, a great number of the mistakes of this type would be spotted by the corrector, whether he was the scribe himself or someone else, whereas other minor changes resulting from careless copying, some of which may have a special importance in a discussion of the OE material, might easily be overlooked. It seems warranted, therefore, if the relative reliability of the various MSS is measured by the number of times that single words are left out, that those cases in which the correct reading is provided by a corrector should also be

[40] By "significant changes of single letters" should be understood all those changes that are not subject to the arbitrariness characteristic of Latin orthography of the early Middle Ages, such as the use of *d* for *t* and *t* for *d*, *e* for *i* and *i* for *e*, and the mixing up of single and double consonants. See below, § 3.

53

included. K leaves out 13 words of which it corrects 4; C leaves out 70 words of which it corrects 25; M leaves out 155 words of which it corrects 135; L leaves out 29 words of which it corrects 22; and B leaves out 71 words and corrects 41. This again confirms the impression that K is amongst the most accurate copies of HE written in the eighth century.

The spread of errors, either corrected or uncorrected, over the folios of the MS is fairly even throughout, and from them not much further proof as to diversity of hands can be drawn, except perhaps another indication of the existence in the script of type three of actually two Hands. When one takes together as one group the instances of change of word-order, omission of single words, and of other significant minor errors, such as the use of the singular of the verb instead of the plural and vice versa, one finds that on 21 r-26 r only one such instance occurs, viz. on 23 v,18-19, where K reads: "dn̄s totus beatitudinis auctor" instead of: "dn̄s totius beatitudinis auctor". This error, though resulting in a totally different reading, may well have to be looked upon as a simple misreading of a -*ti*- ligature for -*t*- in the exemplar. The other folios of this type of script show roughly the same amount of errors as is also found on comparable groups of folios of the MS, viz. over 15[41].

§ 3. Latin Orthography

The number of times a MS deviates in its Latin orthography from the accepted norm may both be an indication of the standard of its copying and, in the case of particular recurrent features, may account for certain peculiarities in its spelling of the OE material. And thirdly,

---

[41] As K shows a text that is earlier in the tradition of the text than that of C, it would theoretically be possible that certain features of the C-type version could be ascribed to particular scribes of K. Such a close connection is not revealed by a detailed study of these features. This is another indication that C is neither directly nor indirectly a copy of K. What may be significant is that of the 22 changes of word-order shared by K and C against the MSS of the M-type text, 14 occur in Book IV and 8 in Book V, which may point to different degrees of thoroughness with which the revision of the original text that resulted in the diversity between C-type text and M-type text was carried out in the respective Books.

it may be possible to identify certain of these peculiarities as characteristic of particular scribes[42].

We give, therefore, first of all an enumeration of the various instances of confusion found in K. There are instances of *a* for *au*, of *a* for *u* and of *u* for *a*, of *a* for *o* and *o* for *a*, of *e* for *ae* and *ae* also spelled *ę* for *e*, of *e* for *i* and *i* for *e*, of *i* for *ii* and *ii* for *i*, of *e* for *oe* and *ae* (*ę*) for *oe*, of *o* for *u* and *u* for *o*, of *u* for *uu* and *uu* for *u*, of simplification and doubling of consonants, of *b* for *u* and *u* for *b*, of *c* for *ch*, of *t* for *d*, of both unassimilated *dt* and assimilated *tt*, of omission and insertion of initial and medial *h*, of the use of both *n* and *m* before bilabials and labio-dentals, of the omission of *n* before *s* and *x*, and of the insertion of *p* between *m* and following *t*. A rough count of the occurrences of spellings which may be marked as incorrect yields a fair measure of the relative reliability as to detail of the various MSS. The number of incorrect spellings is about 100 in L, about 170 in K, about 180 in B, about 250 in M, and about 525 in C. This bears out the conclusion about the relative reliability of K, C, M, L, and B arrived at above, § 2.

Incorrect usage of Latin orthography, when not restricted to the occasional instance, may be indicative of phonological changes and may thus have some bearing on the interpretation of the spelling of the OE material. In this respect attention is drawn to the replacement of *au* by *a*, of *ae* by *e* and *e* by *ae*, of *e* by *i* and *i* by *e*, of *oe* by *e*, and of *d* by *t* and *t* by *d*; to the omission and insertion of *h*, to the omission of *n* before *s*, and the simplification and doubling of consonants, all of them features of the unsettled state of Latin orthography long before Bede's time[43]. Outside the Insular tradition this state of confusion in

[42] In this study spelling-deviations are not evaluated with a view to their possible significance for placing the MS. Such deviations as there are in our MSS are found in post-classical Latin texts from all provinces. Since Ludwig Traube scholars have tended to interpret a fairly great number of such deviations in Insular script as typically Irish. B. Löfstedt, *Der Hibernolateinische Grammatiker Malsachanus* (Acta Universitatis Upsaliensis, Studia Latina Upsaliensia 3), Uppsala 1965, pp. 82 f., points out that such identification is incorrect, except for (p. 107) the insertion of *i* in such words as *staitim* (for *statim*) and *Mairia* (for *Maria*), and the use of *ia* and *ea* instead of *e* in such words as *diciabat* (for *dicebat*) and *profeata* (for *profeta*). For the rest Löfstedt comes to the conclusion that only a *frequent* occurrence of deviations in the orthography of the Latin is a strong indication of Irish origin.

[43] Cf. F. W. Hall, *A Companion to Classical Texts*, Oxford 1913, p. 86; Jeanne Vielliard, *Le Latin des Diplômes Royaux et Chartes Privés de l'Epoque Mérovin-*

Latin orthography led to an extensive corruption of the spelling, which was only ended when scholars returned to classical models at the time of the Carolingian Renaissance. The number of incorrect spellings of any of the types mentioned in K cannot be said to be significant in itself, and varies from about 60 instances of *e* for *ae* and about 15 of *ae* (*ę*) for *e* to only five instances of *a* for *au*, viz. the uncorrected *agustis* on 6v,14 and *cladius* on 48v,6 (the latter of which is also found in C) and the corrected *a^ut* on 6v,25 and 11r,1 and *pa^upe-rib·* on 11r,13. Especially with the latter three instances there is the possibility that they are errors due to the use in the exemplar of superscript *u*. But although the total number of these errors is small in K, their occurrence in itself shows that the scribes were not able to avoid them altogether, a fact which may be of relevance in the discussion of the OE material.

Of the other instances of fluctuation in the spelling of the Latin text it may also be well to remember, when discussing the OE material, that they occur at all. They are, however, small in number and some of them, such as *o* for *a* and *a* for *o*, *u* for *a* and *a* for *u*, and *i* for *ii* and *ii* for *i*[44], are more likely to result from purely visual errors than from any uncertainty as to their phonetic value. A striking example of this is the word *appuruit* on 33r,42, corrected (?later) to *apparuit*; in this case the scribe probably mistook an open *a* of the exemplar for a letter *u*. There are some examples of the spelling of *c* for *ch*. Folio 26r,22 has *micahelis* corrected (?later) to *michahelis*; in agreement with C, K has *euthycetis* on 12r,15, *euthycen* on 12v,7 and *scemate* on 45r,14; in agreement with both M and C *carybdi* on 43v,40; and in agreement with M, but corrected by later hand, *scematibus* on 50r,22[45]. That this confusion has probably to be related to the pronunciation [k] for the digraph *ch* in these words and not to the pronunciation [χ] for *c*, is brought out by the following scribal errors in the consonant cluster *-chr-*, errors which are, moreover,

---

gienne, Première Partie, Phonétique (Bibliothèque de l'Ecole des hautes Etudes 251), Paris 1927; Karl Strecker, *Introduction to Medieval Latin* (English Translation and Revision by Robert B. Palmer), Berlin 1957, pp. 20 ff.; H. W. F. M. Hoppenbrouwers, *La Plus Ancienne Version de la Vie de S. Antoine par S. Athanase*. Etude de Critique Textuelle, Utrecht-Nijmegen 1960, pp. 2 ff.; Löfstedt, *op. cit.*, p. 150; and Dag Norberg, *Manuel pratique de latin médiéval* (Connaissance des Langues IV), Paris 1968, p. 19.

[44] See also above, Chapter 1, § 3.

[45] The part of the text in which this word occurs is missing in both C and B.

typical of K: *sepulcrhi*, 5r,27-28; *sepulcro*, 14r,7; *sepulcro* (corrected to *sepulchro*) on 15r,8; *perpulcrum*, 35r,11; and *sepulcrhum*, 37r,14.

As for significant features in the Latin orthography of the other MSS, it may be worth noting that C, apart from having significantly more incorrect spellings than any of the other MSS, has a fair amount of instances of certain categories of which only occasional instances occur in the other MSS. We may mention here: the incorrect insertion of *h*, the replacement of *a* by *o*, of *a* by *u*, of *t* by *d*, of *u* by *b* and *f*, of *o* by *u* and *u* by *o*, and the use of -*xs*- for -*x*- and the insertion of *p* between *m* and *t*.

Of none of the orthographic features that are represented in K by a fair number of instances have we been able to establish an exclusive or all but exclusive relationship with any of the four Hands we have distinguished. Only of three rare features, viz. *a* for *au*, *c* for *ch*, and -*crh*- and -*cr*- for -*chr*-, may it be said that all the occurrences except one, viz. *micahelis* on 26r,22, are found on folios written by Hand I. The four scribes, therefore, clearly wrote in the same tradition of Latin orthography, in which school to all appearances there was no such freedom of interpretation concerning rules of spelling as there apparently was in the matter of the use of abbreviations.

§ 4. Summary

Plummer distinguishes two recensions of Bede's HE. K clearly belongs to the C-type version with which it shares, against all MSS of the M-type version, all five test passages selected by Plummer and a greater number of similar passages. Against this, however, K shares with the M-type version other passages that may also be called critical. It appears therefore, that the text as found in K is most probably earlier in the line of text-tradition than that of C, which does not necessarily mean that for that reason the MS is chronologically earlier than C. Similarly there is also some indication that the actual origin of the C-type version should be put during Bede's own life-time or very near it; this certainly means that for neither MS the possession of a near-authentic text should be excluded, although it does not prove anything regarding the actual date of composition of either K or C.

When one considers the treatment of minor details in the various MSS, it appears that K has a much more reliable text than C and, moreover, that next to L it is the most accurate MS of HE from the eighth century. This impression of neatness and accuracy is also evident in the MS in as far as the use of Latin orthography is concerned. There is some evidence on the other hand of uncertainty in the application of particular spellings, and it will be necessary to take these instances into account in the discussion of the OE material. None of the peculiarities of Latin orthography can be singled out as being characteristic of any of the four Hands, except perhaps that the very rare instances of three particular features are almost exclusively found on the folios of Hand I. Finally, a critical study of the spread of minor errors over the folios of the MS shows the almost complete absence of errors of this type on 21r to 26r, which is another indication that what was distinguished as the third type of script on solely palaeographical grounds is actually the work of two different Hands.

PART II

THE MATERIAL

EDITORIAL NOTE

1. The aim of the present collation of the OE material of K has been to include not only place-names, river-names and personal names of English origin in the strictest sense, but also those names of other origins that may throw light on the OE material. This is also the policy of both Sweet[1] and Anderson[2], but in this edition it is applied as Anderson applies it, since his selection of name-material is much wider than Sweet's. The interpretation Sweet gives to his statement "Celtic and other foreign names are given only when they throw light on Old English spellings" results in "a good deal of arbitrariness", as Anderson says. Latin names and the Latin translations of OE names are as a rule excluded from this edition, but the selection made is wide enough to include the original Latin forms or the more or less Latinized versions of the names of British rivers and places. Names of Celtic origin have thus all been included. The only OE word of the MS that is not a name, *gae* of 26 v, has also been incorporated.

Every occurrence of the names is recorded fully, even if the same forms are repeated without any variation time and again. Sweet tends to select rigorously in this respect, in contrast to Anderson who looks upon an exhaustive registration as "the only scientific way of editing in a case like this"[3]. Anderson, however, does not adhere strictly to this principle. Of the names of peoples and tribes and of countries he registers only the first few occurrences, if they show no differences of spelling. In this edition the policy with regard to names of peoples and tribes and of countries that are in any way connected with Britain has been that such names are recorded exhaustively if variant forms, however few, show up in any of the six MSS, but that they are not recorded at all if they are of frequent occurrence and of identical appearance in all the MSS. The names of the latter category,

[1] OET 132.
[2] ANDERSON LB 11.
[3] *op. cit.*, p. 12.

and the total number of their occurrences, are: Angli (76), Brettones (10), Cantuarii (15), Mercii (23), Picti (14), Saxones (37), and Scotti (18); Brittania (60)[4], Cantia (14), Fresia (8), Hibernia (14), and Scottia (5); and the related words Brittani (1), Saxonicus (2) and Scotticus (2). These names do, however, figure in PART III.

2. The present collation differs from those provided by OET and ANDERSON LB in that the name-material is arranged alphabetically. Moreover, the material from K and the other MSS is given in parallel columns. The references of the first column are to the folios and lines of K. Cross-references to former editions of the name-material or the MSS themselves, if at hand, are made possible by the two lists appended to this Editorial Note under 4. The first list contains the Book-numberings and Chapter-numberings of HE as found in the edition of CO & MY[5] and against them the corresponding folios and lines in K. In the second list the consecutive folios of K are given against the corresponding folios of M, L, C, and B.

Names omitted in K are not recorded for the other MSS either. Of every name that is recorded, however, the forms that appear in the other MSS are all recorded in full. Instances of omission in MSS other than K are indicated by dashes; question-marks are used in all cases where names or parts of names are illegible. Where scribes have used suprascript strokes as space-saving devices, the omitted letters or syllables are supplied in italics in the present edition.

Corrections of and additions to names may be of three types: a) they definitely stem from the scribes themselves or from contemporary correctors; b) they may possibly stem from the scribes themselves or from contemporary correctors; c) they definitely stem from non-contemporary correctors. In this edition an attempt has been made to avoid all unnecessarily confusing detail. For that reason corrections and additions have not been included in the text of the edition, but are all referred to in the footnotes. In the text the names are recorded in the forms the scribes or the contemporary correctors meant them to take, which means that corrections and additions of type a) have been merged with the names of the edition and are mentioned specific-

[4] In a great number of instances in C one -t- is dotted and another -n- interlined over the word, by second hand.
[5] For Book IV the numbering in CO & MY differs from that in PLUMMER as from Chapter 14 onwards. See for this difference between the two editions PART I, Chapter 2, note 5.

ally only at the bottom of the page, and that the corrections and additions of both type b) and type c) appear in the footnotes only, recognizable as such by the designations "by second hand?" and "by second hand" respectively.

The case-endings of the names may be deduced from what is given of the Latin text in the second column. The aim has been to restrict quotation from the Latin to a bare minimum. No Latin context-material is, therefore, given in column 2 against names in the nominative case or against names that have easily recognizable characteristics of a number of other cases. This means that a name against which no part of the Latin text is given in the second column has the nominative case unless its ending is one of the following: a) *-orum, -arum,* and *-ium*; b) *-um, -am,* and *-em*; c) *-o*; d) *-ae*. Words with the ending of class a) have the genitive plural case, those with the endings of class b) have the accusative singular case, those ending in *-o* have the dative or ablative singular case, and those ending in *-ae* have the genitive or dative singular. In order to preclude any misunderstanding the reader's attention is drawn to two consequences of this system. The first is that names ending in *-i* are to be taken to have the nominative case when no part of the Latin context is found against them in column two, and the second that, conversely, names ending in *-o* or *-ae* that have the nominative case will be accompanied by the relevant part of the Latin text.

The spelling of the Latin text has been normalized when necessary, and it has also been corrected in the case of the scribal errors that are of no importance for the discussion of the OE material. The spelling of the name-material in the text of the edition is a faithful recording of that of the MSS, even where only such variants as *ae, æ,* and *ę* are concerned.

3. The footnotes also serve to register, beside corrections and additions, all instances in which this edition deviates from the previous editions of OET, PLUMMER and ANDERSON LB. Sweet's statement of policy: "Names and readings which repeat the same forms without variation are not registered exhaustively"[6] may lead the user of his edition to wrong conclusions about the appearance of certain names. For of the very many names and readings of names that are not recorded by Sweet many, in fact, do not simply repeat forms already recorded,

---

[6] *op. cit.,* p. 132.

whereas the above quotation at least suggests that in the cases in which only the name as found in M is specifically given in OET that name appears in identical form in both C and B. All such readings, whether identical in form or not to that of M, are in this edition noted as "OET, not recorded." Cases in which names are altogether absent from Sweet's edition are also indicated in the footnotes. In contrast to Sweet Plummer is very definite about his treatment of the names of HE: "In regard to proper names I have, except in one or two cases of obvious blunders which are specially noted, always retained in the text the spelling of M, and have given in the notes the variations of *all* the other three MSS."[7], i.e. of B, C and N. In those cases, therefore, in which Plummer does not give a variant reading for either C or B in his notes, the conclusion must be that the appearance of the name in that MS is, according to Plummer, identical to that of M. In the notes to the present edition the reader will find that Plummer was mistaken in quite a number of cases. Another matter in which Plummer slips up slightly is his treatment of the considerable number of cases in which the MS-reading of B is illegible owing to the burnt state of the Codex. Plummer hardly ever expressly mentions illegibility in his notes, thus creating the impression that in these cases also he has found forms in B identical to those in M. In the present edition notes are attached to such cases in the form: "PLUMMER, as in M.".

4. A. *Book- and Chapter-numbers of HE and the corresponding folios and lines in K*

CO & MY	K	CO & MY	K
IV, capitula	1r,1 - 1v,14	IV,17	12r,14 - 12v,21
IV,1	1v,16 - 2v,11[8]	IV,18	12v,23 - 13r,32
IV,2	2v,11 - 3r,24	IV,19	13r,34 - 14v,13
IV,3	3r,26 - 5r,40	IV,20	14v,15 - 15r,16
IV,4	5r,42 - 5v,32	IV,21	15r,18 - 15r,29
IV,5	5v,34 - 7r,5	IV,22	15r,31 - 16r,18
IV,6	7r,7 - 7r,34	IV,23	16r,19 - 18r,4
IV,7	7r,36 - 7v,26	IV,24	18r,6 - 19r,18
IV,8	7v,28 - 8r,12	IV,25	19r,19 - 20r,33

[7] PLUMMER I, lxxxiv.
[8] The Chapter ends here in the M-type texts. In K and C the Chapter ends in line 14. See PART I, Chapter 2, p. 43.

CO & MY	K	CO & MY	K
IV,9	8r,14 - 8v,29	IV,26	20r,34 - 21r,4
IV,10	8v,31 - 9r,19	IV,27	21r,6 - 21v,26
IV,11	9r,20 - 9v,33	IV,28	21v,28 - 22v,14
IV,12	9v,35 - 10v,7	IV,29	22v,16 - 23r,26
IV,13	10v,9 - 11r,35[9]	IV,30	23r,28 - 23v,33
IV,14		IV,31	23v,35 - 24r,29
IV,15	11r,35 - 11v,7	IV,32	24r,31 - 24v,25
IV,16	11v,9 - 12r,12		
V, capitula	25r,1 - 25v,7	V,13	34v,27 - 35v,11
V,1	25v,11 - 26r,12	V,14	35v,13 - 36r,12
V,2	26r,14 - 26v,27	V,15	36r,13 - 36v,20
V,3	26v,29 - 27r,33	V,16	36v,21 - 37r,24
V,4	27r,35 - 27v,23	V,17	37r,26 - 37v,24
V,5	27v,25 - 28r,8	V,18	37v,26 - 38r,31
V,6	28r,10 - 29r,6	V,19	38r,32 - 41r,27
V,7	29r,8 - 29v,22	V,20	41r,29 - 41v,27
V,8	29v,24 - 30r,19	V,21	41v,29 - 46v,32
V,9	30r,21 - 31r,7[10]	V,22	46v,34 - 47r,42
V,10	31r,9 - 31v,33	V,23	47v,1 - 48r,40
V,11	31v,35 - 32v,3	V,24	48v,1 - 50r,27
V,12	32v,5 - 34v,25	Praefatio	50r,27 - 50r,36[11]

B. *Folios of K and the corresponding folios of M, L, C, and B.*

K	M	L	C	B
1r	70r - 70v	78r - 78v	93r - 93v	111v - 112v
1v	70v - 71r	78v - 79v	93v - 94v	112v - 113r
2r	71r - 71v	79v - 80r	94v - 95r	113r - 114r
2v	71v - 72r	80r - 81r	95r - 95v	114r - 115r
3r	72r - 72v	81r - 81v	95v - 96r	115r - 115v
3v	72v - 73r	81v - 82r	96r - 96v	115v - 116v

[9] No Chapter-division in K or C, which MSS connect it onto Chapter 15. See PART I, Chapter 2, note 5.

[10] The pencil-numbering in K, for which see PART I, Chapter 2, note 5, marks this Chapter as Chapter 10, and is, therefore, from this Chapter onwards one number ahead of the numbering of the other MSS.

[11] Part of Bede's Preface is placed at the end of the work in the C-type version MSS. See PART I, Chapter 2, p. 41.

K	M	L	C	B
4r	73r - 73v	82r - 83r	96v - 97r	116v - 117v
4v	73v - 74r	83r - 83v	97r - 98r	117v - 118r
5r	74r - 74v	83v - 84v	98r - 98v	118r - 119r
5v	74v - 75v	84v - 85r	98v - 99r	119r - 120r
6r	75v - 76r	85r - 86r	99r - 99v	120r - 120v
6v	76r - 76v	86r - 87r	99v - 100r	120v - 121v
7r	76v - 77r	87r - 87v	100r - 101r	121v - 122v
7v	77r - 77v	87v - 88v	101r - 101v	122v - 123v
8r	77v - 78v	88v - 89r	101v - 102v	123v - 124v
8v	78v - 79r	89r - 90r	102v - 103r	124v - 125v
9r	79r - 79v	90r - 90v	103r - 103v	125v - 126v
9v	79v - 80r	90v - 91v	103v - 104v	126v - 127v
10r	80r - 80v	91v - 92r	104v - 105r	127v - 128v
10v	80v - 81r	92r - 93r	105r - 105v	128v - 129r
11r	81r - 83r	93r - 95v	105v - 106r	129r - 132r
11v	83r - 83v	95v - 96r	106r - 107r	132r - 133r
12r	83v - 84r	96r - 97r	107r - 107v	133r - 134r
12v	84r - 84v	97r - 97v	107v - 108v	134r - 134v
13r	84v - 85r	97v - 98v	108v - 109r	134v - 136v[12]
13v	85r - 86r	98v - 99v	109r - 109v	136v - 137v
14r	86r - 86v	99v - 100r	109v - 110v	137v - 138v
14v	86v - 87r	100r - 101r	110v - 111r	138v - 139v
15r	87r - 87v	101r - 102r	111r - 111v	139v - 140v
15v	87v - 88r	102r - 102v	111v - 112v	140v - 141r
16r	88r - 89r	102v - 103v	112v - 113r	141r - 135r[12]
16v	89r - 89v	103v - 104v	113r - 113v	135r - 142r
17r	89v - 90r	104v - 105v	113v - 114v	142r - 143r
17v	90r - 90v	105v - 106v	114v - 115r	143r - 143v
18r	90v - 91r	106v - 107v	115r - 116r	143v - 144v
18v	91r - 92r	107v - 108v	116r - 116v	144v - 145v
19r	92r - 92v	108v - 109r	116v - 117r	145v - 146v
19v	92v - 93r	109r - 110r	117r - 118r	146v - 147r
20r	93r - 93v	110r - 111r	118r - 118v	147r - 148r
20v	93v - 94v	111r - 112r	118v - 119r	148r - 149r
21r	94v - 95r	112r - 113r	119r - 120r	149r - 150r
21v	95r - 95v	113r - 113v	120r - 120v	150r - 151r
22r	95v - 96r	113v - 114v	120v - 121v	151r - 152r

[12] f. 135 of B comes between f. 141 and f. 142.

K	M	L	C	B
22v	96r - 97r	114v - 115v	121v - 122r	152r - 153r
23r	97r - 97v	115v - 116v	122r - 122v	153r - 154r
23v	97v - 98r	116v - 117v	122v - 123v	154r - 155r
24r	98r - 98v	117v - 118r	123v - 124r	155r - 156r
24v	98v - 99r	118r - 118v	124r - 124v	156r - 156v
25r	99r - 99v	119r - 119v	125r - 125v	157r - 157v
25v	99v - 100r	119v - 120v	125v - 126v	157v - 158v
26r	100r - 100v	120v - 121r	126v - 127r	158v - 159v
26v	100v - 101r	121r - 122r	127r - 127v	159v - 160r
27r	101r - 101v	122r - 123r	127v - 128r	160r - 161r
27v	101v - 102r	123r - 123v	128r - 129r	161r - 162r
28r	102r - 103r	123v - 124v	129r - 129v	162r - 163r
28v	103r - 103v	124v - 125v	129v - 130r	163r - 164r
29r	103v - 104r	125v - 126r	130r - 130v	164r - 165r
29v	104r - 104v	126r - 127r	130v - 131r	165r - 166r
30r	104v - 105r	127r - 127v	131r - 132r	166r - 166v
30v	105r - 105v	127v - 128v	132r - 132v	166v - 167v
31r	105v - 106r	128v - 129v	132v - 133r	167v - 168v
31v	106r - 106v	129v - 130v	133r - 133v	168v - 169v
32r	106v - 107v	130v - 131v	134r - 134v	169v - 170v
32v	107v - 108r	131v - 132r	134v - 135r	170v - 171v
33r	108r - 108v	132r - 133r	135r - 136r	171v - 172v
33v	108v - 109r	133r - 134r	136r - 136v	172v - 174r
34r	109r - 110r	134r - 135r	136v - 137v	174v - 175r
34v	110r - 110v	135r - 136r	137v - 138r	175r - 176r
35r	110v - 111r	136r - 137r	138r - 138v	176r - 177r
35v	111r - 111v	137r - 137v	138v - 139v	177r - 177v
36r	111v - 112r	137v - 138v	139v - 140r	177v - 178v
36v	112r - 112v	138v - 139v	140r - 140v	178v - 179v
37r	112v - 113v	139v - 140r	140v - 141r	179v - 180v
37v	113v - 114r	140r - 141r	141r - 142r	180v - 181v
38r	114r - 114v	141r - 141v	142r - 142v	181v - 182v
38v	114v - 115r	141v - 142v	142v - 143r	182v - 183v
39r	115r - 115v	142v - 143v	143r - 144r	183v - 184v
39v	115v - 116r	143v - 144v	144r - 144v	184v - 185r
40r	116r - 116v	144v - 145r	144v - 145r	185r - 186r
40v	116v - 117v	145r - 146r	145r - 146r	186r - 186v
41r	117v - 118r	146r - 147r	146r - 146v	186v - 187v

K	M	L	C	B
41v	118r - 118v	147r - 147v	146v - 147r	187v - 188r
42r	118v - 119r	147v - 148v	147r - 148r	188r - 189r
42v	119r - 119v	148v - 149v	148r - 148v	189r - 190r
43r	119v - 120r	149v - 150v	148v - 149r	190r - 191r
43v	120r - 120v	150v - 151r	149r - 149v	191r - 192r
44r	120v - 121r	151r - 152r	149v - 150v	192r - 193r
44v	121r - 122r	152r - 153r	150v - 151r	193r - 193v
45r	122r - 122v	153r - 154r	151r - 151v	193v - 194v
45v	122v - 123r	154r - 154v	151v - 152r	194v - 195v
46r	123r - 123v	154v - 155v	152r - 153r	195v - 196r
46v	123v - 124r	155v - 156r	153r - 153v	196r - 197r
47r	124r - 125r	156r - 157r	153v - 154r	197r - 198r
47v	125r - 125v	157r - 158r	154r - 154v	198r - 199r
48r	125v - 126r	158r - 159r	154v - 155v	199r - 200r
48v	126r - 126v	159r - 159v	155v - 156r	200r - 201r
49r	126v - 127v	159v - ——[13]	156r - 157r	201r - 201v[14]
49v	127v - 128r	160r - 160v	157r - 157v	
50r	128r	160v - 161r	157v	

[13] At this point a complete folio is missing from L, which is not shown in the numbering of L.
[14] B ends at this point.

		K	M	L	C	B
25v,1		acca	acca	acca	acca[1]	acca[1]
40v,15[1]		acca	acca	acca	acca	acca
40v,20	ad accan presbyterum	accan	accan	accan	accan[1]	accan[1]
41r,41[1]		acca	acca	acca	acca	?[2]
41v,18[1]		acca	acca	acca	acca	acca
48r,17[1]		acca	acca	acca	acca	?[3]
19r,26[1]		adamnanus	adamnanus	adamnanus	adamnanus	adamnanus
25r,28[1]		adamnano	adamnano	adamnano	adamnano	adamnano
36r,16[1]		adamnan	adamnan	adamnan	adamnan	adamnan
36v,8[1]		adamnanum	adamnanum	adamnanum	adamnanum	adamnanum
36v,16[1]		adamnan	adamnan	adamnan	adamnan	adamnan
46r,11[1]		adamnan	adamnan	adamnan	adamnan	adamnan
46r,35[1]		adamnano	adamnano	adamnano	adamnano	adamnano
27v,26	comitis uocabulo addi	addi	addi	addi	addi[1]	aeddi
10v,25	regina nomine aebae	aebae	eabae	eabæ	eabę[1,4]	eabae[1]
13v,14	matri /.../ uocabulo aebbę	aebbae	aebbæ	aebbæ	aebbae[1,5]	?[6]
19v,28		aebbę	aebbę[7]	aebbæ	aebbae[1]	aebbae
20v,21[1]	in monasterio aebber-curnig	aebbercurnig	aebbercurnig	æbbercurnig	aebbercurnig	aebbercurnig
7r,4		aecci	aecci	æcci	aecci[1]	aecci[1]
2v,41		aeddi	aeddi	aeddi	aeddi[1]	aeddi[1]
48r,14[1]		aedilbaldo	aedilbaldo	ædilbaldo	aedilbaldo[8]	aedilbaldo

ms./line							
48v,3?	aedilberct	aedilberctum	?	aedilberctum	aedilberctum	?	accumbercct
47v,4-5[1]	aedilberctum	aedilberctum	aedilberctum	aedilberctum	aedilberhtum	aedilberctum	? berctum[10]
7r,26	aedilburgae	aedilburgae[11]	aedilburgae	aedilburgae[11]	aedilburgae	aedilburgae	aedilburgae[1]
8r,14	aedilburga	aedilburga	aedilburga	aedilburga	aedilburga	aedilburga	aedilburga[1]
8v,25-26 *cum*/.../*mea matre* aedil- burgae	aedilburgae	aedilburge	aedilburge	aedilburge	aedilburgę[12]	aedilburge	aedilburge[1]
8v,31 *successit* /.../ aedilburgi	aedilburgi	aedilburgi	aedilburgi	aedilburgi	aedilburgae	aedilburgi	aedilburgi[1,13]
1r,39	aedilredum	aedilredum	aedilredum	aedilredum	aedelredum	aedilredum	aedilredum[1]
10r,6[1]	aedilraed	aedilred	aedilred	aedilred	aedilred	aedilred	aedilred
10v,7[1]	aedilraed	aedilred	aedilred	aedilred	aedilred	aedilred	aedilred
12r,24[1]	aedilredo	aedilredo	aedilredo	aedilredo	edilredo[14]	aedilredo	aedilredo
15r,18-19[1]	aedilredum	aedilredum[15]	aedilredum	aedilredum[15]	aedilredum	aedilredum	aedilredum
15r,22	aedilred	aedilred	aedilred	aedilred	aedilred	aedilred	aedilred[1]
15r,40[1] ędilredi *regis*	ędilredi	aedilredi	aedilredi	aedilredi	aedilredi	aedilredi	aedilredi
17r,7[1]	aedilredo	aedilredo	aedilredo	aedilredo	aedilredo[16]	aedilredo	aed?redo[17]
34v,29[1]	aedilredum	aedilredum	aedilredum	aedilredum	aedilredum	aedilredum	aedilredum
38r,38[1] *filio* aedilredi	aedilredi	aedilredi	aedilredi	aedilredi	aedilredi	aedilredi	?[18]
40r,22[1]	aedilredo	aedilredo	aedilredo	aedilredo	aedilredo[19]	aedilredo	aedilredo
40v,36[1]	aedilred	aedilred	aedilred	aedilred	aedilred	aedilred	aedilred
40v,37[1]	aedilred	aedilred	aedilred	aedilred	aedilred	aedilred	aedilred
49r,16[1]	aedilredo	aedilredo	aedilredo	aedilredo	aedelredo	aedilredo	—

[1] OET, not recorded. [2] PLUMMER 331, as in M. [3] PLUMMER 351, as in M. [4] PLUMMER 230, eabae. [5] PLUMMER 243, aebbæ. [6] PLUMMER 243, as in M. [7] PLUMMER 264, aebbæ. [8] PLUMMER 350[17]: "aedil-C²(?)." [9] -berct interlined; PLUMMER 353, aedilberct. [10] PLUMMER 348, as in M. [11] -u- over dotted e; OET 142, aedilburgæ, "u over e". [12] -a over final ę; PLUMMER 223[8]: "aedilburgæ C¹; -ga C²." [13] -i altered to -e, by second hand. [14] a letter may have been erased before opening e-; PLUMMER 239², edilredo. [15] PLUMMER 249, aedilredum. [16] PLUMMER 255², aedilredum. [17] PLUMMER 255, as in M. [18] PLUMMER 322, as in M. [19] PLUMMER 327, edilredo.

		K	M	L	C	B
49r,17[1]		aedilred	aedilred	—	aedilred	aedilred
49r,27[1]		ędilred	aedilred	—	aedilred	?.[2]
1r,36		aediltryth	edilthryd	edilthryd	aedildryt	edilthryd[1]
3v,29	*cum regina* aedilthryde	aedilthryde	aedilthryde	aedilthryde	aedeldryda[3]	aedilthryda[4]
13r,34[1]	(in a Latin hymn)	aedilthrydam	aedilthrydam	aedilthrydam	aedeldrydam[5]	aedilthrydam
14v,38[1]		aedilthryda	aedilthryda	aedilthryda	ędildryda	aedilthryda
16r,1[1]		aedilthrydae	aedilthrydæ[6]	aedilthrydæ	aedilthrydae	aedilthrydae
10v,17		ędilualch	aedilualch	aedilualch	aedilualh	aedilualch[1]
11r,18		aedilualch	aedilualch[7]	aedilualch	aedilualh	aedilualch[1]
11r,38[1]	*regem* aedilualch	aedilualch	aedilualch	aedilualch	aedilualh	aedilualch
34v,2		aediluald	ediluald	ediluald	aediluald	ediluald[1]
48r,17[1]		ediluald	ediluald	ediluald	aediluald	ediluald
10r,37[1]	*secundum* ędiluini	ędiluini	ediluini	ediluini[8]	aediluuini	ediluini[9]
20v,30		aelbfled	aelbfled	aelbfled	ęlffled	ael ? fled[1,10]
15r,19		ęlfuini	aelfuini	aelbuini	**aelfuini[11]**	aelbuini[12]
15r,31[1]		aelfuini	aelfuini	aelbuini	**aelfuuine**	aelbini[13]
49r,20		aelfuini	aelfuini	—	**aelfþine**	æluuine[14]
10v,26	*fratris* aenheri	aenheri	aenheri	aenheri	eanheri	aenheri[15]
7v,29	*puer* |.../ aesica *nomine*	aesica	aesica	aesica	aesica[1]	aesica[1]
16v,31		aetla	aetla	aetla	aetla[1]	aetla[1]

72

Folio	Notes					
2r,31[1]		agilberctum	agilberctum	agilberctum	agilberhtum	agilberctum
9v,36[1]		agilberctus	agilberctus	agilberctus	agilberchtus	agilberctus
39v,12[1]		agilbercto	agilbercto	agilbercto	agilberchto	?[16]
39v,18[1]		agilbercto	agilbercto	agilberhto	agilberhto	?[16]
16r,40[1]		aidano	aidano	aidano	aidano	aidano
16v,6[1]		aidano	aidano	aidano	aidano	aidano
16v,11[1]		aidan	aidan	aidan	aidan	aidan
21v,17[1]		aidan	aidan	aidan	aidan	aidan
47r,23[1]		aidanum	aidanum	aidanum	aidanum	aedanum[17]
49r,4[1]		aidan	aidan	—	aidan	aedan[18]
20v,33[1]		aldfrid	aldfrid	aldfrid	aldfrid	aldfrid
26r,11	aldfridi *regis*	aldfridi	aldfridi	aldfridi	aldfridi[1]	aldfridi[1]
29r,8[1]	*regni* aldfridi	aldfridi	aldfridi	aldfridi	aldfridi	aldfridi
34r,38[1]		aldfrido	aldfrido	aldfrido	aldfrido	aldfrido
36r,18[1]		aldfridum	aldfridum	aldfridum	aldfridum	aldfridum
36v,16[1]		aldfrido	aldfrido	aldfrido	aldfrido	aldfrido
37v,26[1]		aldfrid	aldfrid	aldfrid	aldfrid	aldfrid
40r,14[1]	*et secundo anno* aldfridi	aldfridi	aldfridi	aldfridi	aldfridi	aldfridi
40r,22[1]		aldfrido	aldfrido	aldfrido	aldfrido	aldfrido
40v,39[1]		aldfrid	aldfrid	aldfrid	aldfrid	?frid[19]

[1] OET, not recorded. [2] PLUMMER 355, as in M. [3] second e originally was i; according to PLUMMER 208[1], the crossbars of the d's probably stem from the corrector's hand. [4] final -a may well have to be read as -æ; PLUMMER 208, aedilthryde. Cf. also DAHL 173. [5] PLUMMER 243[3]: "aedilthrydam C[1]; aedel-C[2]." [6] PLUMMER 251, aedilthrydae. [7] PLUMMER 232, aedilualch. [8] ANDERSON LB 43, 1.20, ediluini; -d-, however, looks very much like a d. [9] final -i altered to -e, by second hand? [10] PLUMMER 267[6]: "ælbfled B, with b erased." [11] u interlined over -ſu-, by second hand?; both PLUMMER 249[5], and OET 144, aelfuine. [12] PLUMMER 249, aelfuini. [13] u interlined over -bi-, by second hand?; final -i altered to -e, by second hand?; [14] f interlined over -ſu-, by second hand; PLUMMER 355, ælfuini. [15] PLUMMER 249[9]: "aelb'u'ini B[1]; -ne B[2]." [16] PLUMMER 354, aidan. [17] -i- interlined over -e-, by second hand? [18] PLUMMER 355, as in M. [19] PLUMMER 329, as in M.

Folio	Note	K	M	L	C	B
46r,12[1]		aldfridum	aldfridum	aldfridum	aldfridum	aldfridum
49r,29[1]		aldfrid	aldfrid	—	aldfrid	? [2]
39v,31		aldgislo	aldgilso	aldgislo	aldgislo[3]	aldgislo[1,3]
25r,36		aldhelmum	aldhelmum	aldhelmum	aldhelmum[1]	aldhelmum[1]
25r,37[1]	*eiusdem aldhelmi*	aldhelmi	aldhelmi	aldhelmi	aldhelmi	aldhelmi
37v,35[1]		aldhelmo	aldhelmo	aldhelmo	aldhelmo	aldhelmo
38r,2-3[1]		aldhelmo	aldhelmo	aldhelmo	aldhelmo	aldhelmo
38r,5[1]		aldhelm	aldhelm	aldhelm	aldhelm	aldhelm
47v,41		alduino	alduino	alduino	alduino[1]	alduino[1]
48r,6[1]		alduini	alduini	alduini	alduuine	alduin?[4]
12r,25		alduulfo	alduulfo	alduulfo	alduulfo[1]	alduulfo
16r,36	*alduulfi regis*	alduulfi	alduulfi	alduulfi	aldulfi	alduulfi[1]
47v,14[1]		alduulf	alduulf	alduulf	alduulf	alduulf
47v,42		alduulfo	alduulfo	alduulfo	alduulfo	alduulfo[1]
48r,2[1]		alduulf	alduulf	alduulf	alduulf	? [4]
39r,42	*alhfridi regis*	alhfridi	alchfridi	alhfridi	alhfridi[1]	alchfridi[1]
22r,17	*iuxta fluuium* alne	alne	alne	alne	alne[1]	alne[1]
47v,5		alricum	alricum	alricum	alricum[1]	alricum[1]
11r,40		andhuno	andhuno	andhuno	andhuno[1]	andhuno[1]
13r,35[1]		annae	anna	annae	anna	annae[5]

74

36v,3[1]	arcuulfus	arcuulfus	arcuulfus	arcuulfus	arcuulfus
2r,26[1]	arhelas	arhelas	arhelas	arhelas	arhelas
11v,25 arualdi *regis*	arualdi	arualdi	arualdi	arualdi[1]	arualdi[1,6]
23v,35 *frater quidam nomine* badudegn	badudegn	badudegn	badudegn	beaduđegn	badudegn[7]
7r,4	baduini	baduini	baduuini	baduini	baduuini[1,8]
49v,6	baeda	baeda	—	be da[9]	—
39r,36	balthild	baldhild	baldhild	balthild	baldhild[1]
3v,4 *in loco qui dicitur* adbaruae	adbaruae	adbaruae[10]	adbaruae	adbearuae	adbaruae
7r,11-12 *quod dicitur* adbaruae	adbaruae	adbaruæ[11]	adbaruae	adbaruę[11]	adbaruae[1]
17v,9[1] *femina nomine* begu	begu	begu	begu	begu	begu[12]
49r,31	berctfrit	berhtfrid[13]	—	berhtfrid[1]	—[14]
11r,40	bercthuno	bercthuno	berchthuno	berchthuno[1,15]	bercthuno[1]

[1] OET, not recorded. [2] PLUMMER 326, aldgilso. [3] PLUMMER 356, as in M. [4] PLUMMER 350, as in M. [5] PLUMMER 243, anna. [6] o interlined over first a-, by second hand. [7] second -d- altered to -đ-, by second hand?; OET 145, badudegn. [8] final -i altered into e, by second hand? [9] the letter erased between -e- and -d- may have been -a-; PLUMMER 357: "beada C, but with the former a erased." [10] PLUMMER 207, adbaruae. [11] PLUMMER 218, adbaruae. [12] altered to begid, by second hand. [13] PLUMMER 356, berctfrid. [14] B ends imperfectly at a point just before this name; this is not noted by OET. [15] PLUMMER 236, bercthuno.

	K	M	L	C	B
20r,35	bercto	bercto	bercto	berhto	bercto[1]
25,12	berctuald	berctuald	berctuald	berchtuuald[1,2]	berctuald[1]
30,6	berctuald	berctuald	berctuald	berhtuald[1]	berctuald[1]
32r,12[1]	berctualdo	berctualdo	berctualdo	berchtualdo	berctualdo
40v,35[1]	berctuald	berctuald	berctuald	berchtuuald	berctuald
47v,14[1]	berctualdo	berctualdo	berctualdo	berchtualdo	berctualdo
47v,35[1]	berctuald	berctuald	berctuald	berchtuuald	berctuald
49r,37[1]	berctuald	berctuald	—	berhtƿald	—
7r,30 *qui nuncupatur* inberecingum	inberecingum	inberecingum	inberecingum	inbercingum	berecingum[3]
1r,15[1] *in monasterio* bericinensi	bericinensi	bericinensi	bericinensi	bericinensi	bericinensi
26r,17	berichthun	bercthun	bercthun	berhthun[1]	bercthun[1]
26v,29[1]	berichthun	bercthun	bercthun	berhthun	bercthun
10r,30[1]	berniciorum	berniciorum	berniciorum	berniciorum	berniciorum
36r,8-9[1]	berniciorum	berniciorum	berniciorum	berniciorum	berniciorum
11v,20 *cui nomen* bernuuini	bernuuini	bernuuini	bernuuini	berchtuuini[1]	bernuuini[1,4]
12v,26 *adulescens nomine* biscop	biscopo	biscopo	biscopo	biscopo[1]	biscopo[1]
39,6	biscop	biscop	biscop	biscop[1]	? [5]
6r,15	bisi	bisi	bisi	bisi[1]	bisi[1]
6v,40	bisi	bisi	bisi	bisi[1]	bisi[1]

76

		britannyae coniuge sua	britannyae	britannyae	britannyae yae		
21r,17		boisil	boisil	boisil	boisil	bosil	boisil[1]
21r,33		boisil	boisil	boisil	boisil	bosil	boisil[1]
22r,31		boisil	boisil	boisil	boisil	boisel	boisil[1]
30v,2	*sacerdotis* boisili	boisili	boisili	boisili	boisili	boisili	boisili[1]
30v,2		boisil	boisil	boisil	boisil	boisil	boisil[1]
30v,7[1]		boisil	boisil	boisil	boisil	boisil	?[6]
30v,8[1]		boisil	boisil	boisil	boisil	boisil	boisil
30v,24[1]		boisil	boisil	boisil	boisil	boisil	?[6]
30r,31[1]	*sunt* |.../ boructuari	boructuari	boructuarorum	boructuari	boructuari	boructuarii	? tuari[7]
32r,15[1]	*expugnatis* |.../ boruc-	boructuarorum	boructuarorum	boructuarorum	boructuarorum	boructuarorum	boructuarorum
32r,17[1]	tuaris	boructuaris	boructuaris	boructuaris	boructuaris	boructuaris	boructuaris
10r,29		bosa	bosa	bosa	bosa	bosa[1]	bosa[1]
10v,1		bosa	bosa	bosa	bosa	bosa[1]	bosa[1]
16v,31		bosa	bosa	bosa	bosa	bosa[1]	bosa[1]
26v,32[1]	*defuncto* bosa *uiro*	bosa	bosa	bosa	bosa	bosa	bosa
41v,23[1]	bosa |.../ *episcopi*	bosa	bosa	bosa	bosa	bosa	?[8]
49r,19[1]		bosa	bosa	—	bosa	bosa	bosa
10v,31		bosanhamm	bosanhamm	bosanhamm	bosanhamm	bosanham	bosanham
17r,4	*antistes* |.../ *uocabulo*	bosel	bosel	bosel	bosel	bosel[1]	bosel[1,9]
17r,12	bosel	boselum	boselum	boselum	boselum	boselum[1]	boselum[1]

---

[1] OET, not recorded. [2] -t- interlined. [3] *in* rubbed out before the word? OET 142, and PLUMMER 219, in berecingum. [4] final -i altered to -e, by second hand. [5] PLUMMER 323, as in M. [6] PLUMMER 297, as in M. [7] PLUMMER 296, as in M. [8] PLUMMER 332, as in M. [9] PLUMMER 255[1]: "boseli B (?)."

77

Ref		K	M	L	C	B
17r,20		bregosuid	bregusuid	bregusuid	bregusuit	bregusuid[1,2]
47v,39[1]		briudun	briudun	briudun	briuduun	briudun
10v,23-24		burghelm	burghelm	burghelm	burghelm[1]	burghelm[1]
18r,26		caedmon	caedmon	caedmon	cędmon	?[3]
10r,1-2[1]		cędualla	caedualla	caedualla	ceadualla	caedualla
11r,36		cędualla	caedualla	caedualla	ceadualla	caedualla[1]
11v,1	*ab eodem* cędualla	cędualla	caedualla	caedualla	ceadualla	caedualla[1]
11v,2	*post* cęduallan	cęduallan	caeduallan	caeduallan	cęduallam	caeduallan[1]
11v,9		caedualla	caedualla	caedualla	caeduualla	caedualla[1]
25r,9		cędualla	caedualla	caedualla	ceadulla	? ualla[1,4]
29r,8		cęddualla	caedualla	ceadualla	ceadulla	ceadualla
29r,32		caeddual	caedual	caedual	ceadual	ceadual[1]
29v,11		cęddual	caedual	caedual	ceadual[5]	ceadual[1]
29v,15	*abeunte* /.../ cęduualla	cęduualla	caedualla	caedualla	ceadualla[6]	caedualla[1]
29v,24[1]		caeddualla	caedualla	caedualla	ceadualla	caedualla
49r,25		cędualla	caeduald	—	ceadualla	caedualla[1,7]
16r,34[1]	*in monasterio* cale	cale	cale	cale	cale	cale
1r,7[1]		ceadda	ceadda	ceadda	ceadda	ceadda
3r,5[1]		ceadda	ceadda	ceadda	ceadda	ceadda
3r,30[1]	ceadda *episcopum*	ceadda	ceadda	ceadda	ceadda	?. adda[8]
3r,42[1]		ceadda	ceadda	ceadda	ceadda	ceadda
5r,2[1]	*eodem* ceadda	ceadda	ceadda	ceadda	ceadda	ceadda
5r,11	*antistitis* ceadda	ceadda	ceadda	ceadda	ceadda[1]	ceadda[1]
5r,18[1]		ceadda	ceadda	ceadda	ceadda	ceadda

39v,22[1]	ceadda	ceadda	ceadda	ceadda	ceadda
49r,9[1]	ceadda	ceadda	—	ceadda	ceadda
5r,13[1] ceddi *fratris*	ceddi	ceddi	ceddi	ceddi	ceddi
12v,30	ceolfrido	ceolfrido	ceolfrido	ceolfrido[1]	ceolfrido[1]
25v,2	ceolfrid	ceolfrid	ceolfrid	ceolfrid[1]	ceolfridus[1]
41v,39[1]	ceolfridum	ceolfridum	ceolfridum	ceolfridum	ceolfridum
42r,13[1]	ceolfrid	ceolfrid	ceolfrid	ceolfrid	ceolfrid
42r,15[1]	ceolfrid	ceolfrid	ceolfrid	ceolfrid	?[9]
49v,10[1]	ceolfrido	ceolfrido	ceolfrido	ceolfrido	—
49v,18[1]	ceolfrido	ceolfrido	ceolfrido	ceolfrido	—
50r,12[1] *benedicti* ceolfridi	ceolfridi	ceolfridi	ceolfridi	ceolfridi	—
38r,37[1]	ceolredo	ceolredo	ceolredo	ceolredo	?[10]
49r,33[1]	ceolred	ceolred	—	ceolred	—
47v,30[1]	ceoluulfum	ceoluulfum	ceoluulfum	ceoluulfum	ceoluulfum
48r,15	ceoluulf	ceoluulf	ceoluulf	ceoluulf[1]	ceoluulf[1]
7r,28	cerotesei	cerotaesei	cerotæs ei[11]	ceortes ei[12]	cerotaesei[1]
7r,28[1] *id est* ceoroti *insula*	ceoroti	ceroti	ceroti[11]	ceoroti	ceroti
17r,22 *sub rege* |...| cerdice	cerdice	cerdice	cerdice	cerdice[1]	cerdice[1]

[1] OET, not recorded. [2] PLUMMER 255[6]: "uel beorhtsuid B[2]." [3] PLUMMER 259, as in M. [4] PLUMMER 292, as in M. [5] PLUMMER 293[7], ceadualla. [6] PLUMMER 294[4], ceadulla. [7] PLUMMER 355, caeduald. [8] PLUMMER 206, as in M. [9] PLUMMER 333, as in M. [10] PLUMMER 322, as in M. [11] initial *ce-* looks like *æ-* in MS. As ANDERSON LB 42[189] remarks: "If it was meant for an *æ* it is clearly a misreading of the *ce-* of the original." [12] PLUMMER 219[1], cerotesei.

		K	M	L	C	B
6v,15		clofaeshooh	clofeshooch[2]	clofaeshooh	clofeshooh[3]	clofaeshooh
46v,38		coinred	coenred	coinred[4]	coenred[1]	? [5]
47v,2		coinredo	coenredo	coinredo	coenredo	coinredo[1,6]
47v,31[1]	*coinredi regis*	coinredi	coenredi	coinredi	coenredi	coinredi[7]
25r,38		coinred	coinred	coinred	coenred	coinred[1]
34v,29[1]	*temporibus coenredi*	coenredi	coenredi	coenredi	coenredi	coenredi
38r,32[1]		coinred	coinred	coinred	coenred	coinred
38r,38[1]		coinredum	coinredum	coinredum	coenredum	? [8]
40v,37[1]		coenredum	coinredum	coenredum	coenredum	coenredum
49r,28[1]		coinredo	coenredo	—	coenredo	? [9]
49r,30[1]		coinred	coenred	—	—[9]	? [9]
9v,37[1]		coinuualch	coinualch	coinualch	coenualch	coinualch
1r,9[1]		colman	colman	colman	colman	colman
1v,17[1]		colman	colman	colman	colman	colman
5r,42[1]		colmanus	colmanus	colmanus	colmanus	colmanus
5v,16[1]		colmanus	colmanus[10]	colmanus	colmanus	colmanus
49r,8[1]		colman	colman	—	colman	? [11]
1v,2[1]		coludanae	coludane	coludanae	coludanae	coludanae
13v,15[1]	*quem* coludi *urbem nominant*	coludi	coludi	coludi	coludi	coludi
19r,19[1]	*quod* coludi *urbem cognominant*	coludi	coludi	coludi	coludi	coludi
30v,12[1]		columbae	columbae	columbae	columbae	columbae

80

folio							
30v,13¹		columba	columba	columba	columba	columba	columba
30v,16		columba	columba	columba	columba	columba	columba
30v,17¹	*composito a cella et columba nomine*	columba	columba	columbę	columba	columba	? ¹²
30v,26¹		columba	columba	columbae	columba	columbae	? ¹²
48v,26¹		columba	columba	columba	columba	columba	columba
30v,17¹		columcelli	columcelli	columcelli	columcelli	columcelli	? ¹²
41r,4	*abbatis* cudbaldi	cudbaldi	cudbaldi	cudbaldi	cudualdi	cudbaldi	cu ? ¹,¹³
1v,4		cudberct	cudberct	cudberct	cudberct	cudbercht	cudberct¹
20v,4		cudbercto	cudbercto	cudbercto	cudbercto	cudberchto	cudbercto¹
21r,8¹		cudberctum	cudberctum	cudberctum	cudberctum	cudberhtum	? ¹⁴
21r,18¹		cudberct	cudberct	cudberct	cudberct	cudberht	cudberct
21r,20¹		cudberct	cudberct	cudberct	cudberct	cudberht	cudberct
21r,38¹		cudbercto	cudbercto	cudbercto	cudbercto	cudberhto	cudbercto
21v,28¹		cudberct	cudberct	cudberct	cudberct	cudberht	cudberct
22r,42¹		cudberct	cudberct	cudberct	cudberct	cudberht	cudberct
23r,10		cudbercto	cuthbercto¹⁵	cudbercto	cudbercto	cudberchto¹	cudbercto¹
23r,20¹		cudbercto	cudbercto	cudbercto	cudbercto	cudberchto	cudbercto
23r,29¹		cudberct	cudberct	cudberct	cudberct	cudberht	cudberct
23v,9¹		cudberct	cudberct	cudberct	cudberct	cudberht	cudberct
23v,27¹	*patris* cudbercti	cudbercti	cudbercti	cudbercti	cudbercti	cudberchti	cudbercti
24r,10	*patris* cudbercti	cudbercti	cudbercti	cudbercti	cudbercti	cudberchti¹	cudbercti¹
24r,27¹	*corpus* cudbercti	cudbercti	cudbercti	cudbercti	cudbercti	cudberchti	cudbercti
24v,3¹	*patris* cudbercti	cudbercti	cudbercti	cudbercti	cudbercti	cudberchti	cudbercti

¹ OET, not recorded. ² -c- interlined over -oh. ³ PLUMMER 216³: "clofæshooh C." ⁴ -i- over dotted -e-. ⁵ PLUMMER 346, as in M. ⁶ PLUMMER 348, coenredi. ⁷ PLUMMER 349, coenredi. ⁸ PLUMMER 322, as in M. ⁹ PLUMMER 356, as in M. ¹⁰ ending -us interlined, by second hand. ¹¹ PLUMMER 354, as in M. ¹² PLUMMER 297, as in M. ¹³ PLUMMER 330, as in M. ¹⁴ PLUMMER 268, as in M. ¹⁵ PLUMMER 275, cudbercto.

	K	M	L	C	B
25r,1 *successor* cudbercti	cudbercti	cudbercti	cudbercti	cudberhti	cudbercti[1]
25v,11[1] *antistitis* cudbercti	cudbercto	cudbercto	cudbercto	cudberchto	cudbercto
50r,9[1]	cudbercti	cudbercti	cudbercti	cudberchti[2]	—
32v,10-11 *regione/.../quae uocatur* incuneningum	incuneningum	incuneningum	incuneningum	incuneningum[1]	incuneningum[1,3]
11v,31 *presbyter uocabulo* cyniberct	cyniberct	cyniberct	cyniberct	cyneberht[1,4]	cyniberct
10r,38	cyniberctum	cyniberctum	cyniberctum	cyniberchtum[1]	cyniberctum[1]
48r,9[1]	cyniberct	cyniberct	cyniberct	cynibercht	cyniberct
14r,10	cynifrid	cynifrid	cynifrid	cynifrid[1]	cynifrid[1,5]
24r,33 *iuxta amnem* dacore	dacore	dacore	dacore	dacore[1]	dacore[1]
30v,31[1]	danai	danai	danai	danai	?
48v,34 *ad* degsastanae	degsastanae	degsastanæ	?	daegsa stanę	degsastanae[1,6]
26r,18 *monasterii quod uocatur* inderauuda	inderauuda	inderauuda	inderauuda	inderauudu	inderauuda[1]
10r,29[1]	derorum	derorum	derorum	derorum	derorum[1]
26r,18	derorum	derorum	derorum	derorum	deirorum[7]
29r,2[1]	derorum	derorum	derorum	derorum	derorum
22v,24-25 deruuentionis *fluuii*	deruuentionis	deruuentionis	deruuentionis	doruuentionis	deruuentionis[1,8]

Ref.	Lemma							
10v,30[1]	monachus /.../ uocabulo	dicul	dicul	dicul	dicul	dicul	dicul	dicul
16v,33	in episcopatum dorcic cestrae	dorcic cestrae	dorcic caestrae	dorcic caestrae	dorcic caestre	dorciccestre	dorcic cestrae	? [9]
1v,19[1]	ecclesiae doruuernensis	doruuernensis	doruuernensis	doruuernensis	doruuernensis	doruuernensis	doruuernensis[10]	doruuernensis
3r,13-14[1]	doruuernensi ecclesiae	doruuernensi	doruuernensi	doruuernensi	doruuernensi	doruuernensi	doruuernensi[11]	doruuernensi
6r,14[1]	doruuernensis ecclesiae	doruuernensis	doruuernensis	doruuernensis	doruuernensis	doruuernensis	doruuernensis	doruuernensis
29v,31[1]		doruuernensium	doruuernensium	doruuernensium	doruuernensium	doruuernensium	doruuernensium	doruuernensium
12r,28[1]	ciuitatis doruuernis	doruuernis	doruuernis	doruuernis	doruuernis	doruuernis	doruuernis[12]	doruuerni
47v,40[1]	in dorouerni ciuitate	dorouerni	doruuerni	doruuerni	doruuerni	doruuerni	doruuerni	doruuerni
34v,17	frater drycthelme (voc.)	drycthelme	drycthelme	drycthelme	drycthelme	drycthelme	drychthelme[1]	drycthelm[1]
47r,22[1]		duunchado	duunchado	duunchado	duunchado	duunchado	duunchado[13]	duuncado[14]
49r,1[1]		eadbald	eadbald	eadbald	eadbald	eadbald	eadbald	eadbald
47v,5[1]		aadberctum	eadberctum	eadberctum	eadberctum	eadberctum	eadberchtum	eadberctum
23r,21[1]		eadberct	eadberct	eadberct	eadberct	eadberct	eadbercht	? [15]
23r,37		eadbercto	eadbercto	eadbercto	eadbercto	eadbercto	eadberchto[1]	eadbercto[1]
23v,24[1]		eadberct	eadberct	eadberct	eadberct	eadberct	eadbercht	eadberct

[1] OET, not recorded. [2] PLUMMER 359[3], cudberhti. [3] -e- originally was -i-; -g- originally was -c-; -n- interlined. [4] PLUMMER 237[6], cyniberht. [5] first -i- altered to -e-, by second hand?; PLUMMER 245, cynifrid. [6] PLUMMER 353, degsastanae. [7] PLUMMER 283, derorum. [8] o over dotted first -e-, by second hand; PLUMMER 274, deruuentionis. [9] PLUMMER 254, as in M. [10] PLUMMER 201, doruuernensis. [11] PLUMMER 205, doruuernensi. [12] PLUMMER 239: "doro- C, the first o being by C[2] on erasure." [13] PLUMMER 347, duunchado. [14] -h- interlined over ca-, as in M. [15] PLUMMER 275, as in M.

		K	M	L	C	B
25r,35[1]		eadberctum	eadberctum	eadberctum	eadberchtum	eadberctum
38r,27[1]		eadberct	eadberct	eadberct	eadberht	eadberct
48r,4[1]		eadberct	aldberct	aldberct	aldbercht[2]	aldberct
10r,37		eadgarum	eadgarum	eadgarum	eadgarum[1]	eadgarum[1]
7v,33	alloquens eadgyd	eadgyd	eadgyd	eadgyd	eadgyđ	eadgyd[1]
7v,33	alloquens |...\/ eadgyd	eadgyd	eadgyd	eadgyd	—	eadgyd[1]
7v,33	alloquens |...\/ eadgyd	eadgyd	eadgyd	eadgyd	—	eadgyd[1]
10r,33		eadhaed	eadhaed	eadhaed	eadhaet	eadhaed[1]
10r,39		eadhędum	eadhaedum	eadhaedum	eadaedum[3]	eadhaedum[1]
10v,1		eadhaed	eadhaed	eadhaed	eadhaed[1]	? dhaeth[1,4]
10v,6		eadhędum	eadhaedum	eadhaedum	eadhaedum[1]	eadhaedum[1]
49r,19		eadhaed	eadhaeth	—	eadhaet	eadhaed[1,5]
20v,30	cum matre eanflede	eanflede	eanflede	eanflede	eanflede[1]	eanfledae[1]
38v,37[1]		eanfledam	eanfledam	eanfledam	eanfledam	eanfledam
48v,39[1]		eanflęd	eanfled	?	eanfled	eanfled
10v,26	erat autem filia eanfridi	eanfridi	eanfridi	eanfridi	eanfridi[1]	eanfridi[1]
10v,23		eappa	eappa	eappa	eappa[1]	eappa[1]
1v,20		erconberct	erconberct	erconberct	erconbercht	erconberct[1]
13v,37		earconberct	earconberct	earconberct	erconberht	earconberct[1]
38v,41[1]		erconberctum	erconberctum	erconberctum	erconberchtum	erconberctum
49r,7[1]		earconberct	earconberct	—	earconbercht[6]	? [7]

Ref	Context					
Ir,14		erconuald[8]	earconuald	earconuald	earconuald	earconuald[1]
7r,16		erncualdum	earconual*dum*	earconualdum	eorcunualdum	earcon?[1]
9r,34		earconualdo[9]	erconualdo	erconualdo	ercunuualdo[10]	erconualdo[1]
10r,29		eata	eata	eata	eata[1]	eata[1]
10v,1		eata	eata	eata	eata[1]	eata[1]
10v,4	*remamente* eata	eata	eata	eata	eata[1]	eata[1]
21r,14[1]		eata	eata	eata	eata	?[11]
21v,11		eata	eata	eata	eata[1]	?[12]
22r,40[1]		eata	eata	eata	eata	?[13]
26r,14	*defuncto* eata *episcopo*	eata	eata	eata	eata[1]	eata[1]
30v,3	*sub abbate* eata	eata	eata	eata	eata[1]	eata[1]
49r,19[1]		eata	eata	—	eata	eata
3r,32[1]	eboracensis *ecclesiae*	eboracensis	eboracensis	eboracessis	eburacensis	eboracensis
16r,35[1]	eboracensis *ecclesiae*	eboracensis	eboracensis	eboracensis	eburacensis	?[14]
29r,5[1]	eboracensis *ecclesiae*	eboracensis	eburacensis[15]	eburacensis	eburacensis	eburacensis
41v,23[1]	eboracensis *episcopi*	eboracensis	eboracensis	eboracensis	eburacensis	?ensis[16]
48r,16-17[1]	*in* eboracensi *ecclesia*	eboracensi	eburacensi	eburacensi	eburacensi	?racensi[17]
10r,30[1]	*in ciuitate* eboraci	eboraci	eburaci	eboraci	eburaci	eboraci
10v,1[1]	*ordinati sunt* /.../ eboraci	eboraci	eboraci	eboraci	eburaci	eboraci
16v,32[1]	eboraci *fuerit consecratus* eboraci	eboraci	eboraci	eboraci	eburaci[18]	eburaci

[1] OET, not recorded. [2] e interlined initially, by second hand. [3] h interlined over -da-, by second hand. [4] PLUMMER 229[10], eadhaeth. [5] PLUMMER 355, eadhaeth. [6] PLUMMER 354[10], earconberht. [7] PLUMMER 354, as in M. [8] the -e- of the ligature stands out clearly in comparison with the other half, so the scribe may have meant e- only. [9] -a- interlined over er-; an n has been rubbed out over -rc-. [10] PLUMMER 226[1], ercunualdo. [11] PLUMMER 269, as in M. [12] PLUMMER 270, as in M. [13] PLUMMER 273, as in M. [14] PLUMMER 254, as in M. [15] PLUMMER 292, eboracensis. [16] PLUMMER 332, as in M. [17] PLUMMER 350, as in M. [18] PLUMMER 254, eboraci.

	Context	K	M	L	C	B
22r,35[1]	*ordinatio/.../completa est*	eboraci	eboraci	eboraci	eboraci	eboraci
26v,33[1]	*episcopus pro eo eboraci substitutus*	eboraci	eboraci	eboraci	eboraci	eboraci
39v,22[1]	*in episcopatum* eboraci	eboraci	eboraci	eboraci	eburaci	eboraci
40r,4[1]		eboracae	eboracae[2]	eboracae	eburacę[3]	eborace[2]
40r,30[1]		eboracae	eboracę[4]	eboracae	eburacae	? [5]
49r,2[1]	*quondam* eboraci /.../ *antistes*	eboraci[6]	eboraci	?	? raci[7]	eboraci
1r,11[1]	*de morte /.../ et* ecbercti	ecbercti	egbercti	egbercti	ecberchti	egbercti
1v,21[1]		ecbercto	egbercto	egbercto	egberchto[8]	egbercto
2r,37[1]		ecbercto	egbercto	egbercto	egberchto	egbercto
6v,38[1]		ecberct	egberct	egberct	egbercht	egberct
20v,37[1]		egberctum	egberctum	ecberctum	egberchtum	? [9]
20v,41[1]	*filius* egbercti	egbercti	egbercti	egbercti	egberchti	egbercti
21r,2[1]	*filius* egbercti	egbercti	egbercti	egbercti	egberhti	egbercti
47v,3[1]	*filius* ecbercti	ecbercti	egberecti	ecbercti	egber ?[10]	egbercti[10]
49r,12[1]		egberct	egberct	—	egberht	egberct
5r,1[1]			egbercti	egbercti	ecberhti	egbercti
5r,11[1]			egberct	egberct	ecberht	egberct
20v,11[1]			egberctum	egberctum	egberchtum	egberctum
25r,15[1]			egberct	egberct	egbercht	egberct
25v,5[1]			egbercto	egbercto	egberchto	egbercto
30r,22[1]			egberct	egbercto	egberht	egbercto
30v,9[1]			egbercto	egbercto	egberchto	egbercto
30v,18[1]			egberct	egberct	egberht	? [11]
30v,25[1]			egbercto	egbercto	egberhto	egcbe?[11]

egbercti et sociorum

	eius						
31r,9[1]		ecgbercti	ecgbercti	ecgbercti	ecgbercti	ecgberchti	? [12]
46v,41[1]		ecgberct	ecgberct	ecgberct	ecgberct	ecgberht	? [12]
47r,21[1]		ecberct	ecberct	ecberct	ecberct	ecgberht	ecgberct
47r,24[1]		ecbercto	ecbercto	ecbercto	ecbercto	ecgberchto	ecgbercto
47v,27[1]		ecgberct	ecgberct	ecberct	ecgberct	ecgbercht	ecgberct
49r,34[1]		ecgberct	ecgberct	ecbercht	ecgberct	ecgberht	—
49r,37[1]		ecberct	ecgberct	—	ecgberct	ecgberht	—
1r,38		ecfridum	ecgfridum	ecgfridum	ecfridum	ecfridum	ecgfridum[1]
1v,3	de morte ecfridi	ecfridi	ecgfridi	ecgfridi	ecfridi	ecfridi	ecgfridi[1]
6r,1[1]		ecgfridum	ecgfridum	ecgfridum	ecgfridum	ecfridum	ecgfridum
10r,22	regis ecfridi	ecfridi	ecgfridi	ecgfridi	ecgfridi[13]	ecgfridi[13]	ecgfridi[1]
10r,26[1]		ecfridum	ececgfridum[14]	ecgfridum	ecgfridum	ecgfridum	ecgfridum
10r,34[1]		ecfrid	ecgfrid	ecgfrid	ecgfrid	ecgfrid	ecgfrid
11r,28[1]	ecfridi regis	ecfridi	ecgfridi	ecgfridi	ecgfridi	ecgfridi	ecgfridi
12r,22[1]		ecfrido	ecgfrido	ecgfrido	ecgfrido	ecgfrido	ecgfrido
12v,35[1]		ecgfridum	ecgfridum	ecfridum	ecgfridum	ecgfridum	ecgfridum
13r,34[1]		ecfrid	ecgfrid	ecfrid	ecgfrid	ecgfrid	ecgfrid
13v,3[1]		ecfridus	ecgfridus	ecfridus	egfridus	ecgfridus	ecgfridus
13v,14[1]	regis ecfridi	ecfridi	ecgfridi	ecgfridi	ecgfridi	ecgfridi	ecgfridi
15r,18[1]	anno regni ecfridi nono	ecfridi	ecgfridi	ecgfridi	ecgfridi	ecgfridi	ecgfridi
15r,20[1]	regis ecfridi	ecfridi	ecgfridi	ecgfridi	ecgfridi	ecgfridi	ecgfridi
20r,34[1]		ecfrid	ecgfrid	ecfrid	ecgfrid	ecgfrid	ecgfrid
20v,33[1]		ecfrido	ecgfrido	ecgfrido	ecgfrido	ecgfrido	ecgfrido
21r,6[1]		ecfrid	ecgfrid	ecgfrid	ecgfrid	ecgfrid	ecgfrid

[1] OET, not recorded. [2] PLUMMER 326, eboracae. [3] PLUMMER 326[7], eboracae. [4] -c- interlined; PLUMMER 327, eboracae. [5] PLUMMER 327, as in M. [6] dotted h between -c- and -i-. [7] PLUMMER 354, eboraci. [8] PLUMMER 201, ecgbercto. [9] PLUMMER 268, as in M. [10] PLUMMER 348[5]: "defective in C.B." [11] PLUMMER 297, as in M. [12] PLUMMER 298, as in M. [13] -g- interlined over -cf-; PLUMMER 228[11], ecfridi. [14] PLUMMER 229, ecgfridum. [15] -o over dotted final -i.

		K	M	L	C	B
22r,17[1]	regis ecfridi	ecfridi	ecfridi	ecfridi	ecfridi	? [2]
22r,35[1]	regis ecfridi	ecfridi	ecfridi	ecfridi	ecgfridi	ecgfridi
26r,12[1]		ecgfridum	ecgfridum	ecgfridum	ecgfridi	ecgfridum
39v,26[1]		ecgfrido	ecgfrido	ecgfrido	ecgfrido[3]	ecgfrido
40r,14[1]		ecfridum	ecgfridum	ecgfridum	ecfridum	ecgfridum
49r,13[1]		ecgfrido	ecgfrido	—	ecgfrido	ecgfrido
49r,18[1]		ecgfrido	ecgfrido	—	ecgfrido	ecgfrido
49r,23[1]		ecfrid	ecgfrid	—	ecgfrid	ecgfrid
20r,23		edgisl	aedgils	edgisl	edgisl[1,4]	edgisl[1,5]
20v,40		edric	edric	edric	edric[1]	edric[1]
20v,42[1]		edric	edric	edric	edric	edric
16r,26[1]	eduini *regis*	eduini	eduini	eduini	eduini	eduini
48v,40[1]	eduini *regis*	eduini	aeduini	?	eduini	? uini[6]
48v,41[1]		eduini	eduini	?	eduuine	? [6]
48v,42[1]	eduine *rege*	eduine	eduine	eduine	eduine	? [7]
13v,17		elge	elge	elge	elgæ[1,8]	elge
13v,41		elge	elge	elge	elge[1]	elge[1]
14v,7		elge	elge	elge	elge[1]	elge[1]
2r,33[1]	*ad* emme *senonum*	emme	emme[9]	emme	emme	emme
25r,36	*acceperint* /.../ eollan	eollan	eallan[10]	eallan	eollan	eallan[1]
38r,29		eolla	eolla	eolla	eolla[1]	eolla[1]
12r,25		estranglorum	estranglorum	estranglorum	eastranglorum	estranglorum[1]

21r,8	*in insula* farne	farne	farne	farne	farne	farne[1]
23r,14	*insulam* farne	farne	farne	farne	farne[1]	?[11]
23v,10	*in insula* farne	farne	farne	farne	farne[1]	farne[1]
25v,12[1]	*in insula* farne	farne	farne	farne	farne	farne
25v,22[1]	*ad insulam* farne	farne	farne	farne	farne	farne
25v,34[1]	*in ipsa insula* farne	farne	farne	farne	farne	farne
26r,7[1]	*in insula* farne	farne	farne	farne	farne	farne
2r,33-34[1]	*ad faronem meldorum*	faronem	faronem	faronem	faronem	faronem
38r,20		fordheri	fortheri	fordheri	forthere	forthere[1]
48r,5		forthheri	fortheri	fordheri	forthere	fortheri[1]
15v,34[1]	*freso cuidam*	freso	freso	freso	freso	freso
30r,30[1]		fresones	fresones	fresones	fresones	fresones
32r,28[1]	*eidem fresonum genti*	fresonum	fresonum	fresonum	fresonum	?[12]
17v,20		frigyd	frigyd	frigyd	frigyd	?[13]
26v,1		·gae·	gae	gæ	gea[1,14]	gæ[1]
30r,30[1]		garmani	garmani	garmani	garmani	germani
1r,26-27		gemmund	gefmund	gebmund	gemmund	gebmund
10r,20-21		gebmundum	gebmundum	gebmundum	gebmundum[1]	gebmundum[1]
30r,16-17		gebmundo	gebmundo	gebmundo	gebmundo[1]	gebmundo[1]

---

[1] OET, not recorded. [2] PLUMMER 272, as in M. [3] the whole of the word interlined. [4] by second hand; original version erased. [5] PLUMMER 266[1]: "edgisl B(?)." [6] PLUMMER 353, as in M. [7] PLUMMER 354, as in M. [8] PLUMMER 244[2]. [9] n interlined finally, by second hand? elgae. [10] OET 145, eollan. [11] PLUMMER 275, as in M. [12] PLUMMER 302, as in M. [13] PLUMMER 257, as in M. [14] on erasure, by second hand.

		K	M	L	C	B
30r,7	*fluminis* genlade	genlade	genladae	genladæ	genlade[1]	genladae[1]
30r,27[1]		germania	germania	germania	germania	? mania
11r,37[1]		geuissorum	geuissorum	geuissorum	geuissorum	geuissorum
11v,1[1]		geuissorum	geuissorum	geuissorum	geuissorum	geuissorum
11v,6[1]		geuissorum	geuissorum	geuissorum	geuissorum	geuissorum
11v,9[1]		geuuissorum	geuissorum	geuissorum	geuissorum	geuissorum
12r,5[1]		geuissorum	geuissorum	geuissorum	geuissorum	geuissorum
12r,10[1]		geuissorum	geuissorum	geuissorum	geuissorum	geuissorum
39v,12[1]		geuissorum	geuissorum	geuissorum	geuissiorum	geuissorum
30r,14		goduino	goduine	goduine	goduino	?[2]
14r,3		grantacęstir	grantacaestir	grantacaestir	grantacęster[3]	grantacaestir[1]
25v,18		gudfrid	gudfrid	gudfrid	gydfrid	gudfrid
7r,14		gyruiorum	gyruiorum	gyruiorum	gyruiorum[1]	gyruiorum[1]
13r,38		gyruiorum	guruiorum	gyruiorum	gyruiorum[4]	gyruiorum
41v,41	*qui uocatur* ingyruum	ingyruum	ingyruum	ingyruum	ingyruum[1]	ingyruum[1]
49v,7[1]	*ad |.../ et* ingyruum	ingyruum	ingyruum	—	ingyruum	—
17v,7		hacanos	hacanos	hacanos	haconos[1]	hacanos[1]
48r,4		hadulac	hadulac	hadulac	hadulac[1]	hadulac[1]
1r,25		haeddi	haeddi[5]	haeddi[6]	haeddi	haeddi[1,7]
9v,40[1]		hędi	haeddi	haeddi	heddi	haeddi

37v,30		haeddi	haeddi	haeddi	haeddi[1]	? [8]
34r,31	*monachus nomine* hęmgi sl	hęmgi sl[9]	haemgils	haemgisl	haemgils[1]	haemgisl[1]
1r,33	*in campo* hęthfelda	hęthfelda	hæthfelda	hætfelda	haetfeldo	haethf?[1,10]
12r,30		hęthfelth	haethfelth	hæthfelth[11]	haethfeld	haethfelth[1]
49r,21	*in campo* haethfelda	haethfelda	hæthfeltha[12]	—	haetfelda	haethfelda[1,12]
10r,31	*in* hagustaldensi /.../ *ecclesia*	hagustaldensi	hagustaldensi	hagustaldensi	hagustaldensi	? aldensi[13]
10v,3-4[1]		hagustaldensem	hagustaldensem	hagustaldensem	hagustaldensem	hagustaldense*m*
16v,35[1]	hagustaldensis /.../ *ecclesiae*	hagustaldensis	hagustaldensis	hagustaldensis	hagustaldensis	? [14]
21r,16[1]	hagustaldensis /.../ *ecclesiae*	hagustaldensis	hagustaldensis[15]	hagustaldensis	hagustaldensis	? [16]
22r,38[1]	hagustaldensis *ecclesiae*	hagustaldensis	hagustaldensis	hagustaldensis	hagustaldensis	hagustaldensis
22r,41[1]	*ecclesiae* hagustaldensis	hagustaldensis	hagustaldensis	hagustaldensis	hagustaldensis	hagustaldensis
26r,14-15[1]	hagustaldensis *ecclesiae*	hagustaldensis	hagustaldensis	hagustaldensis	hagustaldensis	hagustaldensis
26r,21[1]	*ab* hagustaldensi *ecclesia*	hagustaldensi	hagustaldensi	hagustaldensi	agustaldensi	agustaldensi[17]
26v,31[1]	hagustaldensis *ecclesiae*	hagustaldensis	hagustal*densis*	hagustaldensis	hagustaldensis	hagustaldensis
41r,40-41[1]	hagustaldensis *ecclesiae*	hagustaldensis	hagustaldensis	hagustaldensis	hagustaldensis	? aldensis[18]
48r,17[1]	*in* hagustaldensi (*ecclesia*)	hagustaldensi	hagustaldensi	hagustaldensi	hagustaldensi	? gustaldensi[19]

[1] OET, not recorded. [2] PLUMMER 295, as in M. [3] *-e-* originally was *-i-*; PLUMMER 245, grantacaestir. [4] OET 144, gyruiorum. [5] OET 141, hæddi. [6] *h* interlined. [7] *h* interlined, which is not indicated by PLUMMER 227. [8] PLUMMER 320, as in M. [9] in open space *-l-* probably rubbed out. [10] PLUMMER 238, as in M. [11] first *-h-* interlined. [12] PLUMMER 355, haethfeltha. [13] PLUMMER 229, as in M. [14] PLUMMER 254, as in M. [15] final *-s* interlined. [16] PLUMMER 269, as in M. [17] initial *h* interlined, by second hand?; PLUMMER 283, hagustaldensi. [18] PLUMMER 331, as in M. [19] PLUMMER 351, as in M.

		K	M	L	C	B
16v,4[1]		heiu	heiu	heiu	heiu	heiu
28r,10[1]		herebald	heribald	herebald	herebald	herebald
28r,28[1]		herebald	herebald	herebald	herebald	herebald
1v,8	*presbyter |.../ nomine* hereberct	herebercto	heriberchto	hereberchto	hereberchto	herebercto[1]
22v,23		hereberct	hereberct	hereberct	hereberct[1]	hereberct[1]
22v,31		hereberct	heriberct	hereberct	hereberct[1]	hereberct[1,2]
23r,8[1]		hereberct	heriberct	hereberct	hereberct	hereberct[3]
26v,35		hereburg	heriburg	hereburg	hereburg[1]	hereburg[1]
16r,27	*nepotis |.../ uocabulo* heririci	heririci	hererici	heririci	heririci	heririce[1,4]
17r,21		hereric	hereric	heriric	hereric[1]	hereric[1]
16r,36		herisuid	heresuid	herisuid	heresuit	herisuid[1]
16v,2		herut eu	herut eu	herut eu	herut eu[1]	herut eu[5]
1r,12	*ad locum* herutforda	herutforda	herutforda	herutforda	heorutforda	herutforda[1]
6r,12	*ad* herudforda	herutford	herutford	herutford	heorutford	herudford[6]
49r,13		herudforda	herutforda	—	herudforda	herudforda[1,7]
25r,19	*socii eius* heuualdi	heuualdi	heuualdi	heuualdi	heuualdi[1]	h ? aldi[1,8]
31r,27		heuuald	heuuald	heuuald	heuuald[9]	? [10]
31r,28		heuuald	heuuald	heuuald	hea uald[11]	? [10]
31r,29		heuuald	heuuald	heuuald	hea uuald[12]	? [10]
31r,30		heuuald	heuuald	heuuald	heuuald[13]	? [10]

31v,8[1]		heuualdum	heuualdum	heuualdum	neuualdum	? ?
11v,21	presbyterum nomine	hiddila	hiddila	hiddila	hiddila[1]	hiddila[1]
5v,5[1]	ad insulam hii	hii	hii	hii	hii	hii
30v,14[1]	in hii insula	hii	—	hii	hii	hii
36r,17[1]	in insula hii	hii	hii	hii	hii	hii
36r,28[1]	qui erant in hii	hii	hii	hii	hii	hii
46r,39[1]	in hii insula	hii	hii	hii	hii	hii
46v,34[1]	insulam hii	hii	hii	hii	hii	hii
48v,27[1]	in insula hii	hii	hii	hii	hii	hii
25v,4[1]	hiienses monachi	hiienses	hiienses	hiienses	hiienses	hiienses
36r,33[1]	hienses monachi	hiensium	hiensium	hiensium	hiensium	hiensium
47r,21[1]	hienses monachi	hienses	hiensenses	hienses	hienses	hiienses
49r,34[1]	hienses monachos	hienses	—	—	hienses	hiienses
1r,41		hildae	—	—	hilde[16]	—[17]
16r,20[1]		hild	hild	hild	hild	hild
16v,9[1]		hild	hild	hild	hild	hild
16v,36		hildę	hildae	hildae	hildae[1]	?[18]
17r,15[1]		hild	hild	hild	hild	hild
17v,21[1]	hild abbatissam	hild	hild	hild	hild	hild

[1] OET, not recorded. [2] PLUMMER 274, heribert. [3] PLUMMER 275, heriberct. [4] final -e may have to be read as -i; PLUMMER 252, hererici. [5] heortes ig over the word, by second hand; OET 144, herutei. [6] u dotted and e written over it, by second hand. [7] PLUMMER 354, herutforda. [8] PLUMMER 298, as in M. [9] first -u- altered to a, by second hand; PLUMMER 299, heuuald. [10] PLUMMER 299, heuuald. [11] an erasure between -a- and -u-; OET 146, heauald. [12] an erasure between -a- and -u-; OET 146, heauuald. [13] a over dotted first -u-, by second hand? [14] first -u- altered to a, and another u interlined, by second hand. [15] PLUMMER 300, as in M. [16] PLUMMER 252, hildae. [17] PLUMMER 252, as in M. [18] PLUMMER 254, as in M.

		K	M	L	C	B
49r,22[1]		hild	hild	—	hild	hild
8v,32	*famula nomine* hildilid	hildilid	hildilid	hildilid	hildilid[1]	hildilid[1]
12r,26[1]		hlothario	hlothario	hlothario	lothario	hlothario
1v,3	*de morte* |.../ *et* hlotheri	hlotheri[2]	hlotheri	hlotheri	hlothere	hlotheri[1]
6v,39	*fratre* hlothere	hlothere	hlothere	hlothere	hlothere	hlothere[1]
15v,41	*ad regem* hlotheri	hlotheri	hlotheri	hlotheri	hlotheri[1]	hlotheri[1]
20v,37[1]		hlotheri	hlotheri	hlotheri	hlotheri	? [3]
49r,24[1]		hlothheri	hlotheri	—	hlothere	hlothheri[4]
12r,10	*fluminis* homel·ea·	homel·ea·	homelea	homelea	homelea[1]	homelaea[5]
11v,32		hreutford	hreutford	hreutford	hreutford	hreutford[6]
1r,6[1]	rhofensis ecclesiae	rhofensis	hrofensis	hrofensis	hrofensis	hrofensis
1r,26[1]	rhofensis ecclesiae	rhofensis	hrofensis	hrofensis	rhofensis[7]	hrofensis
25r,14[1]	rhofensi ecclesiae	rhofensi	hrofensi	hrofensi	hrofensi	hrofensi
30r,17[1]	hrofensis ecclesiae	hrofensis	hrofensis	hrofensis	hrofensis	hrofensis
47v,6[1]	hrofensis ecclesiae	hrofensis	hrofensis	hrofensis	hrofensis	hrofensis
47v,42	alduulfo hrofensi	hrofensi	hrofensi	rhofensi	rofensi	rhofensi[1]
49r,3[1]	rhofensis |.../ ciuitatis	rhofensis	hrofensis	—	hrofensis	rhofensis[8]
6r,19	hrofes cestir	hrofes cęstir	hrofes caestir	hrofæs cæstir	hrofes caestir[9]	hrofaes caestir[10]
3r,19[1]	*in ciuitate* hrofi	hrofi	hrofi	hrofi	hrofi	hrofi
10r,9[1]	*ciuitatem quoque* hrofi	hrofi	hrofi	hrofi	hrofi	hrofi
10r,18[1]	*in ciuitate* rhofi	rhofi	hrofi	hrofi	hrofi	hrofi

Folio	Lemma						
10v,7[1]	rhypensi ecclesiae praefecit	rhypensi	hrypensi	rhypensi	hrypensi	rhypensi	hrypensi
25v,14	monasterio quod dicitur inhrypum	inhrypum	inhrypum	inhrypum	inhrypum	inhrypum[1]	in rypum[11]
38v,11[1]	quod dicitur inrhypum	inhrypum	inhrypum	inhrypum	inhrypum	inhrypum	inhrypum
39v,4-5[1]	loco qui uocatur inhrypum	inhrypum	inhrypum	inhrypum	inhrypum	inhrypum	?[12]
41r,5[1]	quod uocatur inhrypum	inhrypum	inhrypum	inhrypum	inhrypum	inhrypum	inhrypum
50r,12	benedicti /.../ et huetbercti	huetbercti	huetbercti	huaetbercti	huaetbercti	huetberhtti[1],[13]	—
10v,25[1]		huicciorum	huicciorum	huicciorum	huicciorum	huicciorum	huicciorum
17r,11[1]		huicciorum	huicciorum	huicciorum	huicciorum	huicciorum	huicciorum
48r,8[1]		huicciorum	huicciorum	huicciorum	huicciorum	huicciorum	? ciorum[14]
48r,13		humbre	hymbræ[15]	humbræ	humbræ	humbræ[16]	humbrae[1]
12r,23		humbronensium	hymbronensium	humbronentium	humbronensium	humbronensium[1]	humbronensium[1],[17]
30r,31[1]		hunni	hunni	hunni	hunni	hunni	hunni
5r,8		hygbald	hygbald	hygbald	hygbald	hygbald[1]	hygbald[1]

---

[1] OET, not recorded. [2] -i over dotted -e. [3] PLUMMER 268, as in M. [4] PLUMMER 355, hlotheri. [5] i a interlined over first part of word, by second hand; PLUMMER 238, homelea; OET 143, homelea. [6] od over dotted -ut-, by second hand; OET 143, hreodford, and OET 143: "od over ut (u dotted)". [7] PLUMMER 227, hrofensis. [8] PLUMMER 354, hrofensis. [9] PLUMMER 215, hrofescaestir. [10] e interlined over final -tr, by second hand; PLUMMER 215: "hrofaescaestir B[1]; -ter B[2]." [11] PLUMMER 281, in hrypum. [12] PLUMMER 325, as in M. [13] PLUMMER 359, huetbercti. [14] PLUMMER 350, as in M. [15] PLUMMER 350, hymbrae. [16] PLUMMER 350[16], humbrae. [17] PLUMMER 239, hymbronensium.

	K	M	L	C	B
3r,27	iarumanno	iarumanno	iarumanno	iarumanno[1]	iarumanno[1]
48v,24[1]	ida	ida	ida	ida	?[2]
15r,34	*iuuenis uocabulo* imma	imma	imma	imma[1]	imma[1]
47v,41	ingualdo	ingualdo	ingualdo	inguualdo[1]	ingualdo[1]
48r,3	inguald	inguald	inguald	inguuald[1]	inguald
11v,2	·ini·	ini	ini	ini[1]	ini[1]
25r,10	ini	ini	ini	ini[1]	ini[1]
29v,15[1]	·ini·	ini	ini	ini	ini
5v,8[1]	inisbofinde	inisboufinde	inhis boufinde	inisbofinde	inhisboufinde
11v,27[1]	iutorum	iutorum	iutorum	iutorum	iutorum
12r,10[1]	iutarum	iutorum	iutorum	iutarum	iutorum
16v,7-8	kęlcacęstir	kælcacaestir	kælcacaestir	kelcacęstir[3]	kaelca cæstir[4]
3r,30-31	*in* laestingę	laestinga e	laestinga e[5]	laestinge	l?stinga e[1,6]
3v,36-37	*quod est in* laestingaei	laestingaeu	laestinga eu	laestingaeu[1]	laestinga eu[1,7]
39v,24	laestingaei	laestinga æi	laestinga æi	laestingaei	laestinga ?[1,8]
1r,25[1]	leutherio	leutherio	leutherio	leutherio	leutherio
6r,19[1]	leutherius	leutherius	leutherius	leutherius	leutherius
9v,35[1]	leutherius	leutherius	leutherius	leutherius	leutherius
9v,38[1]	leutherius	leutherius	leutherius	leutherius	leutherius
3v,7	liccidfelth	lyccidfelth	licidfelth	liccidfeld	liccidfelth[9]

	(alduino liccidfeldensi)	(liccidfeldensi)	(lyccitfeldensi)	(liccitfeldensi)	(liccitfeldensi)	(liccitfeldensi)	(liccitfeldensi[1])
47v,41	alduino liccidfeldensi	liccidfeldensi	lyccitfeldensi	liccitfeldensi	liccitfeldensi	liccitfeldensi	liccitfeldensi[1]
5v,1[1]		lindisfarnensium	lindisfarnensium	lindisfarnensium	lindisfarnensi	lindisfarnensi	lindisfarnensium
10r,31[1]	in /.../ lindisfarnensi ecclesia	lindisfarnensium	lindisfarnensi	lindisfarnensi	lindisfarnensem	lindisfarnensem	lindisfarnensium
10v,4[1]		lindisfarnensem	lindisfarnensem	lindisfarnensem	lindisfarnensium	lindisfarnensium	lindisfarnensi
21r,7[1]		lindisfarnensium	lindisfarnensium	lindisfarnensium	lindisfarnensi	lindisfarnensi	lindisfarnensem
21r,16[1]	lindisfarnensis ecclesiae	lindisfarnensis	lindisfarnensis	lindisfarnensis	lindisfarnensis	lindisfarnensis	?[10]
21v,11[1]		lindisfarnensium	lindisfarnensium	lindisfarnensium	lindisfarnensium	lindisfarnensium	lindis?[11]
22r,20[1]	ecclesiae lindisfarnensis	lindisfarnensis	lindisfarnensis	lindisfarnensis	lindisfarnensis	lindisfarnensis	?[12]
22r,24[1]	de ipsa insula lindisfarnensi	lindisfarnensi	lindisfarnensi	lindisfarnensi	lindisfarnensi	lindisfarnensi	lindisfarnensis
22r,39[1]	lindisfarnensi ecclesiae	lindisfarnensi	lindisfarnensi	lindisfarnensi	lindisfarnensi	lindisfarnensi	lindisfarnensi
22r,42[1]	ecclesiae lindisfarnensis	lindisfarnensis	lindisfarnensis	lindisfarnensis	lindisfarnensis	lindisfarnensis	lindisfarnensi
23r,17[1]	ecclesiae lindisfarnensi	lindisfarnensium	lindisfarnensium	lindisfarnensium	lindisfarnensium	lindisfarnensium	lindisfarnensis
25v,20[1]	in insula lindisfarnensi	lindisfarnensis	lindisfarnensis	lindisfarnensis	lindisfarnensis	lindisfarnensis	lindisfarnensium
26r,8[1]	lindisfarnensis ecclesiae	lindisfarnensi	lindisfarnensi	lindisfarnensi	lindisfarnensi	lindisfarnensi	lindisfarnensis
34v,2[1]		lindisfarnensis	lindisfarnensis	lindisfarnensis	lindisfarnensis	lindisfarnensis	lindisfarnensi
38v,22[1]		lindisfarnensem	lindisfarnensem	lindisfarnensem	lindisfarnensem	lindisfarnensem	lindisfarnensis
48r,17[1]	in lindisfaronensi' (ecclesia)	lindisfaronensi	lindisfaronensi	lindisfaronensi	lindisfaronensi	lindisfaronensi	lindisfaronensi[13]
3r,42		lindisfarorum	lindisfarorum	lindisfarorum	lindisfarorum	lindisfarorum[1]	lindisfarorum[1]
5r,36-37		lindisfarorum	lindisfarorum	lindisfarorum	lindisfarorum	lindisfarorum[1]	lindisfarorum[1]

[1] OET, not recorded.   [2] PLUMMER 353, as in M.   [3] k- may be a correction from h-; cea over dotted ke-, by second hand; PLUMMER 253[8]: "helcacęstir C[1]; cealca- C[2]."; OET 144, helcacęstir, and OET 144[1]: "he over erasure."   [4] PLUMMER 253[8], kaelcacaestir.   [5] accent over final e.   [6] PLUMMER 206, as in M; PLUMMER 206[5] furthermore notes: "-ga e B[1]; -ga ig B[2]".   [7] ig interlined over final -eu, by second hand.   [8] PLUMMER 326[2], laestinga æi.   [9] second c interlined.   [10] PLUMMER 268, as in M.   [11] PLUMMER 269, as in M.   [12] PLUMMER 270, as in M.   [13] -o- interlined over -w-, by second hand; PLUMMER 351, lindisfaronensi.

		K	M	L	C	B
10r,34[1]		lindisfarorum	lindisfarorum	lindisfarorum[2]	lindisfarorum	lindisfarorum
48r,8[1]		lindisfarorum	lindisfarorum	lindisfarorum	lindisfarorum	lindisfarorum
3v,4[1]	*in prouincia* lindissi	lindissi	lindissi	lindissi	lindissi	lindissi
5r,9[1]	*in prouincia* lindissi	lindissi	lindissi	lindissi	lindissi	lindissi
10r,41[1]	*expulsus de* lindissi	lindissi	lindissi	lindissi	lindissi	lindissi
10v,6[1]	*de* lindissi *reuersum*	lindissi	lindissi	lindissi	lindissi	lindissi
39r,9[1]		lugdunum	lugdunum	lugdunum	lugdunum	lugdunum
22v,27[1]		lugubaliam	lugubaliam	lugubaliam	lugubaliam	lugubaliam
47v,41[1]	*ingualdo* lundonensi	lundonensi	lundoniensi	lundoniensi	lundonensi[3]	lundoniensi
7r,16-17[1]	*in ciuitate* lundonia	lundonia	lundonia	lundonia	lundonia	lundonia
9r,33-34[1]		lundoniae	lundoniae[4]	lundoniae	lundoniae	lundoniae
9v,2[1]		lundoniae	lundoniẹ[5]	lundoniae	—[6]	lundoniae
9v,41[1]	*in ciuitate* lundonia	lundonia	lundonia	lundonia	lundonia	lundonia
15v,33[1]		lundoniam	lundoniam	lundoniam	lundoniam	lundoniam
41v,11[1]	*cantatorem │…│ uocabulo* maban	maban	maban	maban	mafan	?[7]
40v,8[1]		maeldum	maeldum	maeldum	mẹldum	meldum
5v,18[1]	*mageo nominatur*	mageo	mageo	mageo	mageo	mageo
38r,6[1]	*quod* maildubi *urbem nuncupant*	maildubi	mailäufi	mailäufi	maildubi	mailäufi

Folio						
21r,14[1]	*monasterium* mailros	mailros	mailros	mailros	mailros	mailros
32v,25[1]	*ad monasterium* mailros	mailros	mailros	mailros	mailros	? [8]
21v,9[1]	*in* mailrosensi *monasterio*	mailrosensi	mailronensi	mailronensi	mailronsensi	mailronsensi
30v,2[1]	*monasterii* mailronensis	mailronensis	mailrosensis	mailrosensis	mailronensis	mailrosensis
2r,26[1]		massiliam	massiliam	massiliam	massiliam[9]	massiliam
10v,20		meanuarorum	meanuarorum	meanuarorum	meanuarorum[1]	meanuarorum[1]
7r,13-14		medeshamstede	medeshamstedi	medeshamstedi	medeshamstede	medeshamstedi[1,10]
2r,34[1]	*ad favonem* meldorum	meldorum	meldorum	meldorum	meldorum	meldorum
12r,24[1]		mercinensium	mercinensium	mercinentium	mercinensium	mercinentium[11]
49r,5	middilengli /.../ *sunt imbuti*	middilengli	middilangli	—	middilaengli	middilengli[1,12]
5v,27[1]	muigeo /.../ *uocatur*	muigeo	muigeo	muigeo	muigeo	muigeo
41v,29[1]		naiton	naiton	naiton	naiton	naiton
42r,15[1]		naitono	naitano	naitono	naitano	? [13]
46v,10[1]		naitono	naitano[14]	naitono	naitano	? [15]
40v,41	*iuxta fluuium* nidd	nidd	nidd[1]	nidd	nidd[1]	nidd[1]

---

[1] OET, not recorded. [2] dotted -n- between -r- and -o-. [3] PLUMMER 350, lundoniensi. [4] PLUMMER 225, lundoniae. [5] PLUMMER 226, lundoniae. [6] PLUMMER 226, as in M. [7] PLUMMER 331, as in M. [8] PLUMMER 304, as in M. [9] PLUMMER 203, as in M. [10] final -i altered into e, by second hand? [11] first -i altered to -e-, by second hand?; PLUMMER 239[8]: "mercinentium B[1]; mercen- B[2]." [12] PLUMMER 354, middilangli. [13] PLUMMER 333, as in M. [14] second -a- may have to be read as -o-; PLUMMER 345, as in M. [15] PLUMMER 345, naitono.

	K	M	L	C	B
1r,27[1]	nordanhymbrorum	nordanhymbrorum	nordanhymbrorum	nordanhymbrorum	nordanhymbrorum
1v,24[1]	nordanhymbrorum	nordanhymbrorum	nordanhymbrorum	nordanhymbrorum	nordan ?[2]
2v,40[1]	nordamhymbrorum	nordanhymbrorum	nordanhymbrorum	nordanhymbrorum	nordanhymbrorum
3r,33[1]	nordanhymbrorum	nordanhymbrorum	nordanhymbrorum	nordanhymbrorum	nordanhymbrorum
5v,35-36[1]	nordanhymbrorum	nordanhymbrorum	nordanhymbrorum	nordanhymbrorum	nordanhymbrorum
6r,17[1]	nordanhymbrorum	nordanhymbrorum	nordanhymbrorum	nordanhymbrorum	nordanhymbrorum
10r,29-30[1]	nordanhymbrorum	nordanhymbrorum	nordanhymbrorum	nordanhymbrorum	nordanhymbrorum
16r,28[1]	nordanhymbrorum	nardanhymbrorum[3]	nordanhymbrorum	nordanhymbrorum	nordanhymbrorum
16v,4-5[1]	nordanhymbrorum	nordanhymbrorum	nordanhymbrorum	nordanhymbrorum	nordanhymbrorum
20r,34-35[1]	nordanbrorum	nordanhymbrorum	nordanhymbrorum	nordanhymbrorum	nordan ?[4]
25r,22[1]	nordanhymbrorum	nordanhymbrorum	nordanhymbrorum	nordanhymbrorum	nordanhymbrorum
26r,12[1]	nordanhymbrorum	nordanhymbrorum	nordanhymbrorum	nordanhymbrorum	nordanhymbrorum
32v,10	nordanhymbrorum	nordanhymbrorum	nordanhymbrorum	nordanhymbrorum[1]	nordanhymbrorum[1]
37v,26[1]	nordanhymbrorum	nordanhymbrorum	nordanhymbrorum	nordanhymbrorum	nordanhymbrorum
39v,25-26[1]	nordanhymbrorum	nordanhymbrorum	nordanhymbrorum	nordanhymbrorum	nordanhymbrorum
40v,39[1]	nordanhymbrorum	nordanhymbrorum	nordanhymbrorum	nordanhymbrorum	nordanhymbrorum
46v,39[1]	nordanhymbrorum	nordanhymbrorum	nordanhymbrorum	nordanhymbrorum	? hymbrorum[5]
47v,2[1]	nordanhymbrorum	nordanhymbrorum	nordanhymbrorum	nordanhymbrorum	nordanhymbrorum
47v,29[1]	nordanhymbrorum	nordanhymbrorum	nordanhymbrorum	nordanhymbrorum	nordanhymbrorum
48r,15[1]	nordanhymbrorum	nordanhymbrorum	nordanhymbrorum	nordanhymbrorum	nordanhymbrorum
48r,31[1]	nordanhymbrorum	nordanhymbrorum	nordanhymbrorum	nordanhymbrorum	nordanhymbrorum
48v,24-25[1]	nordamhymbrorum	nordanhymbrorum	nordanhymbrorum	nordanhymbrorum	nordanhymbrorum
48v,39[1]	nordanhymbrorum	nordanhymbrorum	?	nordanhymbrorum	nordanhymbrorum
49r,9[1]	nordanhymbrorum	nordanhymbrorum	—	nordanhymbrorum	nord.?brorum[6]
49r,11[1]	nordanhymbrorum	nordanhymbrorum	—	nordanhymbrorum	nor.?brorum[7]
49r,24[1]	nordanhymbrorum	nordanhymbrorum	—	nordanhymbrorum	nordan?rum[7]
49r,29[1]	nordanhymbrorum	nordanhymbrorum	—	nordanhymbrorum	nordanhymbrorum
49r,33-34[1]	nordanhymbrorum	nordanhymbrorum	—	nordanhymbrorum	nordanhymbrorum
25r,38	offa	offa	offa	offa[1]	offa[1]

	oiia	oiia	oiia	oiia	oiia	?
58r,40[1]	]uzus /.../ uocabuio oiia					
16v,31	offfor	offfor	offfor	offfor	offfor[1]	offfor[1]
10v,24	oiddi	oiddi	oiddi	oiddi	oiddi	oiddi[1,9]
25r,1	oidiluald	oidiluald	oiduald	oidiluald	oidiluald[10]	oid?[2,11]
25v,13	oidiluald	oidiluald	oidiluald	oidiluald	oidiluald	oidiluald[1,12]
25v,23[1]	oidilualdo	oidilualdo	oidilualdo	oidilualdo	oidilualdo	oidilualdo
25v,35[1]	oidilualdum	oidilualdum	oidilualdum	oidilualdum	oidilualdum	oidilualdum
48v,7[1]	orcadas quoque insulas	orcadas	orcadas	orcadas	orcadas	orcadas
37v,28	osred	osred	osred	osred	osred[1]	osred[1]
38r,32[1]	imperii osredi	osredi	osredi	osredi	osredi	osredi
40v,41[1]	regnante osrede	osrede	osredi	osredi	osrede[13]	osrede[14]
41r,29[1]	osredi regis	osredi	osredi	osredi	osredi	osredi
46v,38[1]	osrede occiso	osrede	osredo	osredo	osredo	osredo
49r,32[1]	osred	osred	—	osred	osred	—
17r,2	osric	osric	osric	osric	osric[1]	osric[1]
47v,1[1]	osrici regis	osrici	osrici	osrici	osrici	osrici
47v,29[1]	osric	osric	osric	osric	osric	?[15]
49r,37[1]	osric	osric	—	osric	osric	—

[1] OET, not recorded. [2] PLUMMER 201, as in M. [3] first -a- altered to -o-, by second hand; PLUMMER 253[6]: "nard- M[1]." [4] PLUMMER 266, as in M. [5] PLUMMER 346, as in M. [6] PLUMMER 353, as in M. [7] PLUMMER 354, as in M. [8] PLUMMER 322, as in M. [9] a over final -i, by second hand; PLUMMER 230[8]: "odda B[2]." [10] -il- interlined over -uu-, by second hand. [11] PLUMMER 281, as in M. [12] æbe interlined over oidi-, by second hand. [13] final -e altered to -o, by second hand. [14] PLUMMER 329, osredo. [15] PLUMMER 349, as in M.

	K	M	L	C	B
15r,21	osthryd	osthryd	osthryd	osthryd	osthryd[1]
49r,2[1]	osuald	osuald	osuald	osuald	osuald
49r,4[1]	osuini	osuini	—	osuine	osuini
1r,11[1] *de morte* osuiu	osuiu	osuiu	osuiu	osuiu	osuiu
1v,24	osuio	osuio	osuio	osuiu	osuio[1]
3r,29[1]	osuio	osuio	osuio	osuiu	osuio
3r,33[1]	osuiu	osuio	osuio	osuiu	osuio
5v,35[1]	osuiu	osuiu	osuiu	osuiu	osuiu
20v,34[1] osuiu *regis*	osuiu	osuiu	osuiu	osuiu	osuiu
39v,17[1] *þatris sui* osuiu	osuiu	osuiu	osuiu	osuiu	?[2]
39v,22[1]	osuio	osuio	osuio	osuiu	osuiu
49r,11[1]	osuiu	osuiu	—	osuiu	osuiu
3v,23 *cui uocabulum erat* ouini	ouini	ouini	ouini	ouini	ouini[1,3]
3v,25	ouini	ouini	ouini	ouini	oui?[1,4]
10v,23	padda	padda	padda	padda[1]	padda[1]
39v,19[1] *parisiacę ciuitatis*	parisiacę	parisiacæ	parisiacæ	parisiacae	?[5]
2r,31[1]	parisiorum	parisior*um*[6]	parisiorum	parisiorum	parisiorum
49r,5[1] *sub principe* peada	peada	peada	—	peada	peada
35v,10	pecthelmo	pecthelmo	pecthelmo	pehthelmo	pecthelmo[1]
37v,34[1]	pecthelm	pecthelm	pecthelm	pehthelm	?[7]
48r,18[1]	pecthelm	pecthelm	pecthelm	pechthelm	pecthelm

Folio						
49r,6[1]	penda	penda	—	penda	penda	penda
31r,15[1]	pippinum	pippinum	pippinum	pippinum	pippinum	pippinum
31v,30[1]	pippin	pippin	pippin	pippin	pippin	pippin
32r,19[1]	pippinum	pippinum	pippinum	pippinum	pippinum	pippinum
32r,25[1]	pippin	pippin	pippin	pippin	pippin	pippin
32r,32-33[1]	pippin	pippin	pippin	pippin	pippin	pippin
27r,37	puch	puch	puch	puch[1]	puch[1]	puch[1]
1r,6	putta	putta	putta	putta[8]	putta[1]	putta[1]
1r,26 *pro putta*	putta	putta	putta	putta[1]	putta[1]	putta[1]
3r,22	putta	putta	putta	putta[1]	putta[1]	putta[1]
6r,18[1]	putta	putta	putta	putta	putta	putta
10r,9[1]	putta	putta	putta	putta	putta	putta
2r,41	quaentauic	quentauic	quentauic	quentauic[1]	quentauic[1]	quentauic[1]
1r,26	quichelm	cuichelm	cuichelm	quichelm	cuichelm[1]	cuichelm[1]
10r,18	quichelmum	cuichelmum	cuichelmum	quichelmum[9]	cuichelmum[1]	cuichelmum[1]
27r,19	quoenburg	quoenburg	quoinburg	quoenburg[1]	quoinburg	quoinburg
30r,8	raculfe	raculfe	raculfe	raculfe	raculfe	raculfe
2r,38	rędfridum	raedfridum	raedfridum	raedfridum	raedfridum	raedfridum

[1] OET, not recorded.　[2] PLUMMER 325, as in M.　[3] final -i altered to -e, by second hand?　[4] PLUMMER 207, as in M.　[5] PLUMMER 325, as in M.　[6] second -i- originally -e-.　[7] PLUMMER 320, as in M.　[8] first -t- interlined.　[9] PLUMMER 228[8], quicelmum.

103

	K	M	L	C	B
31r,3	rathbedo	rathbedo	rathbedo	rathbedo[1]	rathbedo[1]
31r,17[1]	rathbedo	rathbedo	rathbedo	ratbedo	? [2]
31v,10[1]	hreno	rheno	rheno	hreno	hreno
31v,32[1]	rhenum	rhenum	rhenum	rhenum	rhenum
32r,21[1] *in insula quadam rheni*	rheni	hreni	hreni	rheni	hreni
30r,30[1]	rugini	rugini	rugini	rugini	? [3]
48v,36	sabercto	sabercto	sabercto	saeberchto	sabercto[1]
48r,7[1]	sabrinam	sabrinam	sabrinam	sabrinam	sabrinam
1r,13	saxulf	sæxulf	sexulf	saxulf	sexulf
7r,12	saexulfum	sexulfum	sexulfum	saexulfum	sexulfum
10r,12	sexulfum	sexulfum	sexulfum[4]	saexulfum	sexulfum[1]
10r,39	sexulfum	sexulfum	sexulfum	sexulfum	sexulfum[1]
1r,23	sebbi	sebbi	sebbi	sebbi[1]	sebbi[1]
7r,15	sebbe	sebbi	sebbi	sebbe[1]	sebbi[1]
9r,21[1]	sebbi	sebbi	sebbi	sebbi[5]	sebbi
13v,36	sexburg	sexburg	sexburg	saexburg	sexburg[1]
11r,20 *terram |.../ uocabulo* selaeseu	selaeseu	selaeseu	selaeseu	seleseu	selaesei[6]
38r,28	saeleseu	selaeseu	selaeseu	seleseu[1,7]	selaes eu[1,8]
2r,33[1] *ad emme senonum*	senonum	senonum	senonum	senonum	senonum

	signardo	signardo	signardo	signardo	signardo
7r,15	sighere	sigheri	sighere	sighere[1]	sighere[1]
38r,39[1] sigheri *regis*	sigheri	sigheri	sigheri	sighere	sig ?[9]
12r,6	soluente	soluente	soluente	soluente[1]	soluente[1]
39v,3	stanford	stanford	stanford	stanford	?[10]
16r,20	streanaeshalch[11]	strenaeshalc	streanaeshalch	streneshalh	str ?[12]
16v,16	streanaeshalch	streaneshalch	streanaeshalch	streanaeshalh	streanaeshalch
20v,24-25[1] *in* streanaeshalae	streaneshalh	streaneshalch	streaneshalh	streaneshalch	stre ? aeshalch[13]
49r,23	streanaeshalae	streaneshalae	—	streaneshale	streaneshalae[1,14]
30r,13	suaebheardo	suaebhardo	suaebhardo	suebheardo	suaebhardo[1,15]
9v,28	suefredo	suefredo	suefredo	suefredo[1]	suefredo[1]
25r,20	suidberct	suidberct	suidberct	suitbercht[1]	suidberct[1]
32r,7	suidberctum	suidberctum	suidberctum	suidberchtum	suidberctum[1]
32r,14	suidberct	suidberct	suidberct	suitberht	suidberct[1]
24r,34	suidberct	suidberct	suidberct	suitbercht	suidberct[1]
7r,27 *in regione* suthrieona	suthrieona	sudergeona	sudergeona	suthrieona[16]	sudergeona[1,17]

[1] OET, not recorded. [2] PLUMMER 299, as in M. [3] PLUMMER 296, as in M. [4] ANDERSON LB 43, l. 11, sexulfum. [5] final -i over e. [6] PLUMMER 232[4]: "selaesei B[2]." [7] a interlined over -el-, by second hand. [8] -a- not very clear; ig interlined over -eu, by second hand?; PLUMMER 321, selaseu. [9] PLUMMER 322, as in M. [10] PLUMMER 325, as in M. [11] both first -a- and -c- interlined. [12] PLUMMER 252, as in M. [13] PLUMMER 267, as in M. [14] PLUMMER 355, streanaeshalae. [15] PLUMMER 295, suaebhardo. [16] -o- interlined over -ie-, -na half erased; PLUMMER 218[12]: "suthriena C[1], suthri'o'ei C[2]." [17] -i- inserted between -r- and -g-, by second hand; PLUMMER 218[12]: "sudergeona B[1], suderige B[2]."

	K	M	L	C	B
7r,28[1]	tamisam	tamensem	tamensem	tamisam	tamensem
17r,13 *uir /.../ uocabulo* tatfrid	tatfrid	tatfrid	tatfrid	tatfrid[2]	tatfrid[1]
47v,38 *archiepiscopus uocabulo* tatuini	tatuini	tatuini	tatuini	tatuuine[1]	tatuine[1,3]
48r,2[1]	tatuini	tatuini	tatuini	tatuuine	? [4]
49r,38[1]	tatuini	tatuini	—	tatuuine	—
24v,9 *quidam /.../ nomine* thrydred	thrydred	thruidred	thrydred	thrydred	thrydred[1]
31v,23 *cui nomen erat* tilmon	tilmon	tilmon	tilmon	tilmon[1]	tilmon[1]
26r,22 *tino amne*	tino	tino	tino	tino[1]	tino[1]
28r,13[1] *hostium* tini *fluminis*	tini	tini	tini	tini	tini
41v,41 *iuxta amnem* tina	tina	tinam	tina	tina[5]	tina[1,5]
6v,30[1]	titillo	titillo	titillo	titillo	titulo[6]
13r,38 *princeps /.../ uocabulo* tondberct	tondberct	tondberct	tondberct	tondberht[1]	tondberct
8r,16	torctgyd	torctgyd	torctgyd	torchgyd	torhtgyd[1]
8v,8	torctgyd	torctgyd	torctgyd	torchtgyd[7]	torctgyd[1]
13r,25[1]	toronis	toronis[8]	toronis	turonis	turonis
32r,35[1]	traiectum	traiectum	traiectum	traiectum	traiectum

Ref	Lemma							
15r,19	*iuxta fluuium* treanta	treanta	treanta	treanta	treanta	treanta	treanta	treanta
4v,16		trumberct	trumberct	trumberct	trumbercht	trumberct	trumberht[1]	trumberct[1]
10v,5	*cum antistite* trumuine	trumuini	trumuini	trumuini	trumuini	trumuini	trumuini[1]	trumuini[1,10]
20v,19		trumuini	trumuini	trumuini	triumuini	trumuini	trumuini	trumuine[1,11]
22r,23		trumuine	trumuine	trumuine	trumuine	trumuini	trumuine[1]	trumuine[1]
21r,14	tuidi *fluminis*	tuidi	tuidi	tuidi	tuidi	tuidi	tuidi[1]	tuidi[1]
32v,25[1]	tuidi *fluminis*	tuidi	tuidi	tuidi	tuidi	tuidi	tuidi	tuidi
22r,17		adtuifyrdi	adtuifyrdi	adtuifyrdi	adtuifyrdi	adtuifyrdi	adtuifyrdi[1]	adtuifyrde[1,12]
10v,4		tunberctum	tunberctum	tunberctum	tunberctum	tunberctum	tunberchtum[1]	tunberctum[1]
22r,38[1]		tunbercto	tunbercto	tunbercto	tunbercto	tunbercto	tunberhto	tunbercto
15v,7		tunna	tunna	tunna	tunna	tunna	tunna[1]	tunna[1]
15v,8-9		tunnacaestir	tunnacaestir	tunnacaestir	tunnacaestir	tunnacaestir	tunnacaestir[1]	tunnacaestir[1]
9r,34	*antistitem* / ...*/uocabulo* ualdheri	ualdheri	ualdheri	ualdheri	ualdheri	ualdheri	uualdhere	ualdheri[1]
48r,7		ualhstod	ualhstod	ualchstod	ualhstod	ualhstod	uualstod	ualhstod[1]
1r,31[1]		uecta	uecta	uecta	uecta	uecta	uecta	uecta
10v,20[1]		uectam	uectam	uectam	uectam	uectam	uectam	uectam
11v,10[1]		uectam	uectam	uectam	uectam	uectam	uectam	uectam

[1] OET, not recorded. [2] PLUMMER 255[4]: "-friđ C[2]." [3] another u interlined over -u-, by second hand?; final -e may originally have been -i; PLUMMER 350, tatuini. [4] PLUMMER 350, as in M. [5] PLUMMER 332, tinam. [6] -u- on erasure? PLUMMER 249, 217[3]: "titula N. B on erasure." [7] -r- interlined over -oc-. [8] first -o- altered to -u-, by second hand. [9] PLUMMER 249, 217[3]: "titula N. B on erasure." [10] final -i altered to -e, by second hand. [11] final -e may originally have been -i; PLUMMER 267[3]: "-ne B[2]." [12] o over -y-, by second hand; final -e may originally have been -i; PLUMMER 272, adtuifyrdi.

		K	M	L	C	B
11v,34[1]	in insula uecta	uecta	uecta	uecta	uecta	uecta
12r,1[1]		uecta	uecta	uecta	uecta	uecta
40r,13[1]		uectae	uectae	uectæ	uectae[2]	uectae
48r,9[1]		uęctæ	uectæ[3]	uectæ	uectae	uectae
11v,7[1]	in uuenta ciuitate	uuenta	uenta	uenta	uenta	uenta[4]
48r,10[1]		uentę	uentæ[5]	uentæ	uentae	uentae
38r,24[1]		uentanae	uentanæ[6]	uentanæ	uentanae[7]	uentan ?[8]
47v,41[1]		uentano	uentano	uentano	uentano	uentano
26v,35		uetadun	uetadun	uetadun	uetadun[1]	uetadun[1]
25r,16	socius eius uocabulo uictberct	uictberct	uictberct	uictberct	uictbercht	uictberct[1]
30v,40		uictberct	uictberct	uictberct	uictberht	uictberct[1]
31r,11[1]		uictberct	uictberct[9]	uictberct	uihtberht	uictberct·
21r,2		uihtred	uictred	uictred	uuichtred	uictred[1,10]
30r,13		uictredo	uictredo[11]	uictredo	uictredo[1]	? [12]
47v,2[1]		uictred	uictred	uictred	uuichred[13]	uictred[14]
49r,35[1]		uictred	uictred	—	uihtred[15]	—
1r,1		uigheard	uighard	uighard	uuigheard	uighard[1]
1v,25		uuigheard	uighard	uighard	uigheard[16]	uighard[1]
25r,18		uilbrod	uilbrord	uilbrord	uilbrod[17]	uilbrod[1]
25r,20		uilbrod	uilbrord	uilbrord	uilbrod	uilbrord[1]
31r,13[1]		uilbrod	uilbrord	uilbrord	uilbrod	uilbrord
31v,36		uilbrord[18]	uilbrord	uilbrord	uilbrord	uilbrord[1]

32r,26[1]	uilbrord	uilbrord	uilbrord	uilbrord	uilbrord
32r,42[1]	uilbrord	uilbrord	uilbrord	uilbrord[19]	uilbrord
39v,33	uilbrod	uilbrord	uilbrord		uilbrord
1r,28[1]	uilfrid	uilfrid	uilfrid	uilfrid	uilfrid
2v,42[1]	uilfrido	uilfrido	uilfrido	uilfrido	uilfrido
3r,15[1]	uilfrid	uilfrid	uilfrid	uilfrid	uilfrid
3r,31[1]	uilfrido	uilfrido	uilfrido	uilfrido	uilfrido
5v,40[1]	uilfridum[20]	uilfridum	uilfridum	uilfridum	uilfridum
6r,16[1]	uilfrid	uilfrid	uilfrid	uilfrid	uilfrid
10r,27[1]	uilfridum	uilfridum	uilfridum	uilfridum	uilfridum
10v,3[1]	uilfridi	uilfridi	uilfridi	uilfridi	uilfridi
10v,9[1]	uilfrid	uilfrid	uilfrid	uuilfrid	uuilfrid
10v,34[1]	uilfrid	uilfrid	uilfrid	uilfrid	uilfrid
11r,19[1]	uilfrido	uilfrido	uilfrido	uilfrido	uilfrido
11r,25[1]	uilfrid	uilfrid	uilfrid	uilfrid	uilfrid
11v,6[1]	uilfrido	uilfrido	uilfrido	uilfrido	uilfrido
11v,15[1]	uilfrido	uilfrido	uilfrido	uuilfrid	uilfrido
13v,2[1]	uilfrid	uilfrid	uilfrid	uilfrid	uilfrid
13v,16[1]	uilfrido	uilfrido	uilfrido	uuilfrido	uilfrido
14r,9[1]	uilfrid	uilfrid	uilfrid	uilfrid	uilfrid
17r,7[1]	uilfridum	uilfridum	uilfridum	uilfridum	uilfridum
23r,19[1]	uilfrid	uilfrid	uilfrid	uilfrid	uilfrid

abscessionis uilfridi

[1] OET, not recorded. [2] another *u* interlined over *u-*, by second hand; not noted by either OET or PLUMMER. [3] PLUMMER 350, uectae. [4] another *u* interlined over *ue-*, by second hand; PLUMMER 236, uenta. [5] PLUMMER 350, uentae. [6] PLUMMER 321, uectae. [7] another *u* interlined over *u-*, by second hand; PLUMMER 321, uentanae. [8] PLUMMER 321, as in M. [9] first *-c-* interlined over *-it-*. [10] another *u* interlined over *ui-*, by second hand; PLUMMER 268, uictred. [11] *-c-* interlined. [12] PLUMMER 295, as in M. [13] *t* interlined over *-hr-*, by second hand. [14] another initial *u* in the margin, by second hand?; PLUMMER 356[12], uichtred. [15] PLUMMER 348, uictred. [16] PLUMMER 201, uighard. [17] another *u* interlined over *ui-*, by second hand; PLUMMER 201, uighard. [18] second *-y-* interlined. [19] another *u* interlined over *u-*, by second hand; OET 245, uilbrod. [20] in the margin.

	K	M	L	C	B
25r,40[1] uilfridi *episcopi*	uilfridi	uilfridi	uilfridi	uuilfridi	uilfridi
25r,42[1]	uilfrido	uilfrido	uilfrido	uuilfrido	uilfrido
26v,30[1]	uilfrid	uilfrid	uilfrid	uilfrid	uilfrid
32r,9[1]	uilfrid	uilfrid	uilfrid	uilfrid	uilfrid
38r,28[1] uilfridi *episcopi*	uilfridi	uilfridi	uilfridi	uuilfridi	? [2]
38v,7[1]	uilfrid	uilfrid	uilfrid	uilfrid[3]	? [4]
39r,8[1]	uilfridum	uilfridum	uilfridum	uilfridum[5]	uilfridum
39r,35[1]	uilfrid	uilfrid	uilfrid	uilfrid[6]	uilfrid
39r,35[1]	uilfrid	uilfrid	uilfrid	uilfrid[6]	? [7]
39r,38[1]	uilfrid	uilfrid	uilfrid	uuilfrid	uilfrid
39v,25[1]	uilfrido	uilfrido	uuilfritho	uilfrido[8]	uilfrido
40r,1[1]	uilfridum	uilfridum	uilfridum	uilfridum[9]	uilfridum
40r,4[1]	uilfridus	uilfridus	uilfridus	uilfridus[9]	uilfridus
40r,29[1]	uilfridus	uilfridus	uilfridus	uilfridus[9]	uilfridus
40r,34[1]	uilfridus	uilfridus	uilfridus	uilfridus[9]	uilfridus
41r,8[1]	uilfridus	uilfridus	uilfridus	uilfridus	uilfridus
41r,40[1]	uilfrido	uilfrido	uilfrido	uilfrido	? [10]
41v,24[1]	uilfridum	uilfridum	uilfridum	uilfridum	uilfridum
49r,9[1]	uilfrid	uilfrid	—	uilfrit	uilfrid
49r,18[1]	uilfrid	uilfrid	—	uuilfrid[11]	uilfrid
16v,31[1]	uilfrid	uilfrid	uilfrid	uilfrid	uilfrid
29r,5[1]	uilfrido	uilfrido	uilfrido	uilfrido	uilfrido
48r,16[1]	uilfrid	uilfrid	uilfrid	uulfrid[12]	uilfrid
48r,8[1]	uilfrid	uilfrid	uilfrid	uilfrid	uilfrid
32r,34	uiltaburg	uiltaburg	uiltaburg	uiltaburg[1]	uiltaburg[1]
32r,34	uiltorum	uiltorum	uiltorum	uiltorum[1]	uiltorum[1]

99,31	*ut in m.*	.....	.....	.....	.....	.....	.....
49v,7	*ad* uiuraemuda	uiuraemuda	uiuraemuda	uiuraemuda	uiuraemuda	uiuraemuda	—
12v,29	*fluminis* uiuri	uiuri	uiuri	uiuri	uiuri	uiuri[1,14]	uiuri[1]
16r,41	uiuri *fluminis*	uiuri	uiuri	uiuri	uiuri	uiuri[1]	uiuri[1]
41v,40[1]	*ostium* uiuri *amnis*	uiuri	uiuri	uiuri	uiuri	uiuri	uiuri
38v,9	*quae uocatur* inundalum	inundalum	inundalum	inundalum	inundalum	inundalum[1]	inundalum[1]
41r,3	*in prouincia* undalum	undalum	undalum	undalum	undalum	undalum[15]	undalum[1]
3r,26		uulfheri	uulfheri	uulfheri	uulfheri	uulfheri	uulfheri[1,16]
3v,2		uulfheri[17]	uulfheri	uulfheri	uulfheri	uulfhere[1]	uulfheri[1,18]
5r,37[1]		uulfheri	uulfheri	uulfheri	uulfheri	uulfheri	uulfheri[18]
10r,35[1]	uulfhere *fugato*	uulfhere	uulfhere	uulfhere	uulfhere	uulfhere	uulfhere
10v,18[1]	*rege* uulfhere	uulfhere	uulfhere	uulfhere	uulfhere	uulfhere	uulfhere[19]
49r,15[1]		uulfheri	uulfheri	—	uulfheri	uulfheri	uulfheri
1r,13		uynfrido	uynfrido	uynfrido	uynfrido	uynfrido	uynfrido[1]
5r,34		uynfridum	uynfridum	uynfridum	uynfridum	uynfridum[1]	uynfridum[1]
5r,38[1]		uynfrid	uynfrid	uynfrid	uynfrid	uynfrid	uynfrid
6r,20		uynfrid	uynfrid	uynfrid	uynfrid	uynfrid[1]	uynfrid[1]
7r,7[1]		uynfrido	uynfrido	uynfrido	uynfrido	uynfrido	uynfrido
7r,11[1]		uynfrit	uynfrid	uynfrid	uynfrid	uynfrid	uynfrid

[1] OET, not recorded. [2] PLUMMER 321, as in M. [3] another *u* interlined over *u-*, by second hand; PLUMMER 322, uilfrid. [4] PLUMMER 322, as in M. [5] another *u* interlined over *u-*, by second hand; PLUMMER 323, uilfridum. [6] another *u* interlined over *u-*, by second hand; PLUMMER 326, uilfrido. [7] PLUMMER 324, as in M. [8] another *u* interlined over *u-*, by second hand; PLUMMER 331, as in M. [9] another *u* interlined over *u-*, by second hand; not noted by either OET or PLUMMER. [10] PLUMMER 331, as in M. [11] PLUMMER 355, uilfrid. [12] PLUMMER 350[19]: "uuil- C." [13] *u* erased between first *-i-* and *-n-*. [14] PLUMMER 241[1]: "uuiri C." [15] *-a-* was originally *-u-*. [16] *-i* altered to *-e*, by second hand? PLUMMER 206, uulfheri. [17] final *-i* over *-e*. [18] *-i* altered to *-e*, by second hand. [19] dotted *-a-* between *-r-* and *-e-*.

PART III
ETYMOLOGY

INTRODUCTORY

These etymological notes provide the information that is indispensable for the phonological discussion of PART IV. To break new ground in the etymological study of personal names and of place- and river-names is not among the tasks set for the present work. Only little has been added to previous etymological descriptions of the name-material of Bede's HE, such as found in MILLER, KÖHLER, STRÖM, and ANDERSON LB.

All the material of PART II is, without exception, described etymologically. Of all the names and name-els. the historical-phonological setting is established by a summary indication of their connections in OHG and/or OE, and in the case of Celtic names in Old British or related languages. Where general agreement among scholars on a derivation has been encountered, no references to consulted literature have been given. If opinions differ, which is the case almost without exception with uncompounded personal names and with a great many of the place- and river-names, a selection of the suggestions as to etymological derivation and a fairly complete list of references are presented.

Etymological descriptions are also given of such names as ANGLI, BRETTONES etc., which for reasons given in the EDITORIAL NOTE to PART II have not been recorded in the body of the edition of the name-material. The Latin preposition ad, the Latin (possibly OE) preposition in and the suffix ingas are also given separate treatment, because they play an important role in the formation of place-names.

The general principles of name-giving in OE and other Germanic languages will not come up for discussion. Problems such as short-name formation versus by-name construction where uncompounded personal names are concerned, or the use of personal names versus the use of topographical names where the formation of place-names is concerned, are outside the scope of these etymological notes. With regard to the composition of personal names the reader is referred to the works of Stark, Searle, Forssner, Boehler, Redin, Stenton, von Feilitzen, Tengvik, Ström, Bach, Schramm, and Reaney[1]. In

---

[1] The relevant works are listed in the BIBLIOGRAPHY.

this connection attention is drawn to one point, viz. the "meanings" of especially compound personal names. Not too much weight should be attached to the literal meanings of names, for, as is well-known, the name-els. in use among Germanic peoples were restricted in number, and name-els. were combined with each other in the first place to form appellations in which family-relations could be brought out, so that there was an early tendency for their meaning to become weakened. The reader should, therefore, not be surprised to come across seemingly absurd combinations of name-els., and should not, for instance, too readily draw conclusions about the social position of women in Anglo-Saxon society from the frequent use of name-themes connected with warfare in the names of women[2].

For a discussion of principles and problems of the formation of place-names the reader is referred to the works of Zachrisson, Mawer, Stenton, Karlström, Ekwall, Tengstrand, Reaney, Cameron, and Sandred[3]. The Celtic element in English place- and river-names, to which a great deal of attention has been devoted by Förster, Ekwall, and Jackson[3], has always presented special problems. Of late years Krahe's views on what has come to be called "Old European", i.e. what is common pre-Celtic and pre-Germanic but not Indo-European, have also been applied to name-material of the British Isles, in particular by Nicolaisen, and part of the material that so far has generally been classified as Celtic should no doubt be looked upon as pre-Celtic.

Biographical information in the case of personal names and identifications in the case of district-, place-, river-, and tribal-names may be of relevance for the historical-phonological discussion, in so far as regional and dialectal distribution are taken into account. Since information of this kind will often be wanted simultaneously with etymological information and also because in that way space could be saved, such information has also been incorporated in this PART. Biographical notes are restricted to the bare minimum that is necessary to roughly localise persons in time and place. The exact dates of birth, death, etc. are given whenever possible, but no special effort has been made to define such data more closely than in fairly broad terms whenever this was not readily possible. The biographical data are based mainly on the works of Searle, Plummer, Ström, Powicke & Fryde, and Colgrave & Mynors[3].

---

[2] Cf. BOEHLER 192, and STRÖM XXXVI f.
[3] The relevant works are listed in the BIBLIOGRAPHY.

All compound and uncompounded personal names, all place- and river-names, and all name-els. have been brought together in one list alphabetically arranged. Names are printed in boldface capitals, name-els. in boldface small letters. Prepositions that form an integral part of place-names are also printed in small boldface letters, whereas boldface capitals are employed for the main component(s) of such names. This is done to bring out the different character of the component parts. At the same time their close connection is indicated by printing them as one word, as for example with **adBARUAE**[4].

The names of the list are all accompanied by an indication of the number of times they occur in the text of our MS. Information on the number of times name-els. are combined with other els. is also provided.

References to works cited are given in chronological order[5]; references to abbreviated literature are printed in ordinary capital letters.

ACCA (6) Of obscure origin. HOLDER I,14 thinks it may be Celtic. REDIN 81, without specifying further, reckons with "several originally distinct stems", but on p. XXXII names it among a group of lall-names. STRÖM 58 sees three possibilities for it, viz. shortening of compounds in **ac,** which is connected with OHG *eih,* OE *āc* 'oak', such as *Acwulf*; analogical formation with such hypocoristic names as *Ecca* and *Occa*; and thirdly a lall-name. ANDERSON LB 122 looks upon it as a short name from a compound with **alh,** through an intermediary change $/l\chi/ > /lk/$ before a consonant[6], and a subsequent assimilatory change $/lk/ > /kk/$. No evidence is, however, available for the latter change.

> He was a follower of Uilfrid 1 (*s.v.*), whom he accompanied on his wanderings to the Continent after his expulsion around 691/692. He was Bishop of Hexham from 709 to 732, when he had to leave his see. He was one of Bede's close friends. He died in 740.

ad This is the Latin form OE *æt* 'at' takes in HE. Bede observed the rule that original nature-names should be preceded by this preposition when they were

---

[4] Some place-name scholars spell this place-name Adbaruae or ADBARUAE, whereas others prefer to spell Ad Baruae or AD BARUAE. For a discussion of this see FÖRSTER TH 208, n.1.

[5] BOEHLER, published in 1930, was completed in 1918 and is, therefore, placed in accordance with the latter date. DEPN is placed in 1960, the year of its 4th edition. RI & CR was published in 1949, but is the text of a paper read in 1937. JACKSON LHEB has had several reprints, but is placed in accordance with the year of its first publication, 1953.

[6] The same change is assumed by DEPN 6 in such place-names as *Alkham* (K), *Alkerton* (Gl), and *Alkmonton* (Db).

used as habitation-names. *Æt* is followed by the dative, and seems to have been looked upon as an integral part of the place-name. Cf. PLUMMER II,104, EPNE I,5 ff., SMITH ASS 86, CAMERON 30 f., DEPN XIX. The preposition occurs in **adBARUAE** (2) and **adTUIFYRDI** (1).

ADAMNANUS 1 (1)   Of Celtic origin. HOLDER III,502 offers no etymology for the name. FÖRSTER KW 175 suggests that it is a short name with -*an*-derivative from the full-name *Adomnae*, which is connected with *ad-omnae* 'great terror'.

He was an Irish monk at Coldingham around 675.

ADAMNANUS 2 (6)   see **ADAMNANUS 1**

He was the ninth Abbot of Iona, from 679 to 704. He was the biographer of St. Columba.

ADDI (1)   The only occurrence of what is generally considered to be the unmutated variant of **AEDDI**.

A thane who around 690 asked John of Beverley, Bishop of Hexham, to come and consecrate his church.

AEBAE (1)   The other MSS have *Eabae* in its stead, whereas OEBede has *Æbbe*. K's form may be due to a mere scribal error. However, we may also point to the fact that similarly persons named *Aebbae* are sometimes referred to as *Eabbae*, which according to STRÖM 60 indicates that the two names had the same origin, or were substituted for each other because of their similarity in form after their original meanings had become blurred. *Aebae* may thus well be the same name as *Eabae*. According to BOEHLER 208 and 218, *Eabae* cannot be connected with the OE personal name *Abba*, which is derived from Gothic *aba* 'man' and goes back to Primitive Germanic **aƀa*. In her opinion *Eaba* and its variant *Eafa* are related names. REDIN 92 looks upon *Eaba* as probably derived from **auƀa-*, an ancient name-theme arisen from shortening of **Audbalda*. This explanation is accepted as a possibility by ANDERSON LB 95, and also by STRÖM 68 who at the same time mentions the assumption BOEHLER 218 makes, namely that *Eabae* arose from shortening of some such name as *Eanburh*. In this connection Ström repeats Boehler's reference to the fact that Eabae's father was King Eanfrid of the Huiccii (*s.v.*), whose brother was Aenheri (*s.v.*). At any rate the likelihood of **EABAE**, and thus of **AEBAE**, being a short form of a compound name is great.

She was a daughter of King Eanfrid of the Huiccii (*s.v.*). She married King Aedilualch of the South Saxons (*s.v.*) and died in 685.

AEBBAE (2)   REDIN 116 relates it to OE *Ab(b)a*, which is connected with Gothic *aba* (⟨Primitive Germanic **aƀa*) 'man'. Cf. MÜLLER 63. BOEHLER 207 f. proposes shortening of a compound name such as *Aethelburh*. Similarly assimilation of compound names with **aelb/aelf** is suggested by ANDERSON LB 93. STRÖM 60 surveys all these possible derivations, and besides points to similarity with lall-names. It may be assumed that derivation from compound names is more likely. See also **AEBAE,**

> She was a half-sister of King Osuiu of Northumbria (*s.v.*), and a not too successful Abbess of the monastery at Coldingham. She died about 683.

AEBBERCURNIG (1)   The first component of this Celtic place-name goes back to British **adbero-* ⟩ **abbero-* 'river-mouth', whereas the second component is connected with a Celtic *cornu* (⟩ Welsh *corn*) 'a horn', used in the sense of 'promontory' in this connection. Cf. WATSON 16, 458, 461, EKWALL EN 155, GREEN 29, FÖRSTER TH 14 ff., JACKSON LHEB 547, NI, GEL & RI 35 ff.

> Abercorn, Scotland.

AECCI (1)   An *i*-derivative of **ACCA.** Cf. REDIN 130, STRÖM 61, ANDERSON LB 106, 109, 119. With regard to *i*-derivation EKWALL ST I,14 suggests "that many, perhaps most, OE personal names in -*i* (-*e*) go back to earlier -*īn*"; -*īn*, -*īna* is a diminutive suffix, and most of the names it is used with are short forms of compound names. Ekwall denies that names in -*i* are *ja*-stems or *i*-stems, as REDIN 119 seems to hold; according to him they are in all probability *a*-stems. Ekwall's views with regard to *i*-derivation are shared by both DAHL 56 and CAMPBELL 189, n.3.

> Around 675 he and Baduini (*s.v.*) succeeded Bishop Bisi of the East Angles (*s.v.*). His see was Dunwich (Suffolk), the original East Anglian see. He died around 730.

AEDDI (1)   An *i*-derivative of a personal name *Adda*. *Adda* is a fairly common OE name, but scholars do not agree upon its derivation. Celtic origin has been suggested for it by REDIN 82; JACKSON LHEB 418 associates *Adda* of Liber Vitae (OET 158 and 163[1]) with Old Welsh **Adaṽ*, a suggestion also made by FÖRSTER KW 176 who traces it back to the biblical name *Adam*. STRÖM 59 f., who surveys all possible derivations suggested, adds the possibility of lall-name formation. ANDERSON LB 122 is of the opinion that the name arose from shortening of a compound name in **ald**, a view also mentioned by Ström. This requires the introduction of an assimilatory change /ld/ ⟩ /dd/, a change not evidenced elsewhere, but quite possible. For the derivative suffix see **AECCI.**

> One of the chanters of Uilfrid 1 (*s.v.*). He wrote the *Life of Uilfrid* that Bede draws upon for his narrative.

aedil/edil   OHG *adal*, OE *æpele* 'noble, famous'. However, **edil** may have developed as a separate parallel-form, also reflected in OHG **edili**, from which side-form **aedil** may have taken the *il*-suffix; cf. STRÖM 109 ff., ANDERSON LB 93 f., CAMPBELL 82, n.1. It occurs as a first el., in combination with **bald/balt** (1), **berct/berht/berict** (2), **burg** (4), **raed/red** (16) **thryd/thryth** (5), **ualch/ualh** (3), **uald** (2), and **uini** (1). The form **edil** is used once in **EDILUALD.** In the other form *æ* is spelled *ę* four times.

AEDILBALD (1)   aedil/edil; bald/balt.
Succeeded Ceolred as King of Mercia in 716, and by 731 had subjected
all England south of the Humber to his rule. He was murdered in 757.

AEDILBERCT 1 (1)   aedil/edil; berct/berht/berict.
Son of King Eorminric, whom he succeeded as King of Kent in 560.
He died in 616.

AEDILBERCT 2 (1)   aedil/edil; berct/berht/berict.
At his death in 725 King Uictred of Kent (*s.v.*) was succeeded by his
three sons Aedilberct, Eadberct 1 (*s.v.*) and Alric (*s.v.*), according to
HE V,23. Alric is not mentioned at all by later sources. Eadberct's
death is put at 748, so that Aedilberct may have been sole King of Kent
from 748 until his death in 762.

AEDILBURG (4)   aedil/edil; burg.
Sister of Earconuald (*s.v.*), Bishop of London from 675 to 693. According
to HE IV,6 Earconuald founded the monastery of Barking for Aedilburg
before he was consecrated Bishop. Aedilburg died of the plague, possibly
in 664[7].

AEDILRED (16)   aedil/edil; raed/red.
Succeeded his brother Uulfheri (*s.v.*) to the throne of Mercia in 674.
He was married to Osthryd (*s.v.*). He retired to the monastery of Bardney
in 704, where later he was made Abbot.

AEDILTHRYD (5)   aedil/edil; thryd/thryth.
Daughter of King Anna of the East Angles (*s.v.*). After having been
married to Tondberct (*s.v.*), a prince of the South Gyruii, from 652 to
655, she married Ecgfrid (*s.v.*) about the year 660. After twelve years
of marriage she entered the monastery of Coldingham and later founded
a monastery at Ely, where she died around 680.

AEDILUALCH (3)   aedil/edil; ualch/ualh.
King of the South Saxons from before 674. He was killed by Caedualla
(*s.v.*) between 680 and 685.

AEDILUALD (2)   aedil/edil; uald.
After having been Prior and then Abbot of Melrose he was consecrated
Bishop of Lindisfarne in 721. He died in 740.

AEDILUINI (1)   aedil/edil; uini.
He was consecrated Bishop of Lindsey in 680 after having made his
studies in Ireland. He probably held the see until 692.

---

[7] According to PLUMMER II, 400, Aedilburg, the Abbess of Barking, is often
confused with Aethelburg, Abbess of Faremoûtier-en-Brie, who was one of
the four daughters of King Anna of East Anglia (*s.v.*). In CO & MY 597 the two
are not distinguished.

aelb/aelf OHG *alp(b)*, OE *ælf* 'elf, fairy' (⟨Latin *albus* 'white'). It is used as a first el., as **aelb** in combination with **flaed/fled** (1) and as **aelf** with **uini** (3).

AELBFLED (1) aelb/aelf; flaed/fled.

> Daughter of King Osuiu of Bernicia (*s.v.*) and Eanfled (*s.v.*), born in 654. She entered the monastery of Hartlepool, and later went to Whitby, where she and her mother together succeeded Abbess Hild (*s.v.*) in 680. She died around 714.

AELFUINI (3) aelb/aelf; uini.

> Son of King Osuiu of Bernicia (*s.v.*), born about 660. He was probably under-king of Deira under his brother Ecgfrid (*s.v.*). He was killed in the Battle of the Trent in 679.

AENHERI (1) ean/aen; here/heri.

> He and his brother Eanfrid (*s.v.*) were joint rulers of the Huiccii (*s.v.*) under King Aedilred of Mercia (*s.v.*) around the year 680.

AESICA (1) Its etymology is uncertain. REDIN 131 and 155 sees in it an *-ica*-diminutive of an equally obscure *Aese*. ANDERSON LB 71 f. has no doubt that diminutive-derivation from a personal name **Assa*, possibly identical with OE *assa* (⟨ Latin *asinus*) 'ass', has taken place. Although **Assa* is not found independently, EPNE I,13 states that it was used as a personal name and DEPN 15 suggests '*Assa*'s hill' for *Ashingdon* (Ess.). STRÖM 61 f., after having mentioned the preceding derivation, suggests that **AESICA** should be identified with *Aesca*, a short form of compounds in **aesc**, which in its turn is connected with OHG *ask*, OE *æsc* 'ash-tree, spear'. Although the insertion of a svarabhakti between /s/ and /k/ has no parallels in OE, Ström's suggestion is very plausible. There may be an OHG equivalent in **As(i)co* (⟨*Asca*); cf. KAUFMANN UAR 154, KAUFMANN ERG 40.

> In 664 (?) the boy Aesica died of the plague in the monastery of Barking at the age of three.

AETLA (1) Identical with *Attila*, it is a *-(i)la*-diminutive of *Atta* in which the medial vowel was syncopated. *Atta* probably was a lall-name originally, connected with Gothic *atta* 'father'. Cf. MÜLLER 46, 70, SCHÖNFELD 275, REDIN 83, 147, HOLTHAUSEN 13, 417, STRÖM 62, ANDERSON LB 92 f.

> Of Aetla nothing else is known but that he was a monk in the monastery of Streanaeshalch (*s.v.*, = Whitby), and that he was consecrated Bishop of Dorchester around 675. According to PLUMMER II, 245 f. he probably held the see of Dorchester until 685.

agil Of Continental Germanic origin, ultimately either derived from Germanic **agjo-*⟩ OHG *ecka*, OE *egl* 'edge, sword etc.' (modern Dutch *egel*) or from Germanic **agan* 'to fear'. Cf. FÖRSTEMANN I, 14, FORSSNER 11, HOLT-HAUSEN 10, BACH I,1,217, SCHRAMM 148, KAUFMANN UAR 88, KAUF-MANN ERG 20 ff. It is used as a first el. in combination with **berct/berht/berict** (4).

AGILBERCTUS (4)　A Continental Germanic name composed of **agil** and berct/berht/berict.

Agilberctus came from Gaul. He succeeded Birinus as Bishop of Dorchester around 650, and resigned in 660 to return to Gaul. He became Bishop of Paris before 666, and died in 680.

AIDAN (6)　Of Celtic origin. HOLDER III, 527 offers no etymology. However, Old Irish *Aidān* probably was a short name of compounds with Old Irish *aed* 'fire'. Cf. FÖRSTER KW 177, VENDRYES LE A-19.

He was a monk at Iona. In 635 King Osuald of Bernicia (*s.v.*) requested him to come to his kingdom to preach the gospel. He was consecrated Bishop of Lindisfarne and died in 651.

al　STRÖM 5 suggests connection with OHG *all*, OE (*e*)*all* 'all', as a first el. of personal names often appearing in OHG as **ala**. Cf. MÜLLER 100. In K it is as a first el. used in combination with **ric** (1). The name thus constituted could, therefore, be cognate with East Germanic *Alaric*; cf. FÖRSTEMANN I, 53 f., SCHRAMM 36 f., KAUFMANN UAR 88. ANDERSON LB 90 rejects this connection, because in that case the theme would have taken the form *æl in OE. Other explanations of **al** in **ALRIC** are possible, but less likely. A consonant may have been lost between /l/ and /r/, as for example /χ/ of **alh** 'temple, refuge', or the /b/ of **aelb/aelf** 'elf, fairy'. **ALRIC** may also have been a reduction of *Æthelric*. Cf. STRÖM 5, FEILITZEN DB 142, 151, ANDERSON LB 121.

ald　OHG *alt*, OE (*e*)*ald* 'old, eminent'. It is used as a first el. in combination with **frid/frit** (12), **gisl** (1), **helm** (5), **uini** (2), and **uulf** (5). Once, in combination with **berct/berht/berict**, the el. is replaced by **ead/ed/æad**; see **EADBERCT 4 = ALDBERCT**.

ALDFRID (12)　**ald; frid/frit.**

Illegitimate son of King Osuiu of Bernicia (*s.v.*) and an Irish princess. During the reign of his half-brother Ecgfrid (*s.v.*) he remained in Ireland. He came to the throne in 685 and died in 704. He was a scholar and took a great interest in the twin-monasteries of Wearmouth and Jarrow.

ALDGISL (1)　**ald; gisl.**

King of Frisia, who received Uilfrid 1 (*s.v.*) honourably when the latter came to preach in Frisia in 678.

ALDHELM (5)　**ald; helm.**

Born about 639 and connected with the royal family of Wessex. He became Abbot of Malmesbury about 675. He was Bishop of Sherborne from 705 until his death in 709.

ALDUINI (2)　**ald; uini.**

Bishop of Lichfield from between 716 and 727 to 737.

ALDUULF 1 (2)   ald; uulf.
   Son of King Aedilheri of East Anglia and Herisuid (*s.v.*). He was King of East Anglia from about 664 to 713.

ALDUULF 2 (3)   ald; uulf.
   Bishop of Rochester from 727 to 739.

alh   OHG *alah*, OE *(e)alh* 'temple, refuge'.
It is used as a first el. in combination with **frid/frit** (1).

ALHFRID (1)   alh; frid/frit.
   Son of King Osuiu of Bernicia (*s.v.*). He was sub-king of Deira for some time, but is heard of no more after his rebellion against his father in 664.

ALNE (1)   A Celtic river-name. Bede's form is looked upon as the genitive singular of a Latinized *Alna* by EKWALL RN 6, but, as GREEN 33 points out, in HE names always stand in apposition to accompanying words like *fluuium*, and thus *Alne* must be the accusative of an OE form, which probably was *Alun*. The river is recorded as *Alaunos* by Ptolemy around 150. A base **Alauno-* is a likely starting-point, but it is not clear whether the stem is *al-* or *alau-*, as EKWALL RN 8 states. Its origin is, therefore, held to be obscure; cf. EKWALL RN 7, RI & CR 22, EPNE 8, CAMERON 37. NICOLAISEN 225 ff. groups it with Krahe's Old European river-names, and connects it with a stem **al(a)* 'to flow, to stream', to which the compound suffix **-au-no* (⟨*-auo-/ -auā-* and *-no-/-nā-*) has been added. Cf. also KÖHLER 30, MAWER NO & DU 4, FÖRSTER TH 51, n.1, 324, JACKSON LHEB 309.
   A small river in Northumberland that runs from Alnham to the North Sea at Alnmouth.

ALRIC (1)   al; ric.
   He succeeded his father King Uictred of Kent (*s.v.*) in 725 together with his brothers Aedilberct 2 (*s.v.*) and Eadberct 1 (*s.v.*). No further particulars are known about him.

and   The etymology is uncertain. STRÖM 6 reckons with two possibilities. On the one hand derivation from OHG *ando*, OE *anda* 'anger, envy, enmity', on the other derivation from OHG *ant-*, OE *and-* (prefix) 'against; opposite', probably connected with OE *ende* 'end'. The latter is supported by HELLWIG 18 ff. and SCHÖNFELD 20, the former by ANDERSON LB 90. Cf. also FÖRSTEMANN I, 102 and KAUFMANN ERG 34. It is used as a first el. in combination with **hun** (1).

ANDHUN (1)   and; hun.
   Andhun, together with Bercthun (*s.v.*), managed to drive out Caedualla (*s.v.*) who had killed their Lord, King Aedilualch of Sussex (*s.v.*), between 680 and 685. They ruled the kingdom, until they in their turn were overcome by Caedualla.

ANGLI (76)   This tribal name has been connected with OHG *angul*, OE *angel* 'angle, hook'. Cf. EKWALL EN 154 f., HOLTHAUSEN 6, CAMERON 48; cf. also SCHÖNFELD 21. It is used as a component of **MIDDILENGLI** (1).

The Angles.

ANNA (1)   Various explanations have been proposed. HOLDER III, 628 thinks it may be Celtic in origin. MÜLLER 57 f., assuming that the name is the equivalent of *On(n)a*, beside short-name formation suggests a by-name connected with OHG, OE *unnan* 'to grant, to allow'. REDIN 60, BACH I,1,100 and 104, KAUFMANN UAR 138, and KAUFMANN ERG 37 favour derivation from compound names with **arn**, which is connected with OHG *arn*, OE *earn* 'eagle'. Cf. also SCHÖNFELD 22, ANDERSON LB 123. STRÖM 62 f. thinks that lall-name formation is more likely. Modern Frisian *Anne* is probably connected with it.

He was King of East Anglia from around 635 to 654. Aedilthryd (*s.v.*) and Sexburg (*s.v.*) were daughters of his.

ar   Of obscure origin. The spelling of two variants of **ARUALD** in MSS of OEBede, viz. *Aarwald* and *Árwald*, points to a long vowel. STRÖM 6 f. mentions four such *ār* nouns in OE: 1. OHG *ēra*, OE *ār* 'honour, mercy, prosperity'. 2. OHG *ēr*, OE *ār* 'brass, unwrought metal'. 3. Germanic **airō*, OE *ār* 'oar'. 4. Gothic *airus*, OE *ār* 'messenger'. OET 586 prefers *ār* 'honour etc.' as basis for the name-theme, as does ANDERSON LB 72[8]. If obliged to choose, Ström too would choose the first. The name-theme itself, however, may not have existed at all. For no other, absolutely certain, examples of it have come down to us in OE names, nor in names of other Germanic languages. Cf. KAUF-MANN ERG 37. There is much, therefore, that favours Ström's suggestion that **ar** developed from **arn* (: OHG *aro/arn*, OE *earn* 'eagle') through loss of interconsonantal /n/. Cf. SCHRAMM 149 f., BACH I,1,214. There is the possibility that such a loss was merely due to scribal error. The name-theme is used as a first el. in combination with **uald** (1).

arc   Various derivations have been proposed for this Continental Germanic name-theme. Connection has been suggested with OHG *arc/arac* 'avaricious', cf. TENGVIK 180; with OHG *arg*, OE *earg* 'cowardly, useless'; with OHG *archa*, OE *earc(e)* (⟨Latin *arca*) 'ark'; and with OE *earh* (⟨Latin *arcus*) 'arrow', cf. KAUFMANN ERG 38 f. It is used as a first el. in combination with **uulf** (1).

ARCUULFUS (1)   A Continental Germanic name, composed of **arc** and **uulf**. He was a Gaulish Bishop who on his way home from a pilgrimage to the Holy Land was cast onto the coasts of Britain, and thus came into contact with Adamnanus 2 (*s.v.*). Cf. HE V,16 and 17.

---

[8] Anderson justifies his choice with a reference to the length of the vowel, which is not very convincing, seeing that this feature is shared by the vowels of the other three words as well.

124

ARHELAS (1)   A Continental place-name of uncertain origin. Cf. GREEN 36, DAU & ROS 27.

Arles, France.

ARUALD (1)   **ar; uald.**

King of the Isle of Wight when the island was captured by Caedualla (*s.v.*) in 686.

badu   OHG *badu*, OE *b(e)adu* 'fight, battle'. It is used as a first el. in combination with **degn** (1) and **uini** (1).

BADUDEGN (1)   **badu; degn.**

Lay brother of Lindisfarne who was miraculously cured at the tomb of Cudberct (*s.v.*). He lived about the time of Bede's writing. Cf. HE V,31.

BADUINI (1)   **badu; uini.**

Around 675 Aecci (*s.v.*) and Baduini were consecrated Bishops of East Anglia as successors of Bisi (*s.v.*). Baduini went to Elmham, the new see for Norfolk. He died between 693 and 706.

BAEDA (1)   It is generally assumed that the name goes back to shortening of a compound name. It probably arose from a stem **baudi-*, connected with OHG *biotan*, OE *bēodan* 'to bid' and in particular with the preterite *bēad* ⟨**baud*, to which an *i*-suffix was added. Cf. Zimmer[9], MÜLLER 47, REDIN 60 f., 126, LUICK I,180, EKWALL ST I,4 f., STRÖM 63, ANDERSON LB 103, SCHRAMM 138, CAMPBELL 80.

The author of HE.

bald/balt   OHG *bald*, OE *b(e)ald* 'bold, brave'. It is used as a first el. in combination with **hild** (1), and as a second el. in combination with **aedil/edil** (1), **cud** (1), **ead/ed/æad** (1), **here/heri** (2), and **hyg** (1). The form **balt** occurs in the combination with **hild**.

BALTHILD (1)   **bald/balt; hild.**

At one time an Anglo-Saxon slave, she married Clovis II, who was King of the Franks from 638 to 656. She retired as a nun to the monastery of Chelles in 664, where she died in 680.

baru   OHG *baro*, OE *bearu* 'wood, grove'. It occurs in **adBARUAE** (1).

adBARUAE (2)   For the preposition see **ad.** The main component is **baru.** The dative singular of the OE word is *bearwe*.

Barrow-upon-Humber, Lincolnshire.

---

[9] H. Zimmer, "Zur orthographie des namens Beda", *Neues Archiv der Gesellschaft für ältere deutsche Geschichtskunde* 16 (1891), 599-601.

BEGU (1)   An Irish name. HOLDER I,366 offers no etymology. DAHL 116 groups it with pure ō-stems.

> Nun at Hackness for more than thirty years in the first half of the seventh century.

berct/berht/berict   OHG *beraht/berht*, OE *be(o)rht* 'bright, beautiful, noble'. It is used independently once, and as a first el. in combination with **frid/frit** (1), **hun** (3) and **uald** (7). As a second el. it is used in combination with **aedil/edil** (2), **agil** (4), **cud** (19), **cyni** (3), **ead/ed/æad** (7)[10], **earcon/ercon** (4), **ec/ecg** (26), **here/heri** (4), **huaet** (1), **sa** (1), **suid** (4), **tond** (1), **trum** (1), **tun** (2), and with **uict/uiht** (3). The spelling **berht** occurs only once in **AGILBERHT**; **berict** appears in **BERICTHUN** (2).

BERCT (1)   Short form of compounds with **berct/berht/berict** as a first or second el.[11]

> He was sent with an army to Ireland in 684 by King Ecgfrid of Northumbria (*s.v.*).

BERCTFRID (1)   berct/berht/berict; frid/frit.

> Northumbrian ealdorman who fought against the Picts in 711.

BERCTHUN (1)   berct/berht/berict; hun.

> Ruler of Sussex for a short time, together with Andhun (*s.v.*). He was killed by Caedualla (*s.v.*) between 685 and 688.

BERCTUALD (7)   berct/berht/berict;uald.

> He was consecrated Archbishop of Canterbury in 693, and died in 731.

inBERECINGUM (1)   For the preposition see **in**, and for the suffix see **ingas**. The first component is taken to be an unrecorded OE personal name **Berica*, corresponding to OHG *Berico*, probably connected with an OE by-name *Bera* which is identical with OHG *bero*, OE *bera* 'bear', to which the diminutive suffix *-(i)ca* was added. Cf. SCHÖNFELD 50, STENTON EE 47, GREEN 110, ANDERSON LB 74, DEPN 26, EKWALL PNsING 18, CAMERON 67, NI, GEL & RI 18. REANEY OR 1[12], however, prefers to take the name as a toponymic derived from OE *beorc* 'birch', in accordance with the views expressed by Zachrisson[13]. This is shown to be impossible by EKWALL PNsING (*l.c.*).

---

[10] One of these is a mistake for **ald**, see **EADBERCT 4 = ALDBERCT**.

[11] It has been suggested that the bearer of this name is identical with *Berctred* of the annal for 698 in HE V,24, which annal is omitted by C and K. Cf. STRÖM 64, and CO & MY 427, n. 4. Berctred was killed by the Picts in 698.

[12] Also in *The Place-Names of Essex* (EPNS XII), Cambridge 1935, pp. 88 f.

[13] R. E. Zachrisson, "English Place-name Puzzles. A Methodological Investigation into the Question of Personal Names or Descriptive Words in English Place-names", *Studia Neophilologica* V (1932/33), 1-69.

Barking, Essex. OET 540 mistakenly identifies it with the county of Berkshire.

BERICINENSIS (1)   Latinized adjectival form in connection with **inBERE-CINGUM.**

Of Barking, Essex.

BERICTHUN (2)   **berct/berht/berict; hun.**

Abbot of Beverley, Yorks, at the time of Bede's writing. He had founded this monastery together with Bishop John of Hexham.

bern   OHG *baro*, OE *beorn* 'man, warrior', or possibly connected with the tribal name **BERNICII.** It is used as a first el. in combination with **uini** (1).

BERNICII (2)   It is a Latinization of an originally British name. JACKSON LHEB 701 ff. devotes an Appendix to the etymology of this name, and rejects derivation from **brigant-*, a participial stem based on Celtic **brĭg-* 'height', a derivation held by many scholars. He suggests a Celtic stem **bernā/*birnā* (>Old Irish *bern*) 'a gap, a mountain pass'. The meaning would then be something like 'the people of the land of mountain passes'. Cf. also CAMPBELL 55, n. 1, CAMERON 50.

The Bernicii lived in and around the Pennines.

BERNUINI (1)   **bern; uini.**

A nephew of Bishop Uilfrid 1 (*s.v.*); he helped to evangelise the Isle of Wight around the year 686.

BISCOP (2)   A personal name connected with OE *bisc(e)op* (< Latin *episcopus*) 'bishop'. Cf. REDIN 18, n. 1, FEILITZEN DB 202, TENGVIK 238, STRÖM 65, ANDERSON LB 70. The possibility of this by-name has been doubted by PLUMMER II,355 and by MÜLLER 40, who see in it a compound word **bis-scop*. The first el. of this word would then go back to a stem **bis* 'to be exultant' (see also **BISI**) and the second to OHG *scof*, OE *scop* 'poet'.

Benedict Biscop, an Anglian born of noble parents around 630, was founder of the new monastery at Wearmouth in 674. He paid six visits to Rome. He died around 690.

BISI (2)   Of obscure, but certainly native origin; cf. Björkmann[14]. It may be based on a stem **bis* underlying OHG *pison* 'to be exultant'. Cf. REDIN 132, STRÖM 65, and also FÖRSTEMANN I, 308. In a footnote Ström also suggests a possible connection with OE *bisig* 'busy'.

He became Bishop of East Anglia around 669, and when around 675 a serious illness prevented him from executing his duties any further, he was succeeded by Aecci (*s.v.*) and Baduini (*s.v.*).

---

[14] E. Björkmann, *Zur englischen Namenkunde* (Studien zur englischen Philologie 47), Halle 1912; p. 24.

blith   OHG *blīdi*, OE *blīþe* 'cheerful, gay'. It is used as a first el. in combination with **thryd/thryth** (1).

BLITHTHRYD (1)   blith; thryd/thryth. The name is the English reflection of a Continental Germanic name, and as such is not discussed by STRÖM. She was the wife of King Pippin of the Franks (*s.v.*), and is normally known by the name of *Plectrudis*. She tried to seize the kingship at her husband's death in 714. The date of her death is unknown.

BOISIL (8)   The name is an -*il*-diminutive of **BOSA**. Cf. also **BOSEL**. Prior of Melrose; teacher and friend of Cudberct (*s.v.*). He died around 660.

BORUCTUARI (3)   The second el. of this Latinized tribal name, which often appears as *Bructeri*, is **uari**. The first el. is by SCHÖNFELD 54 related to a stem *bṛht-*, probably connected with OHG *brehhan*, OE *brecan* 'to break, to burst', which would give the meaning 'the unruly, the rebellious'[15]. FÖRSTEMANN II,1,578 and 589 connects it with OHG *bruok*, OE *brōc* 'brook, swamp.' Cf. also ANDERSON LB 78 and BACH I,1,191.
   A German tribe.

BOSA (6)   Various etymologies have been proposed for this name. HOLTHAU-SEN 31 connects it with OE *b(e)asu* 'purple', mentioned as a remote possibility by both REDIN 86 and STRÖM 66. Redin, however, prefers derivation from OHG *bōsi* 'angry'; cf. also FÖRSTEMANN I, 329, SCHÖNFELD 52 f. This again is rejected, on account of its stem-vowel, by Ström (*l.c.*) and ANDERSON LB 69, who prefer to identify the name with the Old Norse by-name *Bósi*, which is connected with modern Norwegian *bose* 'big fellow'. According to KAUFMANN UAR 124 f. and KAUFMANN ERG 68 f. the name may well be based on a stem **Bausja*, connected with modern Norwegian *baus* 'brave', which is unlikely because in that case the Umlaut of the stem-vowel could not have resulted in long -*ō*-.
   A monk at Streanaeshalch (*s.v.*, = Whitby), he was consecrated Bishop of York in 678 as one of the three successors of Uilfrid 1 (*s.v.*), when the latter was expelled by King Ecgfrid (*s.v.*). Bosa in his turn was expelled in 686, but restored in 691. He died around 705.

BOSANHAMM (1)   The first component of this place-name is the personal name **BOSA** in the genitive singular. The second component is spelled -*hamm* by both the M-type texts M and L and the C-type text K, so it may safely be assumed that the theme is OE *hamm* and not OE *hām*. Cf. ANDERSON LB 74, GELLING 141. GREEN 46 wavers between the two. From an early date the two themes were almost indistinguishable, which is also the reason why some scholars refrain from identifying the theme in our name; cf. KARL-STRÖM PNsING 48, MA & ST SUS 58, MAGOUN '38 150, DEPN 53. The theme **hamm** has been interpreted as 'enclosure', connected with OE *hemm*

---

[15] Schönfeld assumes that both -*o*- and the first -*u*- may be due to svarabhakti.

'hem (of a garment)', and as 'flat, low-lying river-meadow', connected with modern dialectal English *ham* with the same sense. Cf. MIDDENDORFF 64, ANDERSON HN III, 181, EPNE I,229 ff., CAMERON 191, DEPN 214, EKWALL PNsING 117. GELLING 141 arrives at the conclusion that **hamm** originally meant 'land almost surrounded by water', which then developed into 'river-meadow' and at a later date also came to mean 'an enclosed plot'. GELLING 145 also suggests that on the South coast the theme is even used in the sense of 'promontory' or 'a piece of land in a sharp loop of a river', an example of which would be **BOSANHAMM**.

Bosham, Sussex.

BOSEL (2)   The name is an *-il* ⟩ *-el*, or possibly *-ul* ⟩ *-el*, diminutive of **BOSA**. Cf. MÜLLER 69 f., REDIN 138 f., 141, STRÖM 66, ANDERSON LB 106. Although Redin acknowledges the possibility of derivation from **BOSA**, he thinks that **BOSEL** and **BOISIL** are Celtic in contrast to **BOSA**; cf. also HOLDER I, 495.

He was consecrated Bishop of the Huiccii (*s.v.*) around 680. His see was at Worcester. Ill-health forced him to resign in 691, when he was succeeded by Oftfor (*s.v.*).

bregu   OE *bregu* 'prince', possibly cognate with Old Norse *Bragi*, the name of a god. Cf. BOEHLER 41 f., STRÖM 9 f., ANDERSON LB 95. It is used in combination with **suid** (1).

BREGUSUID (1)   **bregu; suid.**

Wife of Hereric (*s.v.*), nephew of King Eduini of Northumbria (*s.v.*). Her daughter Hild (*s.v.*) was born in 614.

BRETTONES (10)   A Latinized form of the British tribal name **Brittones*, which in OE appears as *Breotone*. Cf. HOLTHAUSEN 34, JACKSON LHEB 567, 672. According to EKWALL EN 150 ff. and DEPN 66 there may be a connection with the Old Welsh word for Picts, viz. *Priten*, which is related to modern Welsh *pryd* 'figure, picture'; the name thus might 'refer to the custom of the ancient Britons to tattoo themselves'. Cf. also HOLDER I, 552.

The original inhabitants of Britain.

BRITTANI (1)   Another Latin equivalent of **BRETTONES**.
The original inhabitants of Britain.

BRITTANIA (60)   Latinized form of the country-name related to **BRETTONES**.
Britain.

BRIUDUN (1)   The first component of the place-name derives from Old British **brigā* 'hill'. Cf. JACKSON LHEB 455, DEPN 62. This element appears in a number of English place-names. The second component is **dun**. HOLDER I, 610 offers no etymological suggestions. The uncertainty about the etymology of **BRIUDUN** is fully represented in the relevant literature. Crawford[16] and MAGOUN '38 151 propose derivation from early British *$d\bar{u}no$-* 'camp', which EKWALL CE 25 and EPNE I, 139 are willing to consider. ANDERSON LB 102, JACKSON LHEB 320, DEPN 62, CAMERON 39, and REANEY OR 75 prefer to connect it with **dun**. GREEN 48 mentions both derivations as possibilities.

Breedon-on-the-Hill, Leicestershire.

brod/brord OHG *brort*, OE *brord* 'point, lance'. The spelling **brod**, which occurs four times, is characteristic of C-type texts. This fluctuation of spelling may have been caused by the related Celtic word which was derived from British **brozdo-s* (> Middle Irish *brot* 'prick'). Cf. FÖRSTER TH 186, n. 3[17]. The abovementioned generally accepted derivation of the name-theme is left for derivation from OHG *brōdr*, OE *brōdor* 'brother' by KAUFMANN ERG 72. It is used as a second el. in combination with **uil** (7).

burg OHG *burg*, OE *burg/burh* 'castle, town', or connected with OHG *bergan*, OE *beorgan* 'to protect'. Cf. MÜLLER 121, BOEHLER 136, REDIN 45, FEILITZEN DB 211, STRÖM 10, ANDERSON LB 98, BACH I, 1, 224, SCHRAMM 159, KAUFMANN ERG 75 f. It is used as a first el. in combination with **helm** (1), and as a second el. in combination with **aedil/edil** (4), **here/heri** (1), **quoen** (1), and **saex/sax/sex**(1). It also occurs as a component of the place-name **UILTABURG** (1).

BURGHELM (1)   **burg; helm.**
He was a priest who helped Bishop Uilfrid 1 (*s.v.*) in the conversion of Sussex around 685.

CAEDMON (1)   A name of Celtic origin, derived from Old British **Catumanos* which is connected with *catu* 'war', used in the sense of 'warrior', the corresponding OE form of which is *headu*. Cf. FÖRSTER KW 179, HOLTHAUSEN 42, STRÖM 92, n. 2, ANDERSON LB 70, 91, FÖRSTER TH 66,n. and 664, n. 1, JACKSON LHEB 272, CAMPBELL 252, n. 1.
He was a member of the monastic community of Hild (*s.v.*) at Streanaeshalch (*s.v.*, = Whitby), and may have been of British descent. He was a poet. The date of his death, for which 680 has been suggested, remains uncertain.

CAEDUALLA (12)   A name of Celtic origin, derived from Old British **Cadwallǫn* which is connected with *catu* 'war' and with the British el. *-ụellaunos* 'powerful'. Cf. HOLTHAUSEN 44, ANDERSON LB 70, FÖRSTER TH 799, JACKSON LHEB 244, 295, 306. Cf. also HOLDER I, 878.

---

[16] O. G. S. Crawford, "Place-Names and Archeology", in: A. Mawer & F. M. Stenton (eds.), *Introduction to the Survey of English Place-Names* (EPNS I, 1), Cambridge 1924, pp. 155 ff.
[17] See below, PART IV, A. I. d.

He was born around 659, and was King of the West Saxons from 685 to 688. In this year he abdicated and went to Rome, where he was baptized shortly before his death in 689[18].

cęstir   Connected with Latin *castra* 'fort, fortified place'. It is used as a second component in the place-names **DORCICCĘSTRAE** (1), **GRANTACĘSTIR** (1), **HROFESCĘSTIR** (1), **KĘLCACĘSTIR** (1), and **TUNNACĘSTIR** (1).

CALE (1)   A Gaulish place-name, which according to FÖRSTER TH 313 goes back to pre-Romanic *Cala*. DAU & ROS 167 connect it with Vulgar Latin **cala* 'shelter under a rock'. Cf. also GREEN 112.
  Chelles, France.

CANTIA (14)   The Latinized form of the Celtic district-name that is connected with British **Cantįon*, Romano-British *Cantium*. Cf. JACKSON LHEB 600, and also ANDERSON LB 91, REANEY OR 71. Relation with modern Welsh *cant* (⟨ **canto-*) 'rim, border' is suggested by DEPN 272. CAMERON 48 gives as a possible meaning of the tribal name 'the hosts', related with modern Welsh *cant* (⟨ **canto-*) 'host, party'. Both meanings are considered possible by EPNE I, 80, but JACKSON RPNs 55, who gives a full survey of the etymologies proposed, shows a preference for 'the hosts'. HOLDER I, 749 and I, 752 and GREEN 52 suggest derivation from Welsh *cant* 'rim, border' and from a stem *canto* 'white, bright' respectively. Holder's latter suggestion is supported by JENSEN AIO 428 f.
  Kent, the county.

CANTUARII (15)   **CANTIA**; **uari**.
  The men of Kent.

CEADDA (9)   Ultimately of Celtic origin, this is a short name of compounds with **catu**, connected with Old British *catu* 'war'; cf. also **CAEDMON**. There has been hypocoristic doubling of the /d/. Its form shows that the name had been completely assimilated into OE. Cf. FÖRSTER KW 179 f., HOLTHAUSEN 44, STRÖM 93, 107, ANDERSON LB 70, 139, n., FÖRSTER TH 802, ARNGART 130, JACKSON LHEB 554, REANEY OR 66, FEILITZEN ST 5. In modern English the name is *Chad*.
  This brother of Cedd (*s.v.*) was Abbot of Lastingham, and then Bishop of York from 664 to 669, and of Lichfield from 669 to 672.

c(e)alc   see **KĘLCACĘSTIR**

CEDD (1)   A name of Celtic origin, derived from compound names with **catu** which is connected with Old British *catu* 'war'; cf. also **CAEDMON**. There has been hypocoristic doubling of the /d/, and *i*-mutation of original /a/ (⟩ /æ/)

---

[18] From his Celtic name it has been concluded that the West Saxon royal family had intermarried with Britons.

to /e/ after the palatal consonant. See also **CEADDA**. Cf. ANDERSON LB 69 f., 94, JACKSON LHEB 554.

> He was a brother of Ceadda (*s.v.*). He founded the monastery of Lastingham near Whitby. Around 654 he was consecrated Bishop of London. He died in 664.

ceol OHG *kiol*, OE *cēol* 'keel, ship'. It is used as a first el. in combination with **frid/frit** (8), **raed/red** (2), and **uulf** (2).

CEOLFRID (8) **ceol; frid/frit.**

> He helped Benedict Biscop (*s.v.*) found the monastery of Wearmouth in 674, and was Abbot of Jarrow from its foundation in 681. He succeeded Benedict Biscop as Abbot of the two monasteries at the latter's death. He resigned in 716, and died in France on his way to Rome in that year.

CEOLRED (2) **ceol; raed/red.**

> Son of King Aedilred of Mercia (*s.v.*), and Osthryd (*s.v.*), he reigned from 709 to 716.

CEOLUULF (2) **ceol; uulf.**

> He was King of Northumbria from 729 onwards. Bede dedicated HE to him. In 731 he was deposed and restored again, and in 737 he resigned and retired to Lindisfarne. He died around 760.

CEOROTESEI (1) **CEOROTUS; ei/eu/ę.** Cf. EKWALL CE 20, GOVER etc. SU 105 ff., MAGOUN '35 78, GREEN 58, ANDERSON LB 70, 74, DEPN 100, CAMERON 31, REANEY OR 66, NI, GEL & RI 71.

> Chertsey, Surrey.

CEOROTUS (1) A Celtic personal name of obscure origin. Cf. HOLDER I, 994.

> It is the first component of the place-name **CEOROTESEI** (1).

CERDIC (1) This name of Celtic origin probably goes back to British **Caratīcos*, which may be connected with Welsh *caredig* 'beloved'. Cf. REDIN 151, EKWALL RN lxviii f., FÖRSTER TH 285, 852, JACKSON LHEB 554, 613 f.

> This King of the British kingdom of Elmete was expelled by King Eduini of Northumbria (*s.v.*). He probably died in 616.

CLOFAESHOOH (1) The first component of this place-name is assumed to be an unrecorded personal name **Kluba* by KÖHLER 37, although he records that OET 580 and MIDDENDORFF 27 suggest connection with OE *clēofan* 'to split'. Other scholars have taken up the latter suggestion and have proposed an OE noun **clof/*clofa* 'crevice', corresponding to Old Norse *klof*, modern Dutch *kloof*. Cf. KARLSTRÖM KIL 131, MAGOUN '35 78 f., ANDERSON LB 74, 98, EPNE I, 99, EKWALL ST III, 20 f., DEPN 113. GREEN 59 mentions the latter derivation, but also suggests that the first component

132

may be connected with a personal name *Ceolf*, a short form of *Ceoluulf*, which may be said to be unlikely .The second component is *hooh*.

In the past this famous meeting-place not far from London has been identified with Cliffe-at-Hoo, Kent. Stenton[19] has shown this to be impossible. EKWALL ST III, 21 suggests "the central part of Hoo Hundred, Hoo St. Werburg (or Hoo) NE of Rochester".

coen/coin OHG *kuoni*, OE *cēne* 'bold, fierce'. It is used as a first el. in combination with **raed/red** (10) and **ualch/ualh** (1). The spelling **coen** occurs twice in **COINRED 2**.

COINRED 1 (3) **coen/coin; raed/red.**
He was a brother of Ceoluulf (*s.v.*), and was King of Northumbria from 716 to 718.

COINRED 2 (7) **coen/coin; raed/red.**
Son of Uulfheri (*s.v.*), he succeeded King Aedilred of Mercia (*s.v.*) in 704. In 709 he abdicated and went to Rome, where he died in the same year.

COINUALCH (1) **coen/coin; ualch/ualh.**
He became King of Wessex in 643. He was in exile in East Anglia from 645 to 648, when he became a Christian. In 648 he was restored, and he probably died in 674.

COLMAN (5) An Old Irish personal name, connected with *Columba*. Cf. HOLDER I, 1066, FORSSNER 55 f., Ekwall[20], STRÖM 92, JACKSON LHEB 509. SMIT 156, n. 26[b], suggests that the name is derived from Old Irish *colum* 'dove' and a diminutive suffix -*an*.

He was an Irishman who became Bishop of Lindisfarne in 661. In 664 he resigned and returned to Ireland. He died in 676.

COLUDANA (urbs) (1) Latinized adjectival form connected with **COLUDI**.
Of Coldingham, Berwickshire (Scotland).

COLUDI (urbs) (2) The etymology of *Colud* is obscure. HOLDER I, 1067, FÖRSTER KW 176, and FÖRSTER TH 313 interpret it as a personal name. EKWALL VC 19 and EKWALL PNsING 158 suggest that *Colud* in itself is an Old British name of the place, from which **COL(U)DINGAS** 'the people at *Colud*' and modern *Coldingham* were formed. GREEN 64 mentions both derivations.
Coldingham, Berwickshire (Scotland).

COLUMBA (6) The Latin form, usually found in Anglo-Saxon sources as

---

[19] F. M. Stenton, *The Place-Names of Berkshire*, Reading 1911, p. 14.
[20] E. Ekwall, *Scandinavians and Celts in the North-West of England* (Lunds Universitets Årsskrift, N. F., Avd. 1, 14:27), Lund 1918; p. 36.

well, of Old Irish **COLUMCELLI**. Cf. FÖRSTER TH 739. The identification with Latin *columba* 'dove' is the more understandable, if one accepts the assumption made by SMIT 156, n. 26[b], that the Irish form originally was *Columbán* 'white dove'.

> This Irish saint founded the monastery of Iona around 565. He died about 597.

COLUMCELLI (1)   This is the regular form the personal name **COLUMBA** takes in Irish sources. It is composed of Old Irish *colum* 'dove' and *cell* (⟨ Latin *cella*) 'church' as also HE V,9 explains. Cf. PLUMMER II, 286, FÖRSTER TH 738 f., SMIT 156, n. 26[b].

> For biographical details see the preceding name.

cud   OHG *kund*, OE *cūþ* 'known, famous'. It is used as a first el. in combination with **bald/balt** (1) and **berct/berht/berict** (19).

CUDBALD (1)   cud; bald/balt.

> He was Abbot of the monastery of Oundle at the time when Uilfrid 1 (*s.v.*) died there in 709[21].

CUDBERCT (19)   cud; berct/berht/berict.

> He first led a solitary life in Farne Island, and then for many years was a monk and Prior at Melrose and Lindisfarne. He was consecrated Bishop of Hexham in 685, and was transferred to Lindisfarne soon after. He died in Farne Island in 687.

cuic   see **quic**

inCUNENINGUM (1)   The etymology of this Celtic district name is unknown. For the preposition see **in**, and for the suffix **ingas**. Cf. WATSON 186, GREEN 114, ANDERSON LB 74, 125, EKWALL PNsING 78 f.

> Cunningham, a district in North Ayrshire (Scotland).

cyni   OHG *kunni*, OE *cyn(n)* 'kin, family', and OHG *kuni-*, OE *cyne-* 'royal'. Cf. MÜLLER 84, BOEHLER 46 f., REDIN 47, STRÖM 11 f., ANDERSON LB 99, SCHRAMM 98, KAUFMANN ERG 86. It is used as a first el. in combination with **berct/berht/berict** (3) and **frid/frit** (1).

CYNIBERCT 1 (1)   cyni; berct/berht/berict.

> A priest who was Abbot of the monastery of Hreutford (*s.v.*) around the year 680.

CYNIBERCT 2 (2)   cyni; berct/berht/berict.

> He was Bishop of Lindsey in the period from 716 until his death in 732. He provided Bede with information on the diocese.

---

[21] His name is recorded by PLUMMER I, 330 as *Cuduald* on the basis of the reading in M; this reading STRÖM 163 also follows.

134

CYNIFRID (1) **cyni; frid/frit.**
A physician who was at the death-bed of Aedilthryd (*s.v.*) in her monastery at Ely, around 680.

DACORE (1) This river-name goes back to a Celtic base **dakru* 'tear', connected with Gothic *tagr*, OE *téar*. In Bede we may have the genitive of a Latinized *Dacora* ⟨ *Dacr*, as EKWALL RN 111 suggests, but more likely is that it is the accusative of OE **Dacor*; cf. GREEN 66, and see **ALNE**. Cf. FÖRSTER TH 325, ARMSTRONG etc. CU I, 10, DEPN 137, JACKSON LHEB 556. HOLDER I, 1213 offers no etymology.
The Dacre is a small river in Cumberland.

DANAI (1) The Latinized form of a Continental Germanic tribal name, usually appearing in Latin as *Dani* and in OE as *Dene*. SCHÖNFELD 70 f. and HOLTHAUSEN 71 connect the name with OE *denu* 'valley', whereas KAUFMANN ERG 91 suggests connection with OHG *tanna* 'fir-tree', which possibly developed a meaning 'spear', or with the related OHG *tan* 'wood'. Cf. also PLUMMER II, 286.
The Danes.

degn OHG *thegan*, OE *þeg(e)n* 'thane, servant, warrior'. It is used as a second el. in combination with **badu** (1).

DEGSASTAN (1) The first component of this place-name is commonly explained as the genitive singular of the short form of a personal name. FÖRSTER TH 810 derives it from a Celtic name **Dagiss-*, connected with Old British *dago-s* 'good', which derivation JACKSON LHEB 560, 612 thinks is very doubtful. MAGOUN '35 80 records both this possibility and the one supported by ANDERSON LB 73, viz. derivation from a name-theme **dag**, which is common in OHG names and is connected with OHG *tag*, OE *dæg* 'day'. The *-s-* of *degsa-* Anderson explains with a reference to OE *dæg* being an old *s*-stem; cf. also HIRT II,57. The second component is **stan**.

> There is uncertainty about the identification. PLUMMER II, 66 and KÖHLER 31 suggest Dawston in Liddesdale, Cumberland, a view shared by BOSWORTH-TOLLER I, 193 f., WATSON 130, Förster (*l.c.*) and HOLTHAUSEN 69. Magoun (*l.c.*) rejects this identification, and GREEN 68, ANDERSON LB 152 and CO & MY 117 think it is doubtful. ARMSTRONG etc. CU I, 39 has no reference to **DEGSASTAN** under Liddesdale, Cumberland.

inDERAUUDA (1) The preposition **in**, and **DERI; uuda.** Cf. GREEN 115, SMITH ERY 12, EKWALL TN 165, EKWALL VC 33.
Beverley, Yorkshire East Riding.

DERI (3) Traditionally connected with Welsh *deifr* 'waters', an obsolete and artificial plural form, from which an Old British word **dovrįā* 'waterland' was constructed which could have led to **DERI**. Cf. HOLDER I, 1260, EKWALL CE 21, FÖRSTER TH 83, HOLTHAUSEN 72, CAMERON 50. JACKSON

LHEB 419 f., however, throws doubt on this etymology, but does not offer anything else in its stead except that the word was very likely a borrowing from a Primitive Welsh *Deir ⟨ *Deiƀr, "probably of some quite different origin".

> Northumbria consisted of Bernicia and Deira. The traditional etymology was taken to suggest that "the centre of the original kingdom was along the rivers flowing into the Humber", cf. CAMERON 50.

DERUUENTIO (1) This Celtic river-name is derived from British *derụā 'oak'; the -nt-ending is obscure. Its meaning may have been something like 'river where oaks grow abundantly'. Cf. KÖHLER 32, FÖRSTER KW 210, EKWALL RN 122 f., GREEN 70, SMITH ERY 2 f., RI & CR 31, ARMSTRONG etc. CU I, 11, JACKSON LHEB 282, CAMERON 38. HOLDER I, 1271 offers no etymology. Another possibility for the first part may be the same derivation JENSEN AIO 429 suggests for **DORUUERNIS**.

> The river Derwent, Yorkshire and Cumberland.

DICUL (1) A Celtic name of obscure origin. Cf. HOLDER I, 1282.

> He was an Irish monk who was Abbot of a small monastery at Bosham, Sussex, around 670.

DORCICCẸSTRAE (1) The first component of this place-name is Celtic, according to DEPN 148 derived from a root derk- 'bright, splendid'. Cf. GREEN 74, and cf. also KÖHLER 32, and Gelling[22]. HOLDER I, 1308 offers no etymology. The second component is cẹstir.

> Dorchester, Oxfordshire.

DORUUERNENSIS (4) Latinized adjectival form synonymous with **DORUUERNIS**.

> Of Canterbury, Kent.

DORUUERNIS (2) This Latinized adjectival form of a Celtic place-name and **DORUUERNENSIS** are used side by side by Bede. They are connected with Old British *duro- 'fort, walled town' and Old British *verno- 'alders, swamp'. The combination means 'the swamp by the fort' according to EKWALL VC 41 and NI, GEL & RI 66 f., and 'the town by the alder swamp' according to EPNE I, 140. Cf. ZACHRISSON RKS 77, GREEN 77, FÖRSTER TH 250, JACKSON LHEB 259 f., EKWALL TN 133 f., EPNE II,230, DEPN 85. JENSEN AIO 429 considers the first component to be an Indo-European ro-adjective from the root dheu- 'to run, to flow'. For a different view of the origin of the second component see ALESSIO 225, who looks upon the second component as a suffix with Mediterranean links. HOLDER I, 1241 offers no etymological suggestions.

> Of Canterbury, Kent.

---

[22] Margaret Gelling, *The Place-Names of Oxfordshire*, Parts I-II (EPNS XXIII-XXIV), Cambridge 1953-1954; I, 152.

136

dryct OHG *truht,* OE *dryht* 'band of retainers'. It is used as a first el. in combination with **helm** (1).

DRYCTHELM (1)   **dryct; helm.**
A saintly man from Cunningham, who was married with children, when about 690 he entered the monastery of Melrose.

dun This place-name el. may be connected with OE *dūn* 'hill', modern Dutch *duin.* This is certainly the origin of the el. in **UETADUN**. Some doubt exists, however, as to its etymology in **BRIUDUN**, since the first component of this name is British. In this case some have suggested derivation from early British **dūno-* 'camp'; cf. HOLDER I, 1375 ff. But at the time of the Anglo-Saxon settlement this word had already changed to Old Welsh *dīn.* Adoption of the form itself cannot have taken place. There is, of course, the possibility that the Anglo-Saxons adapted *dīn* to OE *dūn.* Cf. FÖRSTER KW 166 ff., JACKSON LHEB 320, EPNE I, 139. It is used as a second component in **BRIUDUN** (1) and **UETADUN** (1). See also **LUGDUNUM**.

DUUNCHAD (1)   According to HOLDER I, 1374 this Old Irish personal name is an equivalent of *Dūnŏ-cătŭ-s* 'warrior of the fort'.
He was Abbot of Iona around the year 710.

ea OHG *aha,* OE *ēa* 'river, stream'. It is used as a component in **HOMEL·EA·**(1).

EABAE   see **AEBAE**

ead/ed/æad OHG *ōt* (Gothic *auda*), OE *ēad* 'bliss, happiness; prosperity'. The form **ed** is due to *i*-mutation under the influence of the vowel of the following unstressed component of the name. Cf. MÜLLER 79, LUICK I,167, HOLTHAUSEN 88, STRÖM 12 f., ANDERSON LB 105, CAMPBELL 83, BRUNNER AG 70. BOEHLER 70 reckons with the possibility that **ed** was derived from a separate Primitive Germanic **audi,* of uncertain meaning. It is used as a first el., spelled **ead,** in combination with **bald/balt** (1), **berct/berht/berict** (6), **gar** (1), **gyd** (3), and **haed** (5). It is used in the same way, but spelled **æad,** in combination with **berct/berht/berict** (1), and spelled **ed,** in combination with **gisl** (1), **ric** (2), and **uini** (4).

EADBALD (1)   **ead/ed/æad; bald/balt.**
Son of King Aedilberct 1 of Kent (*s.v.*), whom he succeeded in 616. He died in 640.

EADBERCT 1 (1)   **ead/ed/æad; berct/berht/berict.**
He succeeded his father King Uictred of Kent (*s.v.*) in 725 together with his brothers Aedilberct 2 (*s.v.*) and Alric (*s.v.*). He probably died in 748.

EADBERCT 2 (3)   **ead/ed/æad; berct/berht/berict.**
He was Bishop of Lindisfarne from 688 until his death in 698.

137

EADBERCT 3 (2)   ead/ed/æad; berct/berht/berict.

He was Abbot at Selsey, where he also had his see as Bishop of the South Saxons. He was consecrated Bishop between 709 and 716, and died between 716 and 731.

EADBERCT 4 = ALDBERCT (1)   ead/ed/æad; berct/berht/berict[23].

Aldberct was Bishop of part of East Anglia from between 716 and 731 until between 731 and 747. His see was at Dunwich.

EADGAR (1)   ead/ed/æad; gar.

He was Bishop of Lindsey from around 693 until between 716 and 731.

EADGYD (3)   ead/ed/æad; gyd.

A nun in the monastery of Barking who died shortly after Aesica (*s.v.*), possibly in 664.

EADHAED (5)   ead/ed/æad; haed.

He was a companion of Ceadda (*s.v.*). He was consecrated Bishop of Lindsey in 678. Soon after he was transferred to Ripon. He died in 680.

ean/aen.   Etymology is obscure. STRÖM 13 suggests as the most likely base a Germanic **auna-* (> OHG *ōn-*). ANDERSON LB 68 dismisses derivation from a Germanic base **ahan-*, connected with Germanic **ah* 'sharp, keen', as altogether impossible. Cf. also SCHÖNFELD 177, BJÖRKMANN ST 15 ff., BOEHLER 64. The further etymology of **auna-* has generally been held to be uncertain. SCHRAMM 150 f., however, believes that **auna-* and its parallel form **auni-*, from which the form **aen** could have developed by *i*-mutation, may be looked upon as developments from *awi-* ⟨ **a(g)wjō* 'watery place', also found in Gothic *awi-liuþ* 'song of thanksgiving', a connection supported by HOLTHAUSEN 84. The name-theme occurs as **aen** in combination with **here/heri** (1), and as **ean** in combination with **flaed/fled** (3) and **frid/frit** (1).

EANFLED (3)   ean/aen; flaed/fled.

She was a daughter of King Eduini of Deira (*s.v.*), born in 626, and was married to King Osuiu of Bernicia (*s.v.*). See also **AELBFLED**.

EANFRID (1)   ean/aen; frid/frit.

He and his brother Aenheri (*s.v.*) were joint rulers of the Huiccii (*s.v.*), under King Aedilred of Mercia (*s.v.*), around the year 680.

EAPPA (1)   Probably short form of compound names with **eorp**, which name-theme is connected with OHG *erpf*, OE *eorp* 'brown, swarthy'. Cf. REDIN

---

[23] Four persons called *Eadberct* occur in Bede's HE, three in Books IV and V. Replacement of **ALDBERCT** by **EADBERCT** in itself, therefore, is quite possible. For possible phonological implications of this replacement see PART IV, A. I.a.5, n. 2.

65, STRÖM 14, ANDERSON LB 96, 122. Other formations are, of course, conceivable. Thus the short form could have arisen from *Eadberct*, and in this connection it should be noted that it has been suggested that Eappa is the same man as Eadberct 3 (*s.v.*). Cf. REDIN 65, n. 3.

He was one of the helpers of Uilfrid 1 (*s.v.*) in the conversion of Sussex around 680, and later became Abbot of Selsey.

earcon/ercon   OHG *erchan* 'genuine, excellent', in OE known as a name-theme, and found also in *eorcnan-stān*, variant form *eorcan-stān*, 'precious stone'; cf. BOSWORTH-TOLLER 253, HOLTHAUSEN 92. Cf. MÜLLER 96, FORSS-NER 75, BOEHLER 71, STRÖM 14, ANDERSON LB 96. It is used as a first el. in combination with **berct/berht/berict** (4) and **uald** (3). The form **ercon** occurs twice in each of these two combinations.

EARCONBERCT (4)   earcon/ercon; berct/berht/berict.
Son of King Eadbald of Kent (*s.v.*), whom he succeeded in 640. His wife was Sexburg (*s.v.*), daughter of King Anna of East Anglia (*s.v.*).

EARCONUALD (3)   earcon/ercon; uald.
He was Bishop of London from 675 to 693.

EATA (9)   Short form of compound names with **ead/ed/æad** and a second el. probably opening with a voiceless consonant. Cf. MÜLLER 52, REDIN 64, STRÖM 68, ANDERSON LB 103, 122.
He was one of the English pupils of Aidan (*s.v.*), and was consecrated Bishop of Hexham in 678. In 681 he was transferred to Lindisfarne, where he was Bishop until 685. He died in Hexham in 686.

EBORACENSIS (5)   Latinized adjectival form of **EBORACUM**.
Of York, Yorkshire East Riding.

EBORACUM (9)   The first component of this Celtic place-name may be the common personal name *Eburos*, or the tree-name *eburos* 'yew' from which the personal name may be a derivative. The second component may be a suffix indicating possession, but more likely it is one of the very few instances in Britain of the suffix *-ācon* 'estate, villa', which suffix is common in Gaulish place-names. When taken over by the Anglo-Saxons, the word came to resemble OE *eofor* 'boar', with which it was then popularly identified. Cf. HOLDER I, 1395, Zachrisson[24], GREEN 78, RI & CR 33, SMITH ERY 275 ff., ANDERSON LB 84, FÖRSTER TH 249, JACKSON LHEB 39, 655, EPNE I, 153 f., DEPN 545, CAMERON 57, REANEY OR 24, NI, GEL & RI 197 f.
York, Yorkshire East Riding.

ec/ecg   OHG *ecka*, OE *ecg* 'edge, sword'. It is used as a first el. in combination

---

[24] R. E. Zachrisson, "Some Yorkshire Place-Names. York, Ure, Jervaulx", *The Modern Language Review* XXI (1926), p. 366.

with **berct/berht/berict** (26) and **frid/frit** (25). The spelling **ec** occurs in combination with **berct/berht/berict** 11 times and **frid/frit** 19 times.

ECGBERCT 1 (9)   ec/ecg; berct/berht/berict.
> Son of King Earconberct of Kent (*s.v.*). He succeeded his father in 664 and died around 672.

ECGBERCT 2 (17)   ec/ecg; berct/berht/berict.
> A monk of Iona, greatly admired by Bede. He lived from 639 to 729.

ECGFRID (25)   ec/ecg; frid/frit.
> He was a son of King Osuiu of Northumbria (*s.v.*), born in 645. He succeeded his father in 670, and died in 685.

EDGISL (1)   ead/ed/æad; gisl.
> A priest of the monastery of Coldingham, and in Bede's time of Wearmouth and Jarrow.

EDRIC (2)   ead/ed/æad; ric.
> Son of King Ecgberct of Kent (*s.v.*). He came to the throne in 685, and died in 687.

EDUINI (4)   ead/ed/æad; uini.
> He was a son of King Aelli of Deira, born in 584. He succeeded Aedilfrid as King of both Deira and Bernicia in 616. He died in 632.

eg   see **ei/eu/ę**

ei/eu/ę   OHG *ouwa* (⟨**aujo*⟩), OE *īeg, ēg* 'island'. Normal OE *īeg, ēg* is the form the inflected cases developed from the stem **aujō-*, which was then also used for the nominative; the form **eu**, a Northumbrian development, probably represents the regular development of this stem in the nominative case; **ei** is possibly just another spelling of *ēg*, although according to DAHL 99 ff. and BROOKS 30 it may also have to be understood as a locative of which the preceding preposition has been omitted. The form *ę* in **LAESTINGĘ** must be an amalgamation of final *-a* of *Laestinga* and *e* 'island'; see also **FARNE**. Cf. BROOKS 27 ff., and cf. also MIDDENDORFF 44, LUICK I, 117, GIRVAN 43, HOLTHAUSEN 86, ANDERSON LB 75, 104, FÖRSTER TH 290 ff., BACH II, 1, 276, CAMPBELL 46, DEPN 161, BRUNNER AG 49. DAHL 101, BROOKS 29, and Ekwall[25] have pointed out that the original form assumed by EPNE I, 147 for *ēg*, viz. Primitive Germanic **auhwi-*, is not correct. This place-name el. is used as a component of **CEOROTESEI** (1), **HERUTEU** (1), **LAESTINGAEU** (1; also **-INGĘ** and **-INGAEI** once each), and **SELAESEU** (2). It may also be a component in **FARNE** (7).

---

[25] In a review of EPNE in *Namn och Bygd* 45 (1957), 133-146.

el   OHG *āla*, OE *ǣl/ēl* 'eel'. It is used as a first component of **ELGE** (3).

ELGE (3)   **el; ge.** The confusion of the second component with *ēg* 'island' began in Old English times already. Cf. KÖHLER 30, GREEN 79, ANDERSON LB 99, REANEY CA 213 f., DEPN 166, NI, GEL & RI 90. HOLDER I, 1414 reckons with Celtic origin, which is improbable.
   Ely, Cambridgeshire.

EMME (1)   A name of Continental Germanic origin. Cf. STRÖM 181.
   He was Bishop of Sens, France, from 658 to 675.

EOLLA (2)   Probably a short form of compound names with **eorl**, connected with OHG *erl*, OE *eorl* 'noble warrior', although such names are not recorded in OE. Cf. REDIN 95, STRÖM 69, ANDERSON LB 96, 122.
   He was Bishop of Selsey some time between 717 and 731.

estr   OHG *ōstar*, OE *ēaster* 'east, eastern'. It is used with **ANGLI** (1).

ESTRANGLI (1)   **estr; ANGLI.**
   The East Angles.

fari   Latinized equivalent of OE **faran**, a plural form probably connected with OHG *faro*, OE *ge-fara* 'companion, traveller', although other derivations are possible. Cf. MAGOUN '38 164, FÖRSTER TH 166, ANDERSON LB 76, FORSBERG 137 f., EKWALL TN 145 ff., BACH I, 1, 193, SCHRAMM 168, KAUFMANN ERG 113 f. It occurs as the second component of the tribal-name **LINDISFARI** (4).

farn   see **FARNE**

FARNE (7)   A connection with OHG *farn*, OE *fearn* 'fern' is assumed by most scholars. Cf. OET 484, KÖHLER 32, DAHL 59, ANDERSON LB 75, 91, DEPN 175. HOLDER I, 1493 thinks it may be Celtic, and cf. also MAWER NO & DU 80 f. The interpretation of final *-e*, however, is uncertain. It may be an ending, in which case it probably has to be looked upon as the dative-locative which because of its frequent occurrence in that form also came to be used for the regular nominative-accusative forms. Dahl (*l.c.*) mentions the possibility of interpreting final *-e* as derived from the stem **aujo-* ⟩ OE *ēg* 'island', for which see **ei/eu/ę**, as does also GREEN 82. Anderson (*l.c.*) takes this to be the actual derivation because of the occurrence of the accent over final *-e* of *Farné* in L 60r, providing an exact parallel with *Laestinga é* of L 81 v. This is an acceptable explanation, although the uniformity of appearance of the name in all the MSS is somewhat striking, seeing the irregularity of treatment of **ei/eu/ę** in other names[26].

Farne Island, Northumberland.

FARO (1) A Continental Germanic name, for which see **fari**. Cf. STRÖM 181, DAUZAT NFP 247.

He was Bishop of Meaux, France, from 626 to 672.

feld/felth OHG, OE *feld* 'field, open country'. This place-name el. is used as a second el. in combination with **heath** (3) and with **liccid** (2), for which see **LICCIDFELTH**. The spelling **felth** is used where the el. is in final position.

flaed/fled OHG *flāt*, MHG *vlāt* 'cleanness, beauty', in OE known only as a name-theme. Cf. MÜLLER 133 f., BOEHLER 157, FEILITZEN DB 251, STRÖM 15, KAUFMANN ERG 117. It is used as a second el. in combination with **aelb/aelf** (1) and **ean/aen** (3). In the latter combination it is spelled **fled** once.

for OHG *fuora*, OE *fōr* 'journey'. It is used as a second el. in combination with **oft** (1).

ford/fyrdi OHG *furt*, OE *ford* 'ford'. It is used as the second component of **HERUTFORD** (3), **HREUTFORD** (1), and **STANFORD** (1). For the *i*-mutated form **fyrdi**, which occurs in **adTUIFYRDI** (1), two explanations are possible. Either it is an old locative of *ford* in *-i*, or it is a neuter *ja*-derivative of the stem of *ford*. The former is the more likely explanation. Cf. HOLTHAUSEN 120, DAHL 111, ANDERSON HN III, 176, ANDERSON LB 99, EPNE I, 180 f., DEPN 483 ff.

ford/forth OE *ford* 'forth, forwards'. Cf. OET 575, MÜLLER 101, FEILITZEN DB 252, ANDERSON LB 98. HELLWIG 18 explains its use as a parallel to Latin *per* in *per-magnus* and *per-fidens*. It is used as a first el. in combination with **here/heri** (2), once as **ford** and once as **forth**.

FORDHERI (2) ford/forth; here/heri.

He was Bishop of Sherborne, part of Wessex, from 709 to 737, in which year he resigned in order to go on a pilgrimage to Rome. The date of his death is unknown.

FRESIA (8) Latinized country-name connected with **FRESO**.

Friesland.

---

[26] Dahl's suggestion is based upon a personal communication from Professor Ekwall. The latter, however, has never mentioned this interpretation of final *-e* in any of his writings. BROOKS 30, n., thinks Dahl's suggestion is doubtful, but offers no alternative.

FRESO(NES) (3) This Latinized tribal name occurs twice in the plural and once in the singular. Its OE forms are *Frīsa/Frēsa*. It may be connected with a Germanic stem **frīsiaz* 'curly-haired', and thus possibly refers to a particular hair-fashion of members of this tribe, when going to war. Cf. MIDDENDORFF 54, SCHÖNFELD 95 f., GREEN 83, BACH I, 1, 309, EPNE I, 187 f., KAUF-MANN ERG 123 f.
>   The Frisians.

fri OHG *frī*, OE *frīo/frēo* 'free, noble'. It is used as a first el. in combination with **gyd** (1).

frid/frit OHG *fridu*, OE *frid(u)/friodu* 'peace, security, protection'. It is used as a second el. in combination with **ald** (12), **alh** (1), **berct/berht/berict** (1), **ceol** (8), **cyni** (1), **ean/aen** (1), **ec/ecg** (25), **gud** (1), **raed/red** (1), **tat** (1), **uil** (43), and **uyn** (6). It is spelled **frit** in combination with **berct/berht/berict** (1) and **uyn** (1).

FRIGYD (1) **fri; gyd.**
>   She was Prioress of the monastery at Hackness under Hild (*s.v.*) around
>   680.

gae (1) OHG *jā*, OE *ġéa* 'yes'.

gar OHG *gēr*, OE *gār* 'spear'. It is used as a second el. in combination with **ead/ed/æad** (1).

GARMANI (1) Normally the Latinized form of this tribal name appears as *Germani*. Its etymology is much disputed. HOLDER I, 2011 assumes Germanic origin, whereas SCHÖNFELD 106 assumes Celtic origin. For a full survey of the relevant literature see BACH I, 1, 319 ff.
>   The inhabitants of Germany.

ge OHG *gawi*, OE *gē* 'district, region', in OE only found in place-names. It occurs as the second component of **ELGE** (3). Besides, the theme itself or a derivative of it, corresponding to Gothic *gauja* 'inhabitant of a district', is found in **SUTHRIEONA** (1). Cf. KÖHLER 33, DAHL 98, ANDERSON LB 104, EPNE I, 196 f.

geb OHG *geba*, OE *ġiefu* etc. 'gift'. It is used as a first el. in combination with **mund** (3). In one of the three occurrences final /b/ is assimilated to /m/ under the influence of the opening consonant of **mund**. Cf. FEILITZEN DB 91.

GEBMUND (3) **geb; mund.**
>   He was Bishop of Rochester from 678. The year of his death is often
>   given as 693 on the basis of ASC. This is also held by Powicke & Fryde[27],

---

[27] Sir F. Maurice Powicke & E. B. Fryde (eds.), *Handbook of British Chronology*, 2nd edition, London 1961; p. 247.

although PLUMMER II, 284 thinks this is unlikely, because Gebmund was probably present at the "Council of the Leading Figures" (= *witenagemot*) of Bersted in 696.

GENLAD (1)   The first component of this river-name has been explained as OHG *gegin*, OE *gegn* (adv.) 'again'. The second component is connected with OHG *leita*, OE *lād* 'water-course'. Cf. KÖHLER 34, 38, EKWALL RN 477, WALLENBERG 59, 165, GREEN 85, ANDERSON LB 75, EPNE I, 199, II, 8 f., CAMPBELL 105,n.4, DEPN 284, 542. Ekwall thus arrives at the meaning "'backwater' or the like" for the combination. FORSBERG 28 f., on the other hand, would prefer a connection with Old Norse *gagn-* 'short cut' and the rare OE adjective *gēn* 'direct, short, near (of a road)'. For the combination he suggests 'a watercourse providing a short cut between two larger bodies of water'[28]. HOLDER I, 2001 thinks the name is Celtic.

Ekwall identifies the name as Yantlet Creek or Yenlet in Kent. Forsberg (*l.c.*) suggests that it denotes the Wantsum itself, and not just the Yenlet, its northern arm.

GERMANIA (1)   The Latinized country-name connected with **GARMANI**. Germany.

GEUISSAE (7)   Several derivations have been proposed. HOLDER I, 2017 thinks it may be Celtic in origin. It has been connected with *Visi* in *Visigoths*, which is related to Indo-European **uesu-* 'good, noble'. Cf. HIRT II, 130 and also SCHÖNFELD 268[29]. OET 502 connects it with OHG, OE *(ge)wiss* 'certain, trustworthy', which is tentatively supported by ANDERSON LB 111. These derivations are either rejected or thought less likely by REDIN 30, by whom a connection is assumed with Gothic *gawidan* 'to join' and Gothic *gawiss* 'link, connection', which would give the sense of 'confederates'. This is a very plausible explanation seeing that the name is in fact used for a federation of tribes.

An ancient name of the West Saxons, which is not used in OEBede.

gisl   OHG *gīsal*, OE *gīs(e)l* 'hostage' or Longobardic *gīsil* 'arrow, shaft'. Cf. FÖRSTEMANN I, 647, SCHÖNFELD 30, 110, STRÖM 18, KAUFMANN UAR 93 f. Ström adds in a footnote that it is impossible to decide in the individual cases which of the two derivations applies. ANDERSON LB 100 opts for the former derivation, whereas MÜLLER 131 and ARNGART 132 utter a preference for the latter. SCHRAMM 88 thinks both apply at the same

---

[28] A parallel is found in 1.66 of the *Battle of Maldon*: *lucon lagu-strēamas*, which line means that the two streams of the incoming tide from either side of the Isle of Thanet meet and interlock. Cf. E. D. Laborde, *Byrhtnoth and Maldon*, London 1936; p. 120.
[29] PLUMMER II, 89 supports connection with *Visi* of *Visigoths*, but gives its meaning as 'west', assuming it refers to the "western confederation of Saxon tribes".

time. It is used as a second el. in combination with **ald** (1), **ead/ed/æad** (1), and **haem** (1). All three occurrences have the unmetathesized form.

god   OHG *got*, OE *god* 'God'. Cf. ANDERSON LB 98. Others waver between this explanation and derivation from OHG *guot*, OE *gōd* 'good'. Cf. FORSSNER 118, BOEHLER 77 f., REDIN 14, FEILITZEN DB 262; cf. also SCHÖNFELD 111, KAUFMANN UAR 73 f., KAUFMANN ERG 150 f. It is used as a first el. in combination with **uini** (1).

GODUINI (1)   **god; uini.**
  He was Archbishop of Lyons from about 693 until about 713.

GRANTACĘSTIR (1)   The first component is a river-name *Granta*, which is taken to be Celtic by DEPN 202 and connected with Celtic-Latin *gronna/gromna* 'bog', and may thus be interpreted as 'muddy river'. Cf. GREEN 90 ff., and cf. also HOLDER I, 2039, ANDERSON LB 110. CAMERON 55 thinks the name is pre-Celtic. Celtic origin is called "doubtful" by JACKSON LHEB 221. The second component is **cęstir.** Cf. also REANEY CA 36 f., REANEY OR 25 f., EKWALL VC 13, NI, GEL & RI 66.
  Cambridge, Cambridgeshire.

gud   OHG *gund*, OE *gūþ* 'combat, war'. It is used as a first el. in combination with **frid/frit** (1). See also **gyd**.

GUDFRID (1)   **gud; frid/frit.**
  This Abbot of Lindisfarne was one of Bede's informants. He was probably dead when HE was written.

gyd   Derived from OHG *gundi-* (⟨ **gunthjō-*), connected with OE *gūþ* 'combat, war'. Cf. BOEHLER 161, FEILITZEN DB 155. It is used as a second el. in combination with **ead/ed/æad** (3), **fri** (1), and **torct** (2).

GYRUII (2)   A tribal name connected with OE *gyr* 'mud, fen' and meaning 'fen-dwellers'. Cf. HOLTHAUSEN 141, GREEN 118, ANDERSON LB 97, EKWALL TN 147[30], EPNE I, 212, DEPN 268, REANEY OR 102, EKWALL VC 33, CAMERON 73, NI, GEL & RI 115.
  A tribe in the Peterborough district, in the East Anglian fen area.

inGYRUUM (2)   For the preposition see **in**, and see further the tribal name **GYRUII**. Cf. MAWER NO & DU 124.
  Jarrow, Northumberland[31].

---

[30] See also E. Ekwall, "OE *Gyrwe*", *Beiblatt zur Anglia* 33 (1922), p. 117.
[31] Whether any relationship existed between the Jarrow people and the East Anglian Gyruii remains uncertain. The name can very well have developed independently.

HACANOS (1)   The first component of this place-name is OHG *hāko*, OE *haca* 'hook'. The second component is an OE *nōs, connected with Old Swedish *nos* 'snout, muzzle'. The place-name means 'hook-shaped headland''. Cf. GREEN 93, SMITH ERY XLIX[32], ANDERSON LB 75, 90, 101, EPNE I, 213, II, 52, DEPN 209, and also KÖHLER 35, 40. HOLDER I, 2047 thinks it may be Celtic.

    Hackness, Yorkshire North Riding.

hadu   OHG *hathu*, OE *h(e)aþu* 'war, battle'. It is used as a first el. in combination with **lac** (1). See also **haed** and **CEADDA** for related Celtic *catu*.

HADULAC (1)   hadu; lac.

    He was Bishop of Elmham, East Anglia, from between 716 and 731 until between 731 and 736.

haed   OET 595 connects it with OHG *heida*, OE *hǣþ* 'heath'. More likely, however, is OHG *hathu*, OE *headu* 'battle, combat'. Final *-u* may have been dropped, because the feminine ending seemed to be incompatible with a masculine personal name, so that consequently nothing could prevent a change of /a/ to /æ/. Cf. STRÖM 20, ANDERSON LB 124. It is used as a second el. in combination with **ead/ed/æad** (5).

HAEDDI (3)   An *-i-*(⟨ *-ina*) derivative of *Hadda*, which probably is a short form of compound names with **hadu**, although derivation from compounds with **hard/heard** has also been suggested. For the suffix see **AECCI**. Cf. REDIN 66, STRÖM 69 f., ANDERSON LB 92 f., 106, 122.

    He was Bishop of Winchester from 676 to 705.

haem   OHG *heim*, OE *hām* 'home'. The vowel was mutated under the influence of the vowel of the following name-el. Cf. ANDERSON LB 105, CAMPBELL 83, BRUNNER AG 70. It is used as a first el. in combination with **gisl** (1).

HAEMGISL (1)   haem; gisl.

    He was a companion of Drycthelm (*s.v.*). At the time Bede wrote HE he was probably still alive.

haeth   OHG *heida*, OE *hǣþ* 'heath, open field'. Connection with the personal name-els. **hadu** and **haed** has been suggested by BOEHLER 83. It is used as the first component of **HAETHFELD** (3).

HAETHFELD (3)   haeth; feld/felth. Cf. GREEN 94, GOVER etc. HE 126, ANDERSON LB 103, 122, DEPN 224, NI, GEL & RI 106.

    Hatfield, Hertfordshire.

hagustald   see **HAGUSTALDENSIS**

---

[32] At an earlier date SMITH NRY 112 had explained the first component as a personal name and had interpreted the name as '*nǣss* or headland of one *Hac(c)a*'.

HAGUSTALDENSIS (11)   This is the Latinized adjectival form of a name connected with OHG *hagustalt*, OE *hagust(e)ald* 'warrior, bachelor'. The name, composed of OE *haga* 'enclosure, measure of land' and OE *st(e)ald* which is derived from OE *stealdan* 'to own', originally meant 'owner of an enclosure', but according to EPNE I, 215 came to be used more specifically of "the younger son without inherited property who secured his own holding outside the patrimony or village". Cf. also KÖHLER 35, MILLER 35, OET 471, 491, MAWER NO & DU 114 f., MAGOUN '38 161, ANDERSON LB 90, 114, DEPN 237, CAMERON 137, EKWALL VC 16. A specialised meaning 'one bound by vows to celibacy, a monk' is suggested by GREEN 96 f. with a view to a possibly ecclesiastical origin of the place.

Hexham, Northumberland.

halch/halh   OE *healh* 'a corner, nook, angle'. It is used as the second component of **STREANAESHALCH** (4).

hamm   OE *hamm* 'enclosure etc.'; see for further discussion **BOSANHAMM**.

hamstede   Composed of OHG *heim*, OE *hām* 'home' and OHG *stat*, OE *stede* 'place'. Cf. SANDRED 21. It is used as a component of **MEDESHAMSTEDE** (1).

hard/heard   OHG *hard/herti*, OE *heard* 'firm, brave'. It is used as a second el. in combination with **sig** (1), **suaeb/suef** (1), and **uig** (2). The spelling **hard** occurs with **sig**.

heah   OHG *hōh*, OE *hēah* 'high, illustrious'. It is used as a first el. in combination with **uald** (6) in **HEUUALD**, and it may also occur in **HEIU** (1).

HEIU (1)   A personal name of obscure origin. Since it is not dealt with by OET, REDIN, DAHL, STRÖM, and ANDERSON LB, one may conclude that they consider the name to be Celtic. Cf. also HOLDER I, 2050. BOEHLER 221 f., however, suggests that it may be a Northumbrian short form of names in **heah** (: *hēh* instead of West-Saxon *hēah*) with a strong *u*-ending. This explanation of the name has also been thought of as a possibility by PLUMMER II, 244, according to whom the place-name *Healaugh*, Yorkshire West Riding, may possibly preserve Heiu's name[33].

A nun who founded the monastery of Heruteu (*s.v.*, = Hart or Hartlepool) around the year 650.

helm   OHG, OE *helm* 'helmet, protection, protector'. It is used as a second el. in combination with **ald** (5), **burg** (1), **dryct** (1), **pect** (3), and **quic** (2).

here/heri   OHG *hari/heri*, OE *here* 'army, host'; as a second el. it developed the meaning of 'warrior, fighter', according to BOEHLER 85. It is used as a

---

[33] *Healaugh* is not thus derived by EPNE I, 10, II, 20, DEPN 229, REANEY OR 40, or SMITH WRY IV, 241.

first el. in combination with **bald/balt** (2), **berct/berht/berict** (4), **burg** (1), **ric** (2), and **suid** (1); the spelling **heri** occurs twice only as a first el., viz. in combination with **ric** (1) and **suid** (1). As a second el. it is used in combination with **ean/aen** (1), **ford/forth** (2), **hlot/hloth** (5), **sig** (2), **uald** (1), and **uulf** (6); the spelling **here** occurs in combination with **hlot/hloth** (1), **sig** (1), and **uulf** (2), of which only the combination with **sig** is not an ablative form.

HEREBALD (2)   here/heri; bald/balt.
> At the time Bede was writing HE, Herebald was Abbot of a monastery at Tynemouth. Before that he had been with St. John of Beverley, who was Bishop of Hexham from 687 to 705, and of York from 705 until about 718.

HEREBERCT (4)   here/heri; berct/berht/berict.
> A hermit on an island in Derwentwater, Cumberland, who was a friend of Cudberct's (*s.v.*). He died on the same day as Cudberct in 687.

HEREBURG (1)   here/heri; burg.
> She was Abbess at Uetadun (*s.v.*), around 705.

HERIRIC (2)   here/heri; ric.
> He was a nephew of King Eduini of Northumbria (*s.v.*), and father of Hild (*s.v.*), Abbess of Whitby.

HERISUID (1)   here/heri; suid.
> She was a daughter of Heriric (*s.v.*), and a sister of Hild (*s.v.*). It has generally been held that she was married to King Aedilhere of East Anglia, who was killed in 655, but this has been seriously questioned by Stenton[34].

herud/herut   OHG *hiruz*, OE *heor(o)t* 'hart, stag'. This place-name el. is used as the first component of **HERUTEU** (1) and **HERUTFORD** (3), once in the spelling **herud** in the latter combination.

HERUTEU (1)   herud/herut; ei/eu/ę.   HE has *insula cervi*. Cf. MILLER 37 f., MAWER NO & DU 104, GREEN 99, ANDERSON LB 75, DEPN 222, EKWALL VC 28 f., NI, GEL & RI 104 f.
> Hart or Hartlepool, Durham.

HERUTFORD (3)   herud/herut; ford/fyrdi.   Cf. GREEN 100, GOVER etc. HE 225, ANDERSON LB 113, DEPN 236, NI, GEL & RI 108.
> Hertford, Hertfordshire.

---

[34] F. M. Stenton, "The East-Anglian Kings of the Seventh Century", in: P. Clemoes (ed.), *The Anglo-Saxons: Studies in Some Aspects of their History and Culture. Presented to Bruce Dickins*, London 1959, 43-52; (repr. in: D. M. Stenton (ed.), *Preparatory to Anglo-Saxon England*, being the collected papers of Frank Merry Stenton, Oxford 1970; 394-402).

HEUUALD (6)   heah; uald. Cf. STRÖM 22, ANDERSON LB 103, 121; cf. also HELLWIG 45, ARNGART 131.

The two brothers known by this name were distinguished from each other by the designations *albus* and *niger* respectively, after the colour of their hair. They were English priests who had lived in exile in Ireland and around 700 sailed to preach the Gospel in Old Saxony, where they were martyred.

HIBERNIA (14)   The Latinized corrupt form of British *$\bar{I}\underset{.}{u}eri\acute{o}n$-* ⟩ Modern Welsh *Iwerddon* 'Ireland'. According to HOLDER II, 99 and EKWALL EN 155 f. the name goes back to *$Piveri\bar{o}$*, connected with a root *pi* 'fat', so that the meaning of the name of the country would be 'the fertile country'. Cf. GREEN 101. O'Rahilly[35] suggests that the country took its name from the sun-goddess *$\bar{E}vern\bar{a}$*, whose name is based on the Indo-European root *ei*- 'to move etc.' and means something like 'she who travels regularly'. O'Rahilly stresses that the first vowel of **HIBERNIA** is long. He also notes that one of the traditional explanations of the name of the country is 'the island of the setting sun'. Cf. also JACKSON RPNs 57, JACKSON LHEB 385, 472.

Ireland.

HIDDILA (1)   The diminutive suffix *-ila* was probably added to an OE name *Hidda* ⟨ *$Hilda$*, which is a short form of compound names with **hild**. Cf. MÜLLER 55, REDIN 67, 146, BOEHLER 87, 222, STRÖM 70, ANDERSON LB 96, 108, 122.

He was a priest who in 686 was assigned by Uilfrid 1 (*s.v.*) to Bernuini (*s.v.*), whom he was to help in the evangelisation of the Isle of Wight.

HII (7)   This is the form Celtic *Ioua*, Pictish *Eu*, takes in HE. The origin of this Celtic name is uncertain. WATSON 87 ff. suggests it may mean 'the yew-isle'. Cf. GREEN 102, and cf. also HOLDER II, 66 f., MACBAIN 69, ANDERSON LB 83.

Iona, Scotland.

HIIENSIS (4)   Latinized adjectival form derived from **HII**. In K double *-ii-* is reduced to *-i-* three times.

hild   OHG *hilt*, OE *hild* 'war, combat'. It occurs probably independently in **HILD** (7), and with a diminutive suffix in **HIDDILA** (1). It is used as a first el. in combination with **lid** (1), and as a second el. with **bald/balt** (1).

HILD (7)   In all probability a short-form name derived from compounds with **hild**. Cf. REDIN 7, 40, BOEHLER 222, STRÖM 70, ANDERSON LB 111, ARNGART 131.

She was a daughter of Heriric (*s.v.*) and Bregusuid (*s.v.*). She was Abbess

---

[35] T. F. O'Rahilly, "On the Origin of the Names **ÉRAINN** and **ÉRIU**", *Ériu* XIV (1943), 7-28.

first of Heruteu (*s.v.*) and then of Streanaeshalch (*s.v.*, = Whitby). She died in 680.

HILDILID (1)   **hild; lid.**
She succeeded Aedilburg (*s.v.*) as Abbess of the monastery of Barking in 664 (?). In Bede's own words, HE IV, 10, she reigned "ad ultimam senectutem". From one of Boniface's letters we know that she was still alive in 717.

hlot/hloth   The etymology is uncertain. STRÖM 23 f. and SCHRAMM 17 reckon with non-native origin even. Ström reviews the possibilities that have been put forward, but refrains from choosing between derivation from OE *hlōþ* 'band, troop' (〉 MHG *luot*) and derivation from a form **hluþa* with short vowel which would be connected with Indo-European **kluto* 'famous'. The latter derivation is not supported by OET 641 and is rejected by ANDERSON LB 68 on account of the short vowel. On the other hand SCHÖNFELD 140, HOLTHAUSEN 64, SCHRAMM 18,n.2, and KAUFMANN ERG 189 ff. derive Continental Germanic equivalents from **kluto* 'famous'[36]. BACH I, 1, 224 reckons with long and short variants. It is used as a first el. in combination with **here/heri** (5). The spelling **hlot** occurs four times.

HLOTHARIUS (1)   Latinized form of **HLOTHERI.**

HLOTHERI (5)   **hlot/hloth; here/heri.**
He was a son of King Earconberct of Kent (*s.v.*), and came to the throne in 673. He died in 685.

homel   Probably OHG *hamal*, OE **hamol/*hamel* 'maimed, mutilated', possibly originally 'crooked'. Cf. KÖHLER 36, EKWALL RN 189 f., GREEN 103, ANDERSON LB 75 f., FÖRSTER TH 315, n.1, EPNE I, 231, DEPN 214; cf. also CAMERON 161. It may be suggested that the original sense of the verb connected with this base, i.e. OE *hamelian* 'to mutilate', was 'to cut', so that the meaning in connection with a river-name was something like 'cut deep into'. OET 469 relates the el. to OHG *hamo*, OE *hama* 'covering, coat; slough of a snake'. HOLDER I, 2056 thinks it is Celtic, but offers no etymology. It is used as the first component of **HOMEL·EA·** (1).

HOMEL·EA· (1)   **homel; ea.**
The Hamble, Hampshire.

hooh   OE *hōh* 'heel, spur of land'. It is used as a second el. of the place-name **CLOFAESHOOH** (1).

---

[36] Schramm admits that the vowel of the name-theme is long. This he ascribes to a later development on the analogy of OHG names in **hrod**, which is connected with OHG *hruod*, OE *hrōd*, 'fame'.

150

hreut OHG *hriot*, OE *hrēod* 'reed'. It is used as the first component of **HREUT-FORD** (1).

HREUTFORD (1) **hreut; ford/fyrdi**. Cf. KÖHLER 36, GREEN 104, AN-DERSON HN II, 177, ANDERSON LB 76, DEPN 383, EKWALL VC 12.
Redbridge, Hampshire.

HROFENSIS (7) The Latinized adjectival form of **HROFI**, for which see **HROFESCĘSTIR**. Four times the spelling of the initial consonants is *rh-*.
Of Rochester, Kent.

HROFESCĘSTIR (1) The first component is not a genitive singular form of a personal name connected with OE *hrōf* 'roof', as scholars used to think; cf. MIDDENDORFF 77, KÖHLER 36, OET 580. The first component derives from the original British name of the place, i.e. *Durobrivae*, which consists of the two els. **duro* 'fort, walled town' and *brivā* 'bridge', and which meant 'the bridges of the stronghold'. Through early loss of the initial syllable[37] and the spelling-addition of initial *h*[38] the form **Hrobri* came into existence, which through dissimilation became *Hrofi* and was interpreted as a personal name by Bede himself. Cf. REDIN 21, ZACHRISSON RKS 81, WALLENBERG 3,n.1, MAGOUN '35 86, GREEN 105 f., EPNE I, 140, JACKSON LHEB 267, 558, 647, REANEY OR 80, DEPN 390, NI, GEL & RI 162. The second component is **cęstir**.
Rochester, Kent.

HROFI (3) For the etymology of this place-name component, in our text used in combination with *ciuitas* only, see **HROFESCĘSTIR**.
Rochester, Kent.

HRYPENSIS (1) A Latinized adjectival form of **inHRYPUM**. The spelling of the initial consonants is *rh-*.
Of Ripon, Yorkshire West Riding.

inHRYPUM (4) For the preposition see **in**. The name meant 'place in the territory of the *Hrype*'. The origin of the tribal name *Hrype* is uncertain. Cf. GREEN 119. HOLDER I, 2057 reckons with Celtic origin. EKWALL TN 144 f. assumes a base **hrupi-*, which may stand in ablaut zero-grade relation to OE *hreppan/hrepian* 'to touch', also 'to attack' according to Ekwall. It may well be connected with OHG *roufen*, OE *riepan* 'to rob, plunder', if we assume that the general confusion of *r-* and *hr-* spellings led to the introduction of *h*, for which also compare **HROFESCĘSTIR**. Cf. also KÖHLER 36, ANDERSON

---

[37] British according to JACKSON LHEB 267, English according to DEPN 390.
[38] The general uncertainty as to the pronunciation of initial *h-* is also evidenced in *Beowulf*, in which *hrade* alliterates with *h* normally, but with initial *r-* in ll. 724, 1390, and 1975. Cf. Johannes Hoops, *Kommentar zum Beowulf*, Heidelberg 1932; pp. 92 f.

HN I, 37, MAGOUN '38 162, ANDERSON LB 76, EPNE II, 226, SMITH WRY V, 164 f. and VII, 38 f., CAMERON 73 f., REANEY OR 101 f., DEPN 388, NI, GEL & RI 161.

Ripon, Yorkshire West Riding.

huaet OHG *hwaz*, OE *hwæt* 'sharp, bold, brave'. It is used as a first el. in combination with **berct/berht/berict** (1).

HUAETBERCT (1)   huaet; berct/berht/berict.

Born in Northumbria, he was Abbot of Wearmouth and Jarrow from 716 until after Bede's death.

HUICCII (3)   The origin of this tribal name is obscure. SMITH HW 62 suggests connection with a Germanic root *χwik, surviving in Old Icelandic *hvik* 'a quaking, a wavering' and *hvikari* 'coward'. Cf. also ANDERSON LB 96, EPNE I, 272, DEPN 512 f.

The Huiccii were of Anglian origin and at one time occupied an extensive area in the South West Midlands. They formed a sub-kingdom of Mercia.

HUMBER (1)   The nominative case of this name which is not evidenced in early records, is doubtful. The genitive is frequently *Humbre*, but also *Humbri*, in HE. The origin of the name is uncertain. Scholars generally agree that the name is pre-English. The suggestion of a Celtic base *$*Su\text{-}mbro\text{-} \rangle *Sumbro\text{-}$ giving the sense 'good river', put forward by EKWALL RN 201 ff. and supported by GREEN 107, is called "very doubtful" by JACKSON LHEB 510[39]. Jackson himself (*l.c.*, 519) suggests that the name may be pre-Celtic, i.e. Old European, a suggestion taken up by CAMERON 37. Cf. also HOLDER I, 2057, FÖRSTER TH 307, SMITH ERY 8 f., ANDERSON LB 111, EPNE I, 268, DEPN 256.

The Humber, Yorkshire etc.

HUMBRONENSES (1)   A Latinized adjectival form of **NORDANHYMBRI**. The Northumbrians.

hun Either Old Norse *húnn*, OE *$*hūn$ 'young bear' or OHG *Hūni/Hūn*, OE *Hūne/Hūnas* 'the Huns'. Cf. MÜLLER 114, FÖRSTEMANN I, 929 f., BOEHLER 89 f., REDIN 17, and STRÖM 24 f. SCHÖNFELD 143, FEILITZEN DB 295, ANDERSON LB 102, BACH I, 1, 229, and KAUFMANN ERG 207 f. reject the latter derivation. SCHRAMM 66 thinks that originally such a connection with the Huns cannot have existed, but that possibly the dominating role of the Huns in epic poetry later made the introduction of the theme as a second el. of OHG and OE personal names easier. Besides, in Schramm's opinion the alternative is not Old Norse *húnn*, OE *$*hūn$ 'young bear', but rather Celtic *kūno* 'tall', although in another place, i.e. p. 79, he is willing to

---

[39] Jackson's contention that Ekwall does not consider this possibility is not quite true; cf. Ekwall, *l.c.*, 204.

consider it as a possibility after all; etymologically the two words are probably connected according to Schönfeld (*l.c.*) and HOLTHAUSEN 178. It is used as a second el. in combination with **and** (1) and **berct/berht/berict** (3).

HUNNI (1)   The Latinized form of an Asiatic tribal name, which normally appears as OHG *Hūni/Hūn*, OE *Hūne/Hūnas*. See also **hun**.
    The Huns.

hyg   OHG *hugi*, OE *hyge* 'mind, heart, courage'. It is used as a first el. in combination with **bald/balt** (1).

HYGBALD (1)   **hyg; bald/balt.**
    He was Abbot of Lindsey for some time around 700.

iaru   OHG *garo*, OE *gearu* 'ready, prepared'. It is used as a first el. in combination with **man(n)/mon** (1).

IARUMAN(N) (1)   **iaru; man(n)/mon.**
    He was Bishop of Mercia (Lichfield?) from 662 to 667.

IDA (1)   Probably a short form of unrecorded compound names in **id**, the etymology of which is obscure. It has been connected with OHG *itis*, OE *ides* 'woman, lady, virgin'; with OHG *ītal*, OE *īdel* 'idle'; and with an Old Norse *id* 'activity, work', connected with OE *īdig* 'busy, active'. Cf. FÖRSTEMANN I, 943, FORSSNER 160, REDIN 98 f., BOEHLER 92 f., STRÖM 71, KAUFMANN ERG 213. ANDERSON LB refrains from commenting upon its etymology.
    He was the first King of Bernicia, and reigned from 547 to 560.

IMMA (1)   It is a short form of compound personal names. It has been suggested that the base may be connected with an Old Norse *imr* 'wolf'; cf. MÜLLER 56, HOLTHAUSEN 187, and also SCHÖNFELD 146. An alternative suggestion is derivation from the name-theme **irmin**, connected with OHG *erman*, OE *eormen* 'great'. Cf. FORSSNER 69, REDIN 17, 67, STRÖM 71, ANDERSON LB 97, 122, BACH I,1,100, SCHRAMM 151, KAUFMANN UAR 139 f., KAUFMANN ERG 108 f.
    Imma, a retainer of Aelfuini of Deira (*s.v.*), was severely wounded in the Battle of the Trent in 679.

in   This preposition is sometimes used in HE in combination with regional or tribal names in the sense of 'in, among'. It is followed by a dative case, and just as **ad**(=æt) seems to have formed an integral part of the ensuing (elliptical) place-name. Cf. PLUMMER II, 104, GREEN 210, EPNE I, 5 f., DEPN XIX. The preposition is used in the names **inBERECINGUM** (1), **inCUNENINGUM** (1), **inDERAUUDA** (1), **inGYRUUM** (2), **inHRYPUM** (4), and **inUNDALUM** (1).

ing   Connected with OE *Ing*, the name of a god or a tribal hero and probably a variant of a name-theme **ingua-/ingu-**, also found in the tribal name *Ingvaeones*.

Its further etymology remains uncertain. Cf. FÖRSTEMANN I, 959, MÜLLER 106, SCHÖNFELD 147, BOEHLER 94, HOLTHAUSEN 188, 423, ANDERSON LB 96, BACH I,1,210, SCHRAMM 35,103,154, KAUFMANN UAR 94 f., KAUFMANN ERG 216. It is used as a first el. in combination with **uald** (2).

ingas This suffix is used to form names of peoples who, as EPNE I, 299 has it, were "brought together by dependence on a common leader, living together for their mutual political, economic or defensive advantage". Such names soon came to denote districts held by tribes and, eventually, the principal settlements of these districts. The names may be composed with personal names, but also with names of topographical features, such as rivers. Cf. STENTON EE 47, KARLSTRÖM PNsING 22, EPNE I, 298 ff., SMITH ASS 75 ff., DEPN 263, REANEY OR 107, CAMERON 63 ff., EKWALL PNsING 111 ff., NI, GEL & RI 18. The suffix occurs in **inBERECINGUM** (1), **inCUNENINGUM** (1), and in **LAESTINGAEU** (3).

INGUALD (2)   ing; uald.
>He was consecrated Bishop of London between 705 and 716, and died in 745.

INI (3)   Probably derived from compound personal names with **in**, which name-theme has been connected with the intensifying OE particle *in-* 'very, most', found in *indryhten* 'most noble' and *infrōd* 'very wise'. For the *i*-suffix see **AECCI**. Cf. MÜLLER 68, SCHÖNFELD 146 f., REDIN 123, STRÖM 72, KAUFMANN ERG 216.
>He was King of the West Saxons from 688 to 726. He abdicated and went on a pilgrimage to Rome, where he died.

INISBOFINDE (1)   A name of Celtic origin. The first component is based on ** ĭn-issi-s* 'island', according to HOLDER II, 46, and furthermore on Old Irish *bó* 'cow' and *finde* 'white'; cf. GREEN 120. The translation HE IV, 4 gives of the name in Latin, viz. "insula uitulae albae" ('island of the white heifer'), seems to be correct. Cf. also MACBAIN 236.
>Inishbofin, an island off the coast of county Galway.

IUTAE/-I (2)   K has **IUTARUM** and **IUTORUM** once each. The etymology of this tribal name is uncertain. Cf. BJÖRKMANN ST 21 ff., HOLTHAUSEN 93, ANDERSON LB 105, EKWALL TN 132.
>The Jutes.

KĘLCACĘSTIR (1)   The first component of this place-name is probably an *-ion*-derivative of OE *cealc* 'chalk', i.e. **celce ⟨ *kalkiōn*, in the sense of 'chalky place, chalky ground'. The form the theme takes in this name is probably a genitive singular. Cf. GREEN 123 f., ANDERSON LB 74, 93, 118, 120, EPNE I, 87 f., DEPN 270, and also BOEHLER 43. The second component is **cęstir**.
>The place is usually identified as Tadcaster, Yorkshire West Riding; cf. MILLER 45, SMITH WRY IV, 76 f. and VII, 13n., CO & MY

407, n. 2. Kelk, Yorkshire East Riding, is suggested by Anderson (*l.c.*) and DEPN (*l.c.*).

lac   OHG *lei(c)h*, OE *lāc* 'dance'; in OE the noun has a variety of meanings, such as 'sport; strife; sacrifice; gift', and in modern English it is also found in *wedlock*. It is not clear which of these meanings is to be assumed for the name-theme. Cf. OET 590, FÖRSTEMANN I, 995, MÜLLER 126, FEILITZEN DB 307, STRÖM 27, ANDERSON LB 102, SCHRAMM 61, EKWALL PNsING 208, KAUFMANN ERG 223. It is used as a second el. in combination with **hadu** (1).

lad   see **GENLAD**

laest   OHG *leist*, OE *lǣst* 'track, sole of foot' (〉 modern Dutch *leest*); see further **LAESTINGǢ, -AEU, -AEI**.

LAESTINGǢ, -AEU, -AEI (3)   The first component of this place-name is connected with **laest**. It is a matter of dispute whether the base is an unrecorded OE personal name ***Lǣsta** or the topographical word itself. Cf. SMITH NRY 61 f., KARLSTRÖM PNsING 115, GREEN 125, STRÖM 113, ANDERSON LB 76, 103, FORSBERG 41 f., EPNE I, 301, CAMERON 70, DEPN 289, EKWALL PNsING 155, EKWALL VC 16, Dodgson[40]. For the suffix see **ingas**, and for the final component see **ei/eu/ę**.

Lastingham, Yorkshire North Riding.

LEUTHERIUS (4)   A Continental Germanic name. Cf. FORSSNER 178, STRÖM 181, ANDERSON LB 64 f. PLUMMER II, 488 and CO & MY 609 identify it with an OE personal name *Hlotheri*, for which see **HLOTHERI**, following ASC. FÖRSTEMANN I,1030, SCHÖNFELD 154, and KAUFMANN ERG 232 f., however, connect its first el. with OHG *liut*, OE *lēod* 'people; prince'.

He was a nephew of Agilberctus (*s.v.*), and was sent by the latter from Gaul to be consecrated Bishop of Winchester in 670. He died in 676.

LICCIDFELTH (1)   The first component of this place-name is British in origin. In Romano-British sources it is found as *Letocetum*, corresponding to Old British ***Lētocaiton**, which consists of ***lēto** 'grey' and ***caito** 〉 ***cēto** 'wood'. Its phonological development into OE *liccid-* is traced by JACKSON LHEB 325, 327, 332 ff., 563 f., 647. Jackson also proves that the chronology required by this development makes a first borrowing by the Anglo-Saxons of the name as *Lyccid-* (〈***Luitgēd**) very unlikely, for which FÖRSTER TH 160 f., 588 ff. had built up an ingenious argument on the assumption that the spelling *-y-* (2) in M, the oldest MS, would require such an explanation. The fact that K has *-i-* in agreement with L and the other MSS against M seems to invalidate the

---

[40] J. McN. Dodgson, "Various English Place-Name Formations containing Old English *-ing*", *Beiträge zur Namenforschung*, N.F. 3 (1968), p. 175.

-y-spelling of M, although it should be noted that M does not otherwise mix up the spelling of *y* and *i*, neither in its name-material nor in the Latin text[41]. Cf. also KÖHLER 38 f., HOLDER II, 192, ZACHRISSON RKS 79, EKWALL CE 26 f., MAGOUN '35 88, GREEN 136, RI & CR 37, STRÖM 150, n. 1, ANDERSON LB 100, 120, FORSBERG 103 f., EPNE I, 92, II, 23, DEPN 297, CAMERON 36, REANEY OR 74, NI, GEL & RI 124. DUIGNAN 91 ff. rejects the foregoing etymology and suggests Anglo-Saxon origin also for the first component of the name, viz. connection with OE *lacu* 'pool, pond', and explains the name as 'the boggy field'. The second component is **feld/felth**.

Lichfield, Staffordshire.

LICCIDFELDENSIS (1)   The Latinized adjectival form of **LICCIDFELTH**.
Of Lichfield, Staffordshire.

lid   Probably OHG *lind(i)*, OE *līþe* 'soft, gentle'. Cf. FÖRSTEMANN I, 1058, FORSSNER 120, STRÖM 27, ANDERSON LB 97, 115, 128, BACH I,1,215, SCHRAMM 164, and KAUFMANN ERG 237. It is used as a second el. in combination with **hild** (1).

LINDISFARI (4)   **LINDISSI; fari.**
The people of Lindsey, Lincolnshire.

LINDISFARNENSIS (16)   The Latinized adjectival form of a compound name composed of the tribal name **LINDISFARI** and **eg**. It means 'the island of the *Lindisfaran*'. Cf. FORSBERG 131 ff., JACKSON LHEB 512, EPNE II, 25, CAMERON 74, DEPN 298 f.; cf. also MAWER NO & DU 135. Once, viz. 48r, 17, the name appears as **LINDISFARONENSIS** instead of **LINDISFARNENSIS**, in which all eighth-century MSS of HE agree. The adjective is used substantivally four times in K, in the genitive plural, to designate the monks of the island.

Lindisfarne, or Holy Island, Northumberland.

LINDISSI (4)   A name of Celtic origin, here appearing as the genitive case of a Latin nominative *Lindissum*, according to DAHL 102. Cf. HOLDER II, 228. It is based on Old British **lindo*- 'a pool, water', to which a suffix for tribal and district-names which in Latin is *-ensēs* and in modern Welsh *-wys*, has been added. The ending is not a reduced form of **ge**, as proposed by MILLER 53 f. and KÖHLER 34, nor at this time *ei/eu/e*[42]. Cf. EKWALL CE 20 f., HOLTHAUSEN 203, FÖRSTER TH 166 f., FORSBERG 135 ff., JACKSON LHEB 332, 543, EPNE I, 147, II, 25, DEPN 299, CAMERON 48, 50.

Lindsey, Lincolnshire.

---

[41] C, which shows *y* for *i* regularly in the Latin text, has no instances of it in the name-material.

[42] This ending was added as a component by A.D. 1000 and explains the final part of the name in its present appearance.

LUGDUNUM (1)   It is generally held that the first component of this Continental place-name is the name of the God *Lugus*. Cf. HOLDER II, 307, FÖRSTEMANN II, 2, 143, DAU & ROS 419 f. This name is connected with Welsh *lleu* in *go-leu* 'light' and *lleu-ad* 'noon'; cf. RI & CR 36, JACKSON LHEB 441. A direct connection with the God *Lugus* is thought unlikely by LONGNON 33, who interprets this part of the name as 'luminous'. GREEN 133, besides *Lugus*, also suggests Gaulish **lugos* 'little'. The second component is connected with early British **dūno-* 'camp', for which see **dun**.

Lyons, France.

LUGUBALIA (1)   A place-name of Celtic origin, for which derivation from Gaulish *longos* 'raven' and *valo* 'wolf' was suggested by ZACHRISSON RKS 77. The second el. has also been connected with Old British **vālo-* 'wall'. More plausible, however, seems to be derivation from a personal name composed of *Lugus*, for which see **LUGDUNUM**, and a second el. derived from a root **vălo-* 'to be strong', related to Latin *valeo*. This personal name would thus mean 'strong as the god *Lugus*'. To the compound personal name the Celtic derivative suffix **-jo-* was added, resulting in the meaning 'the town of **Luguvalos*'. Cf. GREEN 134, RI & CR 36, JACKSON RPNs 57, FORSBERG 167 f., ARMSTRONG etc. CU I, 40 ff., JACKSON LHEB 39, DEPN 88, CAMERON 35, REANEY OR 79, NI, GEL & RI 68[43].

Carlisle, Cumberland.

LUNDONENSIS (1)   Latinized adjectival form of **LUNDONIA**. In MSS of the M-type it takes the form *Lundoniensis*.

Of London, Middlesex.

LUNDONIA (5)   A place-name of pre-English, possibly Celtic origin. It has been derived from a personal name **Londinos*, connected with British **lŏndo-* 'wild, bold', and has been taken to mean '*Londinos*'s town'[44]. Cf. HOLDER II, 281, RI & CR 38, DEPN 303, CAMERON 35, REANEY OR 71, NI, GEL & RI 128. The older British form, however, must have been **Lōndonjon* with long *ō* in the base; cf. ZACHRISSON RKS 80, FÖRSTER KW 229 ff., HOLTHAUSEN 207, FÖRSTER TH 165, JACKSON LHEB 258, 308, ALESSIO 223. Because of the long vowel it has seemed necessary to Alessio (*l.c.*, 227 ff.) to look for another etymology. So he suggests **lōndino-* ⟨ **lōna* 'swamp'. With this JENSEN AIO 427 f. agrees. Cf. also FORSBERG 176 ff.

London, Middlesex.

MABAN (1)   A personal name of Celtic origin, connected with Old Welsh

---

[43] By the ninth century Celtic *cair* 'a fortified place' had been added to the name which in the meantime had developed into *Luel* in OE, thus giving rise to modern Carlisle. Cf. also EPNE I, 76.

[44] The place-name would have been formed through adjectivalisation of the personal name, which may have been a typically British way of forming place-names.

mab 'son'. Cf. HOLDER II, 362, WATSON 181, FÖRSTER KW 187, FEILIT-ZEN DB 323, JACKSON LHEB 295, n. 1.

> He was a famous singer of the Gregorian chant, who around 710 was invited by Acca (*s.v.*) to come to Hexham and teach there.

MAELDUM (1)   A Gaulish place-name connected with the tribal name **MELDI**. Cf. LONGNON 102 f., GREEN 137, DAU & ROS 444.

> Meaux (Seine-et-Marne), France.

MAGEO (1)   A place-name of Celtic origin. The first component is Old Irish **mag* (< Latin *magnus*) 'great', and the second is connected with Old Irish *éo* 'yew-trees'. Cf. GREEN 139, VENDRYES LE M-8. Cf. also KÖHLER 39.

> It is a place on the Irish mainland. Later the monastery founded there by Colman (*s.v.*) for his English monks became very large, and was then known as Muigeo (*s.v.*), according to HE IV, 4. But see **MUIGEO**.

MAILDUBI (urbem) (1)   This Celtic personal name is identical with Old Irish *Maeldubh*. Cf. MILLER 79 f., KÖHLER 39, HOLDER II, 389, EKWALL CE 33, FÖRSTER TH 313, REANEY OR 98, DEPN 312. The name is explained as 'with black short hair' by VENDRYES LE M-6, who connects the first el. with Old Irish *mael* 'short-haired' and the second el. with Old Irish *dub* 'black'. Mawer and Stenton[45], however, give its meaning as 'black prince or chief', connecting the first el. with Old Irish *maglo* 'prince'.

> The combination stands for 'the city of *Mailduf*', i.e. Malmesbury, Worcestershire.

MAILROS (2)   The first component of this place-name of Celtic origin is connected with Primitive Welsh **męl* 'bald', which was replaced by Old Irish *mail* by the monks of the Irish foundation at the place. The second component is connected with Primitive Welsh **rôs* 'promontory; wood; moor'. The combination may have had the meaning of 'bare or blunt promontory'. Cf. KÖHLER 39, HOLDER II, 390, WATSON 496, GREEN 141, FÖRSTER TH 378 f., JACKSON LHEB 326 f., 342, VENDRYES LE M-6 f.

> Melrose, Roxburghshire (Scotland).

MAILROSENSIS, -NENSIS (2)   Latinized adjectival form of **MAILROS**.

> Of Melrose, Roxburghshire (Scotland).

man(n)/mon   OHG *mann*, OE *man(n)/mon(n)* 'man'. It is used as a second el. in combination with **iaru** (1) and **til** (1). The second els. of the Celtic personal names **CAEDMON** and **COLMAN** may have been associated with it.

MASSILIA (1)   A Continental place-name of uncertain origin. Cf. GREEN

---

[45] A. Mawer and F. M. Stenton, *The Place-Names of Wiltshire* (EPNS XVI), Cambridge 1939; pp. 47 ff.

144. DAU & ROS 438 suggests derivation from pre-Latin *mas*, probably in the sense of 'spring, source', and a suffix *-alia*.

Marseilles, France.

MEANUARI (1)   The first component of this tribal name is the Celtic river-name *Meon*, which according to EKWALL RN 288 may be related to Gaulish *Moenus* 'Main' and would be based upon a root *mei-* 'to change'. The second component is **uari**. Cf. MILLER 78 f., ANDERSON HN II, 183, ANDERSON LB 105, REANEY OR 106.

The people in the district of the Meon, Hampshire[46].

MEDESHAMSTEDE (1)   DEPN 364 explains the first component of this place-name as the genitive singular of a personal name *Mēde, connected with OHG *muot*, OE *mōd* 'mind, heart, mood'. This view is shared by Gover etc.[47], ANDERSON LB 101, and SANDRED 261. GREEN 145 f. suggests that, should the above derivation be incorrect, another possibility could be OHG *miata*, OE *mēd* 'reward; bribe'. Cf. also KÖHLER 39, NI, GEL & RI 150. The second component is **hamstede**.

Peterborough, Northamptonshire[48].

MELDI (1)   A Gaulish tribal name, also found in the place-name **MAELDUM**.

MERCII (23)   Connected with OHG *marcha*, OE *mearc* 'boundary', and appearing in West-Saxon as *Mierce*. Cf. HOLTHAUSEN 221, ANDERSON LB 94, EKWALL TN 141, EPNE II, 38, CAMERON 48, SMITH HW 62 ff.

The Mercians.

MERCINENSIS (1)   Latinized adjectival form of **MERCII**.

Mercian.

middil   OHG *mittil*, OE *middel* 'middle'. It is used as the first component of **MIDDILENGLI** (1).

MIDDILENGLI (1)   **middil; ANGLI**.

The 'Middle Angles'.

muda   OHG *mund*, OE *mūda* 'mouth'. It is used as the second component of **UIURAEMUDA** (1).

---

[46] They were of Jutish origin, according to HE I, 15. Cf. also JACKSON LHEB 201.

[47] J. E. B. Gover, A. Mawer and F. M. Stenton, *The Place-Names of Northamptonshire* (EPNS X), Cambridge 1933; p. 224.

[48] The original name was lost, when the place was destroyed by the Danes. When rebuilt, it was called *Burg*, to which afterwards the name of the patron saint of the Abbey was added. Cf. EKWALL VC 39, SANDRED 260.

MUIGEO (1) A place-name of Celtic origin. Cf. KÖHLER 39. According to GREEN 139 *Muig-éo* is a dative of *Mag-éo*.
A place on the Irish mainland, see **MAGEO**.

mund OHG *munt*, OE *mund* 'hand, protection'. It is used as a second el. in combination with **geb** (3).

NAITON (3) According to HOLDER II, 696 this Celtic personal name is a variant of *Nechton*, the base of which is an Old Irish adjective *necht* 'pure, white', which is connected with a verb-stem *nig-* 'to wash'; cf. VENDRYES LE N-6 and N-16. Cf. also FÖRSTER TH 120, JACKSON LHEB 410 f., 708.
He became King of the Picts in 706. In his eventful reign he adopted the Roman Easter. He died in 732.

NIDD (1) This pre-English river-name has been derived from British **Nido*, which would be connected with a root **nei-* 'to be brilliant'; cf. EKWALL RN 302 f., GREEN 148, JACKSON LHEB 286, 343, 558, SMITH WRY VII, 132, DEPN 342. Cf. also HOLDER II, 746, FÖRSTER TH 326, 329. Because of the presence of related river-names on the Continent, however, the name has come to be looked upon as Old European and a different root has been proposed for it, viz. **neid-/*nid-* 'to flow'; cf. NICOLAISEN 251 f., Krahe[49], SCHERER AEH 407[50].
The Nidd, Yorkshire West Riding.

nordan OHG *nordana*, OE *norþan* 'north of'. It is the first component of **NORDANHYMBRI** (28).

NORDANHYMBRI (28) nordan; HUMBER.
The Northumbrians.

nos OE **nōs* 'snout, muzzle'. See **HACANOS**.

o OHG *ēo*, OE *ā/ō* 'ever, always'? See **OUINI**.

OFFA (2) Various derivations have been suggested for this common OE personal name. They are reviewed by FEILITZEN DB 334 f. and STRÖM 72 f. Ström's preference is for short-form derivation from compound names with **uulf**; cf. ANDERSON LB 122, ARNGART 131, and also STARK 13. The name could also be derived from compounds with **oht**, possibly connected with OHG *āhta*, OE *ōht* 'persecution, fear', or from compounds with **os** followed by a second

---

[49] H. Krahe, "Die Struktur der alteuropäischen Hydronomie", *Abhandlungen der Geistes- und Sozialwissenschaftlichen Klasse* (Akademie der Wissenschaften und der Literatur) 5 (1962), p. 331.
[50] Also "Britannien und das 'alteuropäische' Flussnamensystem", in: W. Iser & H. Schrabram (eds.), *Britannica, Festschrift für H. M. Flasdieck*, Heidelberg 1960, p. 243.

el. with initial *f-*; cf. HOLTHAUSEN 240, Arngart (*l.c.*). A final possibility is derivation from a base *uƀ as found in OHG *ubil*, OE *yfel* 'evil'; cf. BJÖRK-MANN ST 84, REDIN 101 f., and also MÜLLER 57, SCHÖNFELD 245, BOEHLER 227.

> He was a son of King Sigheri (*s.v.*). He came to the throne after 694 and abdicated in 709 in order to go on a pilgrimage to Rome. There he died soon after his arrival.

oft   OHG *ofto*, OE *oft* 'often'. It is used as a first el. in combination with **for** (1).

OFTFOR (1)   oft; for.

> He had studied in the monastery of Abbess Hild (*s.v.*) at Whitby, and was consecrated Bishop of the Huiccii (*s.v.*) at Worcester in 691. He probably died in 693.

OIDDI (1)   The etymology of this personal name is uncertain. HOLDER II, 840 suggests a British origin for it. STRÖM 73 assumes a Germanic origin, and reviews three possibilities: a short form of compound names with **oidil**; a misspelling for *Oddi ⟨ OE *Odda*; and the use of *oi* instead of *ae*, so that **OIDDI** would be the equivalent of **ÆDDI**. All three possibilities are rejected by ANDERSON LB 71, who explains the name as an *i*-mutated derivative of *Odda*; cf. ANDERSON LB 98, 106 and CAMPBELL 78. *Odda* is a short form of compound names with **ord**, which is connected with OHG *ort*, OE *ord*, 'point, spear'. For the *i*-suffix see **AECCI**. Cf. ANDERSON LB 122, and also REDIN 52, 68 f.

> He was one of the helpers of Uilfrid 1 (*s.v.*) in the conversion of Sussex around 680[51].

oidil   OHG *uodal*, OE *ēdel* 'home, native country'. It is used as a first el. in combination with **uald** (4).

OIDILUALD (4)   oidil; uald.

> A monk in the monastery of Ripon, who went to Farne Island around 685 to lead a solitary life there.

ORCADAS (1)   It is of Celtic origin, probably connected with Old Irish *orc* (⟨ Latin *porcus*) 'pig, boar', possibly through the stage of a folk-name *Orcoi. Cf. HOLDER II, 866, MACBAIN 68, WATSON 28 f., MAGOUN '35 91, GREEN 149, RI & CR 32, VENDRYES LE O-28.

> The Orkney Islands, Scotland.

os   OHG *ans*, OE *ōs* 'divinity, god'. It is used as a first el. in combination with **raed/red** (6), **ric** (4), **thryd/thryth** (1), **uald** (1), **uini** (1), and **uiu** (9).

---

[51] CO & MY 373, 611 actually identifies Oiddi with Bede's Aeddi (*s.v.*).

OSRED (6) os; raed/red.
>He was a son of King Aldfrid of Northumbria (*s.v.*), born in 697. He came to the throne in 705, and died in 716.

OSRIC 1 (1) os; ric.
>He was sub-king of the Huiccii (*s.v.*) around 680.

OSRIC 2 (3) os; ric.
>He was probably a son of King Aldfrid of Northumbria (*s.v.*). He came to the throne in 718 and died in 729.

OSTHRYD (1) os; thryd/thryth.
>She was a daughter of King Osuiu of Northumbria (*s.v.*). Around 679 she married King Aedilred of Mercia (*s.v.*). She was killed in 697.

OSUALD (1) os; uald.
>He was a son of King Aedilfrid of Bernicia, born in 604. Around 633 he came to the throne, and he was killed in the Battle of Maserfelth in 641. He is remembered as St. Oswald.

OSUINI (1) os; uini.
>He was a son of King Osric of Deira. In 644 he came to the throne, and he died in 651.

OSUIU (9) os; uiu.
>He was a son of King Aedilfrid of Bernicia, born in 612. He came to the throne late in 641, and died in 670.

OUINI (2)   If the name is not a misspelling for *Osuini* or an adapted borrowing from a Celtic name connected with modern English *Owen*, the first el. may be connected with OHG *ēo*, OE *ō/ā* 'ever, always'. Cf. STRÖM 29, ANDERSON LB 103. Another possibility is connection with OE *eoh* 'horse', as is tentatively suggested by ANDERSON LB 72 f. Cf. also FEILITZEN DB 343. The second el. is **uini**.
>He was chief of the household of Queen Aedilthryd (*s.v.*), and had come with her to Northumbria at her marriage. Later he entered the monastery of Lastingham near Whitby.

PADDA (1) The origin of this personal name is uncertain. REDIN 105 f. feels inclined to assign it to Celtic, because there is no Germanic theme **paud-*. Then, late OE *Padda* may be a nick-name from OE *pad(d)e* 'toad, frog', although there is no evidence for this word in early OE; cf. FEILITZEN DB 343. STRÖM 74 suggests lall-name formation. And finally, short name formation from a compound name the first el. of which begins with a labial consonant is seriously considered by ANDERSON LB 71, who further remarks that the labial "need not necessarily have been a *P-*". It seems, therefore, that connection with the name-theme **badu**, as suggested by KAUFMANN UAR 37, is quite possible. The name has always been identified with **PEADA** in view of the variant forms with single and double *d*.

He was one of the helpers of Uilfrid 1 (*s.v.*) in the conversion of Sussex around the year 680.

PARISIACUS (1) Adjectival form connected with **PARISII**.
Of the Parisians.

PARISII (1) HOLDER II, 932 assumes for this tribal name an older **Quăr-īsii*, derived from a verbal stem **qari-/*qariu* 'to place, put', and interprets the name as 'the energetic, brave'. Cf. also LONGNON 102, DAU & ROS 519.
The Parisians.

PEADA (1) Probably identical with **PADDA**, the diphthong having arisen through back-mutation of /a/. Cf. REDIN 105 f., STRÖM 75, ANDERSON LB 66, 95, 131, CAMPBELL 87, n. 1. Similar, however, to what has been suggested for **PADDA** and its connection with the name-theme **badu**, the suggestion may be made here that in **PEADA** a name-theme is hidden that is derived from a stem **baudi-*, for which see **BAEDA**. Originally the diphthong would then have been long.
He was a son of King Penda of Mercia (*s.v.*), and was *princeps* of the Middle Angles from around 640 until 656, when he was murdered.

pect OE *Peohtas* 'the Picts', for which see **PICTI**. It is used as a first el. in combination with **helm** (3).

PECTHELM (3) **pect; helm.**
He was Bishop of Whithorn, Galloway (Scotland), from around 730 to 735.

PENDA (1) A personal name of uncertain origin, probably arisen as a short name of compounds with a name-theme **pend**, possibly connected with OHG *pfant* 'pledge' () modern Dutch *pand*). Connection has been suggested with OHG *pfenni(n)c*, OE *pending* 'penny, money', in as far as 'penny' is supposed to have been derived from Penda: 'a piece coined by Penda'. Cf. BOEHLER 106, REDIN 69, STRÖM 75; cf. also MÜLLER 107, BACH I, 1, 298. Derivation from Celtic compound personal names with Old British *penn* 'head' for a first el. has been proposed by FÖRSTER KW 176 f.
He was King of Mercia from between 626 and 632 until 654.

PICTI (14) This Latinized Celtic tribal name has been connected with Latin *pingere* 'to paint' and has been taken to mean 'the painted, tattooed people'. Others have seen in it a parallel of the Gaulish tribal name *Pictaui* of uncertain meaning. Cf. HOLDER II, 993, HOLTHAUSEN 246, STRÖM 31, JACKSON LHEB 576 f. It may be related to **BRETTONES**. As a first el. of personal names it takes the form **pect**. Cf. also MÜLLER 102 f.
The Picts, Scotland.

PIPPIN (5) A Continental Germanic personal name. It has been suggested that nickname formation has taken place from Old French *pepin/pipin* 'seed of a

fleshy fruit'; cf. FORSSNER 204, TENGVIK 224. According to KAUF-
MANN UAR 131 and KAUFMANN ERG 60 it resulted from lall-name
formation on the basis of a name-stem *bib-*.

He established himself as King of the Franks in 687 and died in 714.

PUCH (1)   A Celtic personal name of uncertain etymology. Cf. HOLDER
II, 1051, ANDERSON LB 85.

A *gesith*, whose wife was cured by St. John of Hexham around 700 at
the urgent request of Berichtun (*s.v.*), Abbot of Inderauuda (*s.v.*, =
Beverley).

PUTTA (5)   Opinions differ as to what the origin of this personal name may
have been. REDIN 107 does not wholly reject Celtic origin, but thinks Germanic
origin is more likely. He suggests a number of possibilities: connection with
the modern English verb *to put*; with OE *puduc* 'wart' ((<*pud* 'to swell'); and
with OE *pyttel* 'hawk, kite'. To these STRÖM 75 adds lall-name formation, comparable to Swedish *putte* 'small boy'. Redin's suggestion of by-name formation
from a base **pud* 'to swell' is supported by TENGVIK 329; the suggestion of
connection with OE *pyttel* 'hawk, kite' is taken over by EKWALL ST II, 91,
ANDERSON LB 71, EPNE II, 75, and is thought conceivable by TENGVIK
329, 365. KAUFMANN UAR 46 f. suggests connection, through devoicing of
the initial consonant as in **PADDA**, with a stem **baudi-* (> OHG *bōd-/būd-*)
(for which see **BAEDA**). Such a development of the diphthong, however, is
unlikely for OE. But along the same lines connection may perhaps be suggested
with the stem *but(t)* 'blunt' found in OE *buttuc* 'end, small piece of land etc.',
thought to be the base of the personal name *Byttic* by REDIN 151.

He was Bishop of Rochester from 669 to 676, and Bishop of Hereford
from 676 until possibly 688.

QUAENTAUIC (1)   The first component of this Continental place-name is
a river-name *Quantia* (> modern French *la Canche*), possibly connected with a
Celtic stem *canto* 'white, bright'; cf. GREEN 156. The second component is
uic. Cf. HOLDER II, 1060, ANDERSON LB 119, DAU & ROS 275.

Etaples, France.

quic   OHG *quec*, OE *cwic(u)* 'alive'. It is used as a first el. in combination with
helm (2).

QUICHELM (2)   **quic; helm.**

He was consecrated Bishop of Rochester in 676, and resigned in 678.

quoen   OE *cwēn* (< Gothic *qēns*) 'woman, wife, queen'. It is used as a first el. in
combination with **burg** (1).

QUOENBURG (1)   **quoen; burg.**

She was a nun in the monastery at Uetadun (*s.v.*), where her mother
Hereburg (*s.v.*) was Abbess.

164

RACUULFE (1) A compound place-name wholly of Celtic[52] origin, which in Romano-British took the form *Regulbium*. Cf. HOLDER II, 1113. The first component may be an Old British prefix *ro-* ⟨ Latin *pro*, or an adjectival Old British *ro* 'great'. The second component is connected with a British **gulbio* 'beak'. If we assume borrowing of this name by the Saxons before the migration-period, explaining the change of /g/ to /k/ is no problem. Cf. ZACHRISSON RKS 81, KARLSTRÖM KIL 133 ff., WALLENBERG 12, MAGOUN '35 93, GREEN 157, FÖRSTER TH 191, 846, JACKSON LHEB 559, 661, DEPN 383, CAMERON 35, REANEY OR 80; cf. also ANDERSON LB 84. Most place-name scholars support the derivation of **ro* from *pro*, and give its meaning as 'promontory', but Jackson, Cameron, and Reaney prefer 'great headland'.

  Reculver, Kent.

raed/red OHG *rāt*, OE *rǣd* 'advice, wisdom'. It is used as a first el. in combination with **frid/frit** (1), and as a second el. with **aedil/edil** (16), **ceol** (2), **coen/coin** (10), **os** (6), **suaeb/suef** (1), **thryd/thryth** (1), and **uict/uiht** (4). It is spelled **raed** as a first el., and as a second el. twice in the combination with **aedil/edil**.

RAEDFRID (1) **raed/red**; **frid/frit**.
  He was the prefect of King Ecgberct of Kent (*s.v.*).

RATHBED (2) A Continental Germanic personal name; cf. ANDERSON LB 65. Its first el. goes back to a name-theme **rătha*, which is connected with OHG (*h*)*rad*, OE (*h*)*rǣd* 'quick, clever'; cf. KAUFMANN ERG 282, and also SCHÖNFELD 183. The second el., with long /ē/, must be an Old Frisian development of a name-theme *bōdi-* ⟨ **baudi-*, for which see **BAEDA**; cf. BACH I, 1, 223.
  He was a Frisian King who constantly fought against the Franks, and refused to be baptised. He died in 719.

RHENUS (3) The Latinized form, with unetymological *-h-*, of late Gaulish *Rēnos*, which is probably connected with a root **reinos* 'river'. Cf. HOLDER II, 1130, GREEN 162, BACH II, 2, 54 f. It is considered to be Old European by SCHERER AEH 408 and Krahe[53].
  The Rhine.

ric OHG *rīchi*, OE *rīce* 'powerful', and also in the sense of 'power, kingdom'. The stem has developed from a stem **rīk-*, which was borrowed from Celtic before the assibilation of /k/. The subsequent irregular development may have to be accounted for by the presence of the theme in Celtic names; compare such forms as Gaulish *-rīx* in *Vercingetorix*. Cf. FÖRSTEMANN I, 1253 f., MÜLLER 125, BOEHLER 109, FEILITZEN DB 348, STRÖM 32 f., SCHRAMM 32,

---

[52] MIDDENDORFF 105 and KÖHLER 33 f. assume Germanic origin for the component parts of this place-name.
[53] H. Krahe, *Unsere älteste Flussnamen*, Wiesbaden 1964; pp. 95 f.

and KAUFMANN ERG 289 f. It is used as a second el. in combination with **al** (1), **ead/ed/æad** (2), **here/heri** (2), and **os** (4).

RUGINI (1)   The Latinized form of a Germanic tribal name, which in Latin usually appears as *Rugii*. KAUFMANN ERG 296 connects it with OHG *rocko*, OE *ryǧe* 'rye'. Cf. also PLUMMER II, 287, SCHÖNFELD 195 f., HOLTHAUSEN 265.
>   The Rugians.

sa   OHG *sēo*, OE *sǣ* 'sea, lake'. It is used as a first el. in combination with **berct/ berht/berict** (1).

SABERCT (1)   **sa**; **berct/berht/berict**.
>   He was King of the East Saxons until about 616.

SABRINA (1)   The etymology of this Romano-British river-name, which in OE became *Sæfern* and in modern Welsh is *Hafren*, is unknown. Cf. HOLDER II, 1272, EKWALL RN 358 ff., MAGOUN '35 93, GREEN 166, FÖRSTER TH 245 f., 424, JACKSON LHEB 519, 558, EPNE II, 92, DEPN 413, CAMERON 37, SMITH GL I, 10 and IV, 25, n. 3.
>   The Severn, Wales and Gloucestershire.

saex/sax/sex   OHG *sahs*, OE *seax* 'knife, short sword', and related to the tribal name **SAXONES**, from which the name-theme may actually derive. It is used as a first el. in combination with **burg** (1) and **uulf** (4). In combination with the latter it takes the form **saex** three times and the form **sax** once, whereas it is **sex** in combination with **burg**.

SAEXUULF (4)   **saex/sax/sex**; **uulf**.
>   He was Bishop of Lichfield from 675 until about 691, after having been Abbot of the monastery of Medeshamstede (*s.v.*).

SAXONES (37)   The Latinized form of a Germanic tribal name, which is used in combination with *antiqui, australes, occidentales,* and *orientales* in HE to denote subdivisions of the tribe. It is usually connected with OHG *sahs*, OE *seax* 'knife, short sword', although sometimes its older meaning of 'stone, rock' is preferred. Cf. FÖRSTEMANN I, 1288, SCHÖNFELD 199 f., HOLTHAUSEN 288, STRÖM 33, BACH I,1,201 and 310, EKWALL TN 135 f., DEPN 406, JENSEN GTNs 243. The same stem is found in the name-theme **saex/sax/sex**.
>   The Saxons.

SAXONICUS (2)   Latinized adjectival form of **SAXONES**.
>   Of the Saxons.

SCOTTI (18)   The Latinized form of a Celtic tribal name, the etymology of which is obscure. HOLDER II, 1406 suggests it may be connected with Old

Slavonic *skotŭ* 'cattle, property'. Cf. also EKWALL EN 156, HOLTHAUSEN 282, EKWALL TN 168 f., EPNE II,113, DEPN 408.
>The Irish.

SCOTTIA (5)   This Latinized country-name is connected with **SCOTTI**.
>Ireland.

SCOTTICUS (2)   Latinized adjectival form connected with **SCOTTI**.
>Of the Irish.

SEBBI (3)   For this personal name two short-form derivations have been suggested. The first is derivation from the compound name **SABERCT**, possibly indirectly through the short form *Saba*[54]; cf. REDIN 128, ZACHRISSON RKS 58, STRÖM 76. The other is derivation from compound names in which **saex/sax/sex** is the first el. and in which the second el. begins with a -*b*-; cf. ANDERSON LB 72, 122. For the *i*-suffix see **AECCI**.
>He was King of the East Saxons from 664 – for some time together with Sigheri (*s.v.*) – until about 693.

SEXBURG (1)   **saex/sax/sex; burg.**
>She was a daughter of King Anna of East Anglia (*s.v.*), and wife of King Earconberct of Kent (*s.v.*). Later she succeeded her sister Aedilthryd (*s.v.*) as Abbess of Ely. She died about the year 695.

SELAESEU (2)   The first component of this place-name is connected with OHG *selah*, OE *seolh* 'seal'. Cf. KÖHLER 41, MA & ST SUS 82 f., GREEN 168, ANDERSON LB 77, and *passim*, EPNE II,119, DEPN 411, CAMERON 31. Hille[55] has suggested that the etymology of the first component of this place-name may have to be reconsidered with a view to his proposal for a new etymology of the first el. of the personal name *Seoluini*. For this he assumes a parallel in Old Norse *sjóli* deriving from Primitive Germanic **seƀul-* 'king, chief'. The onomastic grounds Hille adduces for wanting to leave the traditional explanation of the name-theme of both the personal and the place-name are not convincing enough in view of Bede's interpretation of the place-name. Bede translates the name into Latin as "insula uituli marini"; cf. HE IV, 13. The first component appears as *saelęseu* once, viz. 38r,28. For the second component see **ei/eu/ę**.
>Selsey, Sussex.

SENONES (1)   A Continental tribal name of uncertain origin. Cf. HOLDER II, 1485, GREEN 169, DAUZAT NFP 548.
>A tribe in France.

seolh   see **SELAESEU**

---

[54] Saberct (*s.v.*) was called *Saba* by his own sons, according to HE II, 5. Cf. also CO & MY 153, n. 2.
[55] A. Hille, "OE Seoluini and ON Sjóli", *English Studies* 44 (1963), p. 35.

sig OHG *sigi*, OE *sige* 'victory'. It is used as a first el. in combination with **hard/heard** (1) and **here/heri** (2).

SIGHARD (1) **sig; hard/heard.**

He was a son of King Sebbi of the East Saxons (*s.v.*). About 693 he succeeded his father, probably together with his brother Suefred (*s.v.*). He died before 709.

SIGHERI (2) **sig; here/heri.**

He was a son of King Sigberct the Little of Essex. From 664 onwards he reigned over the East Saxons together with Sebbi (*s.v.*). The date of his death is unknown.

SOLUENTE (1) The name is of Celtic, but obscure, origin according to HOLDER II, 1613 and DEPN 430. MILLER 77 f. and KÖHLER 41 connect the first part of the name with OHG *salo*, OE *salu* 'dark, foul'. Cf. also GREEN 170.

The Solent, Hampshire.

stan OHG *stein*, OE *stān* 'stone, rock'. It is the second component of the place-name **DEGSASTAN** (1) and the first component of **STANFORD** (1).

STANFORD (1) **stan; ford.**

The identification of this place with Stamford Bridge, Yorkshire East Riding, is supported by ANDERSON LB 102 and DEPN 436. Neither *Stamford Bridge East* nor *Stamford Bridge West* is connected, however, with Bede's **STANFORD** by SMITH ERY 186, 272. Both PLUMMER II, 528 – tentatively – and CO & MY 615 identify the place as *Stamford, Lincolnshire*, and this is also the identification preferred by GREEN 171.

stod see **UALHSTOD**

STREANAESHALCH (4) The first component of this place-name has not been altogether satisfactorily explained. Bede's own translation of the name as "sinus fari" (HE III, 25) has not helped greatly, since a connection between the first part of the OE name and the meaning of the Latin *farus* 'light-house' is hard to see[56]. So it has been suggested that *fari* should be taken as *farae* from medieval Latin *fara* 'offspring, descent', or as *fori* from *forum* 'market, market-place'. Both corrections would come nearer to the OE word, which could be interpreted as OHG *gi-striuni*, OE *ge-strēon* 'gain, profit; offspring', or as an unrecorded OE personal name *Strēona*, which personal name would be connected with the noun just mentioned either as an agential noun derived from the verb *strēonan/strīenan* 'to acquire, gain' or as a short name formed from compound names such as *Streonberct* and *Streonuulf*. Cf. MILLER 38,

---

[56] Moreover, the presence in the seventh century of lighthouses on the Northumbrian coast seems unlikely. Two lighthouses, both at Dover, are actually known from Roman times. Cf. Ordnance Survey, *Map of Roman Britain*, third edition, Chessington (Surrey) 1956; p. 14.

MÜLLER 82, MIDDENDORFF 128, Liebermann[57], KÖHLER 41, SMITH NRY 13, 126, Mawer[58], MAGOUN '35 59, TENGVIK 356, DAHL 58, STRÖM 101, ANDERSON LB 77, 104, 125, EPNE II,163, DEPN 450, CAMERON 80, NI,GEL & RI 191 f. GREEN 172 ff., having considered the solutions proposed for the problem, prefers to accept the Latin as it stands, assuming that OE *strēon* is here used in an "otherwise unrecorded meaning". The second component is **halch/halh**.

Streanaeshalch survives in Strensall, Yorkshire North Riding, but the place in HE has from an early date been identified with Whitby, Yorkshire North Riding. Beside references given above cf. also PLUMMER II, 184, REANEY OR 180, EKWALL VC 43 f., CO & MY 616.

suaeb/suef OHG *Swāba*, OE *Swǣfas* 'the Swabians', possibly connected with OHG *swās*, OE *swǣs* 'one's own; dear', or more probably with OE *swefan* 'to sleep'. Cf. FÖRSTEMANN I, 1373, SCHÖNFELD 215, REDIN 69, HOLTHAUSEN 331, STRÖM 34 f., ANDERSON LB 99, ARNGART 131, EKWALL TN 150 f., BACH I, 1, 311, KAUFMANN ERG 333. It is used as a first el. in combination with **hard/heard** (1), spelled **suaeb**, and with **raed/red** (1), spelled **suef**.

SUAEBHEARD (1)   suaeb/suef; hard/heard.
According to HE V, 8 he was joint King of Kent together with Uictred (*s.v.*) in the year 692. The dates of his accession and death are unknown.

SUEFRED (1)   suaeb/suef; raed/red.
He was a son of King Sebbi of the East Saxons (*s.v.*). He succeeded his father in 693, probably together with his brother Sighard (*s.v.*). He died before 709.

suid   OHG *swind*, OE *swīþ* 'strong'. It is used as a first el. in combination with **berct/berht/berict** (4), and as a second el. in combination with **bregu** (1) and **here/heri** (1).

SUIDBERCT 1 (3)   suid; berct/berht/berict.
An Anglo-Saxon missionary to the Frisians, who was Bishop of Frisia from 693 until about 713.

SUIDBERCT 2 (1)   suid; berct/berht/berict.
He was Abbot of the monastery near the river Dacre, Cumberland, around the year 730.

suthr   OHG *sundar*, OE **sūþer* 'south'. It is used as a first el. in **SUTHRIEONA**.

---

[57] F. Liebermann, "Streoneshealh", *Archiv für das Studium der neueren Sprachen und Litteraturen* 108 (1902), 368.
[58] A. Mawer, *Problems of Place-Name Study*, Cambridge 1929; pp. 44, 86.

SUTHRIEONA (1)   This is the genitive plural of *Suthrige*. The first component is **suthr**. The second component is **ge**. The name probably originally meant 'the people of the southern district'. Cf. HOLTHAUSEN 330, GOVER etc. SU 1 f., GREEN 176, DAHL 99, ANDERSON LB 98 f., 104, 127, EPNE II,169, DEPN 453, EKWALL TN 130 f.
   Surrey.

TAMISA (1)   This river-name, which in texts of the M-type appears as *Tamensis*[59], is Celtic in origin. It is derived from an Old British *Tamēsa*, which in Primitive OE was understood as *Tamīsa*. By most scholars this base is connected with a stem *tam/*tem 'dark', found in Sanskrit as *tamasā* 'dark', and the name is taken to mean something like 'dark river'. Cf. HOLDER II,1713, EKWALL RN 405, GREEN 177, RI & CR 46, FÖRSTER TH 722 ff., ALESSIO 226 f., JENSEN AIO 430, CAMERON 37 f., REANEY OR 72, DEPN 464, SMITH GL I, 12 f. Another suggestion, however, made by FÖRSTER TH 727 ff. and supported by NICOLAISEN 256 ff., is that the base was derived from Indo-European *tā-/*tə- 'to flow'. The complex etymology of this river-name is further dealt with by EKWALL RN 402 ff., FÖRSTER TH 561 ff., JACKSON LHEB 331, 486, 523, 532, and EPNE II, 175.
   The Thames, Gloucestershire-Essex-Kent.

tat   OHG *zeiz* 'tender, delicate', OE *tāt* 'glad, happy', in OE only known as a name-theme. It is used as a first el. in combination with **frid/frit** (1) and **uini** (3).

TATFRID (1)   **tat; frid/frit.**
   He was Bishop elect of the Huiccii (*s.v.*), but died before his consecration in 680. He had been educated in the monastery of Abbess Hild (*s.v.*).

TATUINI (3)   **tat; uini.**
   He was Archbishop of Canterbury from 731 to 734. He had been a priest in the monastery at Briudun (*s.v.*, = Breedon-on-the-Hill, Leicestershire).

thryd/thryth   OHG *drūd* (⟨*þrūþi⟩), OE *þrȳþ* 'force, strength, majesty'. STRÖM 36 and FORSSNER 81 mention a possible connection with OHG *trūt* 'dear'. In fact the two name-themes were mixed up at a very early date in OHG; cf. BACH I, 1, 208, 226, SCHRAMM 167, and KAUFMANN ERG 98. It is used as a first el. in combination with **raed/red** (1), and as a second el. with **aedil/edil** (5), **blith** (1), and **os** (1). The spelling **thryth** occurs only once, accompanied by the loss of -*h*- in the initial consonant-group, in **AEDILTRYTH** (1r, 36).

---

[59] According to FÖRSTER TH 306, 479 ff. this Latinized adjectival form stems from an incorrect copying of Caesar's *Tamēsis* by Orosius. **TAMISA** would be an Anglo-Saxon Latinization of the correct original base *Tamis*.

170

THRYDRED (1)   thryd/thryth; raed/red.
>He was Abbot of a monastery near the river Dacre, Cumberland, at the time HE was written.

til   OE *til* 'good, excellent', which is connected with OHG *zilōn*, OE *tilian* 'to strive, to gain, to labour, to cultivate etc.', so that the name-theme may also have been interpreted as synonymous with OE *tilia* 'labourer, peasant'. It is used as a first el. in combination with **man(n)/mon** (1).

TILMON (1)   til; man(n)/mon.
>One of the companions of the two missionary brothers Heuuald (*s.v.*).

TINA/TINUS (3)   Only genitive and ablative forms occur in HE of this Latinized river-name. It is generally looked upon as Celtic. Cf. HOLDER II, 1851, MAWER NO & DU 202. The name probably goes back to an Old British base **Tinā*, which is connected with a root **tī-* 'to flow, to dissolve'; cf. also OE *þīnan* 'to dissolve'. Cf. EKWALL RN 425 f., MAGOUN '35 97, GREEN 180, FÖRSTER TH 753, RI & CR 47, DEPN 484, NI,GEL & RI 183. The rivername is taken to be Old European by NICOLAISEN 262 who starts from the same Indo-European root; cf. also CAMERON 37.
>The Tyne, Northumberland-Durham etc.

TITILLO (dat.) (1)   The origin of this name is uncertain. REDIN 144 thinks it may be Celtic. It may, however, be based on **Titta*, which could be a short form of compounds with **tid**, a name-theme connected with OHG *zīd*, OE *tīd* 'time'. The second part is the diminutive suffix *-il(a)*. Cf. STRÖM 76 f., ANDERSON LB 97, 108, DEPN 473 (*s.v. Tidcombe*).
>He was a notary at the Synod of Hertford in 672.

tond   HOLTHAUSEN 342 connects it with OHG *zan(d)*, OE *tōd* 'tooth'. More likely is a connection with such words as OHG *zantaro* 'glowing coal', Old Norse *tandr* 'fire', and OE *on-tendan* 'to kindle'. Cf. MÜLLER 112, BOEHLER 120, STRÖM 37, ANDERSON LB 91. It is unnecessary to assign it to Celtic, as HELLWIG 26 is inclined to do, even if the name-theme is unrecorded in other Germanic languages. It is used as a first el. in combination with **berct/berht/berict** (1).

TONDBERCT (1)   tond; berct/berht/berict.
>He was a prince of the South Gyruii, who married Aedilthryd (*s.v.*) in 652. He died in 655.

torct   OHG *zoraht*, OE *torht* 'bright, illustrious'. It is used as a first el. in combination with **gyd** (2).

TORCTGYD (2)   torct; gyd.
>She was a nun in the monastery at Barking at the time that Abbess Aedilburg (*s.v.*) died of the plague (664?). She herself died three years later.

TORONIS (1) A place-name of Celtic origin, originally appearing as *Turonicum*, which is derived from the tribal name *Turones*. Cf. HOLDER II, 2006, SCHÖN-FELD 244, LONGNON 100, GREEN 187, DAU & ROS 682.

   Tours, France.

TRAIECTUM (1) A Latin place-name, in the sense of 'crossing', used for **UILTABURG**. Cf. HOLDER II, 1903, BACH II, 2, 74.

   Utrecht, The Netherlands.

TREANTA (1) A river-name of Celtic origin, going back to British *Trisantonā*, which in Primitive Welsh became **Trihanton*. Of the two component parts the first is British **trĭ-* 'through, across' and the second may be a stem **santon* in the sense of 'traveller'. Cf. EKWALL RN 415 ff., GREEN 182, JACKSON LHEB 503, 524 f. Ekwall interprets the name as 'the trespasser, river liable to flood'. Cf. also HOLDER II, 1957, DUIGNAN 155 f., MAGOUN '35 97, EPNE II, 187, DEPN 480, CAMERON 38[60], REANEY OR 72.

   The Trent, Staffordshire-Derbyshire etc.

trum OE *trum* 'firm, strong'. It is used in combination with **berct/berht/berict** (1), and **uini** (3).

TRUMBERCT (1)   **trum; berct/berht/berict.**
   This monk of the monastery of Lastingham instructed Bede in the Scriptures. Cf. HE IV, 3.

TRUMUINI (3)   **trum; uini.**
   He was consecrated missionary Bishop of the Picts in 681, and was forced to retire when the Picts recovered their land in 685. He then became a monk of the monastery at Whitby, where he died shortly before 705.

tui OHG *zwi-*, OE *twi-* 'two, double', and see further **adTUIFYRDI**.

TUIDUS (2) This Latinized river-name is of Celtic origin, but its etymology is uncertain. Cf. HOLDER II, 1980, MAWER NO & DU 202[61]. EKWALL RN 421 ff., assuming a long stem-vowel, connects it with an Indo-European root **tevā* 'to swell, to be powerful'; cf. also DEPN 483. FÖRSTER TH 271 ff., assuming a short stem-vowel, ultimately derives it from an Indo-European root **tuei* 'to move up and down'. GREEN 185 records both interpretations. CAMERON 37 assumes a pre-Celtic origin for it.

   The Tweed, Scotland and Northumberland.

adTUIFYRDI (1) For the preposition see **ad**. The first component is **tui**, and its vowel is looked upon as short by OET 566, HOLTHAUSEN 120, 356, and ANDERSON LB 97. Others assume lengthening of the vowel in OE;

---

[60] Also *The Place-Names of Derbyshire*, Parts I-III (EPNS XXVII-XXIX), Cambridge 1959; I, 18.

[61] The name is not discussed by JACKSON LHEB.

cf. KÖHLER 42, LUICK I,120, EPNE II,199, CAMPBELL 120. The second component is **ford/fyrdi**.

It has been identified as Alnmouth, Northumberland. Cf. MAWER NO & DU 4, n. 1, GREEN 28.

tun   OHG *zūn*, OE *tūn* 'enclosure'. It is used as a first el. in combination with **berct/berht/berict** (2), and it also occurs in **TUNNA** (1).

TUNBERCT (2)   **tun; berct/berht/berict.**

He was consecrated Bishop of Hexham in 681, and in 684 he was deposed. Before that he was Abbot of Gilling, Yorkshire North Riding.

TUNNA (1)   This personal name is a short form of a compound name with **tun**, in which gemination of the medial consonant and shortening of the vowel has taken place. Cf. MÜLLER 61, REDIN 56, ANDERSON HN I, 149, STRÖM 77, ANDERSON LB 102, 122 f. HOLDER II, 1992 thinks it may be Celtic.

He was Abbot of the monastery he had founded at Tunnacẹstir (*s.v.*). When his brother Imma (*s.v.*) was severely wounded in the Battle of the Trent in 679, he went out to search for him.

TUNNACẸSTIR (1)   **TUNNA; cẹstir.**

The place was named after Tunna (*s.v.*), and has never been identified. Tunna probably built the monastery on a Roman site.

ualch/ualh   OHG *walh/walah*, OE *w(e)alh* 'foreigner, Briton, slave'. It is used as a first el. in combination with **stod** (1), and as a second el. with **aedil/edil** (3) and **coen/coin** (1). The spelling **ualh** is only found in the combination with **stod**.

uald   Connected with OHG *waltan*, OE *w(e)aldan* 'to rule, to possess'. As a first el. it may be derived more specifically from OE *(ge)weald* 'might, power', and as a second el. from the nomen agentis *wealda* 'ruler'. It is used as a first el. in combination with **here/heri** (1), and as a second el. with **aedil/edil** (2), **ar** (1), **berct/berht/berict** (7), **earcon/ercon** (3), **heah** (6), **ing** (2), **oidil** (4), and **os** (1).

UALDHERI (1)   **uald; here/heri.**

He was Bishop of London from 693 to between 705 and 716.

UALHSTOD (1)   The first el. is **ualch/ualh**. As to the second el., which is not evidenced as a name-theme elsewhere, ANDERSON LB 69 comes to the conclusion that it has a long vowel /ō/, because it appears as *Gwalstawt* as a Welsh loanword. So much is also tentatively suggested by STRÖM 34. The word is probably connected with OE *standan* 'to stand', and may mean something like 'statue; pillar'; its meaning, therefore, comes close to that of the word with short /o/, i.e. *stod* 'post, support'. Both Ström and Anderson interpret the name as a by-name, identical with OE *w(e)alhstod* 'interpreter, mediator', possibly literally 'helper of Britons'. Cf. MÜLLER 135, FÖRSTER TH 157, n. 1.

Ualhstod was Bishop of the peoples west of the Severn from between 727 and 731 to between 731 and 736. His see was at Hereford.

uari OHG *-wari*, OE *-ware/-u* 'settlers, inhabitants'. It is used to form the tribal names **BORUCTUARI** (3), **CANTUARII** (15) and **MEANUARI** (1).

UECTA (7) The Latinized form of a Celtic name, which in British probably was *Ueχta. Cf. HOLDER III, 132. It has been connected with modern Welsh *gwaith*, meaning both 'labour, work' and 'turn, course', which is based on the Indo-European root **wegh-* 'to move'; cf. also Latin *veho* 'to carry' and OE *wiht* 'weight'. FÖRSTER TH 120 f. arrives for the name of the island at the appropriate meaning of 'point at which the water flows into different directions'. Cf. Kökeritz[62]. DEPN 518 and REANEY OR 71 explain the name as 'what has been raised; what rises above the water; the island'. Cf. also JACKSON LHEB 81, 282, 409, CAMERON 48.
  The Isle of Wight.

UENTA (2) A Celtic name of obscure origin. Cf. HOLDER III, 174, JACKSON LHEB 282, 387, CAMERON 36. RI & CR 48 suggests connection with Welsh *gwent* 'field', possibly 'market-place'; cf. also GREEN 191. DEPN 522 suggests it may belong to a root *ven-* 'to enjoy, to love' and that it may have a meaning related to that of Irish *fine* 'kindred'. Cf. also NI, GEL & RI 194.
  Winchester, Hampshire.

UENTANUS (2) The Latin adjectival form of **UENTA**.
  Of Winchester, Hampshire.

uet OE *wǣt/wēt* 'wet'? It occurs in **UETADUN** (1).

UETADUN (1) HOLDER III, 262 sugests Celtic origin, and KÖHLER 43 connection with a tribal name of unknown etymology. However, the first component of this place-name is probably connected with OE *wǣt/wēt* 'wet'. Cf. GREEN 194, SMITH ERY 158, ANDERSON LB 77, 99, 128, EPNE II, 257, DEPN 501. For the second component see **dun**.
  Watton, Yorkshire East Riding[63].

uic OE *wīc* (< Latin *vicus*) 'dwelling-place, village etc.'. It is used as the second component of **QUAENTAUIC** (1), in which place-name, according to Ekwall[64], it may have the specific sense of 'port, harbour'.

uict/uiht Probably OHG, OE *wiht* 'creature, person'. Cf. OET 512, FÖRSTEMANN I, 1590, BOEHLER 127, FEILITZEN DB 413, STRÖM 39, ANDERSON LB 97. Connection, however, with a Celtic name-theme related to **UECTA**

---

[62] H. Kökeritz, *The Place-Names of the Isle of Wight* (Nomina Germanica 6), Uppsala 1940, p. 281.

[63] OE *wēta* was replaced by the related Old Scandinavian *vātr* 'wet' at some time of its later development.

[64] E. Ekwall, *Old English wīc in Place-Names* (Nomina Germanica 13), Uppsala 1964, p. 15.

174

has also been thought possible. Cf. SCHÖNFELD 262, REDIN 72 f., Ström (*l.c.*). And finally it has also been connected with a Primitive Germanic *wihti- 'fight, battle'. Cf. MÜLLER 91, HOLTHAUSEN 426, BACH I,1,190, SCHRAMM 99; cf. also KAUFMANN ERG 402 f. It is used as a first el. in combination with **berct/berht/berict** (3) and **raed/red** (4). The spelling **uiht** occurs once in the latter combination.

UICTBERCT (3)   **uict/uiht; berct/berht/berict.**
> He spent two years as a missionary in Frisia some time before 690. Before and after this he lived as an anchorite in Ireland.

UICTRED (4)   **uict/uiht; raed/red.**
> He was a son of King Ecgberct of Kent (*s.v.*). In 690 he came to the throne, and was at first joint King together with Suaebheard (*s.v.*). He died in 725.

uig   OHG, OE *wīg* 'strife, war'. It is used as a first el. in combination with **hard/heard** (2).

UIGHEARD (2)   **uig; hard/heard.**
> He was sent to Rome around 667 by King Ecgberct of Kent (*s.v.*) and King Osuiu of Bernicia (*s.v.*), to be consecrated Archbishop of Canterbury. He died in Rome.

uil   OHG *willeo*, OE *willa* 'will, desire, pleasure'. It is used as a first el. in combination with **brod/brord** (7) and with **frid/frit** (43).

UILBRORD (7)   **uil; brod/brord.**
> He was educated at Ripon and in Ireland, and went to Frisia as a missionary in 690. In 695 he was consecrated Archbishop of Uiltaburg (*s.v.*, = Utrecht, The Netherlands). He died in 739.

UILFRID 1 (39)   **uil; frid/frit.**
> He was born in 634, and entered the monastery of Lindisfarne in 648. In 669 he became Archbishop of York, and he was expelled in 678. After having been restored in 686, he was expelled again in 691. He died in 709.

UILFRID 2 (3)   **uil; frid/frit.**
> He was educated at Streanaeshalch (*s.v.*, = Whitby) under Hild (*s.v.*). In 718 he was consecrated Archbishop of Canterbury, and in 732 he resigned. He died about 745.

UILFRID 3 (1)   **uil; frid/frit.**
> He was Bishop of the Huiccii (*s.v.*) from 718 until about 745. His see was at Worcester.

UILTABURG (1)   The first component of this Frisian place-name is the genitive

plural of the tribal name **UILTI**. Cf. also KÖHLER 44, BACH II,2,514, and Gysseling[65]. The second component is **burg**.
Utrecht, The Netherlands.

UILTI (1)   The Latinized form of a Continental Germanic tribal name of obscure origin. HOLDER III, 319 suggests Celtic origin, possibly from a stem *vilto-s* 'wild'. FÖRSTEMANN II, 2, 1355 f. connects it with modern German *Quelle* 'source'. Cf. also GREEN 197.
 The tribe that gave its name to Uiltaburg (*s.v.* , = Utrecht, The Netherlands).

uini   OHG *wini*, OE *wine* 'friend, protector'. It occurs independently once, which independent form ANDERSON LB 71 explains as a by-name, but which may equally well be a short form of a compound name with **uini**. Furthermore it is used as a second el. in combination with **aedil/edil** (1), **aelb/aelf** (3), **ald** (2), **badu** (1), **bern** (1), **ead/ed/æad** (4), **god** (1), **o** (?, 2), **os** (1), **tat** (3), and **trum** (3).

UINI (1)   see **uini**
 He was consecrated bishop in Gaul. He was Bishop of the West Saxons for a short time around 663, and after that of London until about 675.

uiu   Either OHG *wīh* 'holy', OE *wīh/wēoh* 'idol, image; holy', or OHG, OE *wīgan* 'to fight'. Cf. KAUFMANN ERG 399 ff. The former derivation is the likelier one, and has been proposed by STRÖM 42, ANDERSON LB 101, 121, 126, and BACH I, 1, 215. The other derivation is supported by SCHÖNFELD 12 and HOLTHAUSEN 402. It is used as a second el. in combination with **os** (9).

UIURAEMUDA (1)   **UIURI**; **muda.**
 Wearmouth, Durham.

UIURI (3)   The genitive singular of the Latinized form of a river-name of Celtic origin. Cf. HOLDER III, 416, MAWER NO & DU 209. It probably goes back to a Primitive Welsh **Uisuro-* or **Uisuris*, based on an Indo-European root ** u̯eis-* 'blood'. The meaning would then be 'water, river'. Cf. EKWALL RN 441 f., GREEN 201, FÖRSTER TH 230,n.5, 276,n., 307, JACKSON LHEB 362, NICOLAISEN 236, DEPN 502. It is assigned an Old European origin by Nicolaisen (*l.c.*); cf. also CAMERON 37.
 The Wear, Durham.

inUNDALUM (2)   For the preposition see **in**. The second component is clearly a tribal name *Undalas* used in the dative plural, but its meaning is uncertain. Cf. GREEN 122. HOLDER III, 30 thinks it is Celtic. DEPN 353 suggests that the name may be composed of the negative OE prefix *un-* and OE *dāl* 'part, share', and as a whole may mean 'that has no share' or 'undivided'.

---

[65] M. Gysseling, *Toponymisch Woordenboek van België, Nederland, Luxemburg, Noord-Frankrijk en West-Duitsland (vóór 1226)*, 2 vols., Tongeren 1960; p. 1079.

Cf. MAGOUN '38 173, ANDERSON LB 77, 98, 102. FÖRSTER TH 199 rejects this derivation on account of the modern pronunciation of the first part of the compound name. Cf. also Gover etc.[66], EKWALL TN 148 f., CAMERON 74.
Oundle, Northamptonshire.

uuda OHG *witu*, OE *widu/wudu* 'wood'. It is used as the second component of **inDERAUUDA** (1).

uulf OHG *wolf*, OE *wulf* 'wolf'. It is used as a first el. in combination with **here/heri** (6), and as a second el. with **ald** (5), **arc** (1), **ceol** (2), and **saex/sax/sex** (4). Reduction of *-uu-* to *-u-* is not evidenced.

UULFHERI (6)   uulf; here/heri.
He was a son of King Penda of Mercia (*s.v.*). Three years after his father's death in 654 he came to the throne. He died in 674.

uyn OHG *wunna/wunni*, OE *wynn* 'joy, delight'. In Latin charters *-y-* is often spelled *-i-*, so that very often there is no way of distinguishing the names with **uyn** from those with **uin(i)**. Cf. BOEHLER 130. It is used as a first el. in combination with **frid/frit** (6).

UYNFRID (6)   uyn; frid/frit.
He was consecrated Bishop of Mercia (Lichfield) in 672 by Archbishop Theodore. In 675 Theodore deposed him.

[66] J. E. B. Gover, A. Mawer and F. M. Stenton, *The Place-Names of Northamptonshire* (EPNS X), Cambridge 1933; p. 213 f.

PART IV

PHONOLOGY

INTRODUCTORY

In this phonological discussion the material is arranged as one finds it in the standard works on OE phonology. This arrangement is also followed by STRÖM and ANDERSON LB. Contrary, however, to what Ström and especially Anderson do, the present study does not discuss separately matters of orthography. The purely palaeographical side has already been gone into in PART I, Chapter 1, and for the rest a clear distinction between orthographical and phonological matters is not always easy to make, so that a discussion of them under separate headings would automatically entail a certain amount of repetition.

In the treatment of the vowel-system a distinction must be made between vowels in stressed and unstressed syllables. Although, especially in the case of personal names, second components had only secondary stress, in the present study, as also in Ström's and Anderson's, they have been grouped with the stressed syllables because the reduction of stress had not materially affected the quality of the vowels. The two categories are separated from each other in the enumerations of material in that vowels of fully stressed syllables are named first. With regard to names quoted it may further be observed that references to number of occurrences and to exact MS place are only added where they may be of interest. All references are to folios and lines of K. Names are sometimes given in a normalised nominative form, especially if the reference is to two or three different occurrences.

Discussion of such matters as the relations between the MSS and the influence of differences in Hands, the influence of Latin orthography and of the origin of the (bearers of the) names, follows immediately where it is relevant. The same holds good for comment with regard to OE phonology in general. This arrangement seemed preferable to saving up all such information for discussion under separate headings. Summaries of the most important findings, and conclusions from these as to place and date of the material will be given in PART V.

A. VOWELS OF STRESSED SYLLABLES

I. *Short vowels*

a. *West Germanic /a/*

1. West Germanic /a/, when uninfluenced by other sounds, is /æ/ (spelled *ae* or *ę*) in *aebbae* (if connected with Gothic *aba*), *aedilbaldo*[1], *aedilberct*, *aedilburga*, *aedilred*, *aedilthryth*, *aedilualch*, *aediluald*, *ędiluini*, *huętbercti*;

and in *eadhaed*.

(1) The vowel of the first component of the Celtic place-name *aebbercurnig* may have undergone the same sound-change.

2. West Germanic /a/, before a back vowel in the following syllable, is /a/ in *acca*, *alricum* (if connected with Continental Germanic *Alaric*), *badudegn*, *baduini*, *hacanos*, *hadulac*, *hagustaldensis*, *padda*;

and in *lindisfaronensi*, *lindisfarorum*, *boructuari*, *cantuarii*, *meanuarorum*.

(1) Continental Germanic *faronem* and *rathbedo*, and Latinized *saxones* and *saxonicus* also belong here.

(2) In unmutated *addi* the /a/ of its base *Adda* is reflected; in B mutated *aeddi* appears.

(3) The vowel is back-mutated in C in *beadudegn*.

(4) In such names of Celtic origin as *dacore* and *maban* the vowel is also preserved.

3. West Germanic /a/, before nasal and before nasal + consonant other than a spirant, is

a) /a/ in *andhuno*, *annae*; cf. also Latinized *angli*, *cantia*, *cantuarii*, *estrangli*;

and in *bosanhamm*, *iarumanno*.

(1) *a* also appears in the Celtic names *colman* and *grantacęstir*.

---

[1] STRÖM 92 groups all the names with the name-theme **aedil** under *i*-mutated West-Germanic /a/, which is correct only if the name-theme is derived from a Germanic base **apuli*. This base is suggested as one of the possibilities by STRÖM 111. For the double umlaut see LUICK I, 183 f., GIRVAN 73, CAMPBELL 82, BRUNNER AG 39, 73. See also below, 7.b.i.

b) /o/ in *homelea, tondberct*;
   and in *tilmon*.

(1) *o* also appears in the Celtic names *caedmon* and *naiton*. The second el. of the former was probably associated with the name-theme **man(n)/mon** of Germanic origin, as was probably also above-mentioned *colman*.

(2)   All three occurrences of *naiton*(*o*) are spelled with *o* by K and L. Only the first is shared by M and C, which have *a* in the other two. B has *naiton* once, being illegible in the passages in which the final two occur.

(3) Confusion of *a* and *o* in the orthography of the Latin is not altogether unusual in any of the four MSS, although C with about 35 instances far surpasses in this respect K, M and B, which have about 10 each, and L, which has about 5.

4. West Germanic /a/, which before /n/ + spirant had developed into nasalised /ã/ in Anglo-Frisian, is /ō/ in *osred, osric, osthryd, osuald, osuini, osuiu*;
   and in *ualhstod*.

5. West Germanic /a/ and breaking:

a) before /l/ + consonant it remains unbroken in *aldfrid*[2], *aldgislo, aldhelm, alduino, alduulf, alhfridi, alricum* (if originally connected with **alh**), *balthild, ualdheri, ualhstod*;
   and in *aedilbaldo, cudbaldi, eadbald, herebald, hygbald, streanaeshalch, hagustaldensis, aedilualch, coinuualch, aediluald, arualdi, berctuald, earconuald, heuuald, inguald, oidiluald, osuald*.

(1) The Celtic names *alne* and *caedualla* also retain *a*.

(2) Absence of breaking before /l/ + consonant is, in the main,

---

[2] The replacement of *aldberct* by *eadberct* may simply be due to a mistake, as we have indicated above, *s.v.* **EADBERCT** 4. In C *aldberct* has interlinear *e* over its first el., but it is not likely that this reflects in any way the situation in C's exemplar or, in combination with *eadberct* of K, the appearance at this point of the parent text of the two MSS, because interlinear *e* was to all appearances inserted by second hand. The use of *eadberct* instead of *aldberct* does not justify the hypothesis that in the exemplar of K or, for that matter, in the speech of the copyist of K a broken form *eald* was present, although it is interesting to note in this connection that *MS. Wolfenbüttel, Herzog-August Bibliothek Weissenburg 34* (see INTRODUCTION, A.) shows the same mistake: it writes *eadhelmum* for *aldhelmum* (25r, 6).

characteristic of Anglian. Cf. BÜLBRING 56, LUICK I, 145 f., GIRVAN 66, CAMPBELL 55, BRUNNER AG 56 f.

b) before /h/ + consonant
i.   *a* appears in *saxuulf* (1r, 13);
ii. *æ* appears in *sæxuulfum* (3×);
iii. and *e* appears in *sexburg* (13v, 16).
iiii. broken /ea/ is lengthened to /ēa/, after the loss of intervocalic /h/ in *homel·ea·*.

(1) *Saxuulf*, which is shared by C and is thus a C-type feature, need not be significant on the phonological level. It may be a Latinization, reminiscent of *Saxones*, but it may also be a mere scribal error, for occasional instances of confusion between *a*- and *e*-spellings are in evidence in all five MSS.

(2) The almost exclusive use of *e*-spellings in the M-type MSS, of which M only has *sæxuulf* (1r, 13) and L *sexuulfum* (10r, 12)[3], against the absence of them in the C-type MSS except for *sexburg* in K, should be noted.

(3) The absence of broken /ea/ in *saex-/sex-*, whether ascribed to 'smoothing' under the influence of the following consonants or not, is a feature of the Anglian dialects. Cf. LUICK I, 213 ff., GIRVAN 83, CAMPBELL 93 ff., BRUNNER AG 96 ff. Some scholars look upon *e*-spellings as a further southern Northumbrian development of /æ/, which was retained in northern Northumbrian. Cf. BÜLBRING 86, LUICK I, 216, ANDERSON LB 137. According to GIRVAN 84 f. there is little evidence for such an inference. At any rate, it would not be very wise to attach too much significance to the name-material of HE in a settlement of this point, for it should be kept in mind that confusion between *e* and *ae* (*ẹ*) is a normal feature of the Latin of the oldest MSS; K has about 75 instances (see PART I, Chapter 2). Cf. also CAMPBELL 17, n. 2. The deviant spelling *homelaea* of B for *homelea* of the other MSS may well have to be similarly explained.

c) before /r/ + consonant.
i.   *a* appears in (*ad*)*baruae, farne, iarumanno*, and Continental Germanic *arcuulfus*;
     and in *lindisfarnensis, sighardo*;
ii. *ea* appears in *suaebheardo* (30r, 13), *uigheard* (1r, 1; 1v, 25).

---

[3] ANDERSON LB 43 (l. 11) has *sexuulfum*.

(1) The three occurrences of -ea- are shared by C only, and may thus well be typical of the C-version. C has another instance in (ad)bearuae. Breaking under these circumstances is not altogether absent in M-type texts: they and C all have beardaneu (1×) and peartaneu (2×) in the part of the text that is lost in K.

(2) The use of a by the side of ea, although not restricted to this dialect, is especially common in Northumbrian. Cf. BÜLBRING 55, WRIGHT 44, LUICK I,146, CAMPBELL 56. The greater number of ea-spellings in K and C need not in itself be an indication of a non-Northumbrian origin of the two MSS. ANDERSON LB 92 suggests that the spelling of the place-names beardaneu and peartaneu (the Lincolnshire place-names Bardney and Partney) may represent the dialect of that area. A similar suggestion could be made for suaebheardo and uigheard (the bearers of these names were Kentish), but is far less likely, because the spellings are only found in the C-type texts.

(3) STRÖM 104, 108 and ANDERSON LB 92 interpret iarumanno different-ly. They assume original /ea/ under the influence of the palatal con-sonant, which falling diphthong /ea/ developed into a rising diphthong /ea̯/, in which process e was absorbed by initial palatal /g/. Such a change of accent within diphthongs, however, is assumed by LUICK I, 240 and BRUNNER AG 106 for West Saxon and later Northumbrian.

6. After initial palatal /k/ and /g/ West Germanic /a/, fronted to /æ/ in pre-historic OE, is

i. /æ/ (spelled ae or ę) in dorciccęstrae, grantacęstir, hrofescęstir, kęlca-cęstir, tunnacęstir; here, no doubt, also belong the Celtic names caedmon and caedualla;

ii. /e/ in genlade.

(1) L has ceadualla twice out of 11 instances, one of which is shared by B, whereas B's reading of the other is illegible. M is in complete agreement with K. C, on the other hand, has 10 instances of ceadualla out of 12.

(2) Diphthongisation of /æ/ under the influence of initial palatal /k/ and /g/ is common in West Saxon, is restricted in Northumbrian, and is altogether absent in the other dialects. Cf. BÜLBRING 60, LUICK I, 160 ff., CAMPBELL 69 f., BRUNNER AG 62. The almost exclusive use of ea in ceadualla by C would thus point to a West Saxon origin for that MS, in which connection it should be noted that Caedualla (s.v.) was a West Saxon King.

(3) Both STRÖM 93 and ANDERSON LB 92 assume that ea of ceadda was

caused by initial palatal /k/. This seems quite plausible, especially if only the appearance of the names in C is considered. But the striking thing is that all nine instances of *ceadda* are spelled with *ea* in all MSS. This fact is also noted by ANDERSON LB 139, n. 1, who suggests that the form was taken over by Bede from another dialect. It is not likely, however, from what we know of the lives of both Ceadda (*s.v.*) and his brother Cedd (*s.v.*), that they were born in the West Saxon area. Moreover, if the form of this name is a loan from the West Saxon dialect, why should *caedualla*, of undisputed West Saxon origin, then have been treated differently? It is proposed, therefore, to explain the diphthong of *ceadda* as due to a phonological influence that could not have been at work in *caedualla*, and to ascribe it to back-mutation (see below, 8).

(4) The river-name *genlade* is a Kentish form. The first component developed from *gægn* to *gegn* in Kentish first, and then medial /j/ was lost with compensatory lengthening. Cf. ANDERSON LB 92, CAMPBELL 105, n. 4.

7. West Germanic /a/ and *i*-mutation:

a) West Germanic /a/ is /æ/ (spelled *ae* or *ę*)

i. in the diminutives *aecci, aeddi, aesica, aetla, haeddi*;

ii. before /l/ + consonant in *aelbfled, aelfuini, kęlcacęstir*, and also *aebbae*, if derived from a compound name with **aelb/aelf**.

(1) The names of the first category are diminutives of such personal names as *acca, adda* etc., in which normal fronting of West Germanic /a/ to /æ/ had not taken place when *i*-mutation set in. The same is true of West Germanic /a/ before /l/ + consonant in Anglian. Cf. LUICK I, 173 f., WRIGHT 43, GIRVAN 73 f., CAMPBELL 73 f., BRUNNER AG 72 ff.

b) West Germanic /a/ is /e/

i. before originally single consonants in *degsastanae, ecgberct, ecgfrid, ediluald* (?), *herebald, hereberct, hereburg, hereric, herisuid*;

and in *aenheri, fordheri, hlotheri*[4], *sigheri, ualdheri, uulfheri, medeshamstede*;

(1) The occasional occurrence in HE names of mutated *edil-* beside the very frequent unmutated *aedil-* has been extensively discussed by STRÖM 109 ff. and also by ANDERSON LB 93 f. The suggestion that parallel-forms existed from an early date and that *aedil* is "a compromise

---

[4] But once Latinized *hlothario* (12r, 26) is used.

between *aedel* (⟨*aþal-*) and *edil* (⟨*aþil-*), with *ae* from the former word and *il* from the latter"[5] is a plausible one. The distinction between the two els. must already have been lost in Bede's time, to which no doubt the confusion in Latin orthography between *ae-* and *e*-spellings contributed. The el. with *e* is used in *edilthryd* (1r, 36), *ediluald* (twice) and *ediluini* (10r, 37) by M, L and B, whereas K has *ediluald* (48r, 17) only and C has no instances[6]. The different usage apparently runs parallel to the distinction between M-version and C-version. The suggestion of ANDERSON LB 94 that the use of *edil*-forms may have had something to do with the origin of the bearers of the names *ediluald* and *ediluini*, and would thus reflect a dialectal feature[7], is for that reason untenable.

ii. before consonants that had caused breaking in *mercii* and possibly also *sebbi* (if derived from compound name with sax/saex/sex);

iii. after palatal /k/ in *ceddi*, a name of Celtic origin;

iv. before nasals in *penda*;

   and in *middilengli*.

(1) The mutated sound was OE /a/, /o/ before nasals, which originally became /æ/ but then soon further developed into /e/. Cf. LUICK I, 170 f., GIRVAN 73, CAMPBELL 74 ff., Kuhn[8], BRUNNER AG 74.

(2) C has the older form *middilaengli*, and M has Latinized *middilangli*. B agrees with K, and L is deficient at this point.

(3) Attention may be drawn to the spelling of the Continental place-name *quaentauic*, which is shared by L, whereas the other MSS have *quentauic*.

8. West Germanic /a/ is /ea/, through back-mutation, in *ceadda* and *peada* (if the name is identical with *Pad(d)a*).

(1) Above, 6.ii., the reasons have been given for finding for the diphthong in *ceadda* another explanation than palatal mutation. Back-mutation is an alternative possibility. Back-mutation of /æ/ is mainly restricted to Mercian. Cf. BÜLBRING 96 f., LUICK I, 210, GIRVAN 87 ff., CAMPBELL 86 ff., BRUNNER AG 83 ff. Although rare under these circumstances, it does also occur before geminates; cf. GIRVAN 89, CAMPBELL 86. The bearer of the name may well have

[5] Cf. STRÖM 111.
[6] C has *edilredo* (12r, 24), but this was probably corrected from *aedilredo*.
[7] STRÖM 110, n. 1, seems to suggest the same.
[8] Cf. Sherman M. Kuhn, "On the Syllabic Phonemes of Old English", *Language* 37 (1961), p. 527.

been born in Mercia. Peada (*s.v.*) was certainly of Mercian origin. (2) Another unquestionable instance of back-mutation is to be found in C, which has *beaduďegn* for *badudegn* of the other MSS.

b. *West Germanic /e/*

1. West Germanic /e/, when developed independently, is /e/ in (*in*) *berecingum, bericinensi, bregosuid*;

   and in *badudegn, haethfelth, liccidfeldensi, liccidfelth, aldhelm, burghelm, drycthelme, pecthelm, quichelm.*

2. West Germanic /e/ and breaking:
a) West Germanic /e/ before /χ/, or /r/ + /χ/, followed by consonant, after breaking and smoothing
i. is /e/ in *bercto, berctfrit, bercthuno, berctuald, pecthelm*;

   and in *aedilberct, cudberct, cyniberct, eadberct, ecgberct, erconberct, hereberct, huẹtbercti, sabercto, suidberct, tondberct, trumberct, tunberct, uictberct*, and Continental Germanic *agilberctus*;
(1) The name *uecta*, of Celtic origin, which was adopted by the Anglo-Saxons at an early date and may thus have undergone the above-mentioned phonological developments, might be added here. Cf. STRÖM 102, ANDERSON LB 95. It is likely, however, that *uecta* was treated as a Latin name by Bede. See below, C. I. f. 5. The occurrence of *ẹ* in *uẹctae* (48r, 9) must be a scribal error due to the confusion between *e*- and *ae*-spellings in the orthography of the Latin.
ii. is /e/, possibly with compensatory lengthening through additional loss of /χ/, in *selaeseu* (11r, 20).
(1) K alone once has *saelẹseu* (38r, 28)[9] which, if the etymology proposed is correct, must be a scribal error, due to the confusion in the orthography of the Latin referred to above. For the loss of /χ/ see GIRVAN 86, ANDERSON LB 95, CAMPBELL 97, BRUNNER AG 181. The latter stresses that compensatory lengthening is not invariably the case at all.

b) West Germanic /e/ before /rk/ appears
i. as *ea* in *earconberct* (13v, 37; 49r, 7), *earconualdo* (9r, 34)[10];
ii. as *e* in *erconberct(um)* (1v, 20; 38v, 41), *erncualdum* (7r, 16);

---

[9] In C interlinear *a* over *sel*- was inserted by second hand.
[10] The *a* of *ear*- is interlined by first hand, whereas interlinear *n* over -*rc*- has been erased.

iii. as *æ* in *ærconuald* (1r, 14), which may, however, have been meant to be *erconuald*.

(1) Worth noting is the different treatment that the name *earconuald* gets in K from that given to *earconberct*, a difference that is to some extent also reflected in C. All four instances of *earconberct* and three instances of *earconuald* are on folios copied by what has been established as Hand I (see PART I). The point is that K renders *earconberct* four times exactly as it appears in the M-type texts, C differing only in that it once has *erconberct* where the others have *earconberct* (13v, 37), and that in K the three occurrences of *earconuald* are all three not only different from the forms in the M-type texts, but also all three show fairly unusual traits in the first el.: *ærcon-* (1r, 14), *ernc-* (7r, 16), and erased interlinear *n* over *earcon-* (9r, 34). Moreover, unusual traits are also found in the first el. of this name in C, viz. *eo* instead of *ea* and *u* instead of *o* in *eorcun-* (7r, 16) and *ercun-* (9r, 34), whereas the M-type texts render the first el. of this name as they render it in the name *earconberct*, i.e. twice *earcon-* and once *ercon-*. See also below B. III. b).

The use of broken forms instead of smoothed *ercon-* in the Bede-MSS should no doubt be ascribed to the origin of the bearers of the names. Earconberct (*s.v.*) was King of Kent and Earconuald (*s.v.*) Bishop of London, and the broken forms may thus stem from Bede's sources, be it that original *eo* was almost invariably replaced by *ea*, which may be a feature of northern Northumbrian. Cf. LUICK I, 138, STRÖM 105 f., ANDERSON LB 132, CAMPBELL 5, BRUNNER AG 25 f. The treatment in K of the spelling of *earconberct*, therefore, most probably faithfully reflects Bede's adaptation of what he found in his sources, as K is in full agreement with the M-type texts. The more striking is the deviant treatment by K and also by C of the name *earconuald*. Difference in hand cannot be blamed for this, since *earconuald* appears on folios by the same hand that also copied the folios in which *earconberct* occurs. The possibility that, after all, the difference in treatment should simply be ascribed to a coincidental accumulation of scribal errors should not be excluded. But if mere coincidence is ruled out, the only way of explaining the different treatment of the two names seems to lie in the assumption that the C-type texts reflect the difference in character of the sources from which Bede derived his information about the two persons concerned. He probably gathered his information on Earconberct, King of Kent, from official documents, whereas the information on Earconuald,

189

Bishop of London and founder of Barking monastery, may have been based on personal communication from Nothelm, a priest of London and later Archbishop of Canterbury (735-739)[11], possibly in combination with what Bede found in a written account of the monastery of Barking, which account he used for Chapters 7 to 11 of Book IV that deal with the monastery[12]. Should this be right, however, then an argument could be made out of this for the C-version to be earlier than the M-version, for the M-version would then show the symptoms of revision.

c) West Germanic /e/ berfore /rn/ is /e/ in *bernuuini*.
(1) Names of Celtic origin such as *berniciorum* and *deruuentionis*[13] were taken over by the Anglo-Saxons after breaking had already taken place. At a later date for some of them OE forms with *eo* were substituted. Cf. CAMPBELL 55, n. 1.

d) West Germanic /e/ before (original) /rl/ is /eo/ in *eolla* (2×).
(1) The first instance is by the M-type MSS rendered as *eallan*(25r, 36). As has already been said in connection with *earcon-* (see above b)), replacement of *eo* by *ea* is considered a feature of northern Northumbrian.

3. West Germanic /e/ after initial palatal consonant is /e/ in *gebmund* (twice).
(1) The circumstances for diphthongisation after initial palatal consonant were for West Germanic /e/ the same as for West Germanic /æ/; cf. above a. 6.ii.

[11] Bede mentions Nothelm in the Preface to HE as one of his helpers. "My principal authority and helper in this modest work has been the revered Abbot Albinus, a man of universal learning who was educated in the Kentish Church by Archbishop Theodore and Abbot Hadrian of blessed memory, both venerable and learned men. There he carefully ascertained, from written records or from the old tradition, all that the disciples of St. Gregory had done in the Kingdom of Kent or in the neighbouring kingdoms. He passed on to me whatever seemed worth remembering through Nothelm, a godly priest of the Church in London, either in writing or by word of mouth." Cf. CO & MY 2 ff.
[12] Cf. Wilhelm Levison, "Bede as Historian", in: A. Hamilton Thompson (ed.), *Bede. His Life, Times and Writings*, Oxford 1935 (repr. 1969), Chapter V, p. 138; and D. P. Kirby, "Bede's Native Sources for the *Historia Ecclesiastica*", *Bulletin of the John Rylands Library* 48 (1965/1966), p. 360.
[13] C's *doruuentionis*, reflected in a correction by second hand in B, is no doubt due to scribal error, probably caused by the similarity with *doruuernensis*.

190

4. West Germanic /e/ does not undergo back-mutation in *heruteu* and *herutford* (3×).

(1) C has *heorutforda* (1r, 12; 6r, 12), where all other MSS have *herut-forda*; *heurdforda* (49r, 13) of B is most likely a scribal mistake. Back-mutation of /e/ before single /r/ is a feature of all OE dialects, although not always indicated in the oldest MSS; cf. LUICK I, 207 ff., CAMPBELL 88 ff. Cf. also BÜLBRING 97, GIRVAN 89 f., BRUNNER AG 85 ff.

(2) *eo* in *ceorotesei* (7r, 28) and *ceoroti* (7r, 28) is probably due to back-mutation, although the names are of Celtic origin. Cf. ANDERSON LB 96, CAMPBELL 88. The forms with *eo* are shared by C only, and are thus a characteristic of the C-version.

c. *West Germanic /i/*

1. West Germanic /i/ is /i/ in *biscop, bisi, geuissorum, hiddila, hild, hildilid, huicciorum, ida* (if not connected with OHG *ītal*, OE *īdel* 'idle', or Old Norse *īđ* 'activity, work'), *inguald, ini, middilengli, quichelm, sighardo, sigheri, tilmon, titillo, (ad)tuifyrdi* (?), *uictberct, uictred, uilbrod, uilfrid, uini*;

and in *aldfrid, alhfridi, berctfrit, ceolfrid, cynifrid, eanfrid, ecgfrid, gudfrid, redfridum, tatfrid, uilfrid, uynfrid, balthild, ediluini, aelfuini, alduini, baduini, bernuuini, eduini, osuini, ouini, tatuini, trumuini, uini,* and Continental *goduino*.

(1) M spells *y* both in *lyccidfelth* and the adjective *lyccitfeldensi* where all the other MSS spell *-i-*. The deviant practice is difficult to account for. Cf. **LICCIDFELTH.**

2. West Germanic /i/, which before /n/ + spirant had developed into nasalised /ī/ in Anglo-Frisian, is /ī/ in *suidberct*;

and in *hildilid, bregosuid, herisuid*.

3. West Germanic /i/ before the breaking-group /r/ + consonant appears i. as *i* in *imma* (if formed from a compound the first el. of which was connected with OHG *erman*, OE *eormen* 'great');

(1) The short form name may, however, have been formed before breaking had taken place.

ii. as *y* in *gyruiorum* (2×) and *(in)gyruum*.

(1) ANDERSON LB 97 takes over Ekwall's[14] suggestion that from

[14] Cf. E. Ekwall, "OE 'Gyrwe'", *Beiblatt zur Anglia* 33 (1922), 116-118.

Primitive Germanic *gerwī-, which underlies OE gyr 'mud, fen', medial /i/ developed which before /rw/ was broken to /iu/; the first el. of the new diphthong was then absorbed by the preceding palatal, after which the remaining /u/ was finally turned into /y/ by i-mutation. The one instance in M of guruiorum (13r, 38) is an unmutated form. This complicated argument seems unnecessary, if we accept a zero-grade form *gr̥wi- which developed into *gurwi.

4. West Germanic /i/ is /ī/ in frigyd (17v, 20).
(1) From *friju- (in inflected forms of the stem *frija-) a diphthong /īu/> /ēo/ developed in OE. For frigyd STRÖM 102 assumes smoothing of/ ēo/ to /ī/ before the palatal /g/ of the second el. Analogical influence from such forms of the OE noun as frīges is, however, more likely; cf. ANDERSON LB 97 f.

5. West Germanic /i/ is /u/ in (in)derauuda (26r, 18).
(1) Under the influence of preceding /w/ West Germanic /i/, whether first changed into /io/ by back-mutation or not, developed into /u/. Cf. BÜLBRING 98, GIRVAN 91, CAMPBELL 92, BRUNNER AG 93 f.

d. West Germanic /o/

West Germanic /o/ is /o/ in clofaeshooh, fordheri, nordanhymbrorum, offa, oftfor, torctgyd, and Continental goduino (if derived from OHG got, OE god 'God');
   and in uilbrod/-brord, herutford, hreutford, stanford, biscop (if connected with OHG scof, OE scop 'poet').
(1) Attention may at this point be drawn to the use by K of -brod four times in uilbrord, the first three of which are shared by C only. The only other occurrence of the name in HE III, 13 is uilbrordum in all MSS, K of course excepted. Thus we have another typical feature of the C-version, which must have originated with the composer of that version.
   An explanation is hard to find, although a clue may be provided by the Irish background of Uilbrord the missionary (s.v.). During his stay in Ireland the second el. of his name may have acquired the pronunciation of the related Irish word, without pre-consonantal r. On his return home this peculiarity may have been preserved in the name as pronounced by Uilbrord's friends and acquaintances. The composer of the C-version, possibly Bede himself, must in that case

192

have known Uilbrord personally or have got his information about him from Uilbrord's circles. This may be another slight indication that the M-version was the corrected, later, version. It should be noted, however, that the name is spelled with *r* in the Codex that contains *The Calendar of St. Willibrord* and *The Hieronymian Martyrology*[15]; it occurs once in a marginal note to the *Calendar* that was probably inserted by the Saint himself (39v), and twice in marginal notes to the *Martyrology* (28v).

e. *West Germanic /u/*

1. West Germanic /u/ is /u/ in *burghelm, putta, trumberct, trumuini, (in)undalum, uulfheri*;

   and in *aedilburga, hereburg, quoenburg, sexburg, gebmund, alduulf, ceoluulf, saexuulf,* and in Continental Germanic *uiltaburg* and *arcuulfus.*
   (1) The /u/ of *uulf* was in other Germanic languages changed to /o/. The name *arcuulfus* probably preserves *u*, because it appears in Latinized form.

2. West Germanic /u/, which before /n/ + spirant had developed into nasalised /ū/ in Anglo-Frisian, is /ū/ in *cudbaldi, cudberct, gudfrid, suthrieona*;

   and in *uiuraemuda.*
   (1) Where the other MSS have *gudfrid* C has *gydfrid*, no doubt due to confusion with the name-el. **gyd.**

3. West Germanic /u/, after *i*-mutation, is /y/ in *cyniberct, cynifrid, drycthelme, gyruiorum,* and *(in)gyruum* (see above c. 3. ii), *hrypensis, (in)hrypum, hygbald, uynfrid*;

   and in *nordanhymbrorum, (ad)tuifyrdi.*

4. West Germanic /u/, which before /n/ + spirant had developed into nasalised /ū/ in Anglo-Frisian, is /ȳ/, after *i*-mutation, in *eadgyd, frigyd, torctgyd.*

---

[15] Cf. H. A. Wilson (ed.), *The Calendar of St. Willibrord* (Henry Bradshaw Society 55), London 1918.

II. *Long Vowels*

a. *West Germanic /ā/*

1. West Germanic /ā/, when uninfluenced by other sounds, is

i. /ē/ in *elge, suefredo, uetadun*;
   and in *aelbfled, eanfled, aedilred, ceolred, coinred, osred, suefredo, thrydred, uictred*;

ii. /ǣ/ (spelled *ae* or *ę*) in *rędfridum* (2r, 28), *suaebheardo* (30r, 13);
   and in *eanflęd* (48v, 39), *aedilraed* (10r, 6; 10v, 7), *coinręd* (25r, 38).

(1) OE /ǣ/ for West Germanic /ā/ is a feature of West Saxon, whereas the other dialects practically always have /ē/. Cf. BÜLBRING 38, LUICK I, 129 f., CAMPBELL 50 f., BRUNNER AG 44 f., PILCH 41.

(2) *rędfridum* and *suaebheardo* are shared by all the other MSS, but the remaining four instances are typical of K. We may assume that the former two stem from Bede himself, and the explanation for their use may be that these names, which both occur only once in HE and both belong to persons of Kentish origin, were incorporated in HE as Bede found them in his possibly West Saxon sources. Cf. ANDERSON LB 65 and the more elaborate treatment by STRÖM 96. Such an explanation is out of the question for the other instances in K, all three of them isolated deviant forms of names that occur a number of times and, moreover, refer to persons of Northumbrian and Mercian origin. They are not characteristic of one Hand only. They must either be instances of the graphic variants that BÜLBRING 38 and LUICK I, 130 have also found outside the West Saxon territory, or be explained as due to the confusion between *e-* and *ae*-spellings in the orthography of the Latin, referred to before.

2. West Germanic nasalised /ā/ is /ō/ (spelled *oo*) in *clofaeshooh*.
(1) M has single -*o*- and interlinear *c* over it. Double *oo* of the other MSS is a graphic means of indicating length. Cf. ANDERSON LB 82 f., CAMPBELL 12 f.

3. West Germanic /ā/ before /n/, after *i*-mutation, is /ǣ/ (spelled *oe*) in *quoenburg* (27r, 19).
(1) L and B spell *quoinburg*. For a discussion of *oi-* and *oe*-spellings see below c. 2.

194

4. West Germanic /ā/ after palatal /g/ is /ǣ/ (spelled *ae*) in *gae* (26v, 1).

(1) *gea* in C is on erasure, by second hand. It would be incorrect to attribute a West Saxon origin to C on account of the spelling of this particle.

b. *West Germanic /ī/*

1. West Germanic /ī/ is /ī/ in *bliththryde, uigheard*;

and in *aldgislo, edgisl, hemgisl, alricum, edric, heriric, osric*, and in the Continental place-name *quaentauic*.

(1) Double *ii* is applied to indicate length in *hii*, of Celtic origin, and once in adjectival *hiienses* (25v, 4). The other three occurrences of the latter have all single *-i-* in K, whereas one has *-ii-* in M and two have *-ii-* in C. L and B have single and double *i* once each, the last occurrence of the adjective not being represented in these MSS.

2. West Germanic /ī/ before original /h/ is /iu/ in *osuiu*.

(1) The assumption is that after /ī/ was broken to /īu/, /h/ was lost before smoothing set in, because it occurred in unstressed position. Cf. STRÖM 97, ANDERSON LB 101. The occasional appearance of *osuiu* as *osuio* will be discussed below, B. II. c.

c. *West Germanic /ō/*

1. West Germanic /ō/, when uninfluenced by other sounds, is /ō/ in *bosa, bosanhamm, bosel, hlotheri* (if connected with OE *hlōþ* 'band, troop');

and in *oftfor, hacanos*.

(1) The /ō/ of *ualhstod* belongs with West Germanic /a/ before /n/ + spirant; ANDERSON LB 101 places it under West Germanic /ō/.

2. West Germanic /ō/, after *i*-mutation, appears as
i. *oi* in *boisil, coinred, coinuualch, oiddi* (if connected with the name-theme oidil[16]), *oidiluald*;
ii. *oe* in *coenred*;
iii. *e* in *medeshamstede* (if the proposed connection with OE *mōd* 'mind, heart, mood' is correct)[17].

---

[16] CAMPBELL 78 assumes that *oiddi* probably contains *i*-mutation of /o/, even if its etymology is less clear.
[17] See, however, below B. II. b.

(1) Unrounding of /œ̄/ had not taken place in the Northumbrian dialect in Bede's days. Cf. BÜLBRING 68, LUICK I, 169, GIRVAN 74. The spelling of *medeshamstede* may, therefore, be a feature of the Mercian dialect of the Peterborough area.

(2) There is some variation of *oe-* and *oi-*-spellings, especially in the name-el. **coen/coin**. The name *boisil* appears invariably in the same form in all MSS, except that C has unmutated *bosil* twice in one passage. The names *oiddi* and *oidiluald* appear with *oi* without exception. For *coinuualch* (9v, 37) only C has *oe*. The treatment of **coen/coin** may, however, be significant in some way. C has *oe* for all instances of the two names Coinred 1 (*s.v.*) and Coinred 2 (*s.v.*). K, L, and B have *oi* for all three occurrences of Coinred 1, whereas M has *oe* only. K, L, and B also have exactly parallel spellings for the occurrences of Coinred 2, *oi* five times and *oe* twice (34v, 29; 40v, 37), whereas M has *oe* three times, of which one (34v, 29) parallel to K, L, and B. From this we may conclude that K, L, and B probably reflect Bede's treatment of the spelling, representing a preference for *oi-* over *oe-*-spellings. The different origins of Coinred 1 (Northumbria) and Coinred 2 (Mercia) cannot very well have played a part in the distinction between the two spellings, although the spellings in K, L, and B, viz. exclusive *oi* for the Northumbrian name and a mixture of *oi* and *oe* for the Mercian name, might seem to point to something of the kind. M's treatment, however, could not possibly be fitted into such an interpretation.

    oi is earlier than *oe*. Cf. GIRVAN 75, CAMPBELL 78, BRUNNER AG 69.

d. *West Germanic /ū/*

1. West Germanic /ū/, when uninfluenced by other sounds, is /ū/ in *tunberctum*;

    and in *briudun, uetadun, andhuno, ber(i)cthun*.

(1) C has *briuduun* (47v, 39), which may be looked upon as one of the exceptional cases in which HE MSS use double vowel-symbols to indicate length. It should be noted that the only other instance of *-uu-* for /ū/ is *duunchado* (47r, 22), shared by all the MSS. *Duunchado* is unquestionably Celtic, while there is some uncertainty as to the interpretation of the second component of *briudun*, of which at least the first component is Celtic (see **dun**). The spelling of C may point towards a Celtic origin of the second component.

196

2. West Germanic /ū/ after *i*-mutation, is /ȳ/ in *thrydred*;
and in *aedilthryth, bliththryde, osthryd.*

(1) M has *thruidred* (24v, 9), where the other MSS write *thrydred*. The combination *ui* for *i*-mutated /ū/ is the older spelling, which at an early date was displaced by *y.* Cf. GIRVAN 76, STRÖM 144 f., CAMPBELL 17 f., 79, BRUNNER AG 69.

3. West Germanic /ū/ is shortened to /u/ in *tunna* and *tunnacęstir.*

III. *Diphthongs*

a. *West Germanic /ai/*

1. West Germanic /ai/ is /ā/ in *arualdi* (for a number of the etymologies proposed), *sabercto, stanford, tatfrid, tatuini*;
and in (*in*)*undalum, eadgarum, medeshamstede, hadulac, genlade, degsastanae.*

(1) Generally the absence of *i*-mutation in *sabercto* is ascribed to syncopation of the thematic vowel /i/ before *i*-mutation set in. Cf. LUICK I, 283 f., Borowski[18], GIRVAN 78, CAMPBELL 83, BRUNNER AG 70 f. In C (48v, 36) the name appears as *saeberchto*, to all appearances with a regularly *i*-mutated vowel of the first el. Luick's suggestion, taken over by Brunner, that in certain name-els. in which the thematic vowel had indeed disappeared before *i*-mutation, *i*-mutated forms could be restored occasionally because of analogy with the appearance of the head-word, seems to apply in this case.

2. West Germanic /ai/ is /ō/ in *ouini* (if its first el. is OE *ā*/*ō* 'ever, always').
(1) How the change from /ā/ to /ō/ was brought about remains unexplained; cf. CAMPBELL 52, n. 3. According to LUICK I, 132 this OE /ā/ ⟨ West Germanic /ai/ may have had a darker quality than normal /ā/ and possibly have shown some lip-rounding, so that it could develop into /ō/ when less stressed. ANDERSON LB 103 suggests that in the name-el. in *ouini* the rounding influence of the following /w/ may have helped.

3. West Germanic /ai/, after *i*-mutation, is /æ/ (spelled *ae* or *ę*) in *hęmgisl, haethfelth, laestingaeu.*

[18] B. Borowski, *Zum Nebenakzent beim altenglischen Nominalkompositum* (Sächsische Forschungsinstitute in Leipzig III, 2), Halle 1921, 66 f.

b. West Germanic /au/

1. West Germanic /au/, when uninfluenced by other sounds, normally becomes /ēa/ and appears

i. as *ea* in *eadbald, eadberct*[19]*, eadgarum, eadgyd, eadhaed, eata, eanfled, eanfridi*;

ii. as *æa* in *æadberctum* (47v, 5);

(1) M has *aea* for *ea* a number of times, but only in the first three Books of HE. This spelling is shown only by the earliest MSS, and has no dialectal implications. Cf. LUICK I, 131, GIRVAN 53, BRUNNER AG 49.

iii. as *e* in *estranglorum* (12r, 25);

(1) C has *eastranglorum*, which may point to a greater distance from Bede's original. The unusual spelling *e-* of the other MSS is probably due to the fact that the word occurs in the text of a Latin document that is cited literally in HE IV, 17[20]. Cf. ANDERSON LB 103.

iv. as *eu* in *heuuald*;

(1) C has *hea(u)uald* twice (31r, 28; 31r, 29), while the other three occurrences of *heuuald* on 31r and 31v of this MS have been tampered with by second hand. The spelling *eu* may be due to the influence of the following /w/, and seems to be restricted to Anglian texts. Cf. BÜLBRING 41, LUICK I, 131, STRÖM 100, ANDERSON LB 103, ARNGART 133.

2. West Germanic /au/, after *i*-mutation, is

i. /ē/ in *edgisl, edric, eduini*;

and in *ceorotesei, farne* (if the second component is connected with OE *ēg* 'island'), *heruteu, laestingaeu, selaeseu, elge, suthrieona*;

ii. possibly /ǣ/ (spelled *ae*) in *aenheri* (10v, 26), *baeda* (49v, 6).

(1) There is some variation between *e-* and *ae-* (*æ-, ę-*) spellings. M has *aedgils* (20r, 23) and *aeduini* (48v, 40) in contrast to the other MSS and to the spelling in M itself of the other three occurrences of *eduini*. C has *elgæ* (13v, 17) for *elge*. M and L have *læstingæi* (39v, 24) against K and C; B is illegible. Finally C has *eanheri* (10v, 26) and *beda* (49v, 6), which may originally have been *beada*.

(2) The *i*-mutated form of West Germanic /au/ is normally /ē/ outside West Saxon; /ǣ/ (spelled *ae, æ, ę*) is restricted mainly to the

---

[19] Once, probably by mistake, appearing instead of *aldberct*; cf. PART III, **EADBERCT 4 = ALDBERCT**, and above, note 2.
[20] Cf. CO & MY 384.

oldest MSS of HE. There is also one instance of *æduini* in the early eighth-century Calendar of St. Willibrord[21]. STRÖM 114 assumes that /æ/-forms actually represent an earlier, different, pronunciation of mutated /au/. LUICK I, 180 and CAMPBELL 80 see them as differences of a merely graphic nature. The latter seems likelier, especially if we take into consideration the confusion between *e*- and *ae*-spellings in the orthography of the Latin, referred to before.

(3) The unmutated form in *eanheri* of C is readily understandable with a view to such names as *eanfridi* and *eanfled*; cf. also **ean/aen**.

c. West Germanic /eu/

West Germanic /eu/ appears as

i. *eo* in *ceolfrid, ceolred, ceoluulf*;

ii. *eu* in *hreutford*[22];

iii. *ea* in *streanaeshalch* (if the first component is connected with OE *ge-strēon* 'gain, profit; off-spring, strain').

(1) C has *hreoutford* (11v, 32). M and C have *strenaeshalc*, in which case the copyist of K 16r, 20 has interlined *a* over *stren-*.

(2) The preservation of *eu*-spellings is a feature of older MSS. Cf. BÜLBRING 42, LUICK I, 135, CAMPBELL 15, 116.

(3) *ea* for *eo* in *streanaeshalch*, which appears once in L as *streunæshalch* and once as *streonaeshalch* in the earlier Books of HE (cf. ANDERSON LB 104), is a regular feature of northern Northumbrian, probably not restricted to the later OE period as BÜLBRING 44 and GIRVAN 52 hold. Cf. LUICK I, 135 f., CAMPBELL 118, BRUNNER AG 25 f.

(4) If the *e*-spelling in *strenaeshalc* of M and C, and partly of K as well, is not simply due to a scribal error or analogy with *i*-mutated forms of /ēa/ ⟨ West Germanic /au/ (and in this connection it is worth noting that the *Wolfenbüttel MS.* (see note 2) spells *strenaes-* in three out of four occurrences), it is hard to see how such early monophthongisation should be accounted for as a regular development.

d. West Germanic /iu/

West Germanic /iu/, which normally developed into OE /īo, ēo/,

[21] Cf. ARNGART 134.
[22] George T. Flom, "Breaking in Old Norse and Old English. With Special Reference to the Relations between them", *Language* 13 (1937), p. 130, mistakes *hreutford* for a back-mutated form of *herutford*.

is not represented in the material, except possibly in the Latinized tribal name *iutarum/iutorum.*

B. VOWELS OF UNSTRESSED SYLLABLES

The arrangement and contents of this section will not closely parallel those of the previous section. In the first place, not all vowels in unstressed position will be dealt with, but only the three vowels that most clearly show signs of the impact of the reduction of stress in the early stages of OE, Primitive OE /i/, /æ/, and /u/. And secondly, two paragraphs of a more general character have been added. The one on Latinization in name-endings will precede the treatment of the three separate vowels – although it contains a fairly full survey of all the endings and not of just those endings of which Primitive OE /i/, /æ/, and /u/ form a part – because in it the sounds that are, or may be, meant to be Latin are singled out. The second, on Parasite Vowels, follows at the end of this section.

The insertion of a third general paragraph, on syncopation of thematic vowels in composition, turned out to be superfluous, for a scrutiny of the material brought to light that K nowhere deviates in any way from the other MSS in this respect. The reader is, therefore, referred to the full discussion of the matter of composition-vowels by STRÖM 118 ff. and to the supplementary remarks by ANDERSON LB 114 ff. Further reference may be made to MÜLLER 143 ff., Borowski[23], LUICK I, 279 ff., GIRVAN 144 ff., DAHL 63 ff., CAMPBELL 145 f., BRUNNER AG 137 f.

I. *Latinization of Case-forms*

In the following discussion it will appear that it is not always feasible to decide whether a particular ending is Latin or OE. This is, of course, the case where the Latin and OE have exactly parallel endings, e.g. where the genitive singular in *hildae* (1r, 41) is concerned. Equally unresolvable, and much more complicated, may be cases in which a particular form could be an undeclined nominative case of the OE word. In the Latin text of HE the OE names are frequently treated as indeclinables, as for example the weak noun *ceadda* in *antistitis ceadda*

---

[23] *op. cit., passim.*

(5r, 11), and *osuiu* in *osuiu regis* (20v, 34), whereas a Latin ablative *osuio* is used in all MSS, C excepted. An instance of an ending that may be interpreted as a Latin oblique form, but also as an undeclined OE nominative case, is *aenheri* in *fratris aenheri* (10v, 26).

Things are made still more complicated by the fact that confusion in the orthography of the Latin between *ae-* and *e*-spellings, and between *e-* and *i*-spellings is also a feature of our MSS, and that we do not know to what extent this confusion is reflected in the spelling of the OE material.

1. The genitive singular of the *ja*-stem *heri*, which in OE name-formations was *heres* from the earliest days instead of the regular *herges* (cf. GIRVAN 216, DAHL 90 f., CAMPBELL 230), appears as *heri* in *fratris aenheri* (10v, 26), *de morte |...| hlotheri* (1v, 3), and *sigheri regis* (38r, 39). The form may be an undeclined OE nominative singular, or a Latinized genitive singular. The fact that C has *-here* in the latter two instances may indicate that the copyist of C took the form to be an OE nominative, although it must be pointed out that unstressed *e* and *i* were also frequently confused in the orthography of the Latin.

2. The dative singular of the *ja*-stem *heri* may be found, as *here* from older *herae*, in *fratre hlothere* (6v, 39), *uulfhere fugato* (10r, 35), and *rege uulfhere* (10v, 18). There are indications that OE datives are used in cases in which an ablative form is expected in the Latin, especially when the OE name is the subject of an ablative absolute construction; cf. DAHL 47, 161 f., STRÖM 141, ANDERSON LB 114. All three instances mentioned above occur in ablative absolute constructions. This, however, also opens the possibility of interpreting these endings as Latin ablatives; they would not be ablatives this time of the second declension, but of the third declension. Both DAHL 161 f. and STRÖM 140 f. prefer to take them as OE dative endings. On the other hand ANDERSON LB 112 f. notes that, should these forms all be looked upon as OE, the number of cases in which OE *-ae* was reduced to OE *-e* would proportionately far outweigh the cases in which OE genitive *-aes* was reduced to *-es*. It is true that all the MSS have invariably *-e* in the above-mentioned instances, one corrected *uulfherae* of B (10v, 18) excepted, while all MSS have OE dative-instrumental *-ae* in *(ad)baruae* (twice); cf. ANDERSON LB 125, CAMPBELL 232. It is not clear, however, why a greater number or reductions of *-ae* to *-e* than

of -*aes* to -*es* should in itself be abnormal. Final -*s* may, after all, have helped to protect the *ae*-sound.

Drycthelme (34v, 17) is clearly a Latin vocative form; OE has no separate form for the vocative, but uses the nominative instead. Likewise there can be little doubt about the Latin nature of the ablative form in *sub rege* /.../ *cerdice* (17r, 22), which by DAHL 46 is classified as a dative singular of an OE pure *a*-stem.

3. Feminine names with *ō*-stems and with *ī*-stems were certainly partly Latinized. There can be no doubt about the nominatives *aedilburga* (8r, 14) and *aedilthryda* (14v, 38), and the accusatives *aedilthrydam* (13r, 34) and *eanfledam* (38v, 37).

Although genitive and dative forms in -*ae* may be both Latin forms of the first declension and early OE forms, one is inclined to assume Latinization in the dative case *aedilburgae* (7r, 26) and the genitive *aedilthrydae* (16r, 1) (as also in the forms *humbre* (48r, 13) and *uiuraemuda* (49v, 7) of Celtic origin), because these spellings are shared by all the MSS.

Where such agreement is absent, as for instance in the genitive *fluminis genlade* (30r, 7) which by the M-type MSS is spelled *genladae*, and in the genitive *hildae* (1r, 41) which by C is spelled *hilde*, it may seem self-evident to reckon with native OE endings. However, in such cases too some reserve is called for, because of the fairly frequent confusion between *ae*- and *e*-spellings in the orthography of the Latin. The conclusion must be that concerning these *ae*- and *e*-endings certainty either one way or the other will never be easy to achieve. Cf. STRÖM 142, CAMPBELL 234, n. 1.

With regard to the variation between *ae* and *e* the following ablative cases may be noted: *cum* /.../ *mea matre aedilburgae* (8v, 25-26; changed to *aedilburga* by second hand in C; M, L, B: *aedilburge*); *cum regina aedilthryde* (3v, 29; C: *aeðelðryda*; B: *aedilthryda*, possibly *aedilthrydæ*); *bliththryde coniuge sua* (32r, 20; M: *bliththrydae*); and *cum matre eanflede* (20v, 30; B: *eanfledae*). There can be little doubt that in these cases we are dealing with OE dative forms, as is also suggested by DAHL 122, STRÖM 141 and CAMPBELL 242, and not with Latin ablative forms, as ANDERSON LB 113 would have us believe, for such Latin forms could only have been taken from the third declension, whereas feminine names normally follow the first declension, as we have seen above. Cf. also STRÖM 140. Some evidence for Anderson's assumption that third declension forms could also be applied with

202

these feminine names, could be found in the dative *aedilburgi* (8v, 31), but it should be noted that C has *aedilburgae* and that a second hand has altered *-i* to *-e* in B. The *i*-form could be interpreted as a scribal error, for confusion of *e* and *i* is common in the orthography of the Latin.

4. With regard to the case-endings of masculine *i*-nouns the following points may be noted.
a) In *middilengli* (49r, 5; M: *middilangli*, C: *middilaengli*) the ending is probably an archaic OE nominative plural, for otherwise the fully Latinized form of the name, *-angli* as in M, might have been expected. Cf. DAHL 163.
b) In *eduini* (16r, 26; 48v, 40) the ending is probably a Latin genitive singular of the second declension, cf. DAHL 161 and CAMPBELL 241, n. 1, although the application of the nominative singular as an indeclinable should not be discarded altogether; cf. STRÖM 142, BRUNNER AG 213.
c) In the ablative combinations *eduine rege* (48v, 42) and *cum antistite trumuine* (22r, 23; L: *trumuini*) it is hard to decide whether these endings are OE dative singular forms or Latin ablative forms of the third declension. *Trumuini* in L may be an archaic OE dative singular, cf. CAMPBELL 241, or an undeclined archaic OE nominative singular, or again an instance of the confusion between *e-* and *i-* spellings in the Latin orthography.

5. The nominative singular of the feminine weak declension occurs in *regina nomine aebae* (10v, 25), shared by all MSS[24]; *-ae* is an archaic form. The name *aebbae* (13v, 14; 19v, 28), shared by the other MSS as well, occurs in genitive and dative (: *matri /.../ uocabulo aebbę*)

[24] Names in this position are not treated by Bede as genitives dependent on *nomine*, but are in apposition to the head-word, which is in this case *regina*. So much is clear from a survey of a great number of cases with the help of P. F. Jones, *A Concordance to the Historia Ecclesiastica of Bede* (The Medieval Academy of America, Publ. no. 2), Cambridge (Mass.) 1929. There can be no doubt about the following examples: *cum episcopo, /..../, nomine Liudhardo*, cf. CO & MY 74; *habentes defensorem nomine Brocmailum*, cf. CO & MY 140; and *a rege /.../ nomine Cuichelmo*, cf. CO & MY 164. The same treatment we find in the combinations with *uocabulo*: *Habuit alterum fratrem uocabulo Ultanum*, cf. CO & MY 276; *habens sororem ipsius coniugem, uocabulo Cyniburgam*, cf. CO & MY 278; *Misit cum eo rex presbyterum suum uocabulo Eadhaedum*, cf. CO & MY 316; and *Erat namque /.../ uir de genere Scottorum, Adamnanus uocabulo*, cf. CO & MY 422.

position respectively, and should probably be taken to be Latin as regards its endings, although it is conceivable that in both cases an undeclined OE nominative form is used. Cf. STRÖM 142.

6. Masculine weak names are treated in the following way[25].

a) The nominative singular appears in -a in acca, aetla, baeda, bosa, cędualla, ceadda, eappa, eata, eolla, ida, imma, offa, padda, penda, putta, and tunna.

b) The normal genitive singular appears in the OE form in the place-name bosanhamm (10v, 31), shared by all MSS; it is an uninflected nominative form in the place-name tunnacęstir (15v, 8-9) and in antistitis ceadda (5r, 11), both cases being shared by the other MSS as well; and finally it exhibits a Latin genitive ending in annae (13r, 35), for which M and C have an undeclined nominative case anna.

c) The normal OE accusative singular form occurs in ad accan presbyterum (40v, 20); in post cęduallan (11v, 2; C: cęduallam, the Latin ending); and in acceperint |...| eollan (25r, 36). In ceadda episcopum (3r, 5) an uninflected nominative case appears.

d) In all nine occurrences of these names in ablative combinations the ending exhibited is invariably -a, which in all probability is the Latin ending, although it may be a nominative singular applied as an indeclinable. Cf. STRÖM 142.

II. *Some Primitive OE Vowels in Unstressed Position*

a. *Primitive OE /i/*

1. Primitive OE /i/, in medial position, occurs both within name-themes and as a composition-vowel between two name-els.

a) Within name-themes it appears

i. as *i* in aedilbaldo, aedilberct, aedilburga, aedilraed, aedilthryth, aedilualch, aediluald, ędiluini, oidiluald, and the Continental Germanic agilberctus;

and in *boisil, hiddila, middilengli, titillo,* and in the formative

---

[25] It may be assumed that the Celtic names *uenta* and *uecta* were looked upon as Latin nouns.

ending -*ing* in (*in*)*berecingum*, (*in*)*cuneningum*, *laestingaeu*[26];

ii. as *e* in the prefix of *geuissorum*;

   and possibly in the diminutive suffix of *bosel* (17r, 4; 17r, 12).

(1) The only deviating spellings occur in C, which has *aeðelredum* (1r, 39), *aeðelredo* (49r, 16), *aeðeldryda* (3v, 29), *aeðeldrydam* (13r, 34), *boisel* (22r, 31). This warrants conclusions as to the date or place of composition of C, or as to both. The change from /i/ to /e/ set in at about the time of the earliest texts and was only gradually completed. Cf. LUICK I, 300 f., GIRVAN 154 f., Storms[27], CAMPBELL 153 f. Moreover, the change was quicker in non-Northumbrian than in Northumbrian. DAHL 191, therefore, concludes that the occurrences of *e* for *i* in C are "irrefutable evidence" for its non-Northumbrian origin.

(2) The use of *e* twice by all MSS in the name *bosel* in contrast to the use of *i* in the eight occurrences of the name *boisil* in all the MSS (one of C excepted), either points to a decisive influence of the non-Northumbrian origin of the bearer of the name, for Bosel (*s.v.*) was Bishop of the Huiccii and had his see at Worcester, or to a different diminutive suffix, *ul* instead of *il*. The latter seems to be more likely.

(3) It may be asked how far the confusion in the orthography of the Latin between *i*- and *e*-spellings influenced the representation of /i/ of Primitive OE in the material. A count of the Latin misspellings in the five MSS has given the following approximate numbers. Incorrect *e* for *i*: K 25, M 30, L 15, C 95, B 24. Incorrect *i* for *e*: K 15, M 60, L 20, C 55, B 30. Seeing these numbers one might have expected a less consistent treatment of the spelling of Primitive OE /i/ in the MSS in general, but especially in M which has twice as many instances of this confusion in the orthography of the Latin as K, L, and B, whereas it is in all but complete agreement with these MSS where the treatment of Primitive OE /i/ is concerned. See, however, b).

b) As a composition-vowel it appears

i. as *i* in *cyniberct*, *cynifrid*, *heririci* (16r, 27), *herisuid*, *hildilid*;

ii. as *e* in *herebald*, *hereberct*, *hereburg*, *hereric* (17r, 21).

---

[26] On the one hand CAMPBELL 34 assigns half-stress to such suffixes "after a long syllable (–́) or its equivalent (◡x), when followed by an unaccented syllable", and on the other hand CAMPBELL 155, in connection with unstressed vowels, states that these suffixes "are generally not subject to the change *i* ⟩ *e*, though *e* is fairly frequent before back vowels".

[27] Cf. G. Storms ,"The Weakening of O.E. Unstressed *i* to *e* and the Date of Cynewulf", *English Studies* 37 (1956), p. 110.

(1) Only C has one instance of *e* in the four occurrences of names with *cyni-, cyneberht* (11v, 31).

M has *heribald* (28r, 10), *heriberct* (1v, 8; 22v, 31; 23r, 8), *heriburg* (26v, 35), whereas L, C, and B agree with K fully in having only *here-* in these three combinations.

The two occurrences of the combination with *-ric* are rendered by *heri-* and *here-* once each in C and B, parallel to the treatment in K. M, on the other hand, exhibits *here-* twice and L *heri-*. In the one occurrence of the combination with *-suid* M and C have *here-* in contrast to K, L, and B.

(2) The greater number of *e*-spellings in C, where other MSS have *i*, bears out the picture of the treatment by this MS of the spelling of Primitive OE /i/ within name-themes.

With regards to the treatment of *heri-/here-* it is further interesting to note a fact pointed out by ANDERSON LB 109. In L the combinations of which the second el. contains /i/, all preserve an *i*-spelling for the composition-vowel; in all other combinations the composition-vowel is spelled *e*. Anderson's suggestion is largely corroborated by K, C, and B. Not, however, by M. As the only MS M has *heri-* in the combinations with *-bald*, *-berct*, and *-burg* five times out of seven, and as the only MS it has exclusively *here-* in the three combinations with *-ric* and *-suid*. This phenomenon can hardly be accounted for by a reference to an earlier date of composition for M than for the other MSS, nor to a different place of origin. Moreover, we have seen above, under a), that taking into consideration the total number of incorrect applications of *e-* and *i*-spellings in the Latin, particularly in M, we must conclude that this confusion had hardly any influence on such spellings in the OE material. More evidence for this will follow below. How are we to account then for the difference in M in connection with the treatment of the composition-vowel? It may perhaps be suggested that the copyist of M produced a number of these mistakes owing to hypercorrectness on his part. From the confused treatment of *i-* and *e*-spellings by M in the orthography of the Latin one may assume such hypercorrectness, especially if one takes into consideration that M is the only MS that has an appreciably larger number of incorrect uses of *i* for *e* than of *e* for *i*.

2. Primitive OE /i/ in final position.

a) The diminutive ending *-i* ⟨*-īna*, added to *a*-stems (see **AECCI**), appears

i. as *i* in *addi, aecci, aeddi, bisi, haeddi, ini, oiddi, sebbi*;
ii. as *e* in *sebbe* (7r, 15).
(1) *Sebbe* in K 7r, 15 is shared by C only, and may thus be a feature
of the C-type version. It seems, however, a bit unusual at this stage
for *-i⟨-īna* to be reduced to *-e*. The context in which the name is
used may provide the clue to an answer, for the name occurs in juxta-
position with *sighere* in: */.../ quibus eo tempore praefuerunt sebbe et
sighere quorum supra meminimus*[28]. See also below.

b) The nominative and accusative cases of the *ja*-stem *heri* appear
i. as *i* in *fordheri, hlotheri, ualdheri, uulfheri*;
ii. as *e* in *sighere* (7r, 15).
(1) C has *forthere* (2×), *hlothere* (49r, 24), *uualdhere* (9r, 34), *uulfhere*
(3v, 2; 49r, 15). The only other deviating form is *forthere* (38r, 20)
in B. It may be noted that two of the forms in K, *hlotheri* (1v, 3)
and *uulfheri* (3v, 2), are corrections of forms with final *-e*.
    The only MS to have "correct" *sigheri* (7r, 15) is M.
(2) K, M, L, and B have invariably final *-i* in the nominative and
accusative, with only the one exception of *sighere* (7r, 15) in K, L,
(C,) and B. It may be deduced that Bede's usage is perfectly represented in this. The irregular form of *sighere* most probably, therefore,
also goes back to Bede himself. For an explanation of this the reader
is reminded of what has just been adduced to account for the nominative form *sebbe* (7r, 15); see under a). It seems that both irregular
nominatives may go back to Bede's original, and that they had best
be explained as direct borrowings by Bede from his source, possibly
from a dialectal area where the change from /i/ to /e/ had progressed
further than in Bede's Northumbrian. It is interesting to find that
the bearers of the names are both East Saxon kings.
(3) With regard to the treatment of Primitive OE /i/ in the nominative and accusative endings of these *ja*-stems the conclusion must
be that, C excepted, not a single MS, not even M, gives us much
cause to assume any influence of the confusion between *i*- and *e*-
spellings in the orthography of the Latin.

c) The genitive and dative singular of *ja*-stems in *-i* have been dealt
with in the preceding section, I. 1. and 2. Here may be added *(ad)tui-*

---

[28] Cf. CO & MY 354.

fyrdi (22r, 17), possibly an old locative. Cf. DAHL 111, ANDERSON LB 109.

(1) B has *(ad)tuifyrde,* which may be a correction of *(ad)tuifyrdi.* Interestingly enough a second hand has interlined *o* over final *-i.*

d) The nominative and accusative singular of masculine *i*-stems appear

i. as *i* in *uini;*

and in *aelfuini, alduini, baduini, bernuuini, eduini, osuini, ouini, tatuini, trumuini;*

ii. as *e* in *medeshamstede.*

(1) C has *aelfuine* (3×), *alduuine* (48r, 6), *eduuine* (48v, 41), *osuine* (49r, 4), *tatuuine* (3×); B has *æl(f)uuine* (49r, 20), which is an altogether unusual spelling for the name in B, and further it has two names in which final *-e* may originally have been *-i, tatuine* (47v, 38) and *trumuine* (20v, 19).

M, L, and B have *medeshamstedi.*

(2) Again we see that K fully agrees with M, and L, and largely with B in that with one exception it has final *-i,* a feature of early texts; cf. CAMPBELL 241. Previous findings with regard to Bede's original, and with regard to the appearance of C are corroborated. It should again be specifically noted that M is quite regular.

e) Nominative plural, and genitive and dative singular of *i*-stems have already been dealt with in the preceding Section, I. 4.

b. *Primitive OE /æ/*

1. Primitive OE /æ/ in medial position.

a) It appears as *e* in *homel·ea·* (if connected with OHG *hamal,* OE **hamol* 'maimed, mutilated').

b) The genitive singular of *a-, ja-,* and *wa*-stems appears

i. as *-aes/-ęs* in *clofaeshooh* (6v, 15), *selaeseu* (11r, 20; 38r, 28), *streanaeshalch* (16r, 20; 16v, 16; 20v, 24-25; 49r, 23);

ii. as *-es* in *ceorotesei* (7r, 28), *hrofescęstir* (6r, 19), *medeshamstede* (7r, 13-14).

(1) M has *clofeshoch* and *streaneshalch* (16v, 16); C has *seleseu* (twice) and *streaneshalch* (4×); B has *streaneshalae* (49r, 23), and L may have

208

had this form but is deficient at this place. M, L, and B have *cerotaęsei* and L and B have *hrofaescaestir*.

(2) The change of Primitive OE /æ/ in unstressed position to /e/ took place about the time of our earliest texts and only in those texts /æ/ is still undisturbed; about the middle of the eighth century the change may have been fully completed. Cf. LUICK 1,299f., GIRVAN 153f., CAMPBELL 153. The predominance in C of -*es* for -*aes* is thus in accord with the conclusions drawn as to its date in the previous Section. Of the three occurrences in K of -*es* that in *medeshamstede* is shared by all the other MSS, even by L. Possibly quite accidentally, the other two occur in names that are Celtic in origin, *ceorotesei* and *hrofescęstir*. The fact that *medeshamstede* is shared by all the MSS may be an indication that the name was taken over by Bede from his source in that form, or perhaps also that the etymology proposed, viz. derivation from a personal name connected with OE *mōd* 'mind, heart, mood', is incorrect. It may be noted that the *i*-mutation of West Germanic /ō/ to /ē/ in *medeshamstede* (see above A. II. c. 2.) is equally generally present in the MSS and is equally rare in the material.

c) The genitive singular of *a*-, *ja*-, and *wa*-stems has been gone into in connection with Latinization of case-forms. Here three remaining names, all three dative-locative forms, should be mentioned: (*ad*) *baruae* (3v, 4; 7r, 11-12), *degsastanae* (48v, 34), *streanaeshalae* (49r, 23). (1) C has *streaneshale*. For the rest there are no differences between the MSS.
(2) The forms are in all probability archaic OE forms.

d) The accusative singular of a pure *ō*-stem appears as -*ae* in *dorciccęstrae* (16v, 33).
(1) C has *dorciccęstre*.
(2) The full context in which the name stands is: *in episcopatum dorciccęstrae fuerit ordinatus*[29]. According to DAHL 119 "the gen. or dat. would also seem possible." In that case one would also have to consider the possibility that it is a Latin case-ending. ANDERSON LB 110f. calls it an accusative singular.
(3) The Celtic river-names *alne* (22r, 17) and *dacore* (24r, 33) are also to be looked upon as accusatives, as they are accompanied by the accusatives *fluuium* and *amnem* respectively with which they most

[29] Cf. CO & MY 408.

probably stand in apposition (see note 24), and not, as EKWALL RN 6, 111 suggests as genitives of Latinized nominatives in -*a*; cf. also DAHL 119. The somewhat striking uniformity of their spelling in all the MSS would also be harder to explain.

e) The genitive and dative forms of *ō*-stems and *ī*-stems, and the nominative singular of the feminine weak declension have been sufficiently dealt with in the previous Section, I, 3 and 5 respectively.

c. *Primitive OE /u/*

1. Primitive OE /u/ in medial position.

a) It appears as *u* in *heruteu, herutford,* and in the dative plural ending of (*in*)*berecingum,* (*in*)*cuneningum,* (*in*)*gyruum,* (*in*)*hrypum.*
(1) In names of Celtic origin *u* appears in *coludanae, coludi, columba, columcelli, dicul, lugubaliam,* but *o* appears in the fourteen occurrences of *eboracensis* and *eboraci.* There is a striking difference between C on the one hand and the other MSS on the other. M, L, and B treat *eboracensis/eboraci* more or less as K does: M spells *-u-* three times, L twice (out of thirteen), and B twice (out of ten). But C spells *-u-* eleven times out of thirteen.

The reduction of Primitive OE /u/ to /o/ was a gradual change, which probably first began at the beginning of the historical period. Cf. BÜLBRING 164, WRIGHT 99, GIRVAN 156, CAMPBELL 155. Two aspects require further attention. In the first place, how should the frequent *o*-spellings of *eboracensis/eboraci* be explained in K, M, L, and B, which are MSS that spell *u* otherwise, especially in names of Celtic origin? And secondly, why should C, i.e. the later MS, almost consistently spell *u*?

The agreement between K and the M-type texts probably means that the *o*-spellings stem from Bede's original. The sound may have been like /o/ in Bede's days more unmistakably in this name than the reduction of Primitive OE /u/ was in other cases. This is in agreement with what JACKSON LHEB 655 says about the adoption of the place-name by the Anglo-Saxons; it was adopted as *Ebor-* as early as the late fifth century. The spellings in C would then have to be marked as aberrant, and one explanation for this might be unfamiliarity on the part of the copyist of C with the name as it was spoken. This could be an indication of a non-Northumbrian origin of the MS.

210

We should note, however, that it is also C that spells *u* without exception in the name *osuiu*, even in the cases in which the other MSS have a Latinized ablative form *osuio* (see below). In the orthography of the Latin C has about twice as many instances of *u* for *o* and *vice versa* than the other MSS, but their number is not exceedingly large in itself (seventeen altogether) to be significant. The *u*-spellings in *eboracensis/eboraci* may, therefore, have to be explained as Latinizations and also be due to hypercorrectness of the copyist of C, as was also suggested for M where it has unusual *i*-spellings instead of *e* of the other MSS (see above a.1.b)).

b) As a composition-vowel it appears
i. as *u* in *badudegn, baduini* (?), *hadulac, hagustaldensis, iarumanno*;
ii. as *o* in *bregosuid*.
(1) All other MSS have *bregusuid*.
(2) It is not clear whether the composition-vowel is preserved or not in *baduini*. The M-type MSS have *baduuini*, and ANDERSON LB 114 assumes that here the vowel has not been syncopated, although this does not necessarily follow from the *uu*-spelling, for double *uu* is also used to represent the semi-vowel /w/ only (see below, C. I.a). STRÖM 122 notes that in OE the composition-vowel of short-syllabic *wō*-stems is commonly preserved, so that *baduini* may be an instance of merely graphic simplification. Ström draws a parallel with *-ulf*- for *-uulf*-spellings, but in both cases it is hard to see how one could consistently apply one symbol for two sounds. The other suggestion made by STRÖM 128 that *baduini* is due to a scribal error, which would then be a scribal error shared by the two C-type texts, is much more acceptable. The occurrence side by side of syncopation of the composition-vowel in K and C and of its preservation in M, L, and B is at least equally acceptable. So much is also assumed by GIRVAN 147 and CAMPBELL 145.
(3) Note the Celtic names *deruuentionis* (22v, 24-25), *doruuernensis* (4×), and *doruuernis* (12r, 28), spelled also *dorouerni* (47v, 40) once. M, L, and B invariably spell *-uu-*. C has double *uu* only in *doruuentionis* (*o* for *e* by mistake), and in *doruuernensium* (29v, 31); finally C spells *dorouernis* (12r, 28). K, M, L, and B, in contrast to C, have very few instances of *uu* representing the semi-vowel /w/, see below C. I.a.2. From this and the occurrence in both K and C of *-ou-* once each it may be concluded that *-uu-* here represents a composition-vowel followed by the semi-vowel: /uw/. The conclusion must then further

211

be that the composition-vowel was syncopated in C, unless one would interpret the four occurrences of single -*u*- as graphic simplifications of -*uu*-.

2. Primitive OE /u/ may occur in final position in *heiu*.
(1) The treatment of the second el. of *osuiu*, in all probability diphthongal (see above A. II.b), may be mentioned in this connection. Of the nine occurrences in K three end in -*o*, all of which are in ablative surroundings: *a rege nordanhymbrorum osuio* (1v, 24), *postulauit a rege osuio* (3r, 29), and *iubente rege osuio* (39v, 22). M agrees with K, and C has only *u*-spellings. L has the same ablative nouns in -*o* as K, but also has -*o* once in a nominative case, *osuio* (3r, 33). B has two of the ablative forms, and agrees with L in having *osuio* (3r, 33), but has *osuiu* instead of the third ablative form. As ANDERSON LB 114 proposes for these forms in L, the three *osuio*-spellings of K should no doubt also be interpreted as Latin case-endings.

III. *Parasite Vowels*

In this Section are placed together the cases in which svarabhakti vowels developed, or could have developed, after an accented syllable between /r/ or /l/ and a following consonant, and the cases in which unaccented vowels developed before syllabic /r/ and syllabic /n/. For discussions of these phenomena see LUICK I, 292 ff., GIRVAN 148 ff., STRÖM 127, ANDERSON LB 116 f., CAMPBELL 150 ff., BRUNNER AG 135 ff.

a) Between /r/ and a following consonant a svarabhakti vowel /i/ has developed in *bericthun* (26r, 17; 26v, 29).
(1) The other MSS have *bercthun*. The only other occurrence of a svarabhakti is in *ecgberecti* (47v, 3) of M. In the great many occurrences of the name-themes **alh**, **berct/berht/berict**, **burg**, **halch**, **halh**, **torct**, and **uaclh/ualh** no further instances of svarabhakti vowels are found neither in M, L, C, and B, nor in K. The presence of the svarabhakti in *bericthun* is the more extraordinary, because it affects only the two occurrences of the name when it refers to the Abbot of Beverley (c. 730), whereas the other occurrence of this compound name, which refers to a Ruler of Sussex, is spelled *bercthuno* (11r, 40). This can hardly be mere coincidence. Neither can it be ascribed to scribal practice regarding svarabhakti vowels in general, even if the two occurrences happen to be by one Hand, because in that Hand several

212

cases without svarabhakti are also evidenced. An explanation of this strange feature could possibly be found in a personal relationship between the bearer of the name and the scribe of the particular passage in K. Although we know that Bericthun (*s.v.*) was one of Bede's sources for HE, the feature cannot stem from Bede personally, because in that case the svarabhakti would certainly also have occurred in the other early MSS. The conclusion seems to have to be that the particular scribe of this passage was closely connected with the monastery of Beverley, Yorkshire East Riding. This may mean that the MS as a whole was copied in that monastery, or, if the MS was composed in another monastery, that this part of the MS was copied by a monk who, for example, was trained at Beverley. In this connection it may be pointed out that the particular Hand which we have recognized as the copyist of folios 25r to 34r, 1-8, was not only characterized by certain physical features of the handwriting, but also by such things as the use of a different type of letters and a different policy where the use of abbreviations was concerned. These are features that may reveal a different schooling and not just a different person.

(2) It may be noted that C drops unstressed vowels in (*in*)*bercingum* (7r, 30) and *ceortesei* (7r, 28). To the former this applies only if its etymology is connected with OE *beorc* 'birch'.

b) Before syllabic /r/ and syllabic /n/
i. an /i/ developed in *grantacęstir, hrofescęstir, kęlcacęstir, tunnacęstir*;
    and an /o/ developed in *earconberct, earconuald* (1r, 14; 9r, 34), and possibly in Continental Germanic *boructuari*;
ii. there is no svarabhakti in the oblique case *dorciccęstrae* (16v, 33), nor in *estranglorum* (12r, 25), *suthrieona* (7r, 27).

(1) B has *hrofaescaestr*, an *e* interlined over -*tr* by second hand. The three M-type texts have *sudergeona* instead of *suthrieona* in K and C. The latter MS has *u* instead of *o* in *ercunuuald* (7r, 16; 9r, 34).

(2) A full discussion of the characteristic appearance of some of the occurrences of *earconuald* in K and C has been given above, A. I. b.2.b). Here it may be noted that *erncualdum* (7r, 16) in K could be due to an error caused by the appearance of the name in K's exemplar as *ercunualdum. Associations with the related OE *eorcnan-stán* 'precious stone' may also have to be blamed.

(3) According to SCHÖNFELD 54 (see Etymology) either *o* or *u* of *boructuari* may be a svarabhakti. ANDERSON LB 117 opts for *o*. From

the appearance of the MSS no conclusion either one way or the other is possible, especially if the Continental origin of the name is taken into account.

C. CONSONANTS

This section, like the preceding one, will deal with only a selection of the OE consonant system and will also be partly devoted to the treatment of a number of general features of the consonants in K.

I. *Some Consonants*

a. *Primitive Germanic /w/*

1. Primitive Germanic /w/
i. has been vocalised in pre-consonantal position in *badudegn, iarumanno*;
ii. may have been syncopated before, or have been amalgamated with, the semi-vowel of the second el. in *baduini* (7r, 4).
(1) M, L, and B have *baduuini*. The question of syncopation of *-u* has been gone into above, B. II.c.1.b).

2. Primitive Germanic /w/, before vowels other than /u/:
a) in initial position appears
i. as *u* in *ualdheri, ualhstod, uetadun, uictberct, uictred, uigheard* (1r, 1), *uilbrod, uilfrid, uiltaburg, uiltorum, uini, uynfrid*, and in the Celtic names *uecta, uentę* (48r, 10), *uentanus, uiuraemuda, uiuri*;
ii. as *uu* in *uuigheard* (1v, 25), and in Celtic *uuenta* (11v, 7).
(1) L has *uuilfritho* (39v, 25). For the rest M, L, and B have no *uu*-spellings in this initial position. C has *uualdhere, uualstod* (sic!), *uuich(t)red* (21r, 2; 47v, 2), *uuigheard* (1r, 1), *uuilfrid* (10v, 9; 13v, 2; 13v, 16; 25r, 40; 25r, 42; 38r, 28; 39r, 38; 49r, 18), *uulfrid* (sic!, 48r, 16), *uuini*, and in the Celtic names *uuiuraemuda* and *uuiuri* (16r, 41).

b) in medial position appears
i. as *u* in *aedilualch, aediluald, berctuald, earconuald, heuuald*[30],

---

[30] For *heu-* see above A. III. b. 1.

214

inguald, oidiluald, osuald, boructuari, cantuarii, meanuari, gyruiorum, ediluini, aelfuini, alduini, baduini, eduini, goduino, osuini, ouini, tatuini, trumuini, geuissorum, osuiu, and in the Celtic names *caedualla* and *soluente,* and in Continental *quaentauic;*

ii. as *uu* in *coinuualch* (9v, 37), *bernuuini* (11v, 20), *geuuissorum* (11v, 9), and in the Celtic name *ceduualla* (29v, 24).

(1) L has *osuuiu* (39v, 17), and B has *æluuine* (sic!, 49r, 20)[31]. Otherwise M, L, and B have no instances of *uu* for /w/ in this position. C has *uu* in *aediluuald* (2×), *berchtuuald* (25r, 12; 40v, 35; 47v, 35), *ercunuualdo* (9r, 34), *heauuald* (31r, 29), *inguuald* (twice), *oidiluuald* (25r, 1; 25v, 13), *gyruuiorum* (13r, 38), *aediluuini, aelfuuine* (15r, 31), *alduuine* (48r, 6), *berchtuuini* (11v, 20)[32], *eduuini* (16r, 26; 48v, 40; 48v, 41), *ouuini* (twice), *tatuuini* (3×), and in the Celtic name *caeduualla* (11v, 9). C, moreover, uses the runic symbol Ϸ in *berhtϷ ald* (49r, 37) and in *aelf ine* (49r, 20), twice in the same passage.

(2) The use of *uu* for /w/ is frequent in C, but occurs very occasionally in K and even less in L. All instances both of initial and medial position in K occur on folios written by Hand I, except *ceduualla* (29v, 24). The introduction of the runic symbol Ϸ is generally considered a later development, evidenced in Mercian and southern, but not in Northumbrian texts. Cf. GIRVAN 16, STRÖM 128, CAMPBELL 26, BRUNNER AG 140, KUHN 42[33]. The interpretation of the many occurrences of *uu* for /w/ in C is not certain; it may be seen as a southern feature or an indication of later origin. Cf. STRÖM 128.

3. Primitive Germanic /w/ before /u/ appears as *u* in *uulfheri;*

and in *alduulf, ceoluulf, saexuulf,* and in Continental Germanic *arcuulfus.*

(1) C simplifies *uu* to *u* in *aldulf* (12r, 25; 16r, 36; 47v, 42), *ceolulf* (twice), and *saexulf* (4×). STRÖM 128 thinks that this "is doubtless merely a graphic simplification". It is more likely that these are instances of actual loss of /w/. Such loss at the beginning of the second els. of compound nouns and names, especially if the meaning had become obscured, is a normal development; cf. GIRVAN 198,

---

[31] Representation of the spirant ƀ by *u* does not occur in the MSS, otherwise we might have single *u* for /w/ after all.

[32] A scribal error for *bernuuini.*

[33] Kuhn does not mention the presence in C of the runic symbol Ϸ, unless this is by him referred to as a *uu*-ligature which "bears no resemblance to the rune" (note 105). But in disagreement with this would be his further statement that he has found the ligature in all the MSS, and not just C only.

CAMPBELL 188, BRUNNER AG 143. Its frequent occurrence in C points to a later date of composition.

b. *Primitive Germanic /ƀ/*

Attention will only be given to the appearance of Primitive Germanic /ƀ/ as a spirant. This sound is always a bilabial stop (spelled *b*) initially, after *m*, and when geminated, and thus does not require separate treatment. Nor need OE /f/ (< Indo-European /p/) be discussed.

Primitive Germanic /ƀ/ appears

i. as *b* in *aelbfled, gebmund* (10r, 20-21; 30r, 16-17), *suaebheardo,* and possibly *aebae;*

(1) The Celtic names *eboracensis/eboraci, maban, maildubi,* and *sabrinam* may be noted in this connection.

ii. as *f* in *aelfuini* (3×), *clofaeshooh, suefredo;*

(1) The Celtic names *hrofensis, hrofescęstir, hrofi,* and *racuulfe* may be noted.

iii. as *m*, in /mm/ < /ƀm/ through assimilation, in *gemmund* (1r, 26-27).

(1) M agrees with K in every respect with the exception that it has *gefmund* for *gemmund*, and, with L and B, Celtic *maildufi*. L and B have *gebmund* for *gemmund* and also spell -*b*- in the combination with -*uini*, three times and twice respectively. C also agrees to a large extent with K, with the exception that it spells *ęlffled* and Celtic *mafan*.

(2) Primitive Germanic /ƀ/, in the earliest stages of OE, developed from bi-labial pronunciation to labio-dental pronunciation. The two pronunciations may have been represented by the symbols *b* and *f* respectively in the earliest texts, but this distinction was certainly not preserved in the MSS of HE. Cf. BÜLBRING 190, LUICK II, 871f., GIRVAN 196, STRÖM 132f., Penzl[34], CAMPBELL 179.

(3) For the assimilation in *gemmund* STRÖM 133 refers to the late OE development of *wīfman* to *wimman*. Cf. WRIGHT 155, LUICK II, 859. The conclusion can, however, hardly be that the assimilation of *gemmund* in K and C is to be looked upon as an indication of a late date of composition for the C-version. Assimilation of this kind took place

---

[34] Cf. H. Penzl, "A Phonemic Change in Early Old English", *Language* 20 (1944), 84-87.

216

in different periods of OE, according to GIRVAN 192, and was not always expressed in spelling, according to CAMPBELL 198.

c. *Primitive Germanic /þ/*

K has no instances of crossed *đ* or the rune *þ* for the spelling of the voiced or voiceless representations of this consonant in OE. It uses either *d* or the digraph *th*, or possibly simply *t* (see below). The symbol *d* stems from the Latin alphabet, and *th* may have been borrowed from Old Irish usage. To some extent the symbols are kept apart, but the distinction is graphic rather than phonetic: neither of the two is exclusively employed to represent either the voiced or the voiceless variants of Primitive Germanic /þ/. Their distinction is more or less one of position. Cf. GIRVAN 14, 16f., STRÖM 128f., ANDERSON LB 86f., CAMPBELL 23ff., BRUNNER AG 161, KUHN 30f.

1. Primitive Germanic /þ/ in initial position:
a) at the beginning of first els. *th* is used in *thrydred*.
b) at the beginning of second els.
i. *th* is used in *aedilthryda* (4×), *bliththryde, osthryd*;
ii. *t* is used in *aediltryth* (1r, 36);
iii. *d* is used in *badudegn*.
(1) M, L, and B invariably use *th*, but agree with K in having *badudegn*. C has *aeđildryd* (3×), *aeđeldrydam* (13r, 34) and only once *aedilthrydae* (16r, 1); it has also *đ* in *beaduđegn*.
(2) The use of *-t-* in *aediltryth* (1r, 36) by K is probably due to a scribal error.

2. Primitive Germanic /þ/ in medial position appears
i. as *d* in *aedilbaldo, aedilberct, aedilburga, aedilred, aedilthryth, aedilualch, aediluald, ędiluini, badudegn, baduini* (?), *hadulac, nordanhymbrorum, oidiluald*;
   and in the inflected forms *aedilthryde* (etc.), *aldfridi* (etc.), *alhfridi, bliththryde, ceolfridi* (etc.), *cudbaldi* (?), *eanfridi, ecgfridi* (etc.), *haethfelda* (2×), *liccidfeldensi, rędfridum, uilfridi* (etc.), *uynfrido* (etc.);
ii. as *th* in *suthrieona* (7r, 27).
(1) M has *hæthfeltha* (49r, 21), and L has *uuilfritho* (39v, 25). M, L, and B have *sudergeona*. For the rest they agree completely with K. C, on the other hand, has a great number of *đ*-spellings: *aeđilbaldo, aeđilburga* (4×), *aeđilred* (10 out of 16), *aeđildryda* (4×), *aeđiluuald*

217

(2×), *norðanhymbrorum* (2v, 40), *oiðuuald* (sic!, 25r, 1), and in *aeðeldryðam* (13r, 34), *bliththryðe*.

(2) C is singled out from the other MSS by its frequent application of the *d* with cross-stroke. This special symbol was common in the eighth and ninth centuries, but less frequently used in Northumbrian. Cf. LUICK I, 77, GIRVAN 16f., ANDERSON LB 86, CAMPBELL 24 f. According to ANDERSON LB 87 the scribes of L were acquainted with *ð*, but used *d* under the influence of the Latin.

3. Primitive Germanic /þ/ in final position.

a) At the end of first els.

i. *d* is used in *cudbaldi, cudberct, fordheri* (38r, 20), *gudfrid, suidberct, thrydred*;

ii. *t* may have been used in *balthild*;

iii. *th* is used in *bliththryde, forthheri* (48r, 5), *haethfelth, hlothheri* (49r, 24), and in Continental Germanic *rathbedo*.

(1) C has *cudberhti* (25r, 1), *gydfrid* (sic!); it also has *haetfelda* (1r, 33; 49r, 21), *ratbedo* (31r, 17), and *suitbercht* (25r, 20; 32r, 14; 24r, 34). M, L, and B have *baldhild*. L shares *haetfelda* (1r, 33) with C. Before *-heri* as final el. the treatment of the consonant varies. Just *th* for the combination is most common: *fortheri* is spelled twice by M and B, and once (48r, 5) by C; *hlotheri* occurs exclusively in M, L (4 times, being deficient 49r, 24), and C, whereas B and K agree in having *hlotheri* 4 times and *hlothheri* once. Finally L has *fordheri* (twice) and C has *fordhere* (38r, 20).

(2) It is uncertain whether *ld* in *baldhild* was pronounced [lþ] or [ld] in Bede's days. STRÖM 130f. assumes that the pronunciation [lþ] is confirmed by the spelling *balthild* in C (and K). This spelling may be accounted for in another way (see below), and ANDERSON LB 120 has pointed out that the uniform appearance of the el. as *-bald* at the end of names seems to contradict Ström's suggestion. Generally speaking the change from /lþ/ to /ld/ is placed very early, even in prehistoric times; cf. LUICK II, 833f., CAMPBELL 169, BRUNNER AG 161. In *Liber Vitae* spellings of *balth-* occur before following *h*; cf. MÜLLER 30. Campbell sees in them preservations of /lþ/, whereas Brunner looks upon them as due merely to orthographic confusion.

(3) The simplification of *th* + *h* to *th* in *fortheri* and *hlotheri* probably represents fusion of the two consonants to /þ/, whether pronounced as a voiceless or as a voiced variety. Cf. STRÖM 130. A connection with the possible change of the fricative consonant to a voiceless plosive

218

in, for instance, *suitberct* in C and *berctfrit* (49r, 31) (see below), as alternatively suggested by STRÖM 131, so that the pronunciation would be [t] + [h], is far less likely. The striking appearance of *d* in *fordheri* in K and L, and of *đ* in C, may be due to the fact that the first el. was still associated with the word in ordinary use.

(4) The reduction in *haetfelda*, in L and C, is by ANDERSON LB 87 explained as "an early instance of the dissimilation of [þf] ⟩ [tf] seen in the modern form *Hatfield*".

b) At the end of second els.

i. *d* is used in *eadbald* (?), *herebald* (?), *hygbald* (?), *aldfrid, ceolfrid, cynifrid, ecgfrid, gudfrid, tatfrid, uilfrid, uynfrid, eadgyd, frigyd, torctgyd, eadhaed, hildilid, bregosuid, herisuid, osthryd*;

ii. *t* is used in *berctfrit* (49r, 31), *uynfrit* (7r, 11);

iii. *th* is used in *aediltryth* (1r, 36), *hethfelth* (12r, 30), *liccidfelth* (3v, 7).

(1) C has *eadgyđ* (7v, 33), *frigyđ, osthryđ, tatfriđ, torchtgyđ* (2×), *uilfriđ* (49r, 9). L has also *đ* in *frigyđ* and *gudfriđ*. C has -*ld* in *haethfeld* (12r, 30) and *liccidfeld*, in contrast to -*lth* in the other MSS. For *berctfrit* and *uynfrit* of K the other MSS have forms with final -*d*. M, L, and B have *edilthryd* (1r, 36), whereas C has *aediлđryt*. More forms with -*t* are exhibited by C in *bregusuit, eadhaet* (10r, 33; 49r, 19), and *herisuit*.

(2) The occasional use of final -*t*, whether of first or second els., is a characteristic feature of K and C. LUICK I, 77 and CAMPBELL 25 record the rare occurrence of *t* for /þ/ and BRUNNER AG 159f. assigns it to the oldest MSS. STRÖM 131 says that it remains an open question whether this spelling possibly represents a voiceless stop developed from the fricative. It should be noted in this connection that the only MSS that confuse *d*- and *t*-spellings in the orthography of the Latin are K and C. K has *d* for *t* once, *t* for *d* 4 times, whereas C has *d* for *t* 8 times and *t* for *d* 6 times. Although the Latin consonants represented by these symbols certainly were plosives, the conclusion can hardly be that this proves a change from /þ/ ⟩ /t/ in the OE names. For how would in that case *tatfriđ* and *uilfriđ* (49r, 9) have to be accounted for? There is little reason to assume that the final el. -*frid* was pronounced differently in the combinations *aldfrid, berctfrit*, and *tatfrid*. Nevertheless, the confusion between *d* and *t* in the ortho-graphy of the Latin may have helped the confusion between these symbols in the spelling of OE names, even if they stood for different phoneme oppositions in the two language systems. In Latin ortho-

graphy the symbols *d* and *t* were very frequently confused since the days of the Republic; cf. Löfstedt[35].

(3) It may be noted that C is the only MS invariably to have final *-ld*, whereas the other MSS sometimes have *-lth*.

d. *Primitive Germanic* /ʒ/

Whether Primitive Germanic /ʒ/ was a spirant or a stop in OE, whether palatal or velar, it is normally spelled *g* in the MSS of HE. The symbol *g* is found, for example, in the names *gebmund, genlade, gudfrid, gyruiorum, sighardo, eadgarum, haemgisl,* and *torctgyd.* As the various MSS do not deviate from normal practice in regard to the representation of these sounds, it will suffice to deal with only the following two phenomena.

1. The palatal spirant is denoted by *i* in *iarumanno* (3r, 27), *suthrieona* (7r, 27).

(1) The spelling in *suthrieona* is shared by C and is thus a feature of the C-version against *g* in *sudergeona* of M, L, and B. It is generally assumed that *i* was spelled to bring out the palatal quality of the sound. Cf. DAHL 98, STRÖM 133, CAMPBELL 25. But not everybody agrees with BÜLBRING 21, GIRVAN 182, ANDERSON LB 120, and CAMPBELL 173 that the *i*-spelling also indicates that the sound was at that time pronounced as the semi-vowel [j]. Cf. LUICK II, 830ff., BRUNNER AG 175f.

2. The palatal geminate appears
i. as *cg* in *ecgberct* (15×), *ecgfrid* (6×);
ii. as *c* in *ecberct* (11×), *ecfrid* (19×).

(1) M and B have no *ec*-spellings at all. C has considerably fewer than K: *ecberct* (3×), and *ecfrid* (4×). L has more than C, but still fewer than K: *ecberct* (6), and *ecfrid* (11×). Finally, C has *eg*- once, in *egfridus* (13r, 34). There is no conformity between K and C as to the occurrence of *ec*-spellings.

(2) If we study the spread of *ec*- and *ecg*-spellings over the folios of K we see that Hands I, III, and IV have a share of both; neither of the two names happens to be represented on folios by Hand II. Further study reveals that only Hand III, folios 21r, 31-42, to 24v, may possibly

---

[35] Cf. B. Löfstedt, *Studien über die Sprache der Langobardischen Gesetze* (Acta Universitatis Upsaliensis, Studia Latina Upsaliensia 1), Uppsala 1961, p. 138.

have applied the two spellings systematically, for all of its four combinations with -*berct* have *ecg*- and the two with -*frid* have *ec*-. We should, of course, bear in mind that the total number of instances in this Hand is relatively small, but that it may at least have some significance is also suggested by the fact that both Hand I and Hand III have an almost equal number of *ec*- and *ecg*-spellings for *ecgberct* on their folios, 8 and 6, and 3 and 5 respectively.

(3) The question arises whether *ec*-spellings for *ecg*- represent a change on the phonological level. Primitive Germanic $/ʒ/$ before a following $/j/$ resulted in a geminate and $/j/$ was lost in the process. The palatalized geminate was a stop and came to be represented by *cg* in OE. The *c* was added instead of a second *g* in order to bring out that the combination represented a plosive and not a spirant. Cf. WRIGHT 138, LUICK II,905, CAMPBELL 27. The use of *c* in this digraph that stands for a *voiced* geminate is "the only considerable trace in OE spelling of the Celtic use of *p, t, c* for voiced stops", according to CAMPBELL 27, n. 1. When in final position the double consonants were simplified in pronunciation, one symbol of the double graphs was frequently dropped. Simplification of the digraph *cg* to *g* would, however, result in confusion with the palatal spirant, which was also represented by a single *g*. The spelling *cg* was, therefore, usually retained in order to distinguish between such pairs as *wecg* 'wedge' and *weg* 'way'. Cf. Moulton[36], KUHN 48. Kuhn also notes that simplification of *cg* to *c* or *g* (as in C: *egfridus* (13r, 34)) is a common feature in the spelling of *ecg*- in the oldest MSS of HE, but apparently appreciates these as merely graphic, as does CAMPBELL 27. STRÖM 134f. fairly tentatively, and ANDERSON LB 120f. fairly definitely, suggest that the *ec*-spellings indicate unvoicing of the consonant, which would be due to assimilation in a combination like *ecfrid* and would then by analogy have been introduced in *ecberct*. It may, however, seriously be doubted whether this is right. To explain the appearance of *ec*- in *ecberct* as due to analogy is not very convincing in the first place, as was also felt by Ström and Anderson, even if the proportion of *ec*-spellings in combination with *frid* is greater than that for combinations with -*berct*: 14 to 6 and 11 to 15 respectively. But more important is that *ec*-spellings are lacking altogether in M and B, which is surprising if the varieties for *ecg* were introduced to render changes

---

[36] Cf. William G. Moulton, "The Stops and Spirants of Early Germanic", *Language* 30 (1954), p. 25.

in the consonant that were taking place at that time or had recently been effected. It would be especially strange for B, which is very close to L in the tradition of the text and most probably later. On the other hand there are indications that it can hardly be a mere matter of scribal error, as STRÖM 130 alternatively proposes, because K and L are the very MSS that are the most correct of the five in all other respects. The conclusion then must be that here, after all, we have instances of mere graphic variation, probably arising from a feeling with some of the scribes that the digraph *cg* was out of place in the orthographic system, since it no longer represented a geminate. An adequate alternative was hard to find, however.

(4) In the orthographic variation of *ecg-* and *ec*-spellings we can, therefore, find no evidence for the assibilation of the voiced palatal stop. The answers to the question at what time assibilation of this sound, and of the OE palatal sound developed from Primitive Germanic /k/ (see below), took place have varied considerably. It has been placed in prehistoric or early OE times, at any rate for the dialects south of the Humber; cf. BÜLBRING 197. At the other extreme WRIGHT 162, 167 has stated that there is no proof at all that such a change had already taken place in OE, and that, therefore, it may well have been very late. Most scholars hold that by the end of the OE period the change had been effected, but that a definite time cannot be given for it. Cf. LUICK II, 904f., GIRVAN 182, CAMPBELL 197, BRUNNER ES I,163, BRUNNER AG 171. The application of diacritical *e* and *i* after *g* and *c* was in the first place a means to indicate palatalisation, independent of whether assibilation had already occurred. It has been proved in the meantime that Bülbring was mistaken in the assumption that assibilation left no traces in Northumbrian; cf. Gevenich[37], Penzl[38], BRUNNER AG 171f. ANDERSON LB 120 attempts to find some evidence for a mid eighth-century date for the assibilation of palatal /k/ in the spelling of the Celtic place-name *liccidfelth*, in which double *cc* represents the assimilation of what originally was /tg/ in Old British, perceived by the Anglo-Saxons as /tk/. JACKSON LHEB 563 f. also indicates that the assimilated sound, taken over by the Anglo-Saxons, was assibilated by them. CAMPBELL 197, n. 1, however, objects that the two sounds were certainly assimilated

[37] Cf. Olga Gevenich, *Die englische Palatalisierung von k ⟩ č im Lichte der englischen Ortsnamen* (Studien zur englischen Philologie 57), Halle 1918.
[38] Cf. H. Penzl, "The Phonemic Split of Germanic *k* in Old English", *Language* 23 (1947), p. 40.

222

by the Anglo-Saxons, but assimilated to palatal /kk/ only, which need not indicate anything as to the date of assibilation. Both Penzl[39] and Watson[40] refrain from statements about the date at which the phonetic change resulting in assibilated consonants was effected. According to PILCH 86, n. 27, assibilation was completed in the eighth century. KUHN 23f. argues that assibilation should be placed about the middle of the seventh century. His argument hinges on the assumption that smoothing could only have taken place before palatalized consonants, which is not, however, the point of view taken by LUICK I, 213f., CAMPBELL 93, BRUNNER AG 97. Finally we may note that Norberg[41] assumes that Bede probably pronounced Latin *c* before *e* and *i* as a stop, which he bases on the fact that in his poetry Bede alliterates *c* in that position with *c* before *a* and before consonants. Conclusions along the same line based on *c*-alliterations in OE poetry are questioned by Penzl[42] with a reference "to a poetic tradition of the kind that is responsible for Modern English 'eye-rhymes'". So far, therefore, the position with regard to the date of assibilation remains uncertain.

e. *Primitive Germanic /k/*

The normal representation of Primitive Germanic /k/, whether palatal or velar, is by *c*. See for example *aecci, ceolred, tunnacęstir, cudbaldi, acca, hacanos,* and the Celtic words *caedmon, ceadda, dacore, liccidfelth.*
The following exceptions may be mentioned.

1. Primitive Germanic /k/ appears as *k* in *kęlcacęstir* (16v, 7-8).
(1) Initial *k* is shared by the other MSS. It stands for velar /k/, which was preserved in this word because Primitive OE /æ/ from West Germanic /a/ was in Anglian retracted to /a/ instead of being broken before /lk/. After palatalisation had already taken place /a/ was *i*-mutated to /æ/ under the influence of /i/ in the derivative suffix -*ion* that had been added. See above, ETYMOLOGY.

---

[39] *op. cit.*, 41 f.
[40] Cf. John W. Watson, Jr., "Non-Initial *k* in the North of England," *Language* 23 (1947), p. 44, n. 6.
[41] Cf. Dag Norberg, *Manuel pratique de latin médiéval* (Connaissance des Langues IV), Paris 1968, pp. 47 ff.
[42] *op. cit.*, p. 34.

(2) For a discussion of the problem whether palatal /k/ had been assibilated in Bede's days, reference may be made to the preceding treatment of Primitive Germanic /ʒ/, d. 2.

2. The combination /kw/ appears as *qu* in *quichelm* (1r, 26; 10r, 18), *quoenburg*, and in Continental *quaentauic*.

(1) *qu* in *quichelm* (2×) is a feature also of C, whereas the M-type MSS all have *cuichelm*.

(2) The use of *qu* for this combination was taken from Latin and occurs only in the oldest MSS. Cf. BRUNNER AG 173, KUHN 25.

f. *Primitive Germanic /h/*

1. Initial pre-vocalic /h/

a) is preserved both in first and second els. in *hacanos, hadulac, haeddi, hęmgisl, haethfelth, hagustaldensis, heiu, herebald, hereberct, hereburg, heriric, herisuid, heruteu, herutford, heuuald, hiddila, hild, hildilid, homel·ea·, hygbald*, and in such Celtic names as *hibernia, hii, hienses, humbrę, humbronensium*;

and in *aenheri, aldhelm, balthild, bercthuno, bericthun, bosanhamm, burghelm, clofaeshooh, drycthelme, eadhaed, fordheri, medeshamstede, nordanhymbrorum, pecthelm, quichelm, sighardo, sighere, streanaeshalch, ualdheri, uigheard, uulfheri.*

(1) C has *agustaldensi* (26r, 21), which in B appears with interlinear *h*, possibly by second hand. C also has *eadaedum* (10r, 39), corrected by second hand. Initial *h* is interlined by first hand in *haeddi* (1r, 25) in both L and B; similarly by L alone in *haethfelth* (12r, 30). M and B may have dropped -*h*- in *hlotheri* (2×); see below.

b) it may have been dropped in *hlotheri* (4×).

(1) For both the appearance of this name in the other MSS and for a discussion of a possible explanation of the disappearance of one *h* from the combination *th + h* in this name and in *hlotheri* in M and B, see above c.3.a).

2. Initial pre-consonantal /h/

a) is spelled *hl*- in combination with /l/ in *hlotheri* and Continental Germanic *hlothario*.

(1) C has *lothario.*

b) is spelled *hu-* in combination with /w/ in *huętbercti, huicciorum.*

c) in combination with /r/
i. it is spelled *hr-* in *hreno* (31v, 10), *hreutford, hrofensis* (3×), *hrofescęstir, hrofi* (2×), *(in)hrypum* (3×);
ii. it is spelled *rh-* in *rhenum* (2×), *rhofensis* (4×), *rhofi* (10r, 18), *rhypensi, (in)rhypum* (38v, 11).
(1) M has *rh-* only in *rheno* (2×). L has *rhofensis* (2×), *rhypensi,* and *rheno* (2×). C has *rhofensi* (1×), *rofensi* (1×), and *rhenum* (2×). B, finally, has *rhofensis* (2×), *rhypensi,* and *rhenum* (1×).
(2) Initial /h/ disappeared before /l/, /n/, /r/, and /w/, after having become a glottal spirant in all Germanic languages. The consonants became voiceless, and *h* was written to indicate this. Cf. CAMPBELL 186, BRUNNER AG 180. Uncertainty as to where to place the symbol is common. The Latin of our MSS, especially that of C, also shows traces of it. The use of unetymological *h* in *hrenus* is also connected with it.

3. Final post-vocalic /h/ appears as *h* in *clofaeshooh.*
(1) M has *clofaeshoch,* of which *c* is interlinear by first hand. Mention may also be made of Celtic *puch* in all MSS.

4. Final post-consonantal /h/ appears
a) at the end of the first els. of compound names as *h* in *alhfridi, ualhstod.*
(1) M has both *alchfridi* and *ualchstod,* and B has *alchfridi.* L agrees with K. C drops /h/ altogether in *uualstod.*
(2) Final /h/, both of first and second els., is in older MSS spelled *ch* which was soon replaced by *h.* Cf. BÜLBRING 189, CAMPBELL 24, BRUNNER AG 185.

b) at the end of the second els.
i. it appears as *ch* in *aediluálch* (3×), *coinuualch, streanaeshalch* (16r, 20; 16v, 16);
ii. it appears as *h* in *streanaeshalh* (20v, 24-25);
iii. it is lost in the inflected form *streanaeshalae* (49r, 23).
(1) M has no instances of *h,* and has *c* in *strenaeshalc* (16r, 20). L agrees with K, but *streanaeshalae* is missing altogether. The only difference between B and K is that B has no instance of *h.* C, on the other hand, has *ch* only in *streaneshalch* (20v, 24-25).
(2) The variation between *h-* and *ch-*spellings does not reflect the

difference between M- and C-version. M chiefly shows the old spelling, and C the new spelling.

5. Primitive Germanic /h/ before /t/ appears
i. as *c* in *aedilberct, berctfrit, bercthuno, bercto, berctuald, cudberct, cyniberct, drycthelme, eadberct, earconberct, ecgberct, hereberct, huętbercti, pecthelm, sabercto, suidberct, tondberct, torctgyd, trumberct, tunberct, uictberct, uictred* (13×), and in Continental Germanic *agilberctus* (3×);
ii. as *h* in *uihtred* (21r, 2), and in *agilberhtum* (2r, 31).
(1) M invariably has *c* except in *berhtfrid*. L has *ch* a number of times: *berchthuno, ecbercht* (47v, 27), *erconbercht* (1v, 20), *hereberchto* (1v, 8), *trumbercht*; it has *h* in *agilberhto* (39v, 18); but in contrast to K it has *c* in *uictred* (21r, 2). B has only *c*, except in *torhtgyd* (8r, 16). In striking contrast to all this C has hardly any instances of *c*, but has about 60 of *ch*, and about 40 of *h*. The instances of *c* in C are *uictbercht* (25r, 16; 30v, 40) and *uictredo* (30r, 13).
(2) It should be noted that Celtic *uecta* is invariably spelled with *c*, strikingly enough also by C. When the name was taken over from the British, the consonant was a spirant already in that language. Cf. JACKSON LHEB 409. The form in which it occurs in HE was apparently looked upon as a Latinization. In this connection it may perhaps be pointed out that the one name-el., **uict/uiht,** that in C is spelled with *c* three out of seven times has by some been related with Celtic **UECTA** (see ETYMOLOGY).
(3) Spelling *c* to represent the spirant in the combination *ct* is a feature of the earliest texts; *h*-spellings later came in its place. Cf. BÜLBRING 188, BRUNNER AG 183, CAMPBELL 24. It should be noted that *h*-spellings began to occur as early as the beginning of the eighth century. Despite this it may be concluded from the all but total absence of *ct*-spellings in C that this MS was composed later than the others.

6. Primitive Germanic /hs/ is spelled *x* in *saexuulf, sexburg,* and in Latinized *saxones* and *saxonicus.*
(1) Scholars generally agree that original /hs/ had developed into /ks/, represented by *x*, by the time our MSS were composed, i.e. after breaking. Cf. LUICK II, 832f., 890, CAMPBELL 170, BRUNNER AG 183f., and cf. also BÜLBRING 189, WRIGHT 171, GIRVAN 14. The suggestion made by KUHN 32 that the change from /hs/ to /ks/ must have been later than the eighth century, because the Vespasian

Psalter gloss is very precise in applying *x* for original /hs/ and *cs* for /ks/, can hardly be reconciled with the simple fact that *x* in Latin orthography represented /ks/. It is inconceivable that the symbol could be used in a Latin text to represent /hs/ in a small number of native OE names.

II. *Assimilation and Dissimilation*

Assimilation has played an important part in the formation of short names from compound names. It has helped to shape such names as **ACCA, AEBBAE, EAPPA,** and **OFFA.** But these formations carry no further information of any importance within the framework of the present study because of their uniformity of appearance which is due to their great age. A general reference to the relevant passages of PART III and to the fuller treatment of assimilation in such names by ANDERSON LB 121 f. may suffice.

Assimilation occurred in OE in various periods and was not always carried out universally. Cf. LUICK II, 854 ff., GIRVAN 192, CAMPBELL 198.

The following points with regards to assimilation in other positions may be noted here.

1. /bm/ ⟩ /mm/ in *gemmund* (1r, 26-27). See above, I.b.iii.

2. /þ/ + /h/ ⟩ /þ/ in *hlotheri* (4×). See above, I.c.3.a). iii.

3. /df/ ⟩ /tf/ in *hreutford* (11v, 32).
(1) *hreutford* is shared by all MSS. In this connection attention is drawn to the spelling *herudforda* (49r, 13) for *herutforda*, where the *d* is due to a scribal error probably caused by the confusion arisen from the assimilation of /df/ ⟩ /tf/, especially where *hreud* and *herut* were so similar in appearance. C shares the spelling of K, and B has *heurdforda*. B has also *herudford* (6r, 12).
(2) M, L, C, and B also have assimilation of /df/ ⟩ /tf/ in *liccitfeldensi* (47v, 41), but all agree with K in having *liccidfelth* (3v, 7).

4. Above, I.d.2., we have already expressed reserve as to the suggestion of Ström and Anderson that *ec*-spellings for *ecg*- are in part due to assimilation.

5. K has no instances of dissimilation of /w/ + /u/ ⟩ /u/ in the name-

theme **uulf** when in second position, which is a characteristic of C alone (see above, I.a.3), nor of /þf/ ⟩ /tf/, which is shown by L and C in *hætfeldo* (1r, 33) and by C alone – L being defective at this point – in *haetfelda* (49r, 21), for which see above, I.c.3.a.).

III. *Other Consonantal Features*

1. The occurrence of *uilbrod* (4 times, the first three shared by C) for *uilbrord* has been gone into above, A.I.d.

2. K spells *t* for *d* in *balthild* (39r, 36), *berctfrit* (49r, 31), and *uynfrit* (7r, 11). The question whether these are instances of unvoicing in final position, has been discussed above, I.c.3.b).

3. Metathesis of consonants is not evidenced in K.
(1) The only instances of metathesis in our MSS occur in the name-theme **gisl**, which by M is invariably spelled as *-gils* in *aldgislo* (39v, 31), *edgisl* (20r, 23), and *hęmgisl* (34r, 31). Note that K at first seems to have spelled *hęmgils*, and that C has the metathesized form.
(2) Metathesis in consonant-combinations with /l/ is especially found in half-stressed and unstressed syllables. The change cannot be accurately dated. Cf. BÜLBRING 230, LUICK II, 919, GIRVAN 186, n. 1.

4. K spells double *-dd-* in *caeddualla* (29r, 8; 29r, 32; 29v, 11; 29v, 24).
(1) This feature is not found in the other MSS, and besides it is restricted to folios copied by Hand IV, which Hand has also two instances with single *-d-*. They all four, in fact, occur in the passages that relate to Caedualla's death in Rome, HE V, 7-8.
(2) The use of double *-dd-* is hard to account for. There is the possibility that it is due to association with the spelling of the related names *ceadda* and *ceddi*. It can hardly be an early instance of the "illogical doubling of consonant symbols" that is well-evidenced in later Northumbrian texts. Cf. GIRVAN 192, CAMPBELL 27.

5. The adjectivalisation of the place-name *mailros* has yielded two different Latin forms, *mailrosensi* (21v, 9) and *mailronensis* (30v, 2), which are both shared by C against the M-type texts.

6. The form *nordamhymbrorum* with *m* for *n* occurs twice in K (2v,

40; 48v, 39) and twice in M (16r, 28; 49r, 33-34). It is probably due to confusion caused by *m* in the following syllable.

7. Loss of /t/ in consonant-groups is not evidenced in K. It is in C, which has *torchgyđ* (8r, 16) and *uuichred* (47v, 2).
(1) By GIRVAN 204f. such loss is associated with later West-Saxon texts. Cf. also FEILITZEN DB 95, CAMPBELL 192.

PART V

SUMMARIES AND CONCLUSIONS

A. SCRIBAL DIFFERENCES

In Chapter 1 of PART I an attempt was made to define more precisely Lowe's statement in CLA VIII, no. 1140, that K was copied "by more than one hand". On palaeographical grounds three Hands were distinguished:
1. 1r-13v; 14v; 15v; 21r, 6-30; 34r,8-42, to 50r.   2.   14r; 15r; 16r-21r, 1-4.   3. 21r, 31-42, to 34r,1-8. Of the many subdivisions within these Hands that further seemed possible on purely palaeographical grounds only that in the third group of folios appeared to be corroborated by other evidence. In the first place, although the whole of this group of folios uses abbreviations sparingly, this holds especially true for folios 25r-34r,1-8. In the second place, folios 21r,31-42, to 24v differ from all other folios in that they have hardly any instances of significant minor errors. On these grounds it seemed justified to distinguish two Hands in the palaeographically fairly similar folios 21r, 31-42, to 34r,1-8, so that eventually four Hands were proposed:
1. Hand I: 1r-13v; 14v; 15v; 21r, 6-30; 34r, 8-42, to 50r.
2. Hand II: 14r; 15r; 16r-21r,1-4.
3. Hand III: 21r, 31-42, to 24v.
4. Hand IV: 25r-34r, 1-8.

On the whole there are few distinctive phonological features that are characteristic of any of these four Hands. The use of double *uu* for the semi-vowel /w/, see PART IV, C.I.a.2.b), is restricted to Hand I except for *uu* in *ceduualla* (29v, 15), but the total number of such occurrences, four in all, is much too small to be reliable. To a lesser degree this also holds true of the sharp distinction between *ec-* and *ecg*-spellings, used with *-frid* and *-berct* respectively, found in Hand IV; see PART IV, C.I.d.2. And finally, the four occurrences of double *-dd-* in *caeddualla* (an exclusive feature of K) are all by Hand IV, but this feature remains unexplained and may be due to other causes; see PART IV, C.III.4.

The only phonological feature of the OE material of K that seems to be particularly relevant in connection with the distinction between the Hands is the occurrence of the svarabhakti vowel in the spelling of *bericthun* (26r and 26v) for the Abbot of Beverley. It has been suggested, PART IV, B.III.a), that this spelling may presuppose a personal acquaintance with Abbot Bericthun (*s.v.*) or with the monastery of Beverley on the part of the particular scribe, i.e. Hand IV.

233

Some of the features of Hand IV appear to represent a somewhat different schooling and the suggestion has been made that Hand IV wrote at Beverley, or was at least trained at Beverley. In this connection it should be remembered that one of the capital letters with crescent finial, which was associated by Lowe with Jarrow, also occurs regularly in this Hand. It may be assumed then that, if this scribe was trained at Beverley, he was probably a monk of Jarrow at the time of copying this part of K.

B. LATIN ORTHOGRAPHY

In Chapter 2 of PART I the various items of confusion in the orthography of the Latin were gone into, among other things with a view to an assessment of a possible reflection of this confusion in the spelling of the OE material.

Generally, in cases in which the possibility of a direct relation between confusion in the orthography of the Latin and confusion in the spelling of OE material has been established as probable, it is hardly ever possible to decide which way the influence has operated. The Latin may have influenced the OE spelling and *vice versa*. This applies in the many instances in which *e*- and *ae*-(*ę*-)spellings have been discussed, as for example in PART IV, A.I.a.7.b), A.I.b.2.a), A.II.a.1., A.III.b.2, and B.II.b.1.b). But it is not in itself self-evident from the material of the present study that the orthography of the Latin and of the OE name-material had any effect upon each other at all. There is on the whole very little evidence to go by and what little evidence there is appears to be contradictory. On the one hand, the exclusive occurrence in K and C of *t*-spellings for *d* in OE names seems to be reflected in an equally exclusive confusion in these MSS between *d* and *t* in the orthography of the Latin; see PART IV, C.I.c.3. b). On the other hand, the relatively frequent confusion in the orthography of the Latin between *e*- and *i*-spellings seems to have left few traces in the OE material of all the MSS, but particularly of M; see PART IV, B.II.a.1. It may, of course, be that the confusion in the orthography of the Latin only influenced the spelling of the OE material in cases in which the scribes became hypercorrect out of uncertainty and were for that reason led to an incorrect treatment of the spelling of comparable sounds in the OE material. This has been suggested as a possible solution to the uncommon treatment

234

by M of *heri-/here-* as a first el., and by C of the representation of the Celtic name *eboraci/eboracensis*; see PART IV, B.II.c.1.

C. THE POSITION OF K AMONG THE OTHER MSS

The value of the OE material of K is in part determined by what relation the MS bears to the other MSS. From a critical study of its relations conclusions can be drawn as to its proximity to the original text composed by Bede, and simultaneously, because such a study entails the comparison of the two versions of HE, conclusions also as to the shape in which the OE material of Bede's original may have appeared. The point of the comparison of K with the other MSS has already been gone into in some detail in PART I, Chapter 2. The results yielded by that comparison of the Latin texts of the MSS may here be summarized briefly:

– K is certainly a text of the C-type version;

– K agrees with M-type texts on a great number of major textual differences as well as minor textual differences, on the score of which it may be said to be nearer than C to the original, which is also thus known to us with more certainty;

– K presents a far more correct text than M and C, but a slightly less correct text than L;

– K and C cannot possibly be descended from one another.

The selection that follows of the agreements and disagreements between the OE material of K and that of the other MSS shows similar conclusions to be drawn with regard to the mutual relations between the MSS, with regard to K's relation to Bede's original, and thus also with regard to the exact shape of the name-material as written down by Bede himself.

1. Only occasionally does K differ from the other four MSS in its representation of the OE material.

a) Four times West Germanic /ā/ is represented as *ae* (*ę*) in the second els. -*flęd* and -*raed*. See PART IV, A.II.a.1. They may be mere graphic variants, possibly due to the confusion of *ae-* (*ę-*) and *e*-spellings in the orthography of the Latin.

b) Twice K has a svarabhakti vowel in *bericthun* (26r, 17; 26v, 29). See PART IV, B.III.a), and also above, A.

c) K has unassimilated /d/ in *liccidfeldensi* (47v, 41) in contrast to

235

the other MSS, which, however, do share with K the spelling of *liccidfelth* (3v, 7). See PART IV, C.II.3.

d) Four times Hand IV of K spells double -*dd*- in *caeddualla*. See PART IV, C.III.4, and also above, A.

e) K twice spells *m* in *nordamhymbrorum*, a feature that also occurs with this name in M, but in different places. See PART IV, C.III.6.

2. C differs from K, M, L, and B as a group in a much greater number of cases. Most of them bear on the place and/or date of composition of the MS. The agreement between K and the MSS of the M-type version is important, because it settles the reading of Bede's original.

a) C has back-mutated *heorutforda* (2×). See PART IV, A.I.b.4.

b) C has *gydfrid* instead of *gudfrid*. See PART IV, A.I.e.2.

c) C has *gea* instead of *gae*. See PART IV, A.II.a.4.

d) C has *bosil* twice instead of *boisil*, probably due to a scribal error on account of the head-word *bosa*. See PART IV, A.II.c.2.

e) C only has *oe*-spellings in the names with *coen-/coin-*, *oe*-spellings being later than *oi*-spellings. The exact parallelism between K, L, and B with regard to the distribution of *oi*- and *oe*-spellings probably reflects their distribution in Bede's original. See PART IV, A.II.c.2.

f) C has *saeberchto* instead of *sabercto*. See PART IV, A.III.a.1.

g) C has normal *eastranglorum* instead of *estranglorum*. See PART IV, A.III.b.1.

h) C has *heau(u)ald* twice instead of Anglian *heuuald*. See PART IV, A.III.b.1.

i) C has unmutated *eanheri* instead of *aenheri*, probably owing to analogy. See PART IV, A.III.b.2.

j) C has *beda* instead of *baeda*. See PART IV, A.III.b.2.

k) C has some instances of unstressed /e/ instead of /i/ in *aedel-*. See PART IV, B.II.a.1.a).

l) C has almost without exception *u* for *o* in *eburaci/eburacensis*. See PART IV, B.II.c.1.a).

m) C has many instances of double *uu* for the semi-vowel /w/, which spelling is rare in the other MSS; it also has the rune $\triangleright$ twice. See PART IV, C.I.a.2.b).

n) C spells single *u* instead of *uu* in -*uulf* as a second el. See PART IV, C.I.a.3.

o) C very regularly uses *đ* for *d/th*. See PART IV, C.I.c.

p) C almost invariably spells final post-consonantal Primitive Germanic /h/ as -*h* instead of -*ch*. See PART IV, C.I.f.4.b).

236

q) C never spells *ct* for Primitive Germanic /h/ + /t/. See PART IV, C.I.f.5.

3. In a number of cases K and C agree with each other against the M-type MSS in the rendering of the OE material. The question then arises which of the readings is to be looked upon as Bede's. The answer to this depends on which version is the earlier. In Chapter 2 of PART I this matter was touched upon from a purely textual point of view. The most important conclusion drawn there is that whichever version is the later it cannot have originated much later than the other version. Should the C-version be the older version, then the M-version cannot have been later than A.D. 737, the date of composition of M. A second conclusion may be that truly authentic material of either version cannot be very different linguistically from that of the other. So much will also appear to be true from the cases that follow. However, the few differences that can be established as authentic of either of the two versions, may be indicators of the earlier version when they are odd or idiosyncratic forms or spellings that would be redressed in the corrected version. In the following enumeration three groups are distinguished, of which the first includes a case that could be interpreted as indicating that the C-version was the corrected version, the second includes cases that point to the M-version as the corrected version, and the third includes cases that seem to point neither way.

i. The use of *qu-* in *quichelm* by the C-texts instead of *cuichelm* of the M-type texts could be interpreted as a corrected form bringing the spelling of this name in line with that of *quoenburg* and *quaentauic*. See PART IV, C.I.e.2. The *qu*-spelling was earlier than *cu-*, so it is also possible to revert the argument.

ii. Of three variant renderings of names in the C-texts it has been suggested that they appear to bear the symptoms of the uncorrected first draft or version.

a) K and C treat the three occurrences of the name *earconuald* in a strikingly aberrant way. See PART IV, A.I.b.2.b).

b) K and C spell *uilbrod* instead of *uilbrord* a number of times, which if it is explained as originating in the Irish connections of St. Willibrord may be the trace of a personal relationship between the composer of this version and the Saint or his circles. The absence of these spellings in the M-version strikes one as a correction. See PART IV, A.I.d.

c) The unusual appearance of *-e* instead of *-i* in the nominative endings

237

of *sebbe* and *sighere*, which together form the subject of a clause, has been explained as a direct borrowing by Bede from his source. See PART IV, B.II.a.2.a) and b).

iii. The following cases do not lend themselves to any tentative interpretation with a view to the question which version is the earlier.

a) K and C have *eollan* against *eallan* in the M-type texts. The second instance of this name appears with *eo* in all MSS. See PART IV, A.I.b. 2.d).

b) K and C have *ceorotesei* and *ceoroti* against *cerotesei* and *ceroti* of the M-type texts. See PART IV, A.I.b.4.

c) K and C have some instances of *t* for *d* at the end of name-themes. See PART IV, C.I.c.3.b).

d) K and C have *suthrieona* for *sudergeona* in the M-type texts. See PART IV, C.I.d.1.

The conclusion may be that there are some indications that the C-version is earlier than the M-version.

D. TRACES OF OTHER DIALECTS IN *HE* AND OF THE STATE OF BEDE'S SOURCES

As CO & MY xxxix f. points out, the Latin text of HE shows that where Bede relied on written sources he, or his amanuensis, sometimes copied the sources so faithfully that errors were also taken over. The OE material too shows instances of this phenomenon in that some names apparently appear in the dialectal form in which they came to Bede in the written or oral sources. Such traces of other dialects need not all be traced back to Bede's sources, for some names were no doubt known all over the country by the form they had in their own dialect. Most of the names mentioned below are also dealt with by ANDERSON LB 63 ff.

1. In a number of cases the reading of K agrees with that of the other MSS, and thus corroborates that certain features of non-Northumbrian origin were certainly introduced by Bede himself.

a) The names *ceadda* and *peada*, both probably showing *ea* caused by back-mutation, may reflect the Mercian origin of the bearers of the names. See PART IV, A.I.a.8. It is not very likely that in the different treatment of the spelling of *coen-/coin-* for the Northumbrian Coinred 1 (*s.v.*) and the Mercian Coinred 2 (*s.v.*) any part was played by either

238

the different origins of the bearers of the names or the state of Bede's sources for the lives of the two kings.

b) The river-name *genlade* shows a Kentish feature, which is in agreement with its origin. See PART IV, A.I.a.6.

c) The absence of smoothing in *earconberct* is a non-Anglian feature. See PART IV, A.I.b.2.b).

d) Unrounded /ē/ in *medeshamstede*, provided the etymology proposed is correct, is a non-Northumbrian feature. See PART IV, A.II.c.2.

e) A West Saxon feature, due to the origin of the bearers of the names, may be detected in the occurrence of long /ǣ/ in *rędfridum* and *suaebheardo*. See PART IV, A.II.a.1.

2. In a number of cases in which K and C agree with each other against the M-type MSS, the reading of the C-version may reflect the way in which Bede copied his sources. Three of them have been mentioned above, under C.2. The fourth is the appearance of breaking in the names *suaebheardo* and *uigheard*, which may be interpreted as due to the Kentish origin of the bearers of the names. See PART IV, A.I.a.5.c). Assuming that the broken forms of these names are indeed non-Northumbrian, one might also on the strength of this think of placing K in a non-Northumbrian area. This would, however, hardly be in accordance with the generally Northumbrian appearance of the rest of the OE name-material of K; see below, under E.

3. In *bericthun* we may have a trace of the source of this particular passage of K. See above, under A.

E. THE DIALECT

The Northumbrian character of the OE material of HE has long been recognized. It is sufficient to refer the reader to STRÖM 146 ff. and ANDERSON LB 136 ff. for some detailed comment on the question of the dialect. In so far as such corroboration is still wanted, it is evident from the foregoing discussion of the material of K that the features of the OE material found in the M-type texts may indeed be looked upon as largely stemming from Bede, because there is such a great measure of agreement between the C-type text K and the M-type MSS. Before some more detailed evidence of this agreement and of the deviant dialectal characteristics of the material of C is given, attention may be drawn to the agreement between L and B, which is such that it is hardly conceivable that these two MSS should have had different origins. The differences shown by M make it the least reliable text of the three M-type MSS; these differences are largely a matter of orthographic variance or scribal error. The differences of dialect that ANDERSON LB 140 assumes for M and L on the basis of M's deviant readings may well be non-existent.

1. The material of K also exhibits the Anglian and Northumbrian features of the material in the M-type texts.

a) Absence of breaking before /l/ + consonant. See PART IV, A. I.a.5.a).

b) Absence of broken /ea/ in *saex-/sex-*. See PART IV, A.I.a.5.b). The interpretation by ANDERSON LB 137 of the *ae*-spellings as possibly typical of northern Northumbrian is ill-founded.

c) Absence of diphthongisation under the influence of the initial palatal consonant in *caedualla*. See PART IV, A.I.a.6.

d) The use of *eu* in *heuuald*. See PART IV, A.III.b.1.

e) The presence of /ē/, sometimes possibly /ǣ/, from West Germanic /au/ after *i*-mutation. See PART IV, A.III.b.2.

f) The spelling of West Germanic /eu/ as *ea* in *streanaeshalch*. See PART IV, A.III.c.

g) The preservation of unstressed Primitive OE /i/ may be a Northumbrian feature in the earliest texts. See PART IV, B.II.a.1.a).

h) The frequent use of unstressed *o* in *eboraci/eboracensis* may be Northumbrian. See PART IV, B.II.c.1.a).

i) The spelling of *u* for the semi-vowel /w/ instead of later *uu* may also be a feature of Northumbrian. See PART IV, C.I.a.2.b).

j) Absence of *đ* for *d* or *th*. See PART IV, C.I.c.2.

2. K has two features in common with C against the M-type texts that may have dialectal implications. The first, *ea* in *suaebheardo* and *uigheard* (2×), is not necessarily indicative of a particular dialect, and, moreover, may be due to the state of Bede's sources. See PART IV, A.I.a.5.c), and above, under D.2. The other is the use of *eo* in *eolla* twice, which once is *eallan* in the M-type texts. *Eallan* may be northern Northumbrian, and the preservation of *eollan* southern Northumbrian. See PART IV, A.I.b.2.d).

Only once does K deviate from all the other MSS, in a feature that, although it has no dialectal connotations, may directly point

240

to the monastery where the MS was copied. It is the spelling of the name of the Abbot of Beverley, Bericthun (*s.v.*). Beverley is southern Northumbrian. The distinction between northern and southern Northumbrian is not a very clear one at this stage of the development of OE and is much disputed. The conclusion of ANDERSON LB 139 that "the dialect peculiarities of L are more definitely south Northumbrian than those of M" would for K fit in with a Beverley origin of the MS, seeing the great measure of agreement between K and L, but the arguments for it are not very convincing. Moreover, the relationship with the Abbot of Beverley that appears to transpire from the spelling of his name in K is not necessarily bound up with the scriptorium of that monastery. See PART IV, B.III.a), and above, under A.

3. That C was written in a different dialect from that of K and the other MSS is evident from a great number of its peculiarities discussed in PART IV. The reader is referred to the paragraphs mentioned under 1.c), d), g), h), i), j), and to the name *beaðudegn* with back-mutation (see PART IV, A.I.a.8) and possibly the loss of /t/ in *torchgyd* and *uuichred* (see PART IV, C.III.7.)

4. In conclusion it may be stated that the OE material points to the same place of composition of K as was tentatively inferred from the palaeographical and codicological evidence of PART I. Its origin must, no doubt, be sought in Northumbria. The close similarity of its OE material with that of the M-type texts, especially of L, possibly points to a Wearmouth-Jarrow origin, which was also suggested by the crescent final of some of its capital letters, a feature shared by L and K. See PART I, Chapter 1, § 6.

F. THE DATE OF THE OE MATERIAL

Defining the date of the phonological features of name-material is not an easy matter. In the INTRODUCTION it has been pointed out that names, especially place-names, tend to quickly become stable once they have arisen. Things are complicated further by the fact that the material in our case occurs in a MS that may have been the copy of a copy etc. etc., and we do not know to what extent the copyists exactly reproduced their exemplars or added features of their own. At any rate, we have already seen above that our MS presents material that is very much similar to that of the M-type MSS. ANDERSON LB 129 ff. has shown that the material of L has in the main features that point to "the earlier half, or about the middle of the 8th century" (p. 130). The great degree of agreement between K and the M-type texts indicates that the material most probably originated with Bede. This would also account for the various archaic forms detected by Anderson in L, for it may be assumed that when Bede wrote HE round about A.D. 730, he often employed spellings that he had acquired a long time before in his life. On the other hand, that name-material was modified by copyists not only of a different dialect but also of a later period may be seen from some of the characteristics of the name-material in C. The close agreement between L and B seems hardly compatible with a date of composition of B that is "probably between fifty and a hundred years later than L and M", as ANDERSON LB 140 is willing to accept from his authorities, although, of course, such faithful copying of all the features of an exemplar by a copyist of much later date remains a remote possibility.

1. The material of K agrees with that of the M-type texts on points that are indicative of an early date.
a) K preserves *eu* in *hreutford*. See PART IV, A.III.c.
b) K almost invariably retains unstressed /i/. See PART IV, B.II.a.1.a).
c) K regularly retains the unstressed ending *-aes*. See PART IV, B. II.b.1.b).
d) K almost invariably spells *-lch* and only seldom the later *-lh*. See PART IV, C.I.f.4.a).
e) K invariably spells *-ct*, and never *-cht* or *-ht*. See PART IV, C.I.f.5.

2. Points on which K differs from the other MSS, whether C is among them or not, never require a later date for its material.
a) K has *æadberctum*, in which *æa* is a variant spelling for *ea* which only occurs in the oldest MSS. See PART IV, A.III.b.1.
b) K and C have assimilated /bm/ > /mm/ in *gemmund* once. Assimilation occurs in various periods of OE. See PART IV, C.I.b.
c) K and C spell *quichelm*. See PART IV, C.I.e.2.

3. A study of the material of C soon reveals a number of features of a later date. Reference may be made to the points mentioned above, under 1.b), c), d), and e), and also to a number of other cases.

242

a) C invariably spells *oe* for *i*-mutated West Germanic /ō/. See PART IV, A.II.c.2.

b) C very regularly spells *uu* for the semi-vowel /w/. See PART IV, C.I.a.2.b).

c) C regularly simplifies *-uulf* to *-ulf*. See PART IV, C.I.a.3.

d) The loss of /t/ in *torchgyd* and *uuichred* may indicate a later date. See PART IV, C.III.7.

4. Palaeographical and codicological evidence pointed towards an eighth-century date for the composition of K; see PART I, § 5. Such a date also fits the evidence from the OE material. The question then arises how early in the eighth century the MS may be placed. As we have remarked above in connection with the close resemblance of B to L, early features of name-material in MSS like K do not necessarily point to an equally early date for the MS itself, although such an early date is fairly likely. Since the material of K consistently shows features of an early date, the date of its composition may safely be fixed at the earliest possible date that could be proposed on palaeographical grounds, i.e. at about A.D. 750.

BIBLIOGRAPHY*

ALESSIO   G. Alessio, "L'origine du nom de *Londres*", in: H. Draye & O. Jodogne (eds.), *Troisième Congrès International de Toponymie & d'Anthroponymie*, vol. II: *Actes et Mémoires* (Bruxelles, 15-19 juillet 1949), Louvain 1951, 223-234.

ANDERSON HN   O. S. Anderson, *English Hundred-Names*. Vol. I: *The English Hundred-Names* (Lunds Universitets Årsskrift 30, 1), Lund 1934; vol. II: *The English Hundred-Names, The South-Western Counties* (Lunds Universitets Årsskrift 35, 5), Lund 1939; vol. III: *The English Hundred-Names, The South-Eastern Counties* (Lunds Universitets Årsskrift 37, 1), Lund 1939.

ANDERSON LB   O. S. Anderson, *Old English Material in the Leningrad Manuscript of Bede's Ecclesiastical History* (Skrifter Utgivna av Kungl. Humanistiska Vetenskapssamfundet i Lund XXXI), Lund 1941.

Ångström, Margareta, *Studies in Old English MSS., with special reference to the delabialization of $\breve{\tilde{y}}$ ($\langle$ $\breve{u}$ + i) to $\breve{\imath}$* (Dissertation), Uppsala 1937.

ARMSTRONG etc. CU   A. M. Armstrong, A. Mawer, F. M. Stenton, & Bruce Dickins, *The Place-Names of Cumberland*, Parts I-III (EPNS XX-XXII), Cambridge 1950-1952.

Arngart, O., *The Leningrad Bede, An Eighth Century Manuscript of the Venerable Bede's Historia Ecclesiastica Gentis Anglorum In the Public Library, Leningrad* (Early English Manuscripts in Facsimile, Second Volume), Copenhagen 1952.

ARNGART   O. Arngart, "The Calendar of St. Willibrord. A little used source of Old English personal names", *Studia Neophilologica* 16 (1943-44), 128-134.

ASC   G. N. Garmonsway (transl.), *The Anglo-Saxon Chronicle*, rev. ed., London 1967.

BACH   A. Bach, *Deutsche Namenkunde*. I, 1-2: *Die deutschen Personennamen*; II, 1-2: *Die deutschen Ortsnamen*; III: *Sachweiser und Register*, Heidelberg 1952-1956.

Baesecke, Georg, *Frühgeschichte des deutschen Schrifttums* (2nd vol. of: Georg Baesecke, *Vor- und Frühgeschichte des deutschen Schrifttums*), Halle 1950/'53.

Baesecke, Georg, "Die Karlische Renaissance und das Deutsche Schrifttum", *Deutsche Vierteljahrschrift für Literaturwissenschaft und Geistesgeschichte* 23 (1949), 143-216.

---

* The Bibliography contains all the works cited and a selection of other works consulted.

Baesecke, Georg, *Der Vocabularius Sti. Galli in der Angelsächsischen Mission*, Halle 1933.

Bains, Doris, *A Supplement to Notae Latinae, Abbreviations in Latin MSS. of 850 to 1050 A.D.*, Cambridge 1936 (repr. and bound in one vol. with LINDSAY, Hildesheim 1963).

Battelli, G., *Lezioni di Paleografia*, Vatican City 1949.

Bauer, Gerd, "The Problem of Short Diphthongs in Old English", *Anglia* 74 (1956), 427-437.

Bazell, C. E., "The Grapheme", *Litera* 3 (1956), 43-46.

Bazell, C. E., "The Phonemic Interpretation of the Old English Diphthongs", *Litera* 3 (1956), 115-120.

Bazell, C. E., (review of Stockwell & Barritt (1951)), *Litera* 1 (1954), 75-77.

Becker, G., *Catalogi bibliothecarum antiqui*, Bonn 1885.

Bévenot, M., "Towards dating the Leningrad Bede", *Scriptorium* 16 (1962), 365-369.

Bévenot, M., *The Tradition of Manuscripts. A Study in the transmission of St. Cyprian's treatises*, Oxford 1961.

Beyerle, Konrad (ed.), *Die Kultur der Abtei Reichenau*, 2 vols., München 1925.

Bieler, L., "Insular Palaeography. Present State and Problems", *Scriptorium* 3 (1949), 267-294.

Bieler, L., *Irland, Wegbereiter des Mittelalters*, Lausanne 1961.

Bieler, L., "Some recent studies on English palaeography", *Scriptorium* 16 (1962), 333-336.

Binz, Gustav, "Ein bisher unbekannter Katalog der Bibliothek des Klosters Fulda", in: *Mélanges offerts à M. Marcel Godet*, Neuchâtel 1937, 97-108.

Bischoff, Bernard, "Paläographie, mit Berücksichtigung des deutschen Kulturgebietes", in: Wolfgang Stammler (ed.), *Deutsche Philologie im Aufriss*, 3 vols. (2nd ed.), Berlin-Bielefeld-München 1962, 379-451.
(the article is also separately available as a photomechanical reprint).

Bischoff, Bernard, & Joseph Hofmann, *Libri Sancti Kyliani. Die Würzburger Schreibschule und die Dombibliothek im VIII. und IX. Jahrhundert*, Würzburg 1952.

Björkmann, E., *Zur englischen Namenkunde* (Studien zur englischen Philologie 47), Halle 1912.

BJÖRKMANN ST   E. Björkmann, *Studien über die Eigennamen im Beowulf* (Studien zur englischen Philologie 58), Halle 1920.

BOEHLER M. Boehler, *Die altenglischen Frauennamen* (Germanische Studien 98), Berlin 1930.

Bolton, W. F., "A Bede Bibliography: 1935-1960", *Traditio* XVIII (1962), 436-445.

Bolton, W. F., *A History of Anglo-Latin Literature 597-1066, vol. I: 597-740*, Princeton, N.J., 1967.

Bonser, W., *An Anglo-Saxon and Celtic Bibliography (450-1087)*, Oxford 1957.

Borowski, B., *Zum Nebenakzent beim altenglischen Nominalkompositum* (Sächsische Forschungsinstitute in Leipzig III, 2), Halle 1921.

BOSWORTH-TOLLER   J. Bosworth & T. N. Toller, *An Anglo-Saxon Dictionary*, Oxford 1898; and *Supplement* (by T. N. Toller), Oxford 1921.

BROOKS K. R. Brooks, "Old English ēa and Related Words", *English and Germanic Studies* 5 (1952-1953), 15-66.

Brosnahan, L. F., *Some Old English Sound Changes: An analysis in the light of modern phonetics* (Dissertation Leiden), Cambridge 1953.

Brower, Christoph, S. J., *Antiquitates Fuldenses*, Antwerpen 1612.

Brower, Christoph, S. J., *Sidera illustrium*, Trier 1616(?).

Brown, T. J., "Latin Palaeography since Traube", *Transactions of the Cambridge Bibliographical Society* III, 5 (1963), 361-381.

Brunner, Karl, "The Old English Vowel Phonemes", *English Studies* 34 (1953), 247-251.

BRUNNER AG Karl Brunner, *Altenglische Grammatik*, nach der Angelsächsischen Grammatik von Eduard Sievers, 3rd ed., Tübingen 1965.

BRUNNER ES Karl Brunner, *Die englische Sprache, ihre geschichtliche Entwicklung*, 2 vols. (2nd ed.), Tübingen 1960.

Bucheler, T., *Benedict Biscop als Pionier römisch-christlicher Kultur bei den Angelsachsen* (Dissertation), Heidelberg 1923.

BÜLBRING K. D. Bülbring, *Altenglisches Elementarbuch*, I. Teil: *Lautlehre*, Heidelberg 1902.

Cameron, K., *The Place-Names of Derbyshire*, Parts I-III (EPNS XXVII-XXIX), Cambridge 1959.

CAMERON K. Cameron, *English Place-Names* (2nd ed.), London 1963.

CAMPBELL A. Campbell, *Old English Grammar*, Oxford 1959.

Cappelli, A., *Dizionario di Abbreviature Latine ed Italiane* (6th ed.), Milan 1961.

Catalogue of Ancient Manuscripts in the British Museum, Part II: Latin, London 1884.

Chambers, R. W., "'Bede', Annual Lecture on a Master Mind", *Proceedings of the British Academy* XXII (1936), 129-156.

Chatman, Seymour, "The *a/æ* opposition in Old English", *Word* XIV (1958), 224-236.

Christ, Karl, *Die Bibliothek des Klosters Fulda im 16. Jahrhundert. Die Handschriften-Verzeichnisse* (Zentralblatt für Bibliothekswesen, Beiheft 64), Leipzig 1933.

Christ, Karl, "Bibliotheksgeschichte des Mittelalters. Zur Methode und zur neuesten Literatur", *Zentralblatt für Bibliothekswesen* 61 (1947), 38-56, 149-166, 233-252.

Christ, Karl, "Handschriftenschätze der Landesbibliothek Kassel", in: Dr. Wilhelm Hopf (ed.), *Die Landesbibliothek Kassel 1580-1930*, Part II, Marburg 1930.

Christ, Karl, "Die Handschriftenverzeichnisse der Fuldaer Klosterbibliothek aus dem 16. Jahrhundert", in: Dr. Joseph Theele (ed.), *Aus Fuldas Geistesleben*, Fulda 1928, 24-39.

Christ, Karl, "Karolingische Bibliothekseinbände", in: *Festschrift Georg Leyh*, Leipzig 1937, 82-104.

CLA E. A. Lowe, *Codices Latini Antiquiores, A Palaeographical Guide to Latin Manuscripts prior to the ninth century*, vols. I-XI, Oxford 1934-1966.

Clark Hall, J. R., *A Concise Anglo-Saxon Dictionary* (4th ed., with a supplement by Herbert D. Meritt), Cambridge 1966.

Clemoes, P. (ed.), *The Anglo-Saxons: Studies in some Aspects of their History and Culture. Presented to Bruce Dickins*, London 1959.

Colgrave, B., *The Venerable Bede and his Times* (Jarrow Lecture), Jarrow: The Rectory 1958.

CO & MY   B. Colgrave & R. A. B. Mynors (eds.), *Bede's Ecclesiastical History of the English People*, Oxford 1969.

Colwell, E. C., & E. W. Tune, "Variant Readings: Classification and Use", *Journal of Biblical Literature* 83 (1964), 253-261.

Crawford, O. G. S., "Place-Names and Archaeology", in: A. Mawer & F. M. Stenton (eds.), *Introduction to the Survey of English Place-Names* (EPNS I, 1), Cambridge 1924, 143-164.

Crawford, S. J., *Anglo-Saxon Influence on Western Christendom 600-800*, Oxford 1933 (repr. Cambridge 1966).

DAHL   Ivar Dahl, *Substantival Inflexion in Early Old English: Vocalic Stems* (Lund Studies in English VII), Lund 1938.

Darby, H. C., "Place-names and the Geography of the Past", in: A. Brown & P. Foote (eds.), *Early English and Norse Studies. Presented to Hugh Smith in Honour of his Sixtieth Birthday*, London 1963, 6-18.

Daunt, Marjorie, "Old English Sound-Changes Reconsidered in Relation to Scribal Tradition and Practice", *Transactions of the Philological Society 1939*, London 1939, 108-137.

Daunt, Marjorie, "Some Notes on Old English Phonology. A Reply to Mr. M. Samuels' paper", *Transactions of the Philological Society 1952*, Oxford 1953, 48-54.

DAUZAT NFP   A. Dauzat, *Dictionnaire étymologique des noms de famille et prénoms de France* (3rd ed.), Paris 1951.

DAU & ROS   A. Dauzat & Ch. Rostaign, *Dictionnaire étymologique des noms de lieu en France*, Paris 1963.

DeCamp, D., "The Genesis of the Old English Dialects. A New Hypothesis", *Language* 34 (1958), 232-244.

Dekkers, E., "Clavis Patrum Latinorum", *Sacris Erudiri* 3 (2nd ed.), Paris 1961.

Denholm-Young, N., *Handwriting in England and Wales*, Cardiff 1954.

DEPN   E. Ekwall, *The Concise Oxford Dictionary of English Place-Names* (4th ed.), Oxford 1960.

Dickins, Bruce, "English names and Old English heathenism", in: D. Nichol Smith (ed.), *Essays and Studies by Members of the English Association* XIX (1934), 148-160.

Dickins, Bruce, "Latin additions to Place- and Parish-Names of England and Wales", *Proceedings of the Leeds Philosophical and Literary Society* (Lit. and Hist. Section III: VI), Leeds 1935, 334-341.

Dobbie, E. van K., *The Anglo-Saxon Minor Poems*, New York 1942.

Dobbie, E. van K., *The Manuscripts of Caedmon's Hymn and Bede's Death Song* (Columbia University Studies in English and Comparative Literature 128), New York 1937.

Dobiache-Rojdestvensky, O., "Un manuscrit de Bède à Leningrad", *Speculum* 3 (1928), 314-321.

Dodgson, J. McN., "The *-ing-* in English place-names like *Birmingham* and *Altrincham*", *Beiträge zur Namenforschung*, N.F., 2 (1967), 221-245.

248

Dodgson, J. McN., "Various English Place-Name Formations containing Old English -ing", Beiträge zur Namenforschung, N.F., 3 (1968), 141-189.

Dodgson, J. McN., "Various Forms of Old English -ing in English Place-Names", Beiträge zur Namenforschung, N.F., 2 (1967), 325-396.

Duckett, E. S., Anglo-Saxon Saints and Scholars, New York 1947.

DUIGNAN   W. H. Duignan, Notes on Staffordshire Place-Names, London 1902.

Ekwall, E.,   see also DEPN

Ekwall, E., "Comparative place-name study", in: H. Draye & O. Jodogne (eds.), Troisième Congrès International de Toponymie & d'Anthroponymie, Vol. II: Actes et Mémoires (Bruxelles, 15-19 juillet 1949), Louvain 1951, 133-141.

Ekwall, E., Contributions to the history of Old English dialects (Lunds Universitets Årsskrift 12:6), Lund 1917.

Ekwall, E., "Notes on the inflexion of Old English place-names", Namn och Bygd 16 (1928), 59-77.

Ekwall, E., "Notes on the palatalisation of k (c) in English", Beiblatt zur Anglia 32 (1921), 155-168.

Ekwall, E., "OE 'Gyrwe'", Beiblatt zur Anglia 33 (1922), 116-118.

Ekwall, E., Old English "wic" in Place-Names (Nomina Germanica 13), Uppsala 1964.

Ekwall, E., "Die Ortsnamenforschung ein Hilfsmittel für das Studium der englischen Sprachgeschichte", Germanisch-romanische Monatsschrift 5 (1913), 592-608.

Ekwall, E., (review of EPNE), Namn och Bygd 45 (1957), 133-146.

Ekwall, E., (review of Olga Gevenich, Die englische Palatalisierung von k ⟩ č im Lichte der englischen Ortsnamen), Beiblatt zur Anglia 30 (1919), 221-228.

Ekwall, E., (review of E. Tengstrand, A Contribution to the Study of Genitival Composition in Old English Place-Names), Studia Neophilologica 16 (1943/44), 147-151.

Ekwall, E., Scandinavians and Celts in the North-West of England (Lunds Universitets Årsskrift, N.F., Avd. 1, 14:27), Lund 1918.

EKWALL CE   E. Ekwall, "The Celtic Element", in: A. Mawer & F. M. Stenton (eds.), Introduction to the Survey of English Place-Names (EPNS I, 1), Cambridge 1924, 15-35.

EKWALL EN   E. Ekwall, "Early Names of Britain", Antiquity 4 (1930), 149-156.

EKWALL PNsING   E. Ekwall, English Place-Names in -ing (Skrifter Ut-givna av Kungl. Humanistiska Vetenskapssamfundet i Lund VI), 2nd ed., Lund 1962.

EKWALL RN   E. Ekwall, English River Names, Oxford 1928 (re-issued 1968).

EKWALL ST I   E. Ekwall, Studies on English Place- and Personal Name s (Kungl. Humanistiska Vetenskapssamfundet i Lund, Årsberättelse 1930-1931; 1-110), Lund 1931.

EKWALL ST II   E. Ekwall, Studies on English place-names (Kungl. Vitter-hets-, historie- och antikvitetsakademiens handlingar 42:1), Stockholm 1936.

EKWALL ST III   E. Ekwall, Etymological Notes on English place-names (Lunds Universitets Årsskrift, N.F., Avd. 1, 53:5), Lund 1959.

EKWALL TN   E. Ekwall, "Tribal names in English place-names", *Namn och Bygd* 41 (1954), 129-177.

EKWALL VC   E. Ekwall, "Variation and change in English place-names", *Vetenskaps-Societetens i Lund Årsbok*, Lund 1962, 3-49.

Emerton, E., *The Letters of St. Boniface*, New York 1950.

EPNE   A. H. Smith, *English Place-Name Elements*, Parts I-II (EPNS XXV-XXVI), Cambridge 1956.

van Essen, A. J., "Some Remarks on Old English Phonology", *Linguistics* 32 (1967), 83-86.

Falk, Franz, *Beiträge zur Rekonstruktion der alten Bibliotheca fuldensis und Bibliotheca laureshamensis* (Zentralblatt für Bibliothekswesen, Beiheft 26), Leipzig 1902.

Farmer, Hugh. "The Studies of Anglo-Saxon Monks (A.D. 600-800)", in: *Los Monjes y Los Estudios, IV Semana de Estudios Monásticos (Poblet 1961)*, Abadía de Poblet 1963, 87-103.

von Feilitzen, O., "Notes on Old English Bynames", *Namn och Bygd* 27 (1939), 116-130.

von Feilitzen, O., *The published writings of Eilert Ekwall* (Lund Studies in English), Lund 1961.

von Feilitzen, O., "Some Continental Germanic Personal Names in England", in: A. Brown & P. Foote (eds.), *Early English and Norse Studies. Presented to Hugh Smith in Honour of his Sixtieth Birthday*, London 1963, 46-61.

FEILITZEN DB   O. von Feilitzen, *The Pre-Conquest Personal Names of Domesday Book* (Nomina Germanica 3), Uppsala 1937.

FEILITZEN ST   O. von Feilitzen, "Some OE Uncompounded Personal Names and Bynames", *Studia Neophilologica* XL (1968), 5-16.

Flom, George T., "Breaking in Old Norse and Old English. With Special Reference to the Relations between them", *Language* 13 (1937), 123-136.

FÖRSTEMANN   E. Förstemann, *Altdeutsches Namenbuch*. I: *Personennamen* (2nd ed.), München 1901 (repr. 1966); II: *Ortsnamen* (3rd ed.), München 1913 (repr. 1967).

Foerster, H., *Abriss der lateinischen Paläographie* (2nd ed.), Stuttgart 1963.

FÖRSTER KW   M. Förster, "Keltisches Wortgut im Englischen", in: H. Boehmer, A. Brandl and others (eds.), *Texte und Forschungen zur englischen Kulturgeschichte. Festgabe für Felix Liebermann*, Halle 1921, 119-242.

FÖRSTER TH   M. Förster, *Der Flussname Themse und seine Sippe. Studien zur Anglisierung keltischer Eigennamen und zur Lautchronologie des Altbritischen* (Sitzungsberichte der Bayerischen Akademie der Wissenschaften, Philosophisch-historische Abteilung, Jahrgang 1941), München 1941.

FORSBERG   R. Forsberg, *A Contribution to a Dictionary of Old English Place-Names* (Nomina Germanica 9), Uppsala 1950.

FORSSNER   T. Forssner, *Continental Germanic personal names in England in Old and Middle English times* (Dissertation), Uppsala 1916.

Franck, J., N. van Wijk, & C. B. van Haeringen, *Etymologisch Woordenboek der Nederlandsche Taal* (en Supplement), 's-Gravenhage 1912-1936.

Funke, Otto, *Englische Sprachkunde, ein Ueberblick ab 1935* (Wissenschaftliche Forschungsberichte, Geisteswissenschaftliche Reihe 10), Bern 1950.

250

Gelling, Margaret, "Place-Names and Anglo-Saxon Paganism", *University of Birmingham Historical Journal* VIII (1962), 7-25.

Gelling, Margaret, *The Place-Names of Oxfordshire*, Parts I-II (EPNS XXIII-XXIV), Cambridge 1953-1954.

GELLING   Margaret Gelling, "The Element hamm in English Place-Names: A Topographical Investigation", *Namn och Bygd* 48 (1960), 140-162.

Gevenich, Olga, *Die englische Palatalisierung von k > č im Lichte der englischen Ortsnamen* (Studien zur englischen Philologie 57), Halle 1918.

GIRVAN   R. Girvan, *Angelsaksisch Handboek* (Oudgermaansche Handboeken 4), Haarlem 1931.

Gottlieb, Theodor, *Ueber mittelalterliche Bibliotheken*, Graz 1890.

Gover, J. E. B., A. Mawer, & F. M. Stenton, *The Place-Names of Northamptonshire* (EPNS X), Cambridge 1933.

GOVER etc. HE   J. E. B. Gover, A. Mawer, & F. M. Stenton, *The Place-Names of Hertfordshire* (EPNS XV), Cambridge 1938.

GOVER etc. SU   J. E. B. Gover, A. Mawer, & F. M. Stenton, *The Place-Names of Surrey* (EPNS XI), Cambridge 1934.

Grandgent, C. H., *An Introduction to Vulgar Latin*, Boston 1907 (repr. 1962).

GREEN   Carleton Green, *The Place-Names in the 'Historia Ecclesiastica' of Bede* (unpublished Dissertation), Harvard 1936.

Grein, C. W. M., *Das Hildebrandslied ... nebst Bemerkungen über die ehemaligen Fulder Codices der Kasseler Bibliothek* (2nd ed.), Kassel 1880.

Gross, F. G. C., "Ueber den Hildebrandslied-Codex der Kasseler Landesbibliothek, nebst Angaben und Vermuthungen über die Schicksale der alten Fuldaer Handschriften-Bibliothek überhaupt", *Zeitschrift des Vereins für hessische Geschichte u. Landeskunde*, N.F., 8 (1880), 143-175.

Gysseling, M., *Toponymisch Woordenboek van België, Nederland, Luxemburg, Noord-Frankrijk, en West-Duitsland (vóór 1226)*, 2 vols., Tongeren 1960.

Hahn, H., *Bonifaz und Lul; Ihre angelsächsische Korrespondenten; Erzbischof Luls Leben*, Leipzig 1883.

Hall, F. W., *A Companion to Classical Texts*, Oxford 1913.

Hallquist, H., *Studies in Old English Fractured ea* (Lund Studies in English 14), Lund 1948.

Hamlin, Frank R., "Bibliographie sommaire des études de toponymie aux Iles Britanniques", *Revue Internationale d'Onomastique* XIV (1962), 299-310.

Harttung, J., "Geschichtliche Aufzeichnungen aus dem Kloster Fulda", *Forschungen zur deutschen Geschichte* 19 (1879), 397-446.

Haselden, R. B., *Scientific Aids for the Study of Manuscripts*, Oxford 1935.

HE   *Historia Ecclesiastica Gentis Anglorum*, in the edition of CO & MY.

Hector, L. C., *The Handwriting of English Documents*, London 1958.

HELLWIG   H. Hellwig, *Untersuchungen über die Namen des nordhumbrischen Liber Vitae I* (Dissertation), Berlin 1888.

Helwig, H., *Einführung in die Einbandkunde*, Stuttgart 1970.

Henry, Françoise, (review art. on T. D. Kendrick and others (eds.), *Evangeliorum Quattuor Codex Lindisfarnensis*, Olten Lausanne 1960), *Antiquity* 37 (1963), 100-110.

Heusinkveld, A. H., & E. J. Bashe, *A Bibliographical Guide to Old English. A selective Bibliography of the Language, Literature, and History of the Anglo-Saxons* (University of Iowa Humanistic Studies IV, 5), Iowa City 1931.

Higounet, Ch., *L'Ecriture* ("Que Sais-Je?" 653), 2nd ed., Paris 1959.

Hill, A. A., "Phonetic and Phonemic Change", *Language* 12 (1936), 15-22.

Hille, A., "OE Seoluini and ON Sjóli", *English Studies* 44 (1963), 28-35.

Hilpisch, S., "Das Kloster Fulda in seiner Kulturbedeutung", in: *Fulda und die Rhön*, Sonderausgabe der illustrierten Monatsschrift "Bayerland", München 1954, 11-13.

HIRT H. Hirt, *Handbuch des Urgermanischen*, 2 vols., Heidelberg 1931-1932.

Hockett, Charles F., "Sound Change", *Language* 41 (1965), 185-204.

Hockett, Charles F., "The Stressed Syllabics of Old English", *Language* 35 (1959), 575-597.

Holder, A., *Die Reichenauer Handschriften*, 3 vols., Leipzig-Berlin 1906-1918.

HOLDER A. Holder, *Alt-celtischer Sprachschatz*, 3 vols., Leipzig 1896-1913.

HOLTHAUSEN F. Holthausen, *Altenglisches Etymologisches Wörterbuch*, Heidelberg 1934 (repr. 1963).

Hoops, Johannes, *Kommentar zum Beowulf*, Heidelberg 1932.

Hopf, Dr. Wilhelm, "Die Landesbibliothek Kassel in ihrer geschichtlichen Entwicklung", in: Dr. Wilhelm Hopf (ed.), *Die Landesbibliothek Kassel 1580-1930*, Part I, Marburg 1930.

Hoppenbrouwers, H. W. F. M., *La Plus Ancienne Version Latine de la Vie de S. Antoine par S. Athanase*, Etude de Critique Textuelle, Utrecht-Nijmegen 1960.

Hunger, Herbert, "Antikes und mittelalterliches Buch- und Schriftwesen", in: Dr. M. Meier and others (eds.), *Geschichte der Textüberlieferung der antiken und mittelalterlichen Literatur*, vol. I, Zürich 1961, 25-147.

Hunter Blair, P., *Bede's "Ecclesiastical History of the English Nation" and its importance today* (Jarrow Lecture), Jarrow: The Rectory 1959.

Hunter Blair, P., *An Introduction to Anglo-Saxon England*, Cambridge 1956.

Hunter Blair, P., *The Moore Bede, Cambridge University Library, MS. Kk. 5.16* (Early English Manuscripts in Facsimile, Ninth Volume), Copenhagen 1959.

Hunter Blair, P., *Roman Britain and Early England 55 B.C. - A.D. 871*, Edinburgh 1963.

Hunter Blair, P., *The World of Bede*, London 1970.

Israel, Friedrich, "Die Landesbibliothek in Kassel", *Hessenland, Zeitschrift für die Kulturpflege des Bezirksverbandes Hessen* 53 (1942), 2-9.

Jackson, K., "Notes on Celtic Place-Names in England", in: C. Battisti & C. A. Mastrelli (eds.), *Atti del VII Congresso internazionale di Scienze onomastiche*, 4 vols., Firenze 1963, II, 189-191.

JACKSON LHEB K. Jackson, *Language and History in Early Britain: a Chronological Survey of the Brittonic Languages 1st to 12th c. A.D.* (Edinburgh University Publications, Languages and Literature 4), Edinburgh 1953 (repr. 1963).

JACKSON RPNs K. Jackson, "On Some Romano-British Place-names", *The Journal of Roman Studies* 38 (1948), 54-58.

James, Montague R., "The Manuscripts of Bede", in: A. Hamilton Thompson (ed.), *Bede. His Life, Times, and Writings*, Oxford 1935 (repr. 1969), 230-236.

JENSEN AIO Knud B. Jensen, "Altindogermanische Ortsnamen in Südeng-

252

land", in: K. Puchner (ed.), *VI. Internationaler Kongress für Namenforschung (München, 24-28. August 1958), Kongressberichte*, 3 vols., München 1961, II, 427-432.

JENSEN GTNs Knud B. Jensen, "Considerations on some Germanic Tribe-Names", in: D. P. Blok (ed.), *Proceedings of the Eighth International Congress of Onomastic Sciences*, The Hague 1966, 243-246.

Jones, Charles W., "Bede as Early Medieval Historian", *Medievalia et Humanistica* 4 (1946), 26-36.

Jones, Leslie W., "Ancient Prickings in Eighth-Century Manuscripts", *Scriptorium* 15 (1961), 14-22.

Jones, Leslie W., "Prickings as Clues to Date and Origin: the Eighth Century", *Medievalia et Humanistica* 14 (1962), 15-22.

Jones, Leslie W., "Pricking Manuscripts: The Instruments and their Significance", *Speculum* 21 (1946), 389-403.

Jones, Leslie W., "Pricking Systems in New York Manuscripts", in: *Miscellanea Giovanni Mercati* (Studi e Testi 126), vol. VI, Vatican City 1946, 80-92.

Jones, Leslie W., "Where are the Prickings?", *Transactions and Proceedings of the American Philological Association* 75 (1944), 71-86.

Jones, P. F., *A Concordance to the Historia Ecclesiastica of Bede* (The Medieval Academy of America, Publication no. 2), Cambridge (Mass.) 1929.

KARLSTRÖM KIL S. Karlström, "Kilvington and Some Related English Place-Names", *Studia Neophilologica* IV (1931/32), 120-140.

KARLSTRÖM PNsING S. Karlström, *Old English compound place-names in -ing* (Uppsala Universitets Årsskrift 2), Uppsala 1927.

KAUFMANN ERG H. Kaufmann, *Ernst Förstemann, Altdeutsche Personennamen. Ergänzungsband*, München 1968.

KAUFMANN UAR H. Kaufmann, *Untersuchungen zu altdeutschen Rufnamen* (Grundfragen der Namenkunde 3), München 1965.

Keller, W., *Angelsächsische Paläographie* (Palaestra XLIII), Berlin 1906.

Kemble, J. M., *On the Names, Surnames and Nicknames of the Anglo-Saxons* (Royal Archaeological Institute of Great Britain and Ireland, Proceedings at Winchester 1845), London 1846.

Ker, N. R., *Catalogue of Manuscripts Containing Anglo-Saxon*, Oxford 1957.

Ker, N. R., (review of Laistner-King, *A Hand-list of Bede MSS.*), *Medium Aevum* XIII (1944), 36-40.

Kindlinger, Nikolaus, *Katalog und Nachrichten von der ehemaligen aus lauter Handschriften bestandenen Bibliothek in Fulda*, Leipzig und Frankfurt a.M. 1812.

King, Robert D., *Historical Linguistics and Generative Grammar*, Englewood Cliffs, New Jersey, 1969.

Kirby, D. P., "Bede's Native Sources for the *Historia Ecclesiastica*", *Bulletin of the John Rylands Library* 48 (1965/1966), 341-371.

Kirby, D. P., "Bede and Northumbrian Chronology", *English Historical Review* 78 (1963), 514-527.

Kirchner, Joachim, *Germanistische Handschriftenpraxis*. Ein Lehrbuch für die Studierenden der deutschen Philologie (2. Auflage), München 1967.

KÖHLER T. Köhler, *Die altenglischen Namen in Baedas Historia Ecclesiastica und auf den altnordhumbrischen Münzen* (Dissertation), Berlin 1908.

Kökeritz, H., "Notes on the Pre-Conquest Personal Names of Domesday Book", *Namn och Bygd* 26 (1938), 25-41.

Kökeritz, H., *The Place-Names of the Isle of Wight* (Nomina Germanica 6), Uppsala 1940.

Krahe, H., "Die Struktur der alteuropäischen Hydronomie", *Abhandlungen der Geistes- und Sozialwissenschaftlichen Klasse* (Akademie der Wissenschaften und der Literatur) 5 (1962), 287-342.

Krahe, H., *Unsere älteste Flussnamen*, Wiesbaden 1964.

Krahe, H., "Vorgermanische und Frühgermanische Flussnamen-Schichten. Mittel zu ihrer Unterscheidung", in: R. Schützeichel & M. Zender (eds.), *Namenforschung. Festschrift für Adolf Bach zum 75. Geburtstag am 31. Januar 1965*, Heidelberg 1965, 192-198.

Krupatkin, Y., "Old English Breaking. A Step to a Phonemic Approach", *Philologica Pragensia* VII (1964), 62-64.

Kuhn, Sherman M., "From Canterbury to Lichfield", *Speculum* 23 (1948), 591-629.

Kuhn, Sherman M., "On the Syllabic Phonemes of Old English", *Language* 37 (1961), 522-538.

KUHN Sherman M. Kuhn, "On the Consonantal Phonemes of Old English", in: James L. Rosier (ed.), *Philological Essays. Studies in Old and Middle English Language and Literature in Honour of Herbert Dean Meritt*, The Hague 1970, 16-49.

Kuhn, Sherman M., & Randolph Quirk, "The Old English Digraphs: A Reply", *Language* 31 (1955), 390-401 (repr. in: Randolph Quirk, *Essays on the English Language Medieval and Modern*, London 1968, 55-69).

Kuhn, Sherman M., & Randolph Quirk, "Some recent interpretations of the Old English digraph spellings", *Language* 29 (1953), 143-156 (repr. in: Randolph Quirk, *Essays on the English Language Medieval and Modern*, London 1968, 38-54).

Laborde, E. D., *Byrhtnoth and Maldon*, London 1936.

Laistner, M. L. W., *Thought and Letters in Western Europe, A.D. 500-900* (rev. ed.), London 1957 (first publ. 1931).

Laistner, M. L. W., & H. H. King, *A Hand-list of Bede Manuscripts*, Ithaca New York 1943.

Langosch, Karl, *Lateinisches Mittelalter. Einleitung in Sprache und Literatur*, Darmstadt 1963.

Langosch, Karl, *Profile des lateinischen Mittelalters*, Darmstadt 1965.

Laur, W., "Namenübertragungen im Zuge der angelsächsischen Wanderungen", *Beiträge zur Namenforschung* XV (1964), 287-297.

Laur, W., "Ortsnamen in England und in den festländischen Stammlanden der Angelsachsen", in: R. Schützeichel & M. Zender (eds.), *Namenforschung. Festschrift für Adolf Bach zum 75. Geburtstag am 31. Januar 1965*, Heidelberg 1965, 300-312.

Lehmann, Paul, "Die alte Klosterbibliothek Fulda und ihre Bedeutung", in: Paul Lehmann, *Erforschung des Mittelalters*, 5 vols., München 1959-1962, I, 213-231 (repr. from: J. Theele (ed.), *Aus Fuldas Geistesleben*, Fulda 1928).

Lehmann, Paul, *Franciscus Modius als Handschriftenforscher* (Quellen und

Untersuchungen zur lateinischen Philologie des Mittelalters III, 1), München 1908.

Lehmann, Paul, "Die Fuldaer Schreibschule und Malschule", *Fulda und die Rhön*, Sonderausgabe der illustrierten Monatsschrift "Bayerland", München 1954, 18-25.

Lehmann, Paul, *Fuldaer Studien* (Sitzungsberichte der Bayerischen Akademie der Wissenschaften, Philosophisch-philologische und historische Klasse, Jahrgang 1925, 3. Abhandlung), München 1925.

Lehmann, Paul, *Fuldaer Studien*, Neue Folge (Sitzungsberichte der Bayerischen Akademie der Wissenschaften, Philosophisch-philologische und historische Klasse, Jahrgang 1927, 2. Abhandlung), München 1927.

Lehmann, Paul, *Johannes Sichardus und die von ihm benutzten Bibliotheken und Handschriften* (Quellen und Untersuchungen zur lateinischen Philologie des Mittelalters 4), München 1911.

Lehmann, Paul, "Lateinische Paläographie. Bis zum Siege der Karolingischen Minuskel", in: Alfred Gercke & E. Norden (eds.), *Einleitung in die Altertumswissenschaft*, 3 vols. (3rd ed.), Leipzig u. Berlin 1927, I, 10; 38-68.

Lehmann, Paul, "Mitteilungen aus Handschriften IX", *Sitzungsberichte der Bayerischen Akademie der Wissenschaften, Philosophisch-historische Klasse* 9 (1950), 1-32.

Lehmann, Paul, "Mittelalterliche Beinamen und Ehrentitel", *Historisches Jahrbuch* 49 (1929), 215-239 (repr. in: Paul Lehmann, *Erforschung des Mittelalters* I, Leipzig 1959, 129-154).

Lehmann, Paul (ed.), *Mittelalterliche Bibliothekskataloge Deutschlands und der Schweiz*, 2 vols., München 1918-1928.

Lehmann, Paul, "Die mittelalterliche Bibliothek der Reichenau", in: Paul Lehmann, *Erforschung des Mittelalters*, IV, Stuttgart 1961, 26-39 (repr. from: Konrad Beyerle (ed.), *Die Kultur der Abtei Reichenau* II, München 1925, 645-656).

Lehmann, Paul, "Quot et quorum libri fuerint in libraria Fuldensi", in: *Bok- och bibliotheks-Historiska Studier tillägnade Isak Collijn*, Uppsala 1925, 47-57.

Lesne, Emile, *Les Livres, "Scriptoria", et Bibliothèques du Commencement du VIIIe à la fin du XIe siècle* (*Histoire de la Propriété ecclésiastique en France*, vol. 4), Lille 1938.

Levison, Wilhelm, "Bede as Historian", in: A. Hamilton Thompson (ed.), *Bede. His Life, Times and Writings*, Oxford 1935 (repr. 1969), Chapter V.

Levison, Wilhelm, *England and the Continent in the Eighth Century*, Oxford 1946.

Liebermann, F., "Streoneshealh", *Archiv für das Studium der neueren Sprachen und Literaturen* 108 (1902), 368.

Lindsay, W. M., "The Abbreviation-symbols of *ergo, igitur*", *Zentralblatt für Bibliothekswesen* 29 (1912), 56-64.

Lindsay, W. M., *Palaeographia Latina*, Part II (St. Andrews University Publications XVI), Oxford 1923.

LINDSAY W. M. Lindsay, *Notae Latinae*. An Account of Abbreviation in Latin MSS. of the Early Minuscule Period (c. 700-850), Cambridge 1915 (repr. Hildesheim 1963).

Löfstedt, B., *Der Hibernolateinische Grammatiker Malsachanus* (Acta Universitatis Upsaliensis, Studia Latina Upsaliensia 3), Uppsala 1965.

Löfstedt, B., *Studien über die Sprache der Langobardischen Gesetze* (Acta Universitatis Upsaliensis, Studia Latina Upsaliensia 1), Uppsala 1961.

LONGNON   A. Longnon, *Les Noms de Lieu de la France. Leur origine, leur signification, leurs transformations*, Paris 1920-1929.

Lowe, E. A.,   see also CLA

Lowe, E. A., "An Autograph of the Venerable Bede?", *Revue Bénédictine* 68 (1958), 200-202.

Lowe, E. A., "An eighth-century list of books in a Bodleian MS. from Würzburg and its probable relation to the Laudian Acts", *Speculum* 3 (1928), 3-15.

Lowe, E. A., *English Uncial*, London 1960.

Lowe, E. A., "Handwriting", in: C. G. Crump & E. F. Jacob (eds.), *The Legacy of the Middle Ages*, Oxford 1926 (repr. 1948), 197-226.

Lowe, E. A., "A Key to Bede's Scriptorium. Some Observations on the Leningrad Manuscript of the 'Historia Ecclesiastica Gentis Anglorum'", *Scriptorium* 12 (1958), 182-190.

Lowe, E. A., "The Oldest Omission Signs in Latin Manuscripts: Their Origin and Significance", in: *Miscellanea Giovanni Mercati* (Studi e Testi 126), vol. VI, Vatican City 1946, 36-79.

Lowe, E. A., "The Script of the Farewell and Date Formulae in Early Papal Documents, as reflected in the oldest manuscripts of Bede's Historia Ecclesiastica", *Revue Bénédictine* 69 (1959), 22-31.

LUICK   Karl Luick, *Historische Grammatik der Englischen Sprache*, 2 vols. (ed. by F. Wild & H. Koziol, with Index), Stuttgart/Oxford 1964 (first publ. 1914-1940).

MACBAIN   A. MacBain, *Place-Names. Highlands & Islands of Scotland*, Stirling 1922.

McGurk, Patrick, "Citation marks in early Latin manuscripts", *Scriptorium* 15 (1961), 3-13 (and Plates 1-4).

McIntosh, Angus, "The Analysis of Written Middle English", *Transactions of the Philological Society 1956*, Oxford 1956, 26-55.

McLaughlin, John, *A Graphemic-Phonemic Study of A Middle English Manuscript*, The Hague 1963.

MAGOUN '35   F. P. Magoun, Jr., "Territorial, Place-, and River-Names in the Old English Chronicle, A-Text", *Harvard Studies and Notes in Philology and Literature* 18 (1935), 69-111.

MAGOUN '38   F. P. Magoun, Jr., "Territorial, Place-, and River-Names in the Old English Annals, D-Text (MS. Cotton Tiberius B. IV)", *Harvard Studies and Notes in Philology and Literature* 20 (1938), 147-180.

Malkiel, Yakov, "Initial Points Versus Initial Segments of Linguistic Trajectories", in: Horace G. Lunt (ed.), *Proceedings of the Ninth International Congress of Linguists* (Cambridge, Mass., August 27-31, 1962), The Hague 1964, 402-406.

Marchand, James W., "Names of Germanic Origin in Latin and Romance Sources in the Study of Germanic Phonology", *Names* (Journal of the American Name Society) VII (1959), 167-181.

Mawer, A., *The Chief Elements Used in English Place-Names* (EPNS I, 2), Cambridge 1924.

Mawer, A., *Problems of Place-Name Study*, Cambridge 1929.

MAWER NO & DU   A. Mawer, *The Place-Names of Northumberland and Durham*, Cambridge 1920.

Mawer, A., & F. M. Stenton (eds.), *Introduction to the Survey of English Place-Names* (EPNS I, 1), Cambridge 1924.

Mawer, A., & F. M. Stenton, *The Place-Names of Wiltshire* (EPNS XVI), Cambridge 1939.

MA & ST SUS   A. Mawer & F. M. Stenton, *The Place-Names of Sussex*, Parts VI-VII, Cambridge 1929-1930.

Meier, H. H., *The Complete Anglist. A Contemporary Linguist's Reorientation* (Inaugural Lecture, Free University Amsterdam), Groningen 1967.

Meyvaert, P., *Bede and Gregory the Great* (Jarrow Lecture), Jarrow: The Rectory 1965.

Meyvaert, P., "The Bede 'Signature' in the Leningrad Colophon", *Revue Bénédictine* 71 (1961), 274-286.

Mezger, F., *Angelsächsische Völker- und Ländernamen* (Dissertation), Berlin 1922.

MIDDENDORFF   H. Middendorff, *Altenglisches Flurnamenbuch*, Halle 1902.

Miller, T.,   see also OEBede

MILLER   T. Miller, *Place Names in the English Bede and the localisation of the MSS.* (Quellen und Forschungen zur Sprach- und Culturgeschichte der Germanischen Völker 78), Strassburg 1896.

Misonne, D., "'Famulus Christi'. A propos d'un Autographe de Bède le Vénérable", *Revue Bénédictine* 69 (1959), 97-99.

Mossé, Fernand, *Manuel de l'Anglais du Moyen Age, I. Vieil-Anglais* (Bibliothèque de Philologie Germanique VIII), Paris 1945 (repr. 1950).

Moulton, William G., "The Stops and Spirants of Early Germanic", *Language* 30 (1954), 1-42.

MÜLLER   R. Müller, *Untersuchungen über die Namen des nordhumbrischen Liber Vitae* (Palaestra IX), Berlin 1901.

Mynors, R. A. B.,   see also CO & MY

Mynors, R. A. B., "The Early Circulation of the Text", in: P. Hunter Blair, *The Moore Bede, Cambridge University Library, MS. Kk. 5.16* (Early English Manuscripts in Facsimile, Ninth Volume), Copenhagen 1959, 33-37.

Neugart, T., *Episcopatus Constantiensis Alemannicus*, Partis I Tomus I, St. Blasien 1803.

Ney, James W., "Old English Vowel Digraph Spellings", *Linguistics* 45 (1968), 36-49.

Nicolaisen, W., *Die morphologische und semasiologische Struktur der Gewässernamen der Britischen Inseln*, I. Teil: *England, Scotland, Wales* (Dissertation), Tübingen 1955.

NICOLAISEN   W. Nicolaisen, "Die alteuropäischen Gewässernamen der britischen Hauptinsel", *Beiträge zur Namenforschung* 8 (1957), 209-268.

NI, GEL & RI   W. Nicolaisen, Margaret Gelling, & M. Richards, *The Names of Towns and Cities in Britain*, London 1970.

Norberg, Dag, *Manuel pratique de latin médiéval* (Connaissance des langues IV), Paris 1968.

OEBede   T. Miller (ed.), *The Old English version of Bede's Ecclesiastical History of the English People*, 4 vols. (EETS 95-96, 110-111), London 1890-1891, 1898.

OET   Henry Sweet, *The Oldest English Texts* (EETS, O.S. 83), London 1885 (repr. 1966).

Okasha, dr. Elisabeth, "The Leningrad Bede", *Scriptorium* 22 (1968), 35-37.

O'Rahilly, T. F., "On the Origin of the Names **ÉRAINN** and **ÉRIU**", *ÉRIU* XIV (1943), 7-28.

Ordnance Survey, *Map of Roman Britain* (3rd ed.), Chessington (Surrey) 1956; *Map of Ancient Britain*, 2 sheets (2nd ed.), Chessington (Surrey) 1964; *Map of Britain in the Dark Ages, 410-870 a.D.* (2nd ed.), Chessington (Surrey) 1966.

Page, R. I., "Language and Dating in OE Inscriptions", *Anglia* 77 (1959), 385-406.

Penzl, Herbert, "The Linguistic Interpretation of Scribal Errors in Old High German Texts", *Linguistics* 32 (1967), 79-82.

Penzl, Herbert, "Orthographic Evidence for Types of Phonemic Change", *Proceedings of the Eighth International Congress of Linguists*, Oslo 1958, 146-148.

Penzl, Herbert, "A Phonemic Change in Early Old English", *Language* 20 (1944), 84-87.

Penzl, Herbert, "The Phonemic Split of Germanic *k* in Old English", *Language* 23 (1947), 34-42.

Pepperdene, Margaret W., "Bede's Historia Ecclesiastica: A New Perspective", *Celtica* IV (1958), 253-262.

Pertz, G. H., "Handschriften der Churfürstlichen Bibliothek zu Kassel", *Archiv der Gesellschaft für ältere deutsche Geschichtskunde* 6 (1838), 203-205.

Pilch, Herbert, "Altenglische historische Lautlehre als phonologisches Problem", *Word* 24 (1968; *Linguistic Studies Presented to André Martinet*, Part Two: *Indo-European Linguistics*), 350-370.

PILCH   Herbert Pilch, *Altenglische Grammatik* (Commentationes Societatis Linguisticae Europaeae I, 1), München 1970.

Plummer, Charles, "Mémoire sur un manuscrit de l'Histoire Ecclésiastique du Peuple Anglais de Bède, dit le Vénérable. Appartenant à la Ville de Namur", *Annales de la Société Archéologique de Namur* 19 (1891), 393-400.

PLUMMER   Charles Plummer, *Venerabilis Baedae Opera Historica* (Historia Ecclesiastica Gentis Anglorum, Historia Abbatum, Epistola ad Ecgberctum, una cum Historia Abbatum Auctore Anonymo), 2 vols., Oxford 1896 (repr. lithographically and published in one vol. in 1946 ff.).

Pope, John C. (ed.), *Seven Old English Poems*, Indianapolis 1966.

Potthast, August, *Wegweiser durch die Geschichtswerke des europäischen Mittelalters bis 1500* (Bibliotheca Historica Medii Aevi I), 2nd ed., Berlin 1896.

Powicke, F. M., & E. B. Fryde (eds.), *Handbook of British Chronology* (2nd ed.), London 1961.

Preisendanz, Karl, "Aus Bücherei und Schreibschule der Reichenau", in: Konrad Beyerle (ed.), *Die Kultur der Abtei Reichenau*, vol. 2, München 1925, 657-683.

Preisendanz, Karl, *Die Schreib- und Buchkunst der Reichenau*, Konstanz 1950.

Prinz, Friedrich, *Frühes Mönchtum im Frankenreich*, Kultur und Gesellschaft in

Gallien, den Rheinlanden und Bayern am Beispiel der monastischen Entwicklung, 4. bis 8. Jahrhundert, München-Wien 1965.

Quirk, Randolph, & C. L. Wrenn, *An Old English Grammar* (2nd ed.), London 1957 (repr. 1963).

Rand, E. K., *A Survey of the Manuscripts of Tours*, vol. I: *Text* (Studies in the Script of Tours I), Cambridge, Mass., 1929.

Reaney, P. H., *A Dictionary of British Surnames*, London 1958.

Reaney, P. H., *The Origin of English Surnames*, New York 1967.

Reaney, P. H., *The Place-Names of Essex* (EPNS XII), Cambridge 1935.

REANEY CA   P. H. Reaney, *The Place-Names of Cambridgeshire and the Isle of Ely* (EPNS XIX), Cambridge 1943.

REANEY OR   P. H. Reaney, *The Origin of English Place-Names*, London 1964.

REDIN   M. Redin, *Studies on Uncompounded Personal Names in Old English* (Uppsala Universitets Årsskrift 2), Uppsala 1919.

van Regemorter, Berthe, "La Reliure Souple des Manuscrits Carolingiens de Fulda", *Scriptorium* 11 (1957), 249-257.

Reskiewicz, A., "The Phonetic Interpretation of Old English Digraphs", *Biuletyn Polskiego Towarzystwa Językoznawczego* 12 (1953), 179-187.

Riché, Pierre, *Education et culture dans l'Occident barbare, VIe-VIIIe siècles* (Patristica Sorbonensia 4), 2nd ed., Paris 1967.

RI & CR   I. A. Richmond & O. G. S. Crawford, *The British Section of the Ravenna Cosmography* (Archaeologia, or Miscellaneous Tracts relating to Antiquity XCIII), London 1949 (paper read in 1937).

Roberts, R. J., "Bibliography of Writings on English Place- and Personal Names", *Onoma*, Bibliographical and Information Bulletin VIII (1958/ 1959), 1*-71*.

Ross, A. S. C., "Old English *æ: a*", *English Studies* 32 (1951), 49-56.

Ruland, A., "Die Bibliothek des alten Benediktinerstifts zu Fulda", *Serapeum* XX (1859), 273-286, 289-298, 305-317.

Ryder, Michael L., "Parchment. Its History, Manufacture and Composition", *Journal of the Society of Archivists* 2 (1964), 391-399.

Samuels, M. L., "The Study of Old English Phonology", *Transactions of the Philological Society 1952*, Oxford 1953, 15-47.

SANDRED   K. I. Sandred, *English place-names in -stead* (Studia Anglistica Upsaliensia 2), Uppsala 1963.

Schapiro, M., "The Decoration of the Leningrad MS. of Bede", *Scriptorium* 12 (1958), 191-207.

Scherer, A., "Britannien und das 'alteuropäische' Flussnamensystem", in: W. Iser & H. Schabram (eds.), *Britannica, Festschrift für H. M. Flasdieck*, Heidelberg 1960.

SCHERER AEH   A. Scherer, "Der Ursprung der 'alteuropäischen' Hydronomie", in: C. Battisti & C. A. Mastrelli (eds.), *Atti del VII Congresso internazionale di Scienze onomastiche*, 4 vols., Firenze 1963, II, 405-417.

Scherer, C., "Der Fuldaer Handschriftenkatalog aus dem 16. Jahrhundert", Beilage zu: Franz Falk, *Beiträge zur Rekonstruktion der alten Bibliotheca fuldensis und Bibliotheca laureshamensis* (Zentralblatt für Bibliothekswesen, Beiheft 26), Leipzig 1902.

Scherer, C., "Die Kasseler Bibliothek im ersten Jahrhundert ihres Bestehens

(16. und 17. Jahrhundert)", *Zeitschrift des Vereins für hessische Geschichte und Landeskunde* 27, N.F. 17 (1892), 225-259.

SCHÖNFELD M. Schönfeld, *Wörterbuch der Altgermanischen Personen- und Völkernamen*, Heidelberg 1911 (repr. Darmstadt 1965).

SCHRAMM G. Schramm, *Namenschatz und Dichtersprache: Studien zu den zweigliedrigen Personennamen der Germanen* (Ergänzungshefte zur Zeitschrift für vergleichende Sprachforschung auf dem Gebiet der indogermanischen Sprachen 15), Göttingen 1957.

Schreiber, H., *Einführung in die Einbandkunde*, Leipzig 1932.

Schützeichel, R., "Zur Bedeutung der Quellenkritik für die Namenforschung", *Beiträge zur Namenforschung* XIII (1962), 227-234.

Searle, W. G., *Onomasticon Anglo-Saxonicum*, A List of Anglo-Saxon Proper Names from the Time of Beda to that of King John, Cambridge 1897.

v. Severus, Emmanuel, *Lupus von Ferrières*, Gestalt und Werk eines Vermittlers antiken Geistesgutes an das Mittelalter im 9. Jahrhundert, Münster 1940.

SMIT J. W. Smit, *Studies on the Language and Style of Columba the Younger (Columbanus)* (Dissertation Nijmegen), Amsterdam 1971.

Smith, A. H.,   see also EPNE

Smith, A. H., "The Survey of English Place-Names", in: H. Draye & O. Jodogne (eds.), *Third International Congress of Toponymy and Anthroponymy*, 3 vols., Louvain 1951, II, 61-69.

Smith, A. H., *Three Northumbrian Poems. Caedmon's Hymn, Bede's Death Song and the Leiden Riddle*, London 1933.

SMITH ASS A. H. Smith, "Place-names and the Anglo-Saxon Settlement", *Proceedings of the British Academy* XLII (1956), 67-88.

SMITH ERY A. H. Smith, *The Place-Names of the East Riding of Yorkshire and York* (EPNS XIV), Cambridge 1937.

SMITH GL A. H. Smith, *The Place-Names of Gloucestershire*, Parts I-IV (EPNS XXXVIII-XLI), Cambridge 1964-1965.

SMITH HW A. H. Smith, "The Hwicce", in: Jess B. Bessinger, Jr., & Robert P. Creed (eds.), *Franciplegius: Medieval and Linguistic Studies in Honor of Francis Peabody Magoun, Jr.*, New York 1965, 56-65.

SMITH NRY A. H. Smith, *The Place-Names of the North Riding of Yorkshire* (EPNS V), Cambridge 1928.

SMITH WRY A. H. Smith, *The Place-Names of the West Riding of Yorkshire*, Parts I-VIII (EPNS XXX-XXXVII), Cambridge 1961-1963.

Sprockel, C., *The Language of the Parker Chronicle*, vol. I: *Phonology and Accidence* (Dissertation Amsterdam), The Hague 1965.

Stark, F., *Die Kosenamen der Germanen*, Wien 1868 (repr. 1967).

Stenton, F. M., *Anglo-Saxon England* (3rd ed.), Oxford 1971.

Stenton, F. M., "The East-Anglian Kings of the Seventh Century", in: P. Clemoes (ed.), *The Anglo-Saxons: Studies in Some Aspects of their History and Culture. Presented to Bruce Dickins*, London 1959, 43-52 (repr. in: D. M. Stenton (ed.), *Preparatory to Anglo-Saxon England*, being the collected papers of Frank Merry Stenton, Oxford 1970, 394-402).

Stenton, F. M., "The Historical Bearing of Place-Name Studies: The Place of Women in Anglo-Saxon Society", *Transactions of the Royal Historical Society* (4th Series) XXV (1943), 1-13 (repr. in: D. M. Stenton (ed.), *Pre-*

paratory to Anglo-Saxon England, being the collected papers of Frank Merry Stenton, Oxford 1970, 314-324).

Stenton, F. M., "Personal Names in Place-Names", in: A. Mawer & F. M. Stenton (eds.), *Introduction to the Survey of English Place-Names* (EPNS I, 1), Cambridge 1924, 165-189.

Stenton, F. M., *The Place-Names of Berkshire,* Reading 1911.

STENTON EE   F. M. Stenton, "The English Element", in: A. Mawer & F. M. Stenton (eds.), *Introduction to the Survey of English Place-Names* (EPNS I, 1), Cambridge 1924, 36-54.

Stockwell, Robert P., "The Phonology of Old English: a Structural Sketch", *Studies in Linguistics* 13 (1958), 13-24.

Stockwell, Robert P., & C. Westbrook Barrit, "The Old English Short Digraphs: Some Considerations", *Language* 31 (1955), 372-389.

Stockwell, Robert P., & C. Westbrook Barrit, "Scribal Practice: Some Assumptions", *Language* 37 (1961), 75-82.

Stockwell, Robert P., & C. Westbrook Barrit, *Some Old English Graphemic-Phonemic Correspondences ... ae, ea and a* (Studies in Linguistics; Occasional Papers 4), Washington, D. C., 1951.

Storms, G., *Compounded Names of Peoples in Beowulf.* A Study in the Diction of a Great Poet, Nijmegen 1957.

Storms, G., "The Weakening of O.E. Unstressed *i* to *e* and the Date of Cynewulf", *English Studies* 37 (1956), 104-110.

Strang, Barbara M. H., *A History of English,* London 1970.

Strecker, Karl, *Introduction to Medieval Latin* (English Translation and Revision by Robert B. Palmer), Berlin 1957.

STRÖM   H. Ström, *Old English Personal Names in Bede's History* (Lund Studies in English VIII), Lund 1939.

Struck, Gustav, "Handschriftenschätze der Landesbibliothek Kassel", in: Dr. Wilhelm Hopf (ed.), *Die Landesbibliothek Kassel 1580-1930,* Part II, Marburg 1930.

Sundén, K., "On the origin of the hypocoristic suffix *-y* (*=ie, =ey*) in English", in: *Sertum philologicum C. F. Johansson oblatum,* Göteborg 1910, 131-170.

Sweet, Henry   see OET

Tangl, Michael, *Bonifatii et Lulli Epistolae* (Monumenta Germaniae historica, Epistolae Selectae I), Berlin 1916.

Tengstrand, E., *A Contribution to the Study of Genitival Composition in Old English Place-Names* (Nomina Germanica 7), Uppsala 1940.

TENGVIK   G. Tengvik, *Old English bynames* (Nomina Germanica 4), Uppsala 1938.

Thompson, A. Hamilton (ed.), *Bede. His Life, Times and Writings,* Oxford 1935 (repr. 1969).

Thompson, E. M., *An Introduction to Greek and Latin Palaeography,* Oxford 1912.

Thompson, James W., *The Medieval Library* (The University of Chicago Studies in Library Science VIII), Chicago 1939.

Traube, L., *Nomina Sacra.* Versuch einer Geschichte der christlichen Kürzung (Quellen und Untersuchungen zur lateinischen Philologie des Mittelalters 2), München 1907.

Twaddell, W. Freeman, "The Prehistoric Germanic Short Syllabics", *Language*

24 (1948), 139-151 (repr. in: M. Joos (ed.), *Readings in Linguistics I*, Washington, D. C., 1957).

Utley, F. L., "The Linguistic Component of Onomastics", *Names* (Journal of the American Name Society) 11 (1963), 145-176.

VENDRYES LE   J. Vendryes, *Lexique étymologique de l'Irlandais ancien*, Dublin 1959.

Vielliard, Jeanne, *Le Latin des Diplômes Royaux et Chartes Privées de l'Epoque Mérovingienne*, Première Partie (Bibliothèque de l'Ecole des hautes Etudes 251), Paris 1927.

Vleeskruyer, R., "Some Notes on Early Anglo-Saxon Handwriting", *English Studies* 40 (1959), 13-18.

Voitl, H., "Die englische Familiennamen in sprachwissenschaftlicher Sicht", *Archiv für das Studium der neueren Sprachen und Literaturen* 202 (1966), 161-177.

Voitl, H., "Die englische Personennamenkunde. Ein Forschungsbericht", I. Teil, *Archiv für das Studium der neueren Sprachen und Literaturen* 199 (1963), 158-167; II. Teil, *idem* 200 (1964), 108-118; III. Teil, *idem* 200 (1964), 436-450.

Wainwright, F. T., *Archaeology and Place-Names and History*. An Essay on Problems of Co-ordination, London 1962.

Wallenberg, J. K., *The Place-Names of Kent*, Uppsala 1934.

WALLENBERG   J. K. Wallenberg, *Kentish Place-Names* (Uppsala Universitets Årsskrift), Uppsala 1931.

Watson, John W., Jr., "Non-Initial *k* in the North of England", *Language* 23 (1947), 43-49.

Watson, John W., Jr., "Northumbrian Old English 'ēo' and 'ēa'", *Language* 22 (1946), 19-26.

Watson, John W., Jr., "Smoothing and Palatalumlaut in Northumbrian", in: *English Studies in Honor of James Southall Wilson* (University of Virginia Studies 5), Charlottesville 1951, 167-174.

WATSON   W. J. Watson, *The History of the Celtic Place-Names of Scotland*, Edinburgh 1926.

Whitelock, Dorothy, *After Bede* (Jarrow Lecture), Jarrow: The Rectory 1960.

Whitelock, Dorothy, *The Beginnings of English Society* (The Pelican History of England 2), London 1952.

Whitelock, Dorothy, *English Historical Documents I, c. 500-1042*, London 1955.

Whitelock, Dorothy, "The Old English Bede", *Proceedings of the British Academy* 48 (1963), 57-90.

Wilson, H. A. (ed.), *The Calendar of St. Willibrord* (Henry Bradshaw Society 55), London 1918.

Wilson, R. M., "The Provenance of the Vespasian Psalter Gloss: The Linguistic Evidence", in: P. Clemoes (ed.), *The Anglo-Saxons: Studies in Some Aspects of their History and Culture. Presented to Bruce Dickins*, London 1959, 292-310.

von Winterfeld, Paul, "De Germanici Codicibus", in: *Festschrift Johannes Vahlen zum 70. Geburtstag gewidmet von seinen Schülern*, Berlin 1900, 391-407.

Woolf, H. B., "The naming of women in Old English times", *Modern Philology* 36 (1938-39), 113-120.

Woolf, H. B., *The Old Germanic Principles of Name-Giving*, Baltimore 1939.

Wrenn, C. L., "The Value of Spelling as Evidence", *Transactions of the Philological Society 1943*, London 1944, 14-39.

Wright, David H., "The Date of the Leningrad Bede", *Revue Bénédictine* 71 (1961), 265-273.

Wright, David H., (review of P. Hunter Blair, *The Moore Bede, etc. ...*), *Anglia* 82 (1964), 110-117.

Wright, David H., (review of E. A. Lowe, *English Uncial*), *Speculum* 36 (1961), 493-496.

Wright, David H., "Some Notes on English Uncial", *Traditio* 17 (1961), 441-456.

Wright, J., & E. Wright, *Old English Grammar* (3rd ed.), London 1925.

Wyld, H., & Mary Serjeantson, "Place-Names and English Linguistic Studies", in: A. Mawer & F. M. Stenton (eds.), *Introduction to the Survey of English Place-Names* (EPNS I, 1), Cambridge 1924, 133-142.

Zachrisson, R. E., "English Place-Name Puzzles. A Methodological Investigation into the Question of Personal Names or Descriptive Words in English Place-Names", *Studia Neophilologica* V (1932/33), 1-69.

Zachrisson, R. E., "Notes on Early English Personal Names", *Studier i modern Sprakvetenskap utgivna av nyfilologiska sällskapet i Stockholm* VI (1917), 269-298.

Zachrisson, R. E., *Some Instances of Latin Influence on English Place-Nomenclature* (Lunds Universitets Årsskrift, N. F., Avd. 1, 7:2), Lund 1910.

Zachrisson, R. E., "Some Yorkshire Place-Names. York, Ure, Jervaulx", *The Modern Language Review* XXI (1926), 361-367.

ZACHRISSON RKS   R. E. Zachrisson, *Romans, Kelts and Saxons in Ancient Britain*. An Investigation into the two dark centuries (400-600) of English History (Skrifter Utgivna av Kungl. Humanistiska Vetenskaps-Samfundet i Uppsala 24:12), Uppsala 1927.

Zimmer, H., "Zur orthographie des Namens Beda", *Neues Archiv der Gesellschaft für ältere deutsche Geschichtskunde* 16 (1891), 599-601.

Zimmermann, E. Heinrich, *Vorkarolingische Miniaturen*, Berlin 1916.

PLATES

For a description of the various Hands
the reader is referred to PART I, Chapter 1, § 3.

Fol. 21 r. Lines 1-4 written by Hand II, lines 6-30 by Hand I, and lines 31-42 by Hand III. (Slightly reduced.)

Fol. 21r, 1-22. Lines 1-4 written by Hand II, lines 6-22 by Hand I.

Fol. 21r, 23-42. Lines 23-30 written by Hand I, lines 31-42 by Hand III.

1. Fol. 5v, 34-42, written by Hand I. 2. Fol. 15r, 18-25, written by Hand II.

1. Fol. 24r, 31-40, written by Hand III. 2. Fol. 31r, 35-42, written by Hand IV.

Fol. 31r, 1-25, written by Hand IV.

INDEX*

* The Index only lists OE material that occurs in K.

273

RATHBED, 104, 165, 182, 218.
RHENUS, 104, 165, 225.
RUGINI, 104, 166.
SABERCT, 104, 166f., 188, 197, 226, 236.
SABRINA, 104, 166, 216.
SAEXUULF, XIX, 46, 104f., 166, 184, 193, 215, 226.
SAXONES, 62, 166, 182, 184, 226.
SAXONICUS, 62, 166, 182, 226.
SCOTTI, 62, 167, 203.
SCOTTIA, 62, 167.
SCOTTICUS, 62, 167.
SEBBI, 104, 167, 187, 207, 238.
SEXBURG, 104, 167, 184, 193, 226.
SELAESEU, 104f., 140, 167, 188, 198, 208.
SENONES, 104, 167.
SIGHARD, 105, 168, 185, 191, 220, 224.
SIGHERI, 105, 168, 186, 191, 201, 207, 224, 238.
SOLUENTE, 105, 168, 215.
STANFORD, 105, 142, 168, 192, 197.
STREANAESHALCH, 105, 147, 168f., 183, 199, 208f., 224f., 240.
SUAEBHEARD, 105, 169, 185, 194, 216, 239f.
SUEFRED, 105, 169, 194, 216.
SUIDBERCT 1, 43, 105, 169, 188, 191, 218f., 226.
SUIDBERCT 2, 105, 169, 188, 191, 218f., 226.
SUTHRIEONA, 105, 143, 170, 193, 198, 213, 217, 220, 238.
TAMISA, 106, 170.
TATFRID, 106f., 170, 191, 197, 219.
TATUINI, 42, 106f., 170, 191, 197, 208, 215.
THRYDRED, 106, 171, 194, 197, 217f.
TILMON, 106, 171, 183, 191.
TINA/TINUS, 106f., 171.
TITILLO, 106f., 171, 191, 204.
TONDBERCT, 106, 171, 183, 188, 226.
TORCTGYD, 106, 171, 192f., 219f., 226, 229, 241, 243.
TORONIS, 106, 172.
TRAIECTUM, 106, 172.
TREANTA, 107, 172.

TRUMBERCT, 107, 172, 188, 193, 226.
TRUMUINI, 107, 172, 191, 193, 203, 208, 215.
TUIDUS, 107, 172.
adTUIFYRDI, 107, 118, 142, 172f., 191, 193, 207f.
TUNBERCT, 107, 173, 188, 196, 226.
TUNNA, 107, 173, 197, 204.
TUNNACESTIR, 107, 131, 173, 185, 197, 204, 213, 223.
UALDHERI, 47, 107, 173, 183, 186, 207, 214, 224.
UALHSTOD, 107, 168, 173, 183, 195, 214, 225.
UECTA, 107ff., 174, 188, 204, 214, 226.
UENTA, 108f., 174, 204, 214.
UENTANUS, 108f., 174, 214.
UETADUN, 108, 137, 174, 194, 196, 214.
UICTBERCT, 108, 175, 188, 191, 214, 226.
UICTRED, 108f., 175, 191, 194, 214, 226, 229, 241, 243.
UIGHEARD, 3, 108f., 175, 185, 195, 214, 224, 239.
UILBRORD, 43, 108f., 175, 191f., 214, 228, 237.
UILFRID 1, 42, 48, 109ff., 175, 191, 214, 217, 219.
UILFRID 2, 110f., 175, 191, 214, 217, 219.
UILFRID 3, 110, 175, 191, 214, 217, 219.
UILTABURG, 110, 130, 172, 175f., 193, 214.
UILTI, 110, 176, 214.
UINI, 111, 176, 191, 208, 214.
UIURAEMUDA, 111, 159, 176, 193, 202, 214.
UIURI, 111, 176, 214.
inUNDALUM, 111, 153, 176f., 193, 197.
UULFHERI, 111, 177, 186, 193, 201, 207, 215, 224.
UYNFRID, 46, 111, 177, 191, 193, 214, 217, 219, 228.